Jakob Hauter

RUSSIA'S OVERLOOKED INVASION

The Causes of the 2014 Outbreak of War in Ukraine's Donbas

With a foreword by Hiroaki Kuromiya

Bibliografische Information der Deutschen Nationalbibliothek
Die Deutsche Nationalbibliothek verzeichnet diese Publikation in der Deutschen Nationalbibliografie; detaillierte bibliografische Daten sind im Internet über http://dnb.d-nb.de abrufbar.

Bibliographic information published by the Deutsche Nationalbibliothek
The Deutsche Nationalbibliothek lists this publication in the Deutsche Nationalbibliografie; detailed bibliographic data are available on the Internet at http://dnb.d-nb.de.

Cover graphic: Russian-led fighter in front of Sloviansk City Council on April 14, 2014.
© Yevgen Nasadyuk. Licensed under CC BY-SA 3.0 (https://creativecommons.org/licenses/by-sa/3.0/).
Available at: https://commons.wikimedia.org/wiki/File:2014-04-14_Sloviansk_city_council_-_3.jpg

ISBN-13: 978-3-8382-1803-8
© *ibidem*-Verlag, Stuttgart 2023
Alle Rechte vorbehalten

Das Werk einschließlich aller seiner Teile ist urheberrechtlich geschützt. Jede Verwertung außerhalb der engen Grenzen des Urheberrechtsgesetzes ist ohne Zustimmung des Verlages unzulässig und strafbar. Dies gilt insbesondere für Vervielfältigungen, Übersetzungen, Mikroverfilmungen und elektronische Speicherformen sowie die Einspeicherung und Verarbeitung in elektronischen Systemen.

All rights reserved. No part of this publication may be reproduced, stored in or introduced into a retrieval system, or transmitted, in any form, or by any means (electronical, mechanical, photocopying, recording or otherwise) without the prior written permission of the publisher. Any person who does any unauthorized act in relation to this publication may be liable to criminal prosecution and civil claims for damages.

Printed in the EU

Soviet and Post-Soviet Politics and Society (SPPS) Vol. 270
ISSN 1614-3515

General Editor: Andreas Umland,
Stockholm Centre for Eastern European Studies, andreas.umland@ui.se

Commissioning Editor: Max Jakob Horstmann,
London, mjh@ibidem.eu

EDITORIAL COMMITTEE*

DOMESTIC & COMPARATIVE POLITICS
Prof. **Ellen Bos**, *Andrássy University of Budapest*
Dr. **Gergana Dimova**, *Florida State University*
Prof. **Heiko Pleines**, *University of Bremen*
Dr. **Sarah Whitmore**, *Oxford Brookes University*
Dr. **Harald Wydra**, *University of Cambridge*

SOCIETY, CLASS & ETHNICITY
Col. **David Glantz**, *"Journal of Slavic Military Studies"*
Dr. **Marlène Laruelle**, *George Washington University*
Dr. **Stephen Shulman**, *Southern Illinois University*
Prof. **Stefan Troebst**, *University of Leipzig*

POLITICAL ECONOMY & PUBLIC POLICY
Prof. **Andreas Goldthau**, *University of Erfurt*
Dr. **Robert Kravchuk**, *University of North Carolina*
Dr. **David Lane**, *University of Cambridge*
Dr. **Carol Leonard**, *University of Oxford*
Dr. **Maria Popova**, *McGill University, Montreal*

FOREIGN POLICY & INTERNATIONAL AFFAIRS
Dr. **Peter Duncan**, *University College London*
Prof. **Andreas Heinemann-Grüder**, *University of Bonn*
Prof. **Gerhard Mangott**, *University of Innsbruck*
Dr. **Diana Schmidt-Pfister**, *University of Konstanz*
Dr. **Lisbeth Tarlow**, *Harvard University, Cambridge*
Dr. **Christian Wipperfürth**, *N-Ost Network, Berlin*
Dr. **William Zimmerman**, *University of Michigan*

HISTORY, CULTURE & THOUGHT
Dr. **Catherine Andreyev**, *University of Oxford*
Prof. **Mark Bassin**, *Södertörn University*
Prof. **Karsten Brüggemann**, *Tallinn University*
Prof. **Alexander Etkind**, *Central European University*
Prof. **Gasan Gusejnov**, *Free University of Berlin*
Prof. **Leonid Luks**, *Catholic University of Eichstaett*
Dr. **Olga Malinova**, *Russian Academy of Sciences*
Dr. **Richard Mole**, *University College London*
Prof. **Andrei Rogatchevski**, *University of Tromsø*
Dr. **Mark Tauger**, *West Virginia University*

ADVISORY BOARD*

Prof. **Dominique Arel**, *University of Ottawa*
Prof. **Jörg Baberowski**, *Humboldt University of Berlin*
Prof. **Margarita Balmaceda**, *Seton Hall University*
Dr. **John Barber**, *University of Cambridge*
Prof. **Timm Beichelt**, *European University Viadrina*
Dr. **Katrin Boeckh**, *University of Munich*
Prof. em. **Archie Brown**, *University of Oxford*
Dr. **Vyacheslav Bryukhovetsky**, *Kyiv-Mohyla Academy*
Prof. **Timothy Colton**, *Harvard University, Cambridge*
Prof. **Paul D'Anieri**, *University of California*
Dr. **Heike Dörrenbächer**, *Friedrich Naumann Foundation*
Dr. **John Dunlop**, *Hoover Institution, Stanford, California*
Dr. **Sabine Fischer**, *SWP, Berlin*
Dr. **Geir Flikke**, *NUPI, Oslo*
Prof. **David Galbreath**, *University of Aberdeen*
Prof. **Frank Golczewski**, *University of Hamburg*
Dr. **Nikolas Gvosdev**, *Naval War College, Newport, RI*
Prof. **Mark von Hagen**, *Arizona State University*
Prof. **Guido Hausmann**, *University of Regensburg*
Prof. **Dale Herspring**, *Kansas State University*
Dr. **Stefani Hoffman**, *Hebrew University of Jerusalem*
Prof. em. **Andrzej Korbonski**, *University of California*
Dr. **Iris Kempe**, *"Caucasus Analytical Digest"*
Prof. **Herbert Küpper**, *Institut für Ostrecht Regensburg*
Prof. **Rainer Lindner**, *University of Konstanz*

Dr. **Luke March**, *University of Edinburgh*
Prof. **Michael McFaul**, *Stanford University, Palo Alto*
Prof. **Birgit Menzel**, *University of Mainz-Germersheim*
Dr. **Alex Pravda**, *University of Oxford*
Dr. **Erik van Ree**, *University of Amsterdam*
Dr. **Joachim Rogall**, *Robert Bosch Foundation Stuttgart*
Prof. **Peter Rutland**, *Wesleyan University, Middletown*
Prof. **Gwendolyn Sasse**, *University of Oxford*
Prof. **Jutta Scherrer**, *EHESS, Paris*
Prof. **Robert Service**, *University of Oxford*
Mr. **James Sherr**, *RIIA Chatham House London*
Dr. **Oxana Shevel**, *Tufts University, Medford*
Prof. **Eberhard Schneider**, *University of Siegen*
Prof. **Olexander Shnyrkov**, *Shevchenko University, Kyiv*
Prof. **Hans-Henning Schröder**, *SWP, Berlin*
Prof. **Yuri Shapoval**, *Ukrainian Academy of Sciences*
Dr. **Lisa Sundstrom**, *University of British Columbia*
Dr. **Philip Walters**, *"Religion, State and Society", Oxford*
Prof. **Zenon Wasyliw**, *Ithaca College, New York State*
Dr. **Lucan Way**, *University of Toronto*
Dr. **Markus Wehner**, *"Frankfurter Allgemeine Zeitung"*
Dr. **Andrew Wilson**, *University College London*
Prof. **Jan Zielonka**, *University of Oxford*
Prof. **Andrei Zorin**, *University of Oxford*

* While the Editorial Committee and Advisory Board support the General Editor in the choice and improvement of manuscripts for publication, responsibility for remaining errors and misinterpretations in the series' volumes lies with the books' authors.

Soviet and Post-Soviet Politics and Society (SPPS)
ISSN 1614-3515

Founded in 2004 and refereed since 2007, SPPS makes available affordable English-, German-, and Russian-language studies on the history of the countries of the former Soviet bloc from the late Tsarist period to today. It publishes between 5 and 20 volumes per year and focuses on issues in transitions to and from democracy such as economic crisis, identity formation, civil society development, and constitutional reform in CEE and the NIS. SPPS also aims to highlight so far understudied themes in East European studies such as right-wing radicalism, religious life, higher education, or human rights protection. The authors and titles of all previously published volumes are listed at the end of this book. For a full description of the series and reviews of its books, see www.ibidem-verlag.de/red/spps.

Editorial correspondence & manuscripts should be sent to: Dr. Andreas Umland, Department of Political Science, Kyiv-Mohyla Academy, vul. Voloska 8/5, UA-04070 Kyiv, UKRAINE; andreas.umland@cantab.net

Business correspondence & review copy requests should be sent to: *ibidem* Press, Leuschnerstr. 40, 30457 Hannover, Germany; tel.: +49 511 2622200; fax: +49 511 2622201; spps@ibidem.eu.

Authors, reviewers, referees, and editors for (as well as all other persons sympathetic to) SPPS are invited to join its networks at www.facebook.com/group.php?gid=52638198614 www.linkedin.com/groups?about=&gid=103012 www.xing.com/net/spps-ibidem-verlag/

Recent Volumes

261 *Andreas Heinemann-Grüder (Ed.)*
Who are the Fighters?
Irregular Armed Groups in the Russian-Ukrainian War in 2014–2015
ISBN 978-3-8382-1777-2

262 *Taras Kuzio (Ed.)*
Russian Disinformation and Western Scholarship
Bias and Prejudice in Journalistic, Expert, and Academic Analyses of East European, Russian and Eurasian Affairs
ISBN 978-3-8382-1685-0

263 *Darius Furmonavicius*
LithuaniaTransforms the West
Lithuania's Liberation from Soviet Occupation and the Enlargement of NATO (1988–2022)
With a foreword by Vytautas Landsbergis
ISBN 978-3-8382-1779-6

264 *Dirk Dalberg*
Politisches Denken im tschechoslowakischen Dissens
Egon Bondy, Miroslav Kusý, Milan Šimečka und Petr Uhl (1968-1989)
ISBN 978-3-8382-1318-7

265 *Леонид Люкс*
К столетию «философского парохода»
Мыслители «первой» русской эмиграции о русской революции и о тоталитарных соблазнах XX века
ISBN 978-3-8382-1775-8

266 *Daviti Mtchedlishvili*
The EU and the South Caucasus
European Neighborhood Policies between Eclecticism and Pragmatism, 1991-2021
With a foreword by Nicholas Ross Smith
ISBN 978-3-8382-1735-2

267 *Bohdan Harasymiw*
Post-Euromaidan Ukraine
Domestic Power Struggles and War of National Survival in 2014–2022
ISBN 978-3-8382-1798-7

268 *Nadiia Koval, Denys Tereshchenko (Eds.)*
Russian Cultural Diplomacy under Putin
Rossotrudnichestvo, the "Russkiy Mir" Foundation, and the Gorchakov Fund in 2007–2022
ISBN 978-3-8382-1801-4

269 *Izabela Kazejak*
Jews in Post-War Wrocław and L'viv
Official Policies and Local Responses in Comparative Perspective, 1945-1970s
ISBN 978-3-8382-1802-1

Acknowledgements

This book is an updated and streamlined version of my PhD thesis (Hauter 2022), which I defended in early February 2022. It is dedicated to all those fighting for a free and democratic Ukraine. Neither my thesis nor this book would have been possible without the people who supported me along the way.

Andreas Umland first inspired me to research the genesis of the Donbas War in a café on Kyiv's Left Bank in summer 2015. Andrew Wilson showed an interest in my project and agreed to supervise me when I decided to go ahead with the PhD endeavor in 2018. He was always there to provide new thoughts and ideas, but he also gave me the space I needed to develop the project in my own way. Ben Noble helped me focus and structure my research and encouraged me to get work published sooner rather than later. His feedback on my drafts always found the right balance between praise and constructive criticism. He and Andrew made the perfect supervisory team.

In addition, Pete Duncan's door was always open, and he was always happy to give advice when I needed it. Kristin Roth-Ey led a great introductory workshop for our PhD student cohort, which covered all the bases. Seth Graham took over from her as graduate tutor and steered the ship through the storm of the pandemic. Oxana Shevel, Dominique Arel, and Vincent Keating were critical but helpful discussants of my presentations at conferences in Ottawa and Paris. Many other conference participants provided helpful feedback as well.

Carolin Heilig, Carlos Gómez del Tronco, Anna Stanisz-Lubowiecka, Ursula Woolley, Julia Klimova, Dave Dalton, Peter Flew, David Rypel, and my other fellow PhD students were great listeners and great company throughout our time together at SSEES. Hiroaki Kuromiya and Mark Galeotti agreed to examine my thesis and raised some important points in their reports and during the viva, which helped me further improve my work. Eyal Weizman, Stefan Laxness, and the great team at Forensic Architecture gave me the opportunity to take part in their investigation of the Battle of Ilovaisk.

My dear Ukrainian friends Artem Shaipov, Vsevolod Mazurenko, Viktoria Savchuk, and Yuliia Shaipova helped me maintain my personal connection with Ukraine, its language, and its people throughout the project. Especially Artem's family showed amazing hospitality when we visited their home in the Donbas in summer 2018. I sincerely hope that one day they will be able to return to a peaceful Bakhmut and rebuild what Russia destroyed.

Finally, my wife Sophie Rust, my parents, my brother, and all my other friends always had my back while I was absorbed by my work and by events in the Donbas. I am very grateful for their love, patience, and support.

Contents

Acknowledgements 5
List of Abbreviations 12
Foreword by *Hiroaki Kuromiya* 13
1. Introduction 21
    1.1. Researching War 23
    1.2. In Defense of Case-Study Analysis 25
    1.3. The Donbas in 2014: Civil War or Invasion? 27
        1.3.1. Why it Matters 30
        1.3.2. The Evidence and Its Shortcomings 32
    1.4. Chapter Conclusion 39
2. The War's Critical Junctures 41
    2.1. A Donbas Conflict Escalation Ladder 41
        2.1.1. Steps and Thresholds 44
        2.1.2. Non-Thresholds 48
    2.2. Six Critical Junctures 50
        2.2.1. Non-Junctures: The Protests of March 2014 52
        2.2.2. Juncture 1: Donetsk and Luhansk,
               Early April 54
        2.2.3. Juncture 2: Sloviansk, Kramatorsk,
               and Surroundings, Mid-April 55
        2.2.4. Juncture 3: Mariupol—Where Separatism
               Failed, Mid-April to Mid-June 58
        2.2.5. Juncture 4: The Fighting Spreads,
               Late May 58
        2.2.6. Juncture 5: Tanks and Heavy Artillery,
               June-July 59
        2.2.7. Juncture 6: The Ukrainian Defeat of
               Late August 59
    2.3. Chapter Conclusion 60
3. Digital Forensic Process Tracing 63

- 3.1. Four Benchmarks for Good Process Tracing 63
  - 3.1.1. Separating Explanations and Evidence 64
  - 3.1.2. Considering Alternative Explanations 65
  - 3.1.3. Practicing Source Criticism 66
  - 3.1.4. Updating Probabilities 66
- 3.2. The Neglect of Source Criticism and Probabilistic Reasoning 67
- 3.3. The Potential of Digital Open Source Information 69
- 3.4. Operationalizing Digital Forensic Process Tracing 72
  - 3.4.1. Five Philosophical Challenges 73
  - 3.4.2. Five Pragmatic Solutions 75
  - 3.4.3. Additional Limitations and Remedies 80
  - 3.4.4. Digital Forensic Process Tracing in Practice 83
- 3.5. Chapter Conclusion 85

4. Of Arms and Barricades: Donetsk and Luhansk in Early April 87
   - 4.1. Enthusiasts or Agents? The Role of Grassroots Activism 91
     - 4.1.1. The Burden of Proof 92
     - 4.1.2. The Chaotic Birth of the Donetsk People's Republic 92
     - 4.1.3. Partisans from Stakhanov? The "Army of the Southeast" in Luhansk 96
   - 4.2. Apathetic Oligarchs: The Role of Local Elites 99
     - 4.2.1. The Yanukovych "Family" 99
     - 4.2.2. Rinat Akhmetov 102
     - 4.2.3. Oleksandr Yefremov 105
     - 4.2.4. Oleksandr Bobkov 108
     - 4.2.5. Other Potential Sponsors 109
   - 4.3. Cossacks, Eurasianists, and Kremlin Advisers: The Role of Russia 110
     - 4.3.1. The Glazyev Tapes 111
     - 4.3.2. Eurasianism and Its Friends in Donetsk 113

- 4.3.3. The Crimean Link 116
- 4.3.4. The Don Cossack Network 117
- 4.3.5. FSB and GRU in Luhansk 118
- 4.4. Chapter Conclusion 122

5. **Enter Igor Girkin: The Occupation of Sloviansk and Kramatorsk** 125
   - 5.1. From Crimea to the Donbas: The Genesis of Girkin's Militia 129
   - 5.2. Girkin's Links to the Kremlin: The Oligarch and the "Prime Minister" 140
   - 5.3. Actions without Consequences: Girkin's Return to Russia 143
   - 5.4. Order or Tacit Approval? On Putin's Role 144
   - 5.5. A Separatist Bandwagon: The Role of Locals 147
   - 5.6. Chapter Conclusion 149

6. **Mariupol: Where Separatism Failed** 151
   - 6.1. Mariupol's Separatist Movement 157
   - 6.2. Oligarchic Resistance? The Role of Rinat Akhmetov 159
   - 6.3. A Handshake and Some Weapons: The Role of Russia 162
   - 6.4. Mariupol Elsewhere: A Counterfactual Thought Experiment 165

7. **The Fighting Spreads** 167
   - 7.1. The Volnovakha Attack: A "Demon" from Russia 170
      - 7.1.1. The Origins of Igor Bezler and His Group 171
      - 7.1.2. Bezler's Second Passport 173
      - 7.1.3. Bezler's Handler: Introducing Vasiliy Geranin 174

- 7.2. Donetsk and Surroundings: Boroday's "Volunteers" 178
  - 7.2.1. Russian Fighters in Donetsk 179
  - 7.2.2. Boroday and Surkov 182
- 7.3. Luhansk City: Where Wagner Meets Orion 185
  - 7.3.1. The Wagner Group in Luhansk 186
  - 7.3.2. Orion, Elbrus, and Pavel Karpov 189
  - 7.3.3. Yevgeniy Prigozhin: Putin's Chef 192
- 7.4. Luhansk Oblast: The Don Cossack Invasion 193
  - 7.4.1. Ataman Nikolay Kozitsyn and the "Cossack National Guard" 193
  - 7.4.2. Pavlo Dromov and Oleksii Mozghovyi 194
- 7.5. The Role of Locals and Kremlin Infighting 197
- 7.6. Chapter Conclusion 198

8. The Calibers Grow 201
- 8.1. From Russia to the Donbas: The First Convoys of Heavy Arms 203
  - 8.1.1. Few Places to Rob: The Unavailability of Ukrainian Heavy Arms 203
  - 8.1.2. From Siberia to the Donbas: The June 12 Tank Convoy 206
  - 8.1.3. Burning Vegetables: The June 13 Grad Attack on Dobropillia 209
  - 8.1.4. Armor Patterns on a Russian Highway: The June 19-21 Tank Convoys 212
  - 8.1.5. The Artemivsk Tank Depot: An Implausible Source 214
- 8.2. Losing Territory, but Gaining Tanks: The Separatists in July 2014 215
- 8.3. Russia's Envoys and the Downing of MH17 217
  - 8.3.1. Civil Society's Tanks: Sergey Kurginyan in Donetsk 217
  - 8.3.2. Appoint More Russians: The Separatist Administrations in Early July 218
  - 8.3.3. MH17 220

    8.4. Chapter Conclusion...221

9. **The Tide Turns: The Ukrainian Defeat of August 2014**..225

    9.1. Prologue I: Cross-Border Shelling 228

    9.2. Prologue II: The Pskov Paratroopers 230

    9.3. The Battle of Ilovaisk...232

    9.4. The Battle of Luhansk 235

    9.5. The Battle of Novoazovsk..238

    9.6. Chapter Conclusion...240

10. **Conclusion** 243

    10.1. Russia's Invasion in Disguise.....................................243
        10.1.1. Donetsk and Luhansk in early April...............244
        10.1.2. Sloviansk and Kramatorsk.................................244
        10.1.3. Mariupol..245
        10.1.4. The Fighting Spreads...246
        10.1.5. Tanks and Heavy Artillery 247
        10.1.6. Ukraine Defeated 247
        10.1.7. Counterfactual Scenarios 248

    10.2. New Ways to Study War 249
        10.2.1. Reviving Escalation Theory...............................249
        10.2.2. Digital Forensic Process Tracing......................251

    10.3. Academic Implications...254

    10.4. How the West Failed Ukraine 258

    10.5. Lessons to Be Learned 260

    10.6. On Multicausality: Concluding Remarks...................262

References 267

List of Abbreviations

COW	Correlates of War project
DNR	Donetsk People's Republic
DOSI	digital open source information
DR	Donetsk Republic
ESM	Eurasian Youth Movement
FSB	Federal Security Service (Russian domestic intelligence service)
GRU	Main Intelligence Directorate (Russian military intelligence service)
JIT	Joint Investigation Committee (for the downing of Malaysian Airlines flight MH17 over the Donbas)
LNR	Luhansk People's Republic
MID	military interstate disputes
NVO	Nezavisimoye Voyennoye Obozreniye (Russian weekly newspaper focusing on military affairs)
OSINT	open source intelligence
OUN	Organization of Ukrainian Nationalists
SBU	Security Service of Ukraine
UCDP	Uppsala Conflict Data Program

Foreword

If the twentieth century marked the apogee and the ultimate demise of imperialism, the twentieth-first century signaled a post-imperialist world. When Moscow annexed Crimea and surreptitiously invaded eastern Ukraine in 2014, the world was shocked, even though with hindsight it should not have been such a surprise. Still one can sympathize with Angela Merkel, the then Chancellor of Germany, who intoned about Russia's military assault on Ukraine:

> Who would've thought that 25 years after the fall of the wall, after the end of the Cold War, after the end of the division of Europe and the end of the world being divided in two, something like that can happen right at [the] heart of Europe? (Smale 2014)

The collapse of any empire is a messy business. It creates complex and tangled territorial, ethnic, linguistic, and a host of other vexing issues, leaving anguished and often spiteful legacies everywhere affected by it. Today the world is coping with these issues and legacies. The collapse of the Russian (Soviet) Empire in 1991 is no exception. Yet, as Edyta Bojanowska (2022) reminds us, "Russia is the only European state that has engaged in a reconquest of its former imperial dominions."

Jakob Hauter's eminently readable book, *Russia's Overlooked Invasion*, examines Russia's attempt to reconquer Ukraine in 2014, focusing on Moscow's clandestine operations in the Donbas, significant parts of which were occupied that year through Russian military operations. The book addresses rigorously both theoretical and empirical issues of the invasion. This preface is intended to help readers comprehend the dramatic and consequential events of 2014 in a broader, historical context.

In the messy aftermath of the collapse of the Soviet Union, no region of the former Soviet Union was left in as contradictory, enigmatic, and even incomprehensible a state as the Donbas. It is important to examine why, if we are to understand how and why the war broke out in the Donbas in 2014. Hauter's book defines the

Donbas as two oblasts in eastern Ukraine, Donetsk and Luhansk, bordering the Russian Federation. In 2014, together they accounted for approximately nine percent of Ukraine's territory and 15 percent of its population. The Donbas is a vast steppe land where the coal and steel industry developed in the 19th and 20th centuries. Its importance as an industrial dynamo was such that during the Stalin years it was called the "All-Union Stokehold." Historically speaking, the Donbas was a Cossack land, the "wild field," so called because the competing political authorities that sought to dominate it, the Polish-Lithuanian Commonwealth, Muscovy, and the Ottoman Empire, could not really control it. The "wild field" symbolized a sort of political vacuum where people could seek refuge and find a degree of freedom. From the sixteenth century onward, those who fled there established military brotherhoods for the purpose of self-defense and came to be called Cossacks (derived from a Turkic word signifying 'free men'). Their center was in Zaporizhzhia, just to the west of the Donbas, in today's Ukraine. While much of today's Donbas belonged to the Zaporizhzhian (Ukrainian) Cossacks, who were only nominally under Polish-Lithuanian control, smaller parts in the eastern Donbas were claimed by a different Cossack group, the (Russian) Don Cossacks, formed and developed at about the same time mainly by those who had fled autocratic Muscovite rule as it expanded and amplified serfdom. Much of this smaller area came under Muscovite rule in the seventeenth century. The Zaporizhzhian Cossack lands (most of today's Donbas) came under Russian rule in the eighteenth century when the Russian Czar Catherine II conquered and subjugated the free men and their lands to Russia's autocratic rule. The vast land grab by Russia at the time included Crimea as well. Catherine called the newly acquired lands on the northern shore of the Black Sea "New Russia," a reflection of nakedly imperialist hubris.

    Since the Donbas was historically a non-Russian land, the Russian government invited ethnic Russians, Germans, and many others to settle in "New Russia." The discovery of vast coal deposits in the Donbas and the subsequent rapid industrialization in the late 19th century and the first half of the 20th century further impacted the ethnic composition of the Donbas. Ethnic Russians began to settle in towns and mines en masse and left a strong cultural and linguistic imprint on the Donbas. The lingua franca of the Donbas as a whole, as of most of "New Russia," became Russian, while the countryside, inhabited largely by ethnic Ukrainians, generally retained the Ukrainian language. Never, however, in the history of the Donbas did ethnic Russians constitute a majority. In the last Soviet census of 1989, for example, ethnic Ukrainians accounted for just over 50 percent. Although sizeable, ethnic Russians constituted at most approximately 44 percent. Since Ukraine's independence, the proportion of ethnic Russians has dropped below 40 percent.

Despite changes wrought by waves of industrialization and brutal Soviet rule lasting from 1918 to 1991, the Donbas never really lost its reputation as the wild and free steppe. The industrialization of the Donbas in both the Czarist and Soviet periods created vast opportunities for all kinds of people who wanted freedom: fortune hunters, criminals, adventurers, the poor and desperate, and those who fled political, economic, and religious persecution. Even during the period of the harshest rule under Stalin, the Donbas retained its reputation as a refuge for freedom-seekers. Many fleeing from Stalin's collectivization and de-kulakisation (dispossession of peasants) hid, both literally and figuratively, in the Donbas underground, as coal miners (Kuromiya 1998). Most interestingly, after World War Two, Ukrainian partisans fighting a losing war against Soviet military forces and unable to escape to the West, were advised to go to the Donbas and hide there (Armstrong 1990, 221). Despite the constant threat of political persecution, the Donbas has remained a land of refuge and freedom through much of its modern history.

The Donbas was and remains an enigma for many outsiders. Nearly every political party has gotten its hand burnt in the Donbas. That was the case in the past and remains so today. In this sense, the Donbas has always been a notorious political playground.

The reason for the notoriety comes down largely to the apparent contradictory nature of the Donbas, representing as it does freedom to some, but enslavement to others, as epitomized by the dangerous, hard, and exploitative labor of the coal mines (Kulchytskyi and Yakubova 2016, 18–20). Equally significant is the powerful prejudice within Ukraine against the Donbas as an "uncultured" brute land. Not long ago one of the most noted contemporary Ukrainian intellectuals dismissed the Donbas as a non-European "proto-cultural wasteland" that "easily succumbs to political manipulation in connection with a black-and-white view of the world," and its people as "medieval-feudal" or "Cro-Magnon-Neanderthal" (Andrukhovych 2005, 3; 2006, 10–11). And while there is no question that wild oppression and naked exploitation existed, the Donbas has continued to stand for freedom, at least until very recently. The Donbas shares this contradiction with America, which oddly embodies both freedom and oppression for many non-Whites. To the chagrin of all political parties, the Donbas as a whole has never adhered to any particular political orientation, just like the Ukrainian Cossacks, whose constantly shifting alliances angered all parties concerned (Poles, Russians, and Ottomans).

Yet the Donbas was and is far from an unprincipled mercenary force, easily manipulated by outside forces. Its seemingly cunning and baffling political orientation actually was and is a well-defined self-defense strategy, typical of border regions in general, to cope with competing outside political forces whom it distrusts. The Donbas as a "free" land never ceased to attract refugees. Indeed, people with nowhere to go tested their luck in the Donbas. Such was the case, even in the late Stalin era, with the father of Anatoly Shcharansky (today an Israeli politician), who could not work in Odesa because of the anti-Semitism and was told to go to the Donbas: "Try your luck in Stalino [today's Donetsk]" (Kuromiya 1998, 325). If freedom constitutes the essence of Ukrainian national identity, the Donbas historically embodies it. It also means that the Donbas has attracted, in addition to those seeking freedom, all kinds of intriguers and political "riff-raff" who could not operate elsewhere. In the years leading up to 2014, Russia almost certainly dispatched, unhindered, such operatives to the Donbas.

True, the Donbas was a problem child for the powers that be. Yet it did not mean that, after the collapse of the Soviet Union, the Donbas rejected integration into Ukraine. On the contrary, in 1991 the Donbas population overwhelmingly supported Ukraine's independence, with over 80 percent of its population voting in favor. While Ukrainian politics ultimately disappointed the Donbas population, and discontent mounted, the people of the Donbas still envisaged their future within the framework of an independent Ukraine. Before 2014, there were few signs of separatist sentiments or movements in the Donbas. Popular separatism emerged only after Russia's intervention in the Donbas in 2014. Hauter is absolutely correct that "while separatist sentiment may cause conflict, conflict may also cause separatist sentiment" (see section 1.3.2.5. of this book). It was conflict brought from outside that introduced popular separatism to the Donbas in 2014.

In the years leading up to 2014, the political integration of the Donbas into the Ukrainian body politic proceeded quietly. Far from separating from Ukraine, the Donbas politicians sought to seize power in the capital, Kyiv. They failed in 2004–5 due to the "Orange Revolution," but they succeeded in 2010 with Viktor Yanukovych, a politician from the Donbas backed by Moscow, elected as Ukraine's President. Through Yanukovych, Moscow sought to control Ukraine. However, as a Ukrainian politician, he was not in agreement with Moscow on all issues. Nevertheless, the policies and the governing style of Yanukovych's administration, which was influenced by Moscow's behind-the-scenes machinations, ultimately led to a mass rebellion in Kyiv in 2013–14 (the "Revolution of Dignity" or "Maidan Revolution"). Initially, Yanukovych did not seem to have had the stomach for killing the protesters, but eventually several dozen protesters died at the hands of the security forces, possibly with the clandestine involvement of Russian operatives. Resisting the orders of Vladimir Putin to cling to his presidential powers, Yanukovych fled. Russia's military occupation of Crimea ensued immediately in February 2014. Shortly thereafter, Russia invaded the Donbas.

Granted, distrust of and discontent with Kyiv was palpable in the Donbas even during the Yanukovych era, yet popular separatism was absent. The people in the Donbas may have helped to elect Yanukovych in 2010, yet he was known there as the "thief from Yenakiieve [Yanukovych's hometown in the Donbas]" and the "shame of the Donbas" (Studenna-Skrukwa 2014, 284–285). Yanukovych and his gang were "bandits," but they were "*our* bandits" (emphasis added). One Donbas worker noted quite revealingly: "Yanukovych is a criminal… all governments are criminal" (Kuromiya 2019, 249).

As for Putin's claims of any animosity toward ethnic Russians or Russian-speaking people in the Donbas, this is nothing short of ludicrous. Even Pavel Gubarev, who had become one of the separatist leaders in the Donbas, openly proclaimed that "here [in the Donbas], there was no ethnic enmity" (Kuromiya 2019, 246).

Lack of ethnic enmity in an ethnically mixed area meant that the Donbas possessed much potential for democratic and civil (as opposed to ethnic) nationalism. During World War Two, Yevhen Stakhiv worked in the Donbas as an Organization of Ukrainian Nationalists (OUN) agent and found that people in the Donbas viewed the OUN ideologue, Dmytro Dontsov, as a "fascist." Under the influence of the Donbas people, Stakhiv, who had once idealized Spain's Franco regime, "abandoned a narrowly defined Ukrainian nationalism and embraced the ideal of a democratic Ukraine without discrimination against its national minorities." Until his death many years later, Stakhiv remained grateful to the Donbas people for his democratic conversion (Stakhiv 1995, 133–134, 308). Far from an anti-democratic bastion, the Donbas exerted a democratizing influence on the Ukrainian body politic.

The open, free, and seemingly indeterminate nature of the Donbas, however, did facilitate stealth political and military intervention from outside. Taking full advantage of the prejudiced views of the Donbas prevalent in Ukraine and beyond, Putin claimed absurdly that the Donbas was not and is not Ukrainian, but rather historically and inherently Russian, with persecution against ethnic Russians and Russophones prevalent. Moreover, Putin, formerly an intelligence officer of the Soviet (Communist) state, asserted facetiously that he would help Kyiv's efforts to "de-communize" Ukraine by destroying Ukraine itself. After all, according to Putin, it was Vladimir I. Lenin who created the "artificial" entity called Ukraine and separated it from Russia; it was also Lenin who in 1918 opposed the separation of the Donbas and the surrounding regions from Ukraine and disbanded the "Donets-Krivoi Rog Republic" (created by a small number of Bolsheviks), incorporating it into Ukraine (Putin 2022a). In other words, Putin now attacks Lenin and the Bolsheviks as anti-Russian and pro-Ukrainian.

Today's Russian military forces use a two-volume textbook on maskirovka (camouflage), which they boast is "three times longer than Leo Tolstoy's War and Peace" (Ash 2015). Disinformation, camouflage, conspiracy, and covert subversion are the essence of Putin's political operations. He inherited them from the grand yet largely unexamined experience of the Soviet state. He deployed all of these in making his grab for "New Russia" in 2014.

Putin's covert operations have fooled many Western academics and observers, who still claim, even after having witnessed Russia's full-scale invasion of Ukraine in 2022, that the war that engulfed the Donbas in 2014 was essentially a civil war. Hauter's meticulous and methodologically rigorous analysis of the events of 2014 makes it abundantly clear that they are wrong: The war was an interstate war initiated by Russia's covert military invasion.

Hiroaki Kuromiya
Indiana University Bloomington, US

1. Introduction

February 24, 2022 will go down in history as the beginning of the war in Ukraine. This is understandable but inaccurate. When Russia launched the all-out invasion of 2022, Ukraine had already experienced almost eight years of armed conflict in its eastern Donbas region.[1]

Violence in the Donbas first broke out in the spring of 2014, shortly after the Maidan Revolution in Kyiv and Russia's annexation of Crimea. Fighting reached its initial peak in August 2014. In the years that followed, hostilities decreased in intensity but never stopped completely. According to UN estimates, between 14,200 and 14,400 people lost their lives between April 2014 and December 2021 as a result of the war (OHCHR 2022, 3).

What happened in the Donbas in 2014 is an inextricable part of the story of the war in Ukraine. To understand the events that shook the world in 2022, it is crucial to understand the reasons behind the initial escalation of violence eight years earlier. These reasons, however, are subject to a heated debate, not only in the political and media discussion surrounding the invasion of 2022 but also in the academic literature. At the core of this controversy lies the question whether the events of 2014 were, first and foremost, a Ukrainian civil war or, in fact, a Russian invasion in disguise. The answer to this question has important implications for the interpretation of the dramatic escalation of 2022 and also for further research on the causes of war in Ukraine and elsewhere. For this reason, it deserves the attention of this book.[2]

At the same time, this book illustrates how research on war can adapt to the growing importance of modern information technology. The 2014 Donbas War was one of the first conflicts of the social media age. This is both a blessing and a curse for researchers

---

[1] This book uses the term Donbas to refer to two administrative regions (*oblasti*) of modern Ukraine—Donetsk Oblast and Luhansk Oblast. This is the most common definition used today. Historically, the term Donbas has also been used to describe a larger area that includes additional parts of modern-day Ukraine and Russia. For an excellent regional history of the Donbas, see Kuromiya (1998).

[2] This book is an updated and streamlined version of my PhD thesis (Hauter 2022), which I defended in early February 2022.

(Hauter 2021c, 1–2). On the one hand, the Internet provides unprecedented access to information from the conflict zone. On the other hand, the prevalence of disinformation makes it difficult to use this information in a way that is both transparent and convincing. As a result, the Internet has the potential to affect the search for the causes of war in two contradicting ways. It can either shed additional light on these causes, or it can further obscure them. Academic research so far has mainly focused on the problem of obfuscation by studying how conflict parties and their supporters have turned the Internet into a propaganda battleground. This book will do the opposite. It will show how an analysis of online media can increase clarity rather than confusion about the causes of a war.

Moreover, this book addresses questions of cause and effect that go beyond the case of Ukraine. How can we differentiate between civil and interstate war if many conflicts feature both internal and international components? How can we identify a primary cause if a war is made possible by many interconnected conditions? And how do we deal with uncertainty and patchy evidence in a heated political climate?

I will proceed in ten chapters. The remainder of this introduction will give a high-level overview of how academic research has approached the causes of war in general and the particular case of the Donbas. Chapter two will develop an escalation sequence model of the Donbas War to illustrate the way the conflict evolved. According to this model, the war's formative phase covered the period between early April and late August 2014 and consisted of six critical junctures. Chapter three will introduce process tracing as the methodology of choice for studying the causes of these critical junctures. It will explain what process tracing is, how it has been used to study the causes of war, and how it can be made fit for the Internet age by incorporating the practice of digital open source information (DOSI) analysis. Chapters four to nine use the developed methodology to investigate the causes of each critical juncture in the escalation sequence model. Each chapter assesses the available open source evidence against the contradicting hypotheses that lie at the bottom of the argument about the war's causes. Two of these chapters find that the critical juncture they investigate was caused primarily by domestic factors. Four of them identify Russia's actions as the primary cause. On this basis, chapter ten concludes that it is appropriate to label the 2014 Donbas conflict first and foremost an interstate war between Russia and Ukraine.

The remainder of this introduction consists of three parts. Firstly, I will give a high-level overview of academic research on types and causes of war. Secondly, I will explain why qualitative research on individual conflicts is an indispensable supplement to quantitative research, especially in the social media age. Thirdly, I will introduce the case of the Donbas in 2014 and the divide between proponents of internal and external causes. I will argue that studies on either side of this divide currently feature theoretical and methodological shortcomings.

1.1. Researching War

Explaining the outbreak of war is one of the big quests of social science research. At the same time, war is a complex and multi-faceted phenomenon. For this reason, many scholars advocate differentiating between different types of wars as a first step toward a better understanding of war in general. Common causes and remedies may be easier to identify among wars which share certain characteristics. Based on this assumption, scholars have created different war typologies. Midlarsky (1990, 173), for example, proposes a distinction between systemic wars and dyadic wars. A systemic war involves "all major powers within the system" and "reaches into the depths of society to involve nearly all civilians." Dyadic wars are more limited conflicts. Another example is the differentiation between regular and irregular war (Kalyvas 2006, 67–70; M. L. R. Smith 2012, 615–616). Regular wars involve open clashes between armed formations on battlefields or along frontlines. In irregular wars, combatants and frontlines are less clearly defined.

The most common and universally accepted typology of war, however, is the differentiation between civil and interstate war. According to Kalyvas (2006, 18–19), the distinction between internal or civil war on the one hand and external or foreign wars on the other has been made throughout European history and was used by thinkers like Thucydides, Plato, Aristotle, Grotius, and Hobbes. Today, most research on war accepts this distinction and the causes of civil and interstate war have been discussed in separate academic debates.

A review by Cederman and Vogt (2017, 1995) finds that the academic literature on the causes of civil war is dominated by three explanatory logics: grievances, greed, and opportunities. Explanations focusing on grievances argue that civil war is the result of injustice. Explanations focusing on greed see civil war as the result of individuals trying to maximize their profits. Explanations focusing on opportunities argue that circumstances favoring the outbreak of civil war are more important than the motives of the actors involved.

Research on the causes of interstate war, on the other hand, mainly focuses on power balances between states and the decision-making strategies of their leaders. Vasquez's (1993) steps-to-war theory, for example, argues that interstate war is the result of arms races and alliance formations—which usually take place between neighbors over territorial disputes—combined with the dominance of hawks over accommodationist decisionmakers at the domestic level. Proponents of offense-defense theory argue that "war is more likely when conquest is easy" (van Evera 1999, 117). Johnson and Tierney (2011, 7) propose a "Rubicon theory of war," according to which decisionmakers switch from a "'deliberative' to an 'implemental' mindset" once they "believe they have crossed a psychological Rubicon and perceive war to be imminent." They argue that this switching of mindsets makes war more likely. Fearon (1995), on the other hand, argues that incomplete information and the inability to trust opponents are the two key factors that make rational actors choose war over peace.

This list of proposed explanations for civil and interstate war is by no means exhaustive. Various reviews of the academic literature have pointed out the diversity of approaches and findings (see, for example, Dixon 2009; Levy 1998; Levy and Thompson 2010; Sambanis 2002; Smith 2004; Suganami 1996, 43–113). To this day, there is little agreement on the relative importance of the various typologies and causes of war proposed by different scholars or the way they in interact with each other. Neither is there agreement on the methods by which such a consensus could be reached.

1.2. In Defense of Case-Study Analysis

Quantitative methods play a central role in the ongoing search for the causes of war. Scholars code characteristics of wars as numbers and run regression analyses to identify correlations. The popularity of this approach has led to the creation of large conflict databases. The most prominent ones are the Correlates of War Project (COW) (Sarkees and Wayman 2010; Dixon and Sarkees 2015; Palmer et al. 2021; Maoz et al. 2019) and the Uppsala Conflict Data Program (UCDP) (Pettersson and Öberg 2020; Gleditsch et al. 2002).

An early criticism of this approach comes from Dessler (1991). He argues that an exclusive focus on correlation leads to a fragmentation of knowledge because of the large variety of ways in which different factors may either interact or randomly coincide. Instead, Dessler calls for a "causal theory of war," which focuses on the mechanisms that underlie correlations. He does not specify what this theory should look like but it is clear that it would require the in-depth study of individual wars.

Twenty years after Dessler's article, the divide between proponents and critics of frequentist approaches persists. Quantitative social science research on war has continued to flourish. In-depth research on individual cases exists alongside it but is often left to historians and area studies specialists. This would not be a problem under two conditions. Firstly, historians and area studies specialists who write about war would have to pay attention to methodology and consider how their research can inform and guide comparative researchers who want to focus on the bigger picture. Secondly, quantitative conflict studies researchers would have to take findings from case studies seriously and take them into account in their coding efforts. In practice, these conditions are rarely met. Scholars like Mahoney (2008) and Seawright (2016) have pointed out compatible aspects and synergy effects of quantitative and qualitative methods. Nevertheless, a lack of interaction between the two continues to be a problem, in research on war and in the social sciences in general. Quantitative research often dismisses the need to study individual cases in depth. Qualitative case-study research, on the other hand, often dismisses the need to look beyond the nuances of the individual case, which results in a lack of conceptual and methodological rigor.

A closer look at the quantitative conflict studies literature and the potential ambiguities surrounding a conflict's most basic parameters clearly illustrates the need for high-quality case studies and quantitative-qualitative dialogue. An example is a conflict's start date. Defining the beginning of a war can be a difficult task – sometimes even in cases with a seemingly obvious start date, such as a formal declaration of war or the landing of an invasion force. Violence may predate such events, or it may only erupt with a significant delay. In other cases, there may not be an obvious start date at all. Violence may simply creep in as tensions rise. Nevertheless, scholars engaging in quantitative research need a precise definition of its beginning. Complex coding rules are the result. The UCDP, for example, records the day of the first battle-related death as the first start date of an armed conflict. The day when the total number of battle-related deaths exceeds 25 is recorded as the second start date. An armed conflict is retroactively categorized as a war if the total number of battle-related deaths exceeds 1000 in a given year (Pettersson 2020, 5–6).[3] Under these coding rules, the start date of a war depends on three decisions by the researchers who do the coding. Firstly, they have to choose data sources which supply accurate casualty figures. Secondly, they have to check that these casualties were battle-related and not, for example, the result of a massacre that only involved armed violence from one side. Thirdly and most importantly, they have to decide how to handle instances in which different sources provide contradictory information. The complexity of these decisions depends on the information environment in which the conflict takes place. The higher the number of available sources and the greater the conflict parties' efforts to distort the information leaving the conflict zone, the more complex the coding decisions become.

In cases of particularly contradictory information environments, the complexity of these coding decisions reaches a level that

---

[3] This distinction between war and armed conflict is not relevant for any arguments made in this book. For this reason, I use the terms "war", "armed conflict", and "conflict" interchangeably.

can no longer be dealt with sufficiently in a footnote or methodological annex. Such cases require a separate qualitative inquiry to justify coding decisions. What is more, coding challenges are not limited to comparatively straightforward units like the exact start date of a war or the exact number of casualties. They may also concern more fundamental and complex parameters, such as the conflict's type or the role of actors participating in it. Categorizing a war and establishing the role of the actors involved requires more conceptual and methodological groundwork than the counting of battle-related deaths. It requires a closer look at questions of cause and effect and at the definitions and rationales behind conflict typologies. As a result, there are many cases where quantitative conflict studies researchers can only make accurate coding decisions through a dialogue with historians and area studies specialists who can contribute case-study research based on their regional expertise. Unfortunately, however, such a dialogue does not appear to be part of the current practices of the UCDP or the COW.

1.3. The Donbas in 2014: Civil War or Invasion?

A prime example of a war in need of an in-depth qualitative case study with a focus on causality is the war that began in 2014 in eastern Ukraine's Donbas. The abundant but murky information environment in which this conflict unfolded and the political and academic controversies surrounding its nature and causes make it an extreme case (Gerring 2007, 101–105) regarding the complexity of coding decisions. However, this extreme may well become the new normal as the Internet increasingly shapes knowledge about contemporary conflict. This would turn the Donbas conflict into a typical case (Gerring 2007, 91–97) of a war fought in the age of modern information technology. Either way, the case of the Donbas in 2014 is ideal to illustrate how comparative research on the causes of war can benefit from regional expertise and the in-depth study of individual cases.

The political messaging surrounding the outbreak of militarized violence in the Donbas is characterized by fundamental disagreements about the conflict's nature and causes. The Ukrainian authorities have portrayed the war as a Russian act of aggression from its very beginning. When Ukraine's then Acting President, Oleksandr Turchynov, announced on April 13, 2014 that his administration had initiated a military operation in the east of the country, he said that this decision had been made after "terrorist units coordinated by the Russian Federation" occupied several administrative buildings in Donetsk Oblast (Turchynov 2014b). Ever since, Kyiv's line has remained the same: Ukraine has been defending itself against Russia since 2014, when Russia attacked Ukraine's southeast with special forces operatives as well as regular armed forces. Locals fighting against forces loyal to Kyiv were "terrorists" or "mercenaries" in Moscow's service. The Russian authorities, on the other hand, deny any involvement in the pre-2022 conflict beyond humanitarian aid for suffering civilians. They have admitted the presence of some volunteers with Russian citizenship among the separatist forces in the Donbas but claimed that these volunteers joined the conflict on their own private initiative and had no links whatsoever to the Russian state. According to Moscow, the conflict that started in 2014 was a civil war. The people of the Donbas rebelled against an illegitimate regime of Western-backed nationalists that had conducted a coup d'état in Kyiv. The regime brought in the military to oppress the rebellion, which led to the outbreak of war. Russia was a mediator—an advocate for civilians affected by Kyiv's military operation—but by no means a conflict party. President Putin not only reiterated this narrative when he announced the invasion of February 24, 2022 but even used it to justify his decision. "For eight years, for eight endless years we have been doing everything possible to settle the situation by peaceful political means," Putin said. He then went on to claim that the purpose of Russia's all-out invasion was "to protect people who, for eight years now, have been facing humiliation and genocide perpetrated by the Kiev regime" (Putin 2022b).

The two diametrically opposed narratives coming out of Kyiv and Moscow shaped the way in which the conflict was discussed and analyzed in politics and media between 2014 and 2022. Supporters of either side tried to give credence to their narrative and discredit the narrative of their opponents. Propaganda battles of this kind are not a new phenomenon. What is new, however, is the ease with which both information and disinformation about a war can be created and disseminated. The outbreak of war in the Donbas in 2014 was subject to an unprecedented level of attention from news outlets as well as local residents and freelance conflict analysts posting on social media. This has dramatically increased the diversity of source material available to researchers. Hence, academic research on this war has to operate in an information environment that is murky on the one hand but abundant on the other. In previous cases of information murkiness, researchers could point out that there was a lack of reliable information and wait for the relevant military archives to open. In the case of the Donbas, however, a lack of reliable information is not the problem. On the contrary, the volume of valuable primary information from the conflict zone is larger than ever before. This means that separating facts from fiction becomes a challenge worth tackling.

So far, academic research has tackled the challenge posed by the Donbas War's abundant but murky information environment with limited success. Of course, the academic debate on the war's causes is more nuanced than the positions of Kyiv and Moscow. Most scholars accept that the conflict that started in 2014 was caused by an interplay between domestic and foreign factors. They reject the idea that the Kremlin was entirely uninvolved and unaware while also rejecting the idea that the war played out according to a masterplan devised and implemented by Vladimir Putin in person. They acknowledge that a variety of actors within Russia interacted with a variety of actors within Ukraine in a rapidly evolving crisis situation. However, concerning the relative importance of these actors and the role of the Russian state as a fragmented yet collective entity, the academic debate shows a divide that is similar to the divide in the political discourse.

The majority of Western academic research published between 2014 and 2021 on the causes of the Donbas War is closer to Moscow's narrative than to Kyiv's. It supports what I call the civil war hypothesis—the claim that, despite a certain degree of Russian meddling, the war in the Donbas was primarily a homegrown phenomenon and an internal Ukrainian conflict. A smaller share of academic publications make the opposite claim, labelling the war primarily as a Russian invasion.

Table 1: Contradicting Hypotheses on the Donbas War's Causes

Civil war hypothesis	Despite a certain degree of Russian meddling, the war in the Donbas is primarily a homegrown phenomenon and an internal Ukrainian conflict.
Invasion hypothesis	Although domestic factors play an important auxiliary role, the war in the Donbas is primarily a Russian invasion of Ukraine.

Source: the author

1.3.1. Why it Matters

This divide in the academic literature should be addressed for two main reasons. First and foremost, the question what kind of war broke out in the Donbas in 2014 has important political implications. Labelling the conflict up to 2022 as a civil war does not justify Russia's subsequent actions, but it has the potential to relativize their severity at least to some extent. It would leave space for the argument that the attack of 2022 was, perhaps, an overreaction based on legitimate underlying concerns regarding the situation in Ukraine, which then developed a life of its own. It would also make it possible to place at least some responsibility on Ukraine by saying that Kyiv should have focused on sorting out its domestic issues by non-violent means to prevent a deterioration of relations with Russia. At the same time, it would cast doubt on the Ukrainian standpoint that attempts to reconquer territories lost in 2014 would qualify as legitimate self-defense efforts. Most importantly, defining the pre-2022 conflict as primarily internal would keep the hope alive that there could be a diplomatic solution to the 2022 invasion in which Russia withdraws and accepts Ukraine's sovereignty without the need for substantial military deterrence.

Labelling the events of 2014 as an invasion, on the other hand, would mean that Russia's narrative of a pre-emptive intervention after eight years of peaceful conflict resolution efforts loses any last shred of credibility. It would suggest that the attack of 2022 was the continuation of an aggressive imperialist policy rather than an overreaction or a temporary change in Russia's attitude toward Ukraine. It would mean that, within one decade, Russia made two military attempts to destroy Ukraine as a free and independent state. In turn, this would dramatically decrease confidence in any future agreements with the current Russian regime and in any Russian assurance not to use force against Ukraine or other neighboring countries in the future. Diplomatic conflict regulation based on assurances and trust in adherence to international law would appear as an increasingly futile approach. The importance of military deterrence to save Ukraine from future attacks would grow significantly.

Secondly, the correct classification of the Donbas conflict has important implications for academic research. Not only is it important for the historical record, but it is also an issue of data quality for those using the Donbas for comparative research on the causes of war. As discussed above, conflict datasets like the UCDP and the COW are currently the key sources for many scholars conducting quantitative analyses of armed conflict. Because quantitative research can only be as good as the data it is based on, the correct coding of an individual conflict in datasets is extremely important. The differentiation between civil war and interstate war is firmly established among conflict studies scholars. Labelling the Donbas conflict as one or the other will therefore predetermine which other wars it will be subsequently compared to.

Moreover, different characterizations of the war that started in 2014 affect the focus of researchers trying to explain the invasion of 2022. A civil war in 2014 would suggest that 2022 marked a dramatic change in direction for both conflict parties. It would suggest that Russia decided to invade after keeping its distance from the conflict for many years. At the same time, it would suggest that Ukraine suddenly succeeded in resisting an all-out invasion after struggling to contain a domestic rebellion. This would imply that academic research needs to supply an explanation for sudden and dramatic change. It would encourage researchers to contrast post-2022 with pre-2022 events and treat the invasion of 2022 as a distinct phenomenon with distinct causes.

An invasion in 2014, on the other hand, would suggest that the events of 2022 resembled an accelerated movement along a pre-existing trajectory rather than a dramatic change of direction. What changed was the scale of events and not the fact that Russia attacked and Ukraine resisted. This would encourage researchers to look at the events of 2014 and the events of 2022 as part of the same continuum. It would highlight 2014 rather than 2022 as the key watershed moment in Russia-Ukraine relations. The dramatic escalation of 2022 would appear more predictable and less surprising in hindsight. As a result, the search for the war's causes would have to focus more on 2014. In relation to 2022, the key question would be not so much what changed. It would be what failed to change after 2014 to prevent the war's further escalation.

1.3.2. The Evidence and Its Shortcomings

From an academic perspective, the question of whether the war that started in 2014 was primarily internal or international has remained unresolved because the existing literature on both sides of the civil war-invasion divide suffers from several shortcomings. These shortcomings affect the power of either side's argument. They can be divided into six categories.

1.3.2.1. Blurry Definitions

Research on the Donbas conflict often supports or rejects the use of the civil or interstate war label without a clear definition of either. Many contributions to the literature describe certain instances of local mobilization or foreign meddling but do not make clear why the highlighted instances are crucial for the characterization of the conflict. However, an invasion can involve local collaboration, and a civil war can involve foreign intervention (see also Hauter 2019). For this reason, a study that highlights instances of domestic mobilization or foreign intervention cannot make a compelling argument without specifying why the described events are compatible with the definition of one conflict type but not the other.

Scholars who try to develop criteria of this kind include Kudelia (2016) and Katchanovski (2016), who argue that the nationality of combatants is key to the character of a war. They argue that the Donbas conflict in 2014 was a civil war because, according to their assessment, most combatants on either side were Ukrainian citizens. However, this focus on nationality is problematic. It is questionable whether the citizenship of combatants is sufficient to define a conflict as primarily internal. Accepting combatant citizenship as the decisive indicator would imply that any invasion will turn into a civil war if enough local collaborators join the invader.

The COW's definition of interstate war (Sarkees 2010; Palmer et al. 2020) is problematic for a similar reason. It emphasizes that an interstate war must involve the "regular" forces of two states. This raises the question of how to treat covert military operations that involve, for example, mercenaries acting on behalf of a state. The COW's coding manual acknowledges this problem but does not offer a coherent solution.

1.3.2.2. Historical Determinism

Another problem is the fact that many works on the Donbas War prioritize structural conditions over immediate causes. They do not focus their analysis on the investigation of causal relationships between events in the conflict zone at the time of conflict escalation. Instead, they focus on a broader historical or geopolitical narrative and then present the Donbas conflict as an episode which blends into that narrative. This prioritization of the macro-level may lead to historical determinism in the sense that the presented historical narrative affects the interpretation of the facts of the case. Loshkariov and Sushentsov (2016), Sakwa (2015; 2017), and Sotiriou (2016), for example, emphasize longstanding identity cleavages in post-Soviet Ukraine. This focus in the choice of historical narrative inevitably sets the scene for a stronger focus on domestic conflict dynamics when it comes to the analysis of the conflict itself. In the work of scholars like Wilson (2014) or Kuzio (2017), on the other hand, an emphasis on nationalist and irredentist tendencies in Russia's recent history implicitly supports an interpretation of the conflict that focuses more on Russia's actions.

Studies of how historical developments did or did not affect the conflict are very important. However, they are more effective after the immediate causes of the war have been established through a more inductive analysis. A deductive framework that starts off by integrating the conflict into a wider historical narrative increases the risk of overlooking or mischaracterizing causal processes at the micro-level during the outbreak of the conflict itself.

1.3.2.3. Evading the Question

Other works feature a related type of determinism. They preselect certain aspects of the conflict and thereby predetermine an emphasis on either domestic or foreign causes. Matveeva (2016, 25) writes that her article "acknowledges the Russian government's role to be a big issue, but abstains from examining it, concentrating on [the] internal dynamic instead." This means that Matveeva (2016, 35) arrives at her conclusion that the Donbas conflict "was leaderless and not spearheaded by [an] elite" within a framework of analysis that completely ignores Russia's actions. In contrast, Hosaka's (2019) focus on Kremlin adviser Vladislav Surkov's involvement in the conflict emphasizes Russia's role as the key actor from the start.

Other analyses restrict their framework in different ways. Melnyk's (2020) insightful study of the conflict's causes is constrained by the fact that it only covers the run-up to the conflict but does not investigate the actual outbreak and escalation of militarized violence. Mykhnenko (2020) starts off by defining economic factors as the only possible domestic explanation for the war, which means that disproving economic explanations becomes sufficient proof of the primacy of Russia's role. And Yurchenko's (2018) Marxist framing of the conflict defines Ukraine's post-Soviet transformation by Western capitalism as the primary cause of the war and turns Russian intervention into a subordinate factor by default.

1.3.2.4. Lack of Regional Expertise

An important methodological problem relates to the coding procedures of the two major armed conflict data projects. These procedures are inadequate for the categorization of a war featuring the abundant but murky information environment surrounding events in the Donbas. The UCDP bases its coding decisions on media reporting data from all over the world as aggregated by the Factiva database. In addition, the project draws on NGO reports and some area-specific sources not included in Factiva. The data is filtered by "a string of search terms designed to produce all news articles reporting the use of violence." The results are then manually read and coded (Sundberg, Eck, and Kreutz 2012, 354–355).

The question that arises here is whether the UCDP had the time, resources, and expertise to adjust its data gathering to the specific information environment of the Donbas and then analyze the gathered data in a way that leads to transparent results. The

UCDP's writing on the conflict suggests that this was not the case. It does not represent the in-depth qualitative inquiry that would be required to justify coding decisions in a complex case like the Donbas. The reports lack references, provide a rather high-level overview of events, and appear to take certain claims made in the media—such as the supposed unification of separatist forces into the "United Armed Forces of Novorossiya" in September 2014—at face value, without examining whether they had any impact on the actual course of the conflict (UCDP n.d.a; n.d.b; n.d.c; see also Brik 2021, 203–204, 209–214). A dataset of the source material used to analyse the initial phase of the Donbas conflict can be downloaded from the UCDP's website. It includes 152 events covering the time between April 13 and September 16, 2014. The event catalogue is based exclusively on reporting from English-language sources. Most of these sources are major news agencies. Only one of them is based in Ukraine and none of them focuses specifically on the Donbas or is known for region-specific insights.

Similarly, most of the sources used by the coders of the COW's Military Interstate Disputes (MID) dataset are also major international English-language news agencies and newspaper websites (Palmer et al. 2021, 3). The resulting "dispute narrative" for interstate tensions between Russia and Ukraine in 2014 (dispute No. 4682) is even shorter than the UCDP's description (Palmer et al. 2020). Moreover, the MID narrative omits any claim of Russian military operations in Ukraine that is denied by the Kremlin. This results in an incoherent account of events that is incompatible with any of the conflict narratives proposed in the academic literature.

1.3.2.5. Correlation versus Causation

Another methodological problem consists of a conflation of correlation and causation resulting from an overreliance on public opinion poll data. Kudelia (2016), Katchanovski (2016), and Giuliano (2018) cite opinion polls as evidence that separatist sentiment among the Donbas population was an important factor in the outbreak of the war. Kudelia (2016, 9–12) and Giuliano (2018) both cite an opinion poll conducted between April 8 and 16, 2014 by the Kyiv International Institute of Sociology (KIIS 2014a), which suggests that separatist sentiment was more widespread in the Donbas than in other regions of Ukraine. However, as Giuliano (2018, 158) points out, only a minority of respondents supported separatist views according to this survey. Katchanovski (2016, 484), on the other hand, argues that another opinion poll commissioned by him and conducted by the same polling institute in April–May 2014 (KIIS 2014b), showed that "the majority of Donbas residents backed various forms of separatism."

Discrepancies of this kind are not surprising. The wording of the questions differs between the two surveys, and they were conducted almost a month apart. At the time, conflict escalation in the Donbas was already underway, and it is possible that rising tensions were leaving a mark on public opinion. In other words, while separatist sentiment may cause conflict, conflict may also cause separatist sentiment. Moreover, even if separatist ideas are widespread, this does not necessarily mean that people will act on these ideas. And the reverse is true as well: Armed conflict can be triggered by a small group of fanatics who do not enjoy wide public support. Finally, it also seems reasonable to assume that Russia, if it were planning an invasion, would choose Ukraine's most pro-Russian regions as a first point of attack.

All this does not mean that public opinion is unimportant. The fact that separatist ideas appeared to be more popular in the Donbas than in other parts of Ukraine in April 2014 needs to be considered in any assessment of the conflict's causes. On its own, however, this correlation between separatist sentiment and war does not have much causal significance because it leaves the most important question open: What were the processes that connected separatist sentiment to mobilization, militarization, and the outbreak of war?

1.3.2.6. Insufficient Source Criticism
The most important shortcoming of academic research on either side of the civil-interstate war debate is a lack of transparency and attention to detail in the discussion of sources and the evidence they provide. Most of the existing literature treats sources as an affirmatory afterthought to a narrative rather than treating them as the data that creates this narrative in the first place. Hardly any works engage in explicit source criticism. Bowen (2019, 325–333), for

example, uses a selection of investigative online news articles to support his narrative. However, a critical appraisal of this source material is not a central part of his study. This approach is problematic. Investigative journalism is an indispensable source of evidence in the context of covert military activity. However, the claims of online news sources must not be taken at face value. They must be critically assessed according to four questions: What evidence do they provide? Is this evidence convincing? How does this evidence prove their claims? And how does this evidence disprove claims to the contrary? If an author fails to discuss these questions, their analysis inevitably becomes more susceptible to attacks from critics, who can simply question the quality of the cited source material. Moreover, an explicit and transparent appraisal of the available evidence also forces a researcher to reflect more on the credibility of their sources and thereby lowers the risk of cherry picking and unconscious bias.

This also applies to other data sources of academic research. Matsuzato (2017, 190–200), for example, relies on his visits to the self-proclaimed separatist republics and his interviews with separatist leaders. Matveeva (2018, 301–303) also relies on interviews with separatist leaders and fighters, Donbas residents, and Russian and Ukrainian experts. However, neither of them includes a critical assessment of their sources' reliability in their empirical narrative, although Matveeva (2018, 307–308) discusses some limitations of interview-based research in a brief methodological annex. This absence of source criticism from the empirical narrative is a problem. A critical reflection on the credibility of gathered interview data is crucial in a conflict situation, in which various actors may have instructions or personal motives to misrepresent certain facts. Just because a separatist denies links to the Russian state, it cannot be assumed that they do not exist. Just because a visitor to Donetsk cannot see Kremlin interference on first sight, it cannot be assumed that there is no Russian presence. And just because a local expert voices an opinion, it cannot be assumed that this opinion is grounded in facts.

Davies (2016, 733–743) and Robinson (2016, 509–512) face a similar problem. They use official statements by Russia's leadership to show the Kremlin's desire to regulate the conflict and highlight discrepancies between Moscow's rhetoric and separatist actions to demonstrate lack of control. However, it is problematic to rely on a literal reading of official statements from Moscow to reach conclusions about the conflict, since the Kremlin's statements may diverge from its capabilities, intentions, and actions.

A lack of source criticism becomes even more problematic when there are multiple steps to the primary source. As Brik (2021, 198) correctly points out, referencing chains create the risk that "pieces of low-quality information from media reports could undergo a transformation into unquestioned common knowledge after a few circles of cross-referencing." For example, an important source cited by several supporters of the invasion hypothesis (Bowen 2019, 324; Mykhnenko 2020, 529; Wilson 2016, 647–649) is a briefing paper produced by Igor Sutyagin (2015) for the Royal United Services Institute. This paper provides detailed figures of Russian troop numbers in Ukraine and the specific units involved. However, the paper's sourcing is patchy. The only sources cited are a Ukrainian news website article, an interview with an unnamed Ukrainian Armed Forces official, and some statements by US military officials. Another key source that is frequently cited to emphasize Russia's role (Gentile 2020, 14; Kuromiya 2019, 258; Mykhnenko 2020, 529; Wilson 2016, 647–649) is a study by Mitrokhin (2015). This study, in turn, relies on a selection of investigative online news articles and social media posts but lacks source criticism (Hauter 2021a, 222). It is, of course, possible that Sutyagin possesses additional insider information from sources that cannot be named for confidentiality reasons and that the sources cited by Mitrokhin are useful and reliable. However, when secondary sources are used to support an argument, the sources of these sources — or their lack of sources — need to be discussed. As far as possible, referencing chains should be avoided. Evidence should be traced back and attributed to its primary source and the credibility of this source should be addressed explicitly. As I will discuss further in chapter three, this type of source criticism is a key component of process tracing and DOSI analysis. Nevertheless, it is virtually absent from the academic literature on the Donbas conflict and from the wider academic literature on the causes of war.

1.4. Chapter Conclusion

This introductory chapter has provided an overview of the academic debate on the causes of armed conflict and explained the choice of the 2014 Donbas War as a case study. I have argued that the events of 2014 are extremely important for a better understanding of the dramatic escalation of the war in 2022. Moreover, they are an ideal case to show how social science research can adapt to the abundant but murky information environments that characterize war in the social media age. I have then explained the divide between proponents of domestic and external causes that characterizes both the political and the academic debate on the causes of the war in 2014. Finally, I have outlined why academic research on either side of the civil war-invasion divide suffers from a lack of theoretical and methodological rigor.

The divide in the literature on the Donbas War has the potential to create two self-reinforcing echo chambers in the academic discourse. The remainder of this book aims to counter this trend by providing a transparent analysis based on openly available primary information from the conflict zone. To enable this analysis, the next two chapters will address the theoretical and methodological deficits which I identified in the current academic discourse. Chapter two will develop an analytical framework for the investigation of the war's causes. At the same time, it will provide an overview of how the conflict escalated in the spring and summer of 2014. Chapter three will then propose a methodology to investigate the causes of key moments in this escalation sequence. At the same time, it will discuss underlying questions of how to evaluate cause and effect in the context of an armed conflict. On this basis, the six empirical chapters will identify the causes of the war.

2. The War's Critical Junctures

This chapter will provide an overview of how violence in the Donbas escalated in the spring and summer of 2014.[4] At the same time, it develops an analytical framework for the further investigation of the conflict's causes. It is divided into two parts. The first part will use conflict escalation theory to develop an escalation ladder for the Donbas conflict. The second part will turn this ladder into a two-dimensional escalation sequence model consisting of six critical junctures. I will argue that these critical junctures are the key episodes that moved the Donbas from a state of tense calm in February 2014 to a state of full-scale war in August. For this reason, the causes of each critical juncture are the constituent parts of the causes of the war as a whole.

2.1. A Donbas Conflict Escalation Ladder

A useful starting point for an analytical framework underpinning an investigation of the Donbas conflict's causes is the work of scholars who see war as a process of escalating violence. Escalation became a prominent topic of strategic studies research during the Cold War. Scholars studied escalation processes to assess the likelihood of nuclear war between the two superpowers and to find ways to prevent it. Kahn (1965, 39–40), for example, suggests that possible scenarios of an armed conflict between the United States and the Soviet Union can be conceptualized through an "escalation ladder" consisting of 44 steps. The ladder starts with the exchange of diplomatic notes and ends with the indiscriminate use of all available nuclear firepower. The steps are grouped into seven units, which are divided by thresholds. These thresholds signify "very sharp changes in the character of the escalation" (Kahn 1965, 40). An obvious key threshold is the use of nuclear weapons, but examples of other thresholds are attacks on the adversary's home territory or the deliberate targeting of civilians. Whereas Kahn only

---

[4] A previous version of this chapter was published as a journal article in *The Soviet and Post-Soviet Review* (Hauter 2021b).

defines escalation in terms of examples, Smoke (1977) develops a precise definition. This definition draws on Schelling's (1966) work on "limited war." Smoke's (1977, 32) interpretation of Schelling's work is that virtually all wars are restrained by certain limits which the conflict parties choose not to exceed. He calls these war-restraining limits "saliencies." On this basis, Smoke (1977, 35) defines escalation as "an action that crosses a saliency which defines the current limits of a war."

Based on a combination of Smoke's (1977) definition of escalation and Kahn's (1965) ladder analogy, I created an escalation ladder for the Donbas in 2014 (Table 1). For simplicity's sake, I omitted Kahn's subdivision into steps and units of escalation. Instead, my ladder only consists of steps. Each of these steps represents a development which crossed a threshold beyond the limits that previously defined the conflict. Considering that the term "saliency," which Smoke uses, is not very intuitive, I followed Kahn's terminology and used the term "threshold" to describe the war-restraining limits that are crossed by escalatory steps. At the same time, I followed Angstrom and Petersson's suggestion (2019, 287) that Smoke's definition of escalation should be extended to include actions "both within and outside war." This makes sense because it enables the inclusion of escalatory dynamics that precede the first armed clashes.

The creation of a conflict-specific escalation ladder is an inductive process and requires a context-specific justification of each step. For each step, it has to be specified what threshold was crossed and why this threshold consisted of limits which previously defined the conflict. This is what differentiates an escalation ladder from a simple event timeline. The ladder only includes events which crossed limits that previously defined the conflict. Events that do not meet this criterion are excluded, even if they appear important on first sight and received attention in the political debate and the academic literature. I discuss some of these excluded non-thresholds in further detail below.

I created the escalation ladder based on a dataset of online media reports that were published at the time of the events. Unlike secondary sources, these media reports consist of real-time information that has not been subject to selection and interpretation in light of subsequent developments. Naturally, a problem that remains is the potential political bias of media outlets and potential gaps in media coverage (Althaus et al. 2011; Gladun 2020). The impact of this, however, can be mitigated through a diverse sample of region-specific media sources that represent the views of all major conflict actors. Moreover, the events on the ladder can subsequently be checked against the academic literature to further minimize the risk of omissions.

I created a first draft of the ladder based on the manual review of a dataset containing 6430 media reports from the Ukrainian news website *Ukrainska Pravda* and the Russian state news agency *TASS*. These two sources represent the view of a high-profile Ukrainian news outlet with pro-Western views as well as the view of the Russian state. I gathered the dataset using Python programming language code, which downloaded all articles about the Donbas published on the two websites between February 22, and September 5, 2014. The former date marks the replacement of Ukraine's pro-Russian President Viktor Yanukovych by the Maidan Revolution. The latter date marks the First Minsk Agreement which introduced a shaky ceasefire after the intense fighting of August 2014.

To test whether the steps on the first draft ladder really crossed limits which previously defined the conflict, I created a set of keywords relating to each step. I then searched for these keywords in an extended dataset containing 58,003 media reports. This led to the merger and reordering of some parts of the first draft ladder and produced the refined Donbas escalation ladder shown in Table 1 below.

The extended dataset includes Donbas-focused reporting from eight news websites representing a broad spectrum of affiliations and ideological viewpoints. In addition to the initial small dataset, it includes all reports published between February 22 and September 5, 2014 on the local Donbas news websites *Novosti Donbassa, Ostrov, Novorosinform.org,* and *Novorossia.su*, and on the Donbas sections of the Ukrainian national newspaper websites *Vesti* and *Segodnya*. *Novosti Donbassa* and *Ostrov* support a united, pro-European Ukraine. *Novorosinform.org* and *Novorossia.su* cover events from the perspective of Russian imperialism, which provided an ideological framework for separatism in the Donbas.

Because these two news websites only started working properly in late May 2014, I also included *Vesti* and *Segodnya* to represent reporting on the earliest stages of unrest in the region from sources critical of the new Kyiv authorities. Both *Vesti* and *Segodnya* are linked to oligarchs who had been allies of the replaced President Viktor Yanukovych.

2.1.1. Steps and Thresholds

Table 1 shows the refined escalation ladder for the Donbas conflict in 2014. It cites reports from the extended dataset. In cases where the dataset contains numerous reports on one event, the report containing the most information is cited. Multiple reports are cited when there is no single report that covers all key aspects of an event. When a report consists exclusively of information that was copied from another source outside the dataset and the original source could be easily located, this original source is cited. When a report cites YouTube videos, or when a YouTube search produced videos that provide a better overview of an event than a report from the dataset, these videos are cited instead of the report.

The escalation ladder and the subsequent escalation sequence model are supposed to act as a framework for more in-depth research on the war's causes. They are not supposed to predetermine the result of such research. As far as possible, they remain agnostic about contentious issues. Events that are denied by one of the conflict parties are marked as alleged. An in-depth investigation of specific events and their causes, which will follow later in this book, will require a more elaborate methodology. However, for the identification of general escalation trends and the selection of cases that warrant closer scrutiny, the approach adopted here is sufficient.

Table 2: Refined Donbas Conflict Escalation Ladder

Background and baseline: The Euromaidan protests in Kyiv started in November 2013 after President Yanukovych decided to suspend the pursuit of an Association Agreement with the EU in favor of closer ties with Russia. The Yanukovych Administration's attempts to disperse the protests by force backfired. The protest movement grew dramatically and shifted its focus from EU integration toward general discontent with regime corruption and police brutality. At the same time, the more radical wing of the protest movement resorted to more militant means like the construction of barricades, the occupation of buildings, and the use of violence against the police.

The standoff between protesters and the regime continued throughout the winter. It culminated in a dramatic escalation of violence in late February. Firearms including sniper rifles were used against the protest movement. Around 100 people, most of them protesters, were killed between February 18 and 20 (BBC News 2020; UINP 2022). However, the violence did not disperse the protests. Neither were the protesters willing to accept an agreement on constitutional reform and early presidential elections between the regime and the opposition that was brokered by the foreign ministers of Germany, France, and Poland and signed on February 21. On the same evening, President Yanukovych left Kyiv for Kharkiv and fled to Russia a few days later. Many of Yanukovych's allies in parliament defected. On February 22, a clear majority voted to remove him from office and scheduled early presidential elections for May 25. An interim government formed by opposition politicians assumed office over the following days.

In the immediate aftermath of Yanukovych's removal, the situation in the Donbas was characterized by protest activity from both supporters and opponents of the new Kyiv authorities. According to the extended dataset, the largest protest in the last week of February took place on February 23 in Donetsk. According to Segodnya (2014a), about 3000 opponents of the change of power in Kyiv gathered. However, the pictures accompanying the report as well as video footage from YouTube (2014b) suggest that the number of attendants was smaller. The footage shows scattered groups of protesters without a united message or agenda beyond opposition to what was happening in Kyiv. The most serious altercation during this initial period was a brawl in Luhansk on February 22, which reportedly left two to four people injured (Ostrov 2014a; Ukrainska Pravda 2014a; 0642.ua 2014a). Moreover, there were some reports of activists recruiting people to volunteer "self-defense units" to guarantee public order and defend the region against supposed nationalist radicals from Kyiv and Western Ukraine (Novosti Donbassa 2014a; Ostrov 2014b; Segodnya 2014b).

Step	Threshold	Justification
1. Large protest events supporting separatism	No vocal challenge to Ukrainian state sovereignty over the Donbas	The Donbas did not have a previous history of significant separatist activism. Even during the immediate aftermath of President Yanukovych's departure on February 22, regional expressions of discontent focused on support for the old regime and fear of unrest spreading from Kyiv. Separatist demands were still limited to individuals or small groups. A large protest event in Donetsk on March 1 was the first large-scale challenge to the status of the region. Protesters shouted pro-Russian slogans and applauded the proclamation of "People's Governor" Pavlo Hubariev and his intention to hold a referendum on independence or joining Russia (YouTube 2014g; 2014e). A similar rally with Russian flags and "referendum" slogans was held in Luhansk on the same day (YouTube 2014f; 2014d). This moved separatism from the fringes to the center of local politics.
2. Occupation of state buildings	No disruption of state institutions' work or acts of vandalism against them	Opponents of the regime change in Kyiv initially called for public order and were firmly opposed to the idea of revolutionary unrest in the Donbas. Separatist activists who stormed and temporarily occupied administrative buildings in Luhansk and Donetsk on March 2 and 3 (Vesti 2014a; YouTube 2014h; 2014j; 2014i) removed this limit by showing that some people were prepared to use force and mirror the actions of activists during the earlier Maidan protests in Kyiv for the purpose of a separatist agenda.
3. Authorities arrest separatist leaders	Authorities tolerate separatist activity and refrain from interfering	The authorities did not interfere in the protests and the first occupation of buildings. With the arrests of Donetsk "People's Governor" Pavlo Hubariev on March 6 (Novosti Donbassa 2014c), the security forces crossed this non-interference threshold and took action to counter separatist activism.
4. Major violence among protesters	No loss of life or more than four people injured at a protest event	During the initial protests and occupations of buildings, violence had been limited to acts of vandalism and occasional minor altercations between protesters. Violence did not exceed the baseline level of four injured activists. Mass brawls between pro-Russian and pro-Kyiv protesters in Luhansk on March 9 and in Donetsk on March 13, crossed this threshold and significantly raised the conflict's level of violence. One anti-separatist activist died and several dozen people were injured (Ostrov 2014g; Ukrainska Pravda 2014c).

5. Appearance of armed groups	Absence of military-grade weaponry	The appearance of separatist armed groups in early to mid-April raised the challenge to state authority to a new level. The groups consisted of armed men in camouflage equipped with military-grade weaponry, who permanently occupied and fortified state buildings (YouTube 2014ac; 2014ag). Even at the height of earlier unrest in Kyiv in February, protesters had never gained access to military-grade weaponry.
6. Ukrainian military deployed	No involvement of the Ukrainian Armed Forces	The mid-April decision to send the Ukrainian Armed Forces to the Donbas (Turchynov 2014b) created the possibility of armed clashes between the military and the armed groups. It crossed another limit that had been firmly in place even at the height of earlier unrest in Kyiv, where President Yanukovych had refrained from involving the armed forces.
7. Armed clashes	No battle-related casualties	The first battle-related casualties in mid-April (Turchynov 2014b; Vesti 2014c) mark the outbreak of armed conflict according to the Uppsala Conflict Data Program's methodology. Accordingly, these first armed clashes represent a key threshold between war and peace in the Donbas.
8. Use of air force, tanks, or heavy artillery	Neither side uses air force, tanks, or heavy artillery	Airstrikes, tanks, and heavy artillery, first observed in the Donbas between late May and mid-June (Segodnya 2014c; 2014d; 2014e), have a higher destructive potential than light weapons. Their absence from the battlefield is an important sign of restraint because their use dramatically increases the number of potential casualties and the likelihood of collateral damage.
9. Artillery fire affecting urban centers	Conflict parties avoid fighting in densely populated areas	Keeping hostilities away from urban centers is another important sign of restraint because fighting in densely populated areas increases the likelihood of civilian casualties and the destruction of civilian infrastructure. Artillery fire from or at urban areas in Sloviansk was first reported at the end of May (Vesti 2014g). Regular artillery fire from or at urban areas in Luhansk began in early July (Ostrov 2014q) and in Donetsk in mid-July (YouTube 2014bo).
10. Cross-border shelling from Russia (alleged)	No shelling of Ukrainian positions from Russian territory	Shelling from Russian territory, first alleged by Ukrainian forces in mid-July (Ukrainska Pravda 2014o; Segodnya 2014f), would increase the theater of war across international borders. It would mean that Ukrainian positions came under fire from places that were out of bounds for retaliatory strikes because the Russian leadership, which denies that any cross-border shelling took place, would have portrayed such a strike as an act of aggression.

| 11. Invasion by regular Russian troops (alleged) | No direct involvement of Russia's regular armed forces | An invasion by regular Russian troops, which allegedly took place in late August (Ostrov 2014r), would have added the firepower and expertise of Russia's regular armed forces to the conflict. This would have removed the limiting effects of the covert nature of manpower and equipment supplies that may have taken place during previous steps. |

Source: the author

2.1.2. Non-Thresholds

Many accounts of the Donbas conflict also highlight other events. At first sight, some of these could be interpreted as escalation threshold crossings. A closer analysis, however, suggests that they were not part of the escalation sequence.

2.1.2.1. The Euromaidan Protests

When investigating the causes of the Donbas conflict, it makes sense to limit the initial analysis to the time after February 22, 2014. Rather than escalating the conflict in the Donbas, the sudden regime change that happened in Kyiv on that day created a baseline from which the conflict could escalate in the first place. This is an important difference. There were no signs of war in the Donbas on February 22, 2014. Manifestations of public discontent were moderate considering that the country had just experienced a revolution. The crucial question of conflict escalation in the Donbas is how the region transitioned from this post-revolutionary state of tense calm to a state of war. An analysis of the previous Euromaidan protest wave and its violent escalation in Kyiv diverts attention from this question and leads to conceptual overstretch. It dissolves the specific issue of the Donbas conflict in a broader analysis. Of course, the Euromaidan was a necessary condition for the war – just like, for example, the 2012 re-election of Vladimir Putin as president of Russia or the breakdown of the Soviet Union. However, this does not mean that it is useful to view all these preceding events as part of the Donbas conflict. On the contrary, identifying their place in an overarching explanation of the war is only possible after analyzing the transition from peace to war in the region itself.

2.1.2.2. The Geneva Agreement

On April 17, 2014, representatives of the European Union, the United States, Ukraine, and Russia issued a statement after multilateral talks in Geneva (Ukrainian Foreign Ministry 2014). The statement called for the disarmament of all illegal armed groups, the return of all illegally seized buildings, and an inclusive process of constitutional reform in Ukraine. At first sight, the statement could be perceived as an instance of de-escalation. However, when looking at events in the region at the time, it becomes clear that the statement had no discernible de-escalating impact. Over the following weeks, the region witnessed unprecedented levels of violence.

2.1.2.3. The Separatist "Referenda"

Another prominent development came in the shape of the May 11 separatist independence "referenda" in the self-proclaimed Donetsk and Luhansk People's Republics. Although these "referenda" received significant media attention, their significance in terms of conflict escalation was negligible. The two "republics" had already been proclaimed. Armed men had already occupied buildings in the regional centers and were engaging in armed combat with Ukrainian security forces in Sloviansk and Mariupol. In this context, a symbolic vote was not a step that pushed the level of violence across limits that had previously defined the conflict.

2.1.2.4. Events after the First Minsk Agreement

August 2014 was the deadliest month of the war up to February 2022. It was followed by the September 5, 2014 First Minsk Ceasefire Agreement (OSCE 2014). This Agreement marks the end of the conflict's initial escalation sequence. Autumn 2014 was a period of relative calm. This was followed by another escalation uptick in early 2015, which led to the Second Minsk Agreement (OSCE 2015). However, fighting did not reach the scale observed in July and August 2014 and, from February 2015 onward, the war continued to de-escalate.[5] Hence, the First Minsk Agreement of September 2014

---

5   Detailed Ukrainian casualty statistics for 2014–2021 are available from the Memory Book for Ukraine's Fallen volunteer project (Memorybook.org.ua n.d.a). For a compilation of frontline maps produced by the Ukrainian military, see TSN (2019a).

marks the highest level of escalation observed in the Donbas before February 2022. It also marks the emergence of the key features that characterized the armed conflict for the following eight years: hostilities of varying but generally decreasing intensity which were contained along a defined contact line that was not subject to major changes. For this reason, it is reasonable to choose September 5, 2014 as the cut-off point for an analysis of the conflict's formative phase. Extending the analysis further to include the subsequent de-escalation process is unlikely to provide significant added value regarding the identification of the conflict's causes.

2.2. Six Critical Junctures

The one-dimensional escalation ladder shown in Table 2 provides a basic framework for the analysis of the Donbas conflict. However, this framework is still too simplistic to be an adequate model of the escalation of violence in the region. The ladder has to be extended to take account of the fact that the actual escalation sequence in the Donbas was spread unevenly across space and time. Different thresholds were crossed in different places at different points in time with the involvement of different actors. Some thresholds were crossed in close succession while others were further apart.

Neither does the escalation ladder address questions of causality. It cannot simply be assumed that the ladder is a causal sequence in which one step causes the next. The causal significance of each step, both for subsequent steps and for the conflict as a whole, remains an open question.

The concept of critical junctures is helpful to improve my framework and analyze escalation in terms of actors and causality. Collier and Munck (2017, 2) define a critical juncture as "a major episode of institutional innovation" which leaves an "enduring legacy." Capoccia and Kelemen (2007, 348) add that a critical juncture is short compared to its legacy and that, during the juncture, actors' choices have a higher impact than during the legacy period.

War is not usually analyzed as an institution. However, social scientists often define institutions as rules or constraints that regulate human interactions, which is similar to Schelling's (1966) and Smoke's (1977) definition of limited war. North (1991, 1) describes institutions as "humanly devised constraints that structure political, economic and social interaction." According to Hodgson (2006, 18), they are "systems of established and embedded social rules." Moreover, three of the four criteria that define a critical juncture automatically apply to escalation steps as described by Kahn (1965) and Smoke (1977). Firstly, an escalation step constitutes a major episode of innovation in the context of an armed conflict because any redefinition of the limits of a war represents a major change to the implicit rules that restrain violence. Secondly, choices that cross a threshold which defines the current limits of a war are, by definition, more impactful than choices that stay within these limits. Thirdly, an act of escalation in war can only leave an enduring legacy if this legacy is long compared to the act itself.

Leaving an enduring legacy, however, is the key criterion from the definition of critical junctures that is not part of the definition of escalation. Some escalation steps could be followed by de-escalation, or they could be superseded by further escalation steps without leaving an enduring legacy. Other escalation steps, however, do leave an enduring legacy. This legacy could consist of hostilities that continue for a long period of time or of damage that takes a long time to repair. Alternatively, or simultaneously, it could consist of further escalation—of making additional critical junctures possible, which then leave an enduring legacy of violence further down the line. Steps that leave an enduring legacy in either of these ways are of particular importance for the analysis of the Donbas War's causes. Their further scrutiny can provide answers regarding the role played by domestic and foreign factors during the war's formative phase.

The idea that critical junctures leave an enduring legacy is closely linked to causality in terms of necessary conditions. Actors' choices can only leave an enduring legacy on the further course of events if this course of events would not have been the same without their impact. They do not have to be a sufficient condition. Necessity, however, is crucial.

In practice, this means that the events on the escalation ladder must be analyzed across different points in time and different locations according to their impact and the causal relationships between them. This analysis results in an escalation sequence model that divides the formative phase of the Donbas War into six critical junctures. The model is illustrated in Figure 1 and explained in detail in the following sections.

2.2.1. Non-Junctures: The Protests of March 2014

My Donbas escalation ladder includes events that precede the outbreak of militarized violence. To qualify as critical junctures, such pre-conflict escalation steps would have to be necessary conditions either for the start of the armed conflict or for its subsequent further escalation. A closer look at the relevant events suggests that, up to the permanent and armed building occupations of April 6, 2014, none of the developments in the region meet this criterion.

2.2.1.1. Mass Protests Against the Kyiv Authorities

On the weekend of March 1–2, 2014, large protest rallies against the new Kyiv authorities took place in several locations across the Donbas. The largest rallies were reported from the regional centers of Donetsk and Luhansk with 10,000 people reported in each city (Ostrov 2014d; 2014e). However, turnout did not increase further. On the contrary, by early April, the pro-Russian protest movement had lost rather than gained momentum.

This becomes particularly apparent when comparing videos of the crowd that had gathered in front of the Donetsk Oblast State Administration on March 1 and April 6 while activists stormed the building. On the former date, protesters filled the entire square (YouTube 2014c). On the latter date, they constituted a scattered group of people that only occupied a small section of it (YouTube 2014q; 2014r). A calculation of the square's area on Google Earth combined with crowd size models provided by crowd safety expert Keith Still (2013) suggests that 2000 people is a generous maximum estimate for the April 6 event.

Footage from Luhansk from April 6 presents a similar picture. The crowd of protesters was limited to a relatively small area that could hardly hold more than 2000 people (YouTube 2014p; 2014v). Gatherings of this size were not significantly above the baseline of protest activity in the Donbas in the immediate aftermath of the replacement of President Yanukovych in late February. Hence, the protest rallies in March do not qualify as a necessary condition for the conflict's further escalation in April. A core group of radicalized activists could have escalated the conflict in April regardless of the scale of earlier protest activity.

2.2.1.2. The Occupation of State Buildings

Initial incidents of protesters storming state buildings in Donetsk and Luhansk in early March were temporary. Activists vacated the occupied buildings after a few hours or days. None of these attempts had a lasting impact—besides media attention, the arrest of some separatist leaders, and some damage to property. Moreover, there were no reports of building seizures in Donetsk and Luhansk between March 16 and April 6. This suggests that the events of April 6—when people stormed buildings, stayed in these buildings, built barricades, and obtained arms—should be analyzed as separate events and not as the consequence of previous building occupations.

2.2.1.3. The Arrest of Separatist Leaders

Arresting protest leaders could cause further escalation of a conflict either by radicalizing an initially moderate protest movement or by strengthening a protest movement because new people join to demand freedom for the leaders. Neither was the case in the Donbas. The separatist movement in Donetsk and Luhansk did not begin with a moderate agenda but with temporary building seizures and calls for a complete power transfer to the local level and referenda on independence or joining Russia. These demands and methods, which were completely unacceptable for the Kyiv authorities, remained unchanged after the arrests of early March. There is no reason to assume that the arrested separatist leaders or their supporters would have changed course and become more moderate had the arrests not happened. Neither did the arrests of early March galvanize further public support. As argued above, the protest movement lost rather than gained momentum throughout the course of the month.

2.2.1.4. Violence among Protesters

There is no plausible causal connection between the violence against pro-European activists at protests in mid-March and the appearance of armed groups. Violence among protesters could have caused further escalation either if protesters had obtained arms as a result or if it had resulted in the security forces using violence to stop further protests from taking place. Neither was the case in the Donbas. The first arms appeared not at protest events but in occupied buildings and at no point did the security forces use violence against protesters. This means that the first critical juncture of the conflict took place in early April because none of the events of March qualify.

2.2.2. Juncture 1: Donetsk and Luhansk, Early April

On April 6, 2014, separatist activists stormed the building of the Oblast State Administration in Donetsk and the regional headquarters of the Security Service of Ukraine (SBU) in Luhansk. Unlike in previous instances of building seizures in the Donbas, the activists did not vacate the two buildings after a short period of time but started to build barricades around them (Ostrov 2014i; YouTube 2014z). More importantly, they armed themselves with automatic rifles seized from the SBU (62.ua 2014; YouTube 2014ac). This was the first appearance of military-grade equipment in separatist hands in the Donbas. The Ukrainian authorities responded with threats of "antiterrorist measures" (Turchynov 2014a) but did not take any action. Instead, representatives from Kyiv travelled to Donetsk and Luhansk to oversee negotiations with the separatists (Ukrainska Pravda 2014e; 2014g; 2014i; 2014k).

Although it took almost another two months until armed clashes reached Donetsk and Luhansk, the armed occupation of state buildings in early April created the first militarized separatist footholds in the two cities. Without these footholds, the Ukrainian security forces could have taken control of the regional centers without the risk of armed resistance and civilian casualties. Hence, the initial militarization of separatism in Donetsk and Luhansk was a necessary condition for the later spread of armed conflict to the two cities, even though the first fighting took place elsewhere.

2.2.3. Juncture 2: Sloviansk, Kramatorsk, and Surroundings, Mid-April

On April 12, armed men in camouflage seized police stations in the towns of Sloviansk and Kramatorsk in the northwest of Donetsk Oblast (YouTube 2014ag; 2014ai). The following morning, a group of these men attacked SBU operatives just outside Sloviansk. One person died and several were injured. On the same day, Ukraine's Acting President Turchynov announced the launch of an "antiterrorist operation" with the involvement of the Ukrainian Armed Forces (Hromadske TV 2014b; LifeNews 2014b; 2014a; Turchynov 2014b). Regular armed clashes between Ukrainian troops and separatist forces commenced in early May (Memorybook.org.ua n.d.a), and the area around Sloviansk became the central theater of armed conflict in the Donbas until the separatists' withdrawal on July 5 (Novorosinform.org 2014c).

Because this episode of conflict escalation featured the crossing of three escalation thresholds — the appearance of armed groups, the deployment of the military, and armed clashes — in close succession, it makes sense to group these events together in one critical juncture. There can be no doubt that what happened around Sloviansk in mid-April left an enduring legacy of armed conflict. It was in the context of these events that the Ukrainian military was first mobilized, and for over two months the most intense fighting took place around Sloviansk. It was in this area that heavy artillery and tanks were first used in late May and early June (Ostrov 2014o; Segodnya 2014d). Even if the whole armed conflict had been limited to this episode, it would have left a legacy of violence and destruction that was unprecedented in Ukraine since World War Two.

Figure 1: Donbas Conflict Escalation Sequence

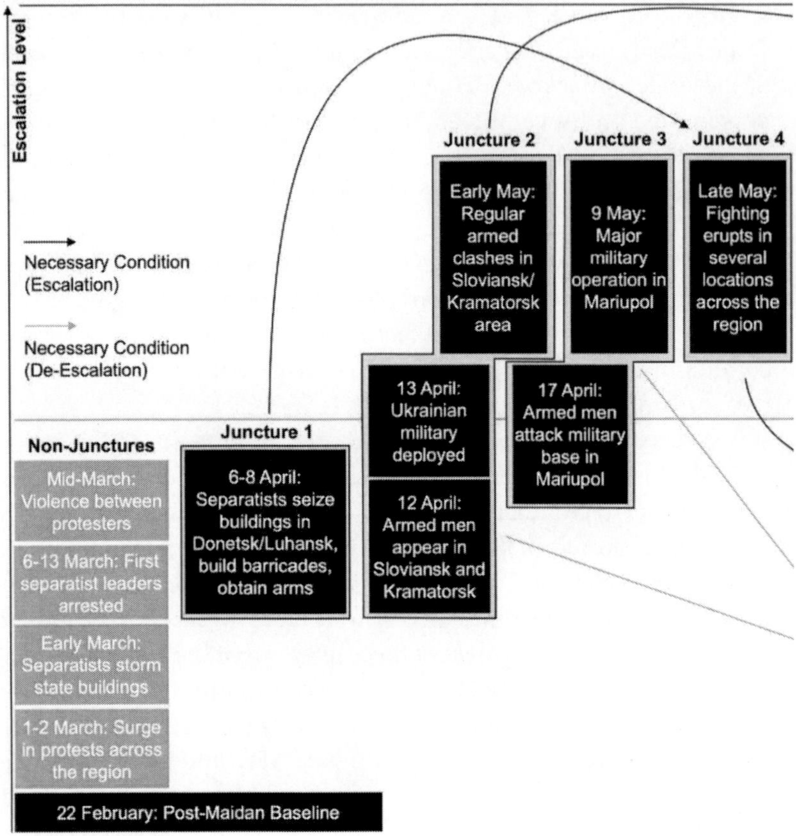

Escalation Level

→ Necessary Condition (Escalation)

⇢ Necessary Condition (De-Escalation)

Non-Junctures
- Mid-March: Violence between protesters
- 6-13 March: First separatist leaders arrested
- Early March: Separatists storm state buildings
- 1-2 March: Surge in protests across the region
- 22 February: Post-Maidan Baseline

Juncture 1
- 6-8 April: Separatists seize buildings in Donetsk/Luhansk, build barricades, obtain arms
- 12 April: Armed men appear in Sloviansk and Kramatorsk
- 13 April: Ukrainian military deployed
- 17 April: Armed men attack military base in Mariupol

Juncture 2
- Early May: Regular armed clashes in Sloviansk/Kramatorsk area

Juncture 3
- 9 May: Major military operation in Mariupol

Juncture 4
- Late May: Fighting erupts in several locations across the region

Source: the author

The War's Critical Junctures 57

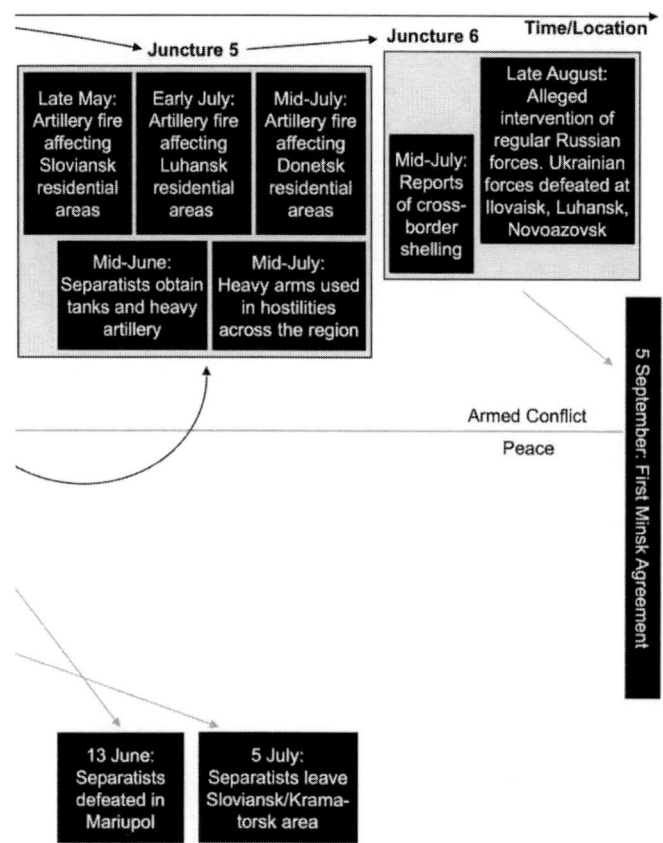

2.2.4. Juncture 3: Mariupol—Where Separatism Failed, Mid-April to Mid-June

After Sloviansk, the southern port city of Mariupol was the first place in the Donbas where tensions crossed the armed conflict threshold (Novosti Donbassa 2014d; Vesti 2014c; 2014f). Like in the Sloviansk area, the appearance of armed groups, the deployment of the security forces, and the first armed clashes happened in close succession. However, the level of violence and separatist control never reached the level observed in other areas of the Donbas and the Kyiv authorities consolidated their control over the city as early as mid-June (Novorosinform.org 2014b; Liga.Novosti 2014a). Nevertheless, the fighting that occurred left a legacy of armed conflict in this city that was unprecedented since World War Two. This legacy was only superseded in spring 2022, when Russian forces destroyed most of Mariupol. The 2014 escalation of violence in Mariupol is also interesting from a comparative perspective because of its relatively short duration. Analyzing it may indicate why armed separatism was less successful in Mariupol than in other parts of the Donbas.

2.2.5. Juncture 4: The Fighting Spreads, Late May

For the first month of armed conflict, fighting in the Donbas was limited to the Sloviansk area and to Mariupol. However, from late May onward—around the time of the Ukrainian presidential election—hostilities rapidly spread to several other locations across the Donbas. The most important new theatres of violence were Volnovakha (Ostrov 2014n), Karlivka (Novosti Donbassa 2014f), Donetsk Airport (TASS 2014a), parts of Luhansk city (Novosti Donbassa 2014h; TASS 2014b), an urban agglomeration northwest of Luhansk (Ukrainska Pravda 2014m), and rural areas near the Russian-Ukrainian border in the south of Donetsk and Luhansk Oblasts (Novosti Donbassa 2014e; Glavkom 2014). This sudden increase in theaters of war not only led to a significant number of casualties but also paved the way for continuing hostilities in these new hotbeds. Each incident of fighting spreading to a new location could be defined as a separate critical juncture. However, to avoid a fragmentation of the analysis and to emphasize that all these incidents share the legacy of expanding the theater of war, it makes sense to group them into one juncture.

2.2.6. Juncture 5: Tanks and Heavy Artillery, June-July

The Ukrainian Armed Forces first used airstrikes during armed clashes at Donetsk Airport on May 26 (Segodnya 2014c). The use of heavy artillery was first reported near Sloviansk on May 29 (Ostrov 2014o), and the combat deployment of Ukrainian tanks in this area was confirmed on June 6 (Segodnya 2014d). In mid-June, first reports of tanks and artillery under separatist control appeared (YouTube 2014aw; Segodnya 2014e). Soon, the use of tanks and heavy artillery on both sides became a common occurrence across the battlefield and, simultaneously, began to affect densely populated areas. Heavy arms left a particularly devastating legacy because they were responsible for most of the damage and loss of life in the Donbas during the course of the armed conflict in 2014. Again, each instance of heavy arms use in a new location could be defined as a new critical juncture. However, like in the previous case, it makes sense to group all incidents of heavy arms use initially into one juncture.

2.2.7. Juncture 6: The Ukrainian Defeat of Late August

The Ukrainian Armed Forces first voiced allegations of cross-border shelling from Russian territory in mid-July after an attack on Ukrainian positions near the village of Zelenopillia (Ukrainska Pravda 2014o). This attack and subsequent incidents of alleged cross-border shelling may have slowed the advance of the Ukrainian forces, but they were insufficient to turn the tide of the conflict. However, the tide did turn in late August when many Ukrainian soldiers lost their lives while trying to leave an encirclement near Ilovaisk and Ukrainian forces lost control over the areas south of Luhansk and east of Mariupol. Kyiv claimed that a Russian invasion force was responsible for this sudden defeat (Ostrov 2014r; Segodnya 2014g).

Moscow denies any cross-border shelling and any invasion. However, the question of Russian involvement can be sidestepped at this initial stage. Regardless of Russian involvement, fighting along the border in July and August led to the crossing of escalation thresholds in several additional locations. And, regardless of Russian involvement, the intensity of fighting in the Donbas peaked during the battles that marked the sudden Ukrainian defeat of late August. These battles left an unprecedented legacy of violence in the region and Ukrainian society as a whole. At the same time, the defeat of late August prevented the Ukrainian Armed Forces from regaining control over the whole of the Donbas. Hence, it was a necessary condition for the continuation of the armed conflict at a lower level over the years that followed. For this reason, the Ukrainian defeat of late August 2014 and the intensification of hostilities leading up to it represent a final critical juncture in the initial, formative stage of the war.

2.3. Chapter Conclusion

This chapter has provided an overview of how the Donbas conflict escalated in 2014. It has also developed a framework for the further investigation of the war's causes. I have combined conflict escalation theory with the concept of critical junctures to create an escalation sequence model of the war's initial formative phase. I have argued that this model covers the time period of early April to late August 2014 and comprises six critical junctures.

My escalation sequence model is a benchmark for attempts to explain the outbreak of the war in 2014. Any convincing explanation must be able to explain the six critical junctures outlined in this chapter. For this reason, my further investigation of the role of domestic factors on the one hand and Russian interference on the other will focus on these critical junctures.

None of the events included in my escalation sequence are controversial in the sense that either side of the conflict, their affiliated media outlets, or any part of the academic literature, dispute their occurrence. For example, in virtually all cases of fighting, all sides agree that an armed clash occurred. What is disputed are the details of the event – the actors involved, their motivation and the nature, sequence, and consequences of their actions. In most cases, the question of Russian involvement is at the core of such controversies, and this is precisely what the nature of the war depends on.

If most critical junctures in the escalation of the war took place primarily because of internal factors, the conflict should be considered a civil war. If the primary cause of most critical junctures were the actions of the Russian state, the war should be considered an invasion. In other words, an investigation into the nature of the 2014 Donbas War has to look at each of the six critical junctures outlined in this chapter and answer the following question: Were the separatist groups who fought against the Ukrainian security forces agents of the Russian state in the sense that the Russian state's actions were the primary cause of their actions?

However, this question can only be answered after a more thorough discussion of causal relationships and ways to identify them. Before I can proceed with the investigation of the war's critical junctures, I have to explain how I have decided whether one cause is more important than another. I also have to clarify what kind of evidence I use to reach my conclusions. This is what I will do in the following chapter.

3. Digital Forensic Process Tracing

This chapter will take a closer look at questions of cause and effect and at the way in which digital information sources can be used to identify causal relationships.[6] The result will be a methodological framework for the investigation of the six critical junctures that shaped the Donbas War in 2014. I will proceed in four steps. Firstly, this chapter will introduce process tracing as the methodology of choice for the in-depth study of individual cases. I will argue that process tracing can be defined by four benchmarks—separating explanations and evidence, considering alternative explanations, practicing source criticism, and using probabilistic reasoning. Secondly, this chapter will argue that existing studies neglect the latter two of these benchmarks and fail to pay sufficient attention to online sources. Thirdly, this chapter will introduce digital open source information (DOSI) analysis—a way of doing research that has gained popularity among journalists and NGO activists in recent years. It will highlight the synergy effects of merging DOSI analysis and process tracing into *digital forensic process tracing*. Fourthly, I will discuss some assumptions about the nature of cause and effect that underpin the application of digital forensic process tracing to the Donbas conflict. In this final section, I will also discuss the methodology's limitations and possible mitigation techniques and explain how I use digital forensic process tracing in practice.

3.1. Four Benchmarks for Good Process Tracing

Process tracing is a social science methodology which tries to open the black box between cause and effect. In contrast to frequentist approaches to causality, which infer cause and effect from the correlation of variables across multiple cases, process tracing takes a detailed look at individual cases and tries to find evidence of how a cause brings about an outcome. Process tracing relies heavily on the concept of "causal mechanisms" to describe what is inside the black box between cause and effect. Despite the central role of this

---

6 Parts of this chapter were previously published in Hauter 2021c, 2–6.

concept, however, there is no consensus on what a causal mechanism actually is. Hedström and Ylikoski (2010, 51) list as many as nine different definitions, most of which are either very abstract or very general or both at the same time. Beach and Pedersen (2013, 29) draw on some of these definitions and make the concept more concrete and precise. They define a causal mechanism as a set of entities that engage in activities which transmit causal force from a cause to an outcome. They argue that a causal mechanism can be compared to a machine with toothed wheels (the entities), the movement of which (their activities) transmits causal force through the machine. To illustrate this analogy, they use the example of a car engine. They define the motor as the cause and the movement of the car as the outcome. The causal mechanisms are the wheels and the driveshaft, which, through their movement, transmit the motor's impulse into the movement of the car (Beach and Pedersen 2013, 30).

Defined in its broadest sense, process tracing includes any academic writing that underpins a claim about cause and effect with a detailed case-based narrative. According to this definition, the academic literature that uses process tracing for the study of armed conflict is vast. At the same time, some scholars have made attempts to formulate practice-oriented standards that define process tracing in a narrower way. In general terms, this methodological literature develops four benchmarks for methodologically rigorous process tracing research.

3.1.1. Separating Explanations and Evidence

Beach and Pedersen (2013, 33) stress that process tracing has to go beyond a mere empirical narrative. It must compare the empirical evidence of the particular case to the hypothetical evidence a researcher would expect to see if a particular causal mechanism were at work. This mechanism can be formulated at the start to be tested against the empirical evidence, or it can be developed deductively after the analysis of the empirical evidence (Beach and Pedersen 2013, 11–22). Either way, the crucial point is that the analysis keeps empirical evidence and theoretical causal mechanism separate and explicitly points out how the former supports the latter.

3.1.2. Considering Alternative Explanations

Bennet and Checkel's list of best practices for process tracing research (2015, 23-31), places particular emphasis on the importance of investigating alternative hypotheses. They argue that "failing to consider a potentially viable explanation that readily occurs to the readers and critics of a case study can make the process tracing unconvincing" (Bennett and Checkel 2015, 23). An important tool for the evaluation of evidence in light of competing hypotheses is a typology of tests devised by Stephen van Evera. Bennet and Checkel (2015, 17), as well as Beach and Pedersen (2013, 100-105) and Mahoney (2015, 207-212) describe this typology as an integral component of process tracing. The typology groups evidence into four categories (van Evera 1997, 31-32):

- Evidence which can disprove but not prove a hypothesis. The presence of this evidence does not rule out alternatives to the hypothesis in question, but the absence of this evidence rules out the hypothesis. Van Evera argues that evidence of this kind represents a "hoop test" because the evidence represents a hoop that the hypothesis has to "jump through."
- Evidence which can prove a hypothesis but not disprove it through its absence. Van Evera calls this a "smoking gun test," because "a smoking gun seen in a suspect's hand moments after a shooting is quite conclusive proof of guilt, but a suspect not seen with a smoking gun is not proven innocent."
- Evidence which can both prove and disprove a hypothesis. Van Evera calls this a "doubly-decisive test." This evidence presents the hypothesis with a hoop test and a smoking-gun test at once: "passage strongly corroborates an explanation, a flunk kills it."
- Evidence which can "weigh in the total balance" but is not decisive either way. Van Evera calls this a "straw-in-the-wind test."

The application of this typology forces researchers to spell out how and to what extent their empirical evidence favors their proposed explanation rather than alternative hypotheses.

3.1.3. Practicing Source Criticism

Process tracing analysts should be wary of taking their sources at face value. Bennet and Checkel's (2015, 24–25) process tracing guidelines urge researchers to "consider the potential biases of evidentiary sources." Beach and Pedersen (2013, 125–129) argue that, in order to turn observations into evidence, process tracing researchers have to "assess the content" and "evaluate the accuracy" of observations. They also argue that the reliability of different types of sources can depend on a variety of contextual factors which process tracing researchers need to take into account (Beach and Pedersen 2013, 132–143). Fairfield and Charman (2017, 370) go a step further and argue that "testimonial evidence in process tracing is best analyzed by including the source in the definition of the evidence." They suggest that "evidence E should typically take the form 'source S stated X'." What this means is that, rather than postulating evidence as a statement of fact that is referenced to a source, process tracing analysts should evaluate the context and background of both the source and the evidence contained in it. In other words, they should follow the example of historians by practicing rigorous source criticism. This benchmark is of particular importance for research on armed conflict and especially for research in the context of the abundant but murky information environment that characterizes the Donbas War.

3.1.4. Updating Probabilities

Questioning the accuracy of source material inevitably creates uncertainty, which can be addressed through the use of probabilistic language. For this reason, the same process-tracing theorists who advocate source criticism also advocate the use of Bayesian inference (Beach and Pedersen 2013, 83; Bennett and Checkel 2015, 16; Fairfield and Charman 2017). Bayes' Theorem postulates that the probability of a hypothesis being true increases or decreases as pieces of evidence for or against it accumulate. In the words of Bennett (2009, 8), "the more unlikely a piece of evidence [E] is in light of alternatives to explanation H, the more that evidence [E] increases our confidence that H is true if the evidence proves consistent with H." Bennett (2009, 8) summarizes Bayes' theorem with a formula which can be spelled out as follows:

Probability that H is true in light of E = H's prior probability $\times \dfrac{\text{E's probability in light of H}}{\text{E's prior probability}}$

Bayes' theorem provides a tool for formal probabilistic reasoning in qualitative case study research. Theoretically, the continued application of the above formula until all available evidence has been considered should lead researchers with divergent starting positions regarding the probability of H to the same final probability (Bennett 2009, 9). Of course, this is unlikely to work in practice because researchers may assign different probabilities to different pieces of evidence. Also, there is a controversy about whether or not there is any benefit in researchers assigning specific numerical probabilities to qualitative evidence (Barrenechea and Mahoney 2019, 453; Beach 2017, 15; Befani and Stedman-Bryce 2017, 52–53; Fairfield and Charman 2017).

Nevertheless, applying the general principles of Bayesian inference is another benchmark for process tracing research. Applying these principles either mathematically or verbally forces researchers to spell out the probabilistic reasoning behind their evaluation of evidence, which makes clear where exactly their assessments converge and differ. Moreover, using probabilistic reasoning allows for a more nuanced assessment than the mere use of van Evera's typology of tests (Befani and Stedman-Bryce 2017, 53). This makes Bayesian inference particularly useful in cases where there are major gaps or contradictions in the available evidence, which may result in numerous straw-in-the-wind tests pointing in different directions.

3.2. The Neglect of Source Criticism and Probabilistic Reasoning

Naturally, these four benchmarks are an ideal type that few if any empirical studies are able to meet. Limits imposed by time, space, research design, and data availability force researchers to prioritize certain benchmarks while neglecting others. For this reason, it is appropriate to define any research that meets at least one of the four benchmarks as process tracing.

Most studies on the causes of war that engage in process tracing as defined above only meet either the first or the second benchmark. However, it is the third and fourth benchmarks which make process tracing the methodology of choice for research that exploits online media to investigate the facts of a contemporary war like the Donbas conflict. The volume of information available online and the prevalence of disinformation make it essential to explicitly assess the reliability of source material and to spell out the probabilistic conclusions that a researcher can draw from this assessment. This is not to say that the authors of existing process tracing research on war are careless in their treatment of sources and have not sufficiently considered limitations and potential biases in their data. It simply means that source criticism and Bayesian updating are not key components of their empirical narratives. This may not be necessary within the specific research designs and source environments of many existing studies. However, source criticism and Bayesian updating are essential for process tracing research that aims to navigate the abundant but murky online information environment that characterizes the Donbas conflict and other wars of the social media age.

Chapter two of this book has already used online information as the empirical basis for the Donbas War's escalation sequence. However, it sidestepped the need for source criticism and Bayesian updating by leaving all controversial questions open. The events included in the escalation sequence model are either not disputed by any conflict party or they are labelled as disputed and requiring further investigation. Neither does the model specify the actors responsible for each critical juncture. While the creation of the model meets some aspects of the first two benchmarks, its process tracing efforts remain incomplete because it omits a causal mechanism's most crucial part—the causes. For this reason, chapter two on its own would not qualify as fully-fledged process tracing research that uses online information to investigate the causes of war.

At present, process tracing research of this kind, which aims to use online information from a conflict zone as the main data source to study a war, is virtually non-existent. Process tracing research on armed conflict draws primarily on interview data gathered during fieldwork as well as archival material and secondary literature. Newspaper articles or news agency reports are used by some authors but play a secondary, supplementary role. This is a gap worth filling. It is crucial that academic process tracing research on armed conflict adapts to modern information technology and treats online media and related qualitative data as an important information source. By doing so, it could make use of a huge repository of primary information that is currently not used according to its full potential. Moreover, a focus on online media would also enable timely research in cases in which it would be unsafe to travel to the conflict zone or in which key participants are unavailable for interviews.

3.3. The Potential of Digital Open Source Information

Academic process tracing research on armed conflict can be made fit for the Internet age by incorporating digital open source information (DOSI) analysis. DOSI refers to the vast amount of information that the Internet has made available to the general public in the form of text, picture, and video material posted on news websites or on social media platforms such as Twitter, Facebook, or YouTube. It also includes the information available in public online databases, such as the flight tracking website Flightradar24, the Internet Archive project, or the annotated satellite imagery platform Wikimapia. DOSI analysis is the analytic technique that is used to identify, structure, and verify this type of data.

Even though DOSI is related to and often used synonymously with open source intelligence (OSINT), it makes sense to differentiate between the two terms. The origins of the term OSINT lie in the work of government intelligence agencies, where it is used to describe information gathered from publicly available sources as opposed to, for example, information received from informants (Gibson 2013). In recent years, OSINT analysis has become a popular term to describe not only the work of government agencies but also investigations by activists and journalists based on openly available information. However, some researchers are uncomfortable with the use of OSINT as a label for work carried out beyond government intelligence agencies. Clem (2017, 608), for example, refers to "public-sourced information" and restricts the term OSINT "to the analysis of public information within intelligence agencies." Toler (2020b) calls OSINT a "silly term" and voices the suspicion that it is "used by people who want to cosplay as intel[ligence] officers." He proposes "digital research/investigation" as an alternative.

It is understandable that researchers want to draw a clear line between the work of government intelligence officers, on the one hand, and journalists and NGO activists, on the other. Moreover, it makes sense to differentiate between the different purposes for which government intelligence agencies on the one hand and journalist and activists on the other use openly available information. This is made particularly clear in the Berkeley Protocol on Digital Open Source Investigations (United Nations 2020). This protocol is a set of principles and best practices published by the Human Rights Center of the UC Berkeley School of Law and the UN Office of the High Commissioner for Human Rights. It differentiates between DOSI and OSINT by defining the latter as a subcategory of the former. OSINT is openly available information which is "collected and used for the specific purpose of aiding policymaking and decision-making, most often in a military or political context" (United Nations 2020, 7). I will follow this differentiation and use the term DOSI rather than OSINT to refer to the vast amount of information that the Internet has made available to researchers.

The most famous examples of high-quality DOSI analysis are the publications of the investigative journalist group Bellingcat. Long before an official report came to the same conclusion, Bellingcat succeeded in confirming the Russian origin of the missile launcher that downed Malaysian Airlines flight MH17 over the Donbas in July 2014. The key source of their investigation was photo and video material of the launcher that was published online around the time the plane was shot down (Allen et al. 2014). This success story of DOSI analysis did not go unnoticed in the academic literature (Sienkiewicz 2015). However, even though DOSI analysis has been the subject of academic work (see also Dyer and Ivens 2020; Hayes and Cappa 2018; McDermott, Koenig, and Murray 2021; Pastor-Galindo et al. 2020; Senekal and Kotzé 2019; Wheatley

2018), its synergies with process tracing methodology have remained unnoticed. Naturally, the use of DOSI analysis by journalists and advocacy groups does not focus on academic debates and methodologies. At the same time, there is no academic work so far that explicitly incorporates DOSI analysis into process tracing methodology to answer research questions.

The methodological approach of DOSI analysis mirrors the requirements of the third and fourth process tracing benchmarks outlined in this chapter. Source criticism and the principles behind Bayesian updating are an integral part of any qualitative evaluation of DOSI. The Berkeley Protocol illustrates this. The protocol's "open source investigation cycle" (United Nations 2020, 55–68) includes a "preliminary assessment" stage, at which the investigator should check whether the discovered information appears to be "prima facie" relevant and reliable. This is followed by a "verification" stage, which features an in-depth assessment of a source's content and context. Moreover, the protocol also stresses that analytical reports based on DOSI need to address gaps and uncertainties and include relevant caveats (United Nations 2020, 72).

The added value of DOSI analysis for process tracing lies in its focus on the potential of online sources. In many cases, all it takes to harness this potential is the skillful use of online search engine algorithms to find primary sources of evidence followed by careful contextual analysis and cross-checking of these sources (Myers 2020; Toler 2020a). In cases where a topic has already received significant attention from secondary sources, DOSI analysis can check whether these secondary sources rely on openly available online material. If they do, DOSI analysis can evaluate and cross-check this material to either validate or refute the conclusions of the secondary source. In some cases, DOSI researchers may also use certain tools to make source discovery and verification more effective. Examples are reverse image search engines like TinEye, satellite imagery tools like GoogleEarth or SunCalc, and the photo and video verification toolkit InVID. A broader overview of available DOSI analysis tools is provided by Bellingcat's (n.d.a) Online Investigation Toolkit database.

The incorporation of DOSI analysis enhances process tracing research on the causes of war in two important ways. Firstly, it shifts the empirical focus toward the abundance of primary information from conflict zones that is available on the Internet in general and on social media in particular. Secondly, it shifts the methodological focus to source criticism and Bayesian updating.

In other words, the incorporation of DOSI analysis applies the forensic components of process tracing in a digital source environment. The term "forensic" generally refers to the investigation of a crime. Several process tracing theorists point out this is a good analogy for some aspects of process tracing research. Bennett (2009, 4) argues that the work of a process tracing researcher is "closely analogous to a detective attempting to solve a crime." Similarly, Befani and Stedman-Bryce (2017, 46–47) suggest that process tracing researchers should approach their research as if they were facing a trial in which they had to present evidence to a jury. These analogies are convincing. Process tracing can be approached in a forensic way. A particular outcome can be treated like a crime that requires investigation, and a hypothetical cause can be treated like a suspect whose guilt needs to be proven. However, this only works if process tracing researchers pay attention to the third and fourth benchmark of my definition and engage in source criticism and Bayesian updating. It is not sufficient for a detective or prosecutor to theorize how a crime may have unfolded and discuss different hypotheses in general terms. To convince a judge or a jury, they must subject their sources to critical scrutiny and spell out the probabilistic reasoning behind their assessment of the available evidence.

Based on these considerations, I define my proposed methodology as *digital forensic process tracing*. By incorporating DOSI analysis, my approach makes process tracing fit for the digital age. At the same time, my approach enables process tracing to live up to its forensic ambitions by focusing on source criticism and Bayesian updating.

3.4. Operationalizing Digital Forensic Process Tracing

The remainder of this chapter will discuss some further assumptions and specifications to prepare digital forensic process tracing for its application to the critical junctures of the 2014 Donbas War. Before attempting to use digital forensic process tracing to study the war's causes, it is important to revisit some of the philosophical foundations of process tracing and discuss potential objections. For this purpose, it is useful to return to Beach and Pedersen's (2013, 30) analogy, which compares a causal mechanism to a car engine. This car engine analogy is not only a clear, practice-oriented example of how causal mechanisms can be conceptualized; it can also be used to illustrate five key problems associated with any study of causation.

3.4.1. Five Philosophical Challenges

The first problem in need of clarification is the relationship between a causal mechanism and a causal sequence. Beach & Pedersen (2013, 29) acknowledge that their car engine analogy has limits. Causal mechanisms "are not necessarily neutral transmission belts." They "can have effects that cannot merely be reduced to the effect of X [the initial cause]." This raises the question of whether there is a qualitative difference between cause and outcome, on the one hand, and the steps of the causal mechanism connecting them, on the other. In other words, is there any difference between a causal mechanism and an expandable causal sequence? Could what is a step in one causal mechanism, become a cause in another — and vice versa, in the context of different research designs?

The second problem is what King, Keohane, and Verba (1994, 86) describe as "infinite regress" — the problem that "there always exists in the social sciences an infinity of causal steps between any two links in the chain of causal mechanisms." What this means is also evident in the analogy of the car engine. It could be argued that the car is not moved directly by the spinning of the wheels but by the force of static friction between tires and asphalt. This force, in turn, is the result of molecular adhesion, which takes the causal chain right down to an atomic scale. The number of causal steps might not be literally indefinite, but King, Keohane, and Verba are correct in the sense that it is certainly not feasible to break down complex social science problems into causal steps that happen at the level of particle physics.

The third problem consists of a slightly different form of infinite regress. Rather than analyzing ever smaller units of causal force transfers, it is theoretically possible to identify causes further and further back in time. A rather extreme illustration of this is Fearon's thought experiment (1991, 190), posing the questions of whether "the gene controlling the length of Cleopatra's nose was a cause of World War I." According to this causal logic, the shape of Cleopatra's nose led to Antony's affection for her which led to the Battle of Actium which then affected the further course of European history. While this specific example is questionable in several ways, it clearly illustrates a problem with causal mechanisms that is also apparent in the car engine analogy. The cause of the car's movement could be defined as the motor, the turning of the ignition key, the driver's decision to go for a ride, or even the manufacturing of the car itself.

The fourth problem is what Roberts (1996, 89–90) calls "indiscriminate pluralism." Roberts argues that "a set of conditions" rather than an event causes an outcome: "Not a lighted match, but a lighted match and a pile of paper and the presence of oxygen causes a fire" (Roberts 1996, 89). Roberts (1996, 90) further argues:

> If one allows the absence of certain conditions to be a necessary condition, then the number of conditions that must be enumerated is limited only by a person's imagination. One might even insist on including the fact that a comet did not destroy the earth a moment before the fire.

In the context of the car engine analogy, this is illustrated by the fact that it is not only the running motor that makes the car move but also the release of the clutch pedal and parking brake combined with the absence of a wheel clamp.

The fifth and final problem concerns the impact of equifinality on the definition of necessary conditions. In their car engine analogy, Beach and Pedersen (2013, 30) describe the driveshaft and the wheels as "insufficient but necessary parts of an overall mechanism." Either of these parts on its own is "insufficient to produce an outcome," because "it only functions together with the rest of the machine." The four problems discussed above mainly relate to the definition of sufficiency. They illustrate the challenge of determining the engine's confines and the number of parts included in it. On first sight, necessity seems to be a relatively straightforward concept compared to this challenge. Without a necessary part, the engine won't work. But what about alternative parts? Is a driveshaft strictly necessary if, in theory, it could be replaced by a chain to achieve a similar outcome? Things become even more complicated if parts are divided into multiple components. According to Mahoney (2008, 418), a house can burn down "either because of a short circuit combined with wooden framing or because of a gasoline can combined with a furnace." By no means is this an exhaustive list of scenarios that can cause a fire. Consequently, the question arises whether any condition can ever be a truly necessary part of a causal mechanism if, in theory, this condition—or any of its components—could be replaced by a counterfactual alternative which would lead to the same outcome.

3.4.2. Five Pragmatic Solutions

All five problems discussed above relate to fundamental questions in the philosophy of science. Answering them on a general theoretical level is, if at all possible, far beyond the scope of this book. However, all five problems must be considered and addressed in the context of the Donbas War before I can use digital forensic process tracing to study the causal mechanisms that led to its outbreak.

Regarding the first problem, my study does not define an inherent qualitative difference between the nature of cause and outcome, on the one hand, and the nature of the causal mechanism connecting them, on the other. In general terms, war is the outcome and local separatist sentiment versus Russian interference are the two hypothetical causes to be tested in the context of this book. In between the outcome and the two possible causes lies a series of events consisting of actors who engage in activities that transmit causal force. However, the two possible causes, as well as the outcome, could also be described in terms of actors engaging in activities. Local separatist sentiment consists of Donbas residents developing a desire to break away from the Ukrainian state. Russian interference consists of Russian state structures deciding that the situation in Ukraine requires them to take action. War consists of clashes of opposing military forces in the Donbas, which affect all actors involved in a variety of ways. It is my study's level of analysis that determines what is defined as cause and effect and what is defined as the mechanism in between. The scope of this book is the only reason why I define war, local separatism, and Russian interference as generalized concepts rather than as concrete actors engaging in activities. In a research project of a larger scale, these concepts could feature as actors engaging in activities within a causal mechanism that connects different causes and outcomes. In a research project of a smaller scale, events that are components of my causal mechanism could turn into cause and outcome. For this reason, I will follow the approach of Mahoney (2015, 205), who treats "mechanisms in the same way as cause and outcome" and argues that the former differ from the latter only "because of their temporal position." In other words, a causal mechanism is identical to a causal sequence.

The second problem—King, Keohane, and Verba's (1994, 86) interpretation of infinite regress—largely loses its relevance in the context of a practice-oriented approach to the study of armed conflict. It is true that certain parts of a causal sequence can be broken down into smaller steps. In fact, I utilize this in my research by breaking down the Donbas War into a series of critical junctures, each of which will face further subdivision in the empirical chapter devoted to it. However, this procedure of exploring a causal sequence within a step of another causal sequence soon reaches limits. These limits are defined by data availability and disciplinary boundaries as well as common sense. Establishing that a certain actor made a decision to act in a certain way requires a certain amount of data. A far larger amount of data is required to establish the exact circumstances of the decision-making process. Even more data, as well as psychological expertise, is required to go further and investigate the cognitive processes within the decision-maker's mind at the time. Such data might not be available in the context of an armed conflict, but this is not a problem. It is not necessary to understand every procedural detail of the decision-making process or the inner workings of a decision-maker's mind in order to decide whether the Donbas conflict was primarily a domestic or an international phenomenon. For example, Russian state responsibility does not depend on the details of decision-making procedures within the Kremlin. As long as the involvement of the Russian state apparatus is evident, it does not matter whether Vladimir Putin personally initiated certain actions, whether he approved someone else's initiative, or whether he was kept out of the decision-making process altogether. On the contrary, going into this kind of depth would require a completely different research design that could no longer focus on the causes of the Donbas War as a whole. To use another example, it might be relatively straightforward to establish that a certain building was destroyed by artillery fire from a certain direction at a certain point in time. However, the exact process of how the building collapsed as a result of the shelling might require data that is not available as well as expertise in structural engineering. At the same time, the fact that the building was destroyed by artillery fire from a certain direction at a certain point in time would be entirely sufficient in the context of a study on the causes of war. Further details of the collapse process would be superfluous. These examples show that infinite regress to the micro level is not a problem for a process tracing analysis of armed conflict. This is because any study will relatively quickly reach a point where a further zooming in on a causal sequence is either no longer feasible or no longer useful, or both at the same time.

The third problem — concerning infinite regress back in time — also loses most of its salience in the context of a specific research question regarding the causes of armed conflict. Even if a solid argument could be made that the shape of Cleopatra's nose was a cause of World War One, this finding would be just as useful as attributing the war to the Big Bang itself. The supposed cause is simply too far removed from the research puzzle to yield any useful insights. Fearon himself (1991, 191) relativizes the validity of his thought experiment for this reason. He admits that the number of influencing factors increases dramatically while following a causal chain back in time. In turn, this means that the determinative importance of each individual factor decreases, which reduces its explanatory power. Roberts (1996, 111) goes a step further and argues that "analytical philosophers dreamed up the problem of infinite regress." According to him, historians easily circumvent it by stopping "the backward search for the ultimate cause at the point where the state of affairs, whose alteration they seek to explain, flourished." To some extent, this choice of words is an oversimplification. Seemingly flourishing peace can be deceptive, and it is very well possible that important reasons for a war predate its outbreak. However, Roberts raises an important point in the sense that there is limited analytical value in attributing the alteration of a state of affairs to factors that are simultaneously causes of the very same state of affairs in the first place. Instead, he says, historians should focus their search for causes on elements of change that disrupt one state of affairs and bring about another. In the context of this book, this means that there is little analytic value in attributing the war in the Donbas, for example, to the collapse of the Soviet Union. While there can be little doubt that this collapse eventually led to the conditions of April 2014, which made war possible, it also led to the conditions of, for example, April 2013, when war seemed extremely unlikely. Moreover, the collapse of the Soviet Union is a precondition for both Ukraine's domestic politics and Russia's foreign policymaking in spring 2014 and is thus unable to indicate which factor played a stronger role in the escalation of violence. As argued in chapter two, the same logic leads to the exclusion of the Euromaidan protests in Kyiv from my study of the war's causes. It is not the purpose of this book to list all historical events that made the war possible. Its purpose is to investigate how the Donbas transitioned from a state of tense calm after the February 2014 regime change in Kyiv to a state of full-scale war six months later.

Concerning the fourth problem—indiscriminate pluralism—Roberts (1996, 96) argues that a focus on "abnormal" events is the mitigation strategy of choice. He argues that a complex web of causal factors can be reduced to a simple causal chain by singling out those factors that were most abnormal and thus most disruptive to the state of affairs that underwent change—a technique that he calls "linear colligation" (Roberts 1996, 109–110). Naturally, the resulting causal sequence will be a simplification of reality. It will not represent all causal factors that contributed to a particular outcome but only the factor that was most disruptive at each stage of the process. It is an illustration of what was key rather than a comprehensive depiction of all relevant facets. In the context of historical explanation, this degree of simplification prevents an understanding of the complexities of the particular case. For this reason,

Roberts (1996, 97) proposes a less radical application of abnormalism that uses a set of abnormal conditions for multicausal explanations while ignoring those conditions that do not depart from the normal course of events. He returns to the example of a fire to illustrate this point:

> To leave debris in an alley is more common than throwing lighted matches into alleys, but less common than the presence of oxygen. The historian should probably mention it in an explanation of the fire though not as prominently as the carelessly thrown match.

What follows from this is the construction of more complex causal sequences that include a selection of disruptive factors. These sequences can converge, diverge, or run parallel to each other (Roberts 1996, 112–133). The definition of causal sufficiency in this context depends on the desired level of specificity. From a historian's point of view, a sufficient explanation should include all factors in the hierarchy of abnormal conditions that illustrate the specifics of the particular historical case. In contrast, the simplicity of linear colligation can be an advantage in political science process tracing. Precisely because of its simplicity, linear colligation is well suited to test competing hypotheses about the relative importance of different causal factors and to categorize phenomena into mutually exclusive typologies. It is exactly this kind of reduction to the most significant causal sequence that is required to investigate the nature of armed conflict at the borderline between civil and interstate war. Hardly anyone denies that both domestic and foreign factors were at work during the escalation of the Donbas conflict. The controversial question is which factors were more important. A process tracing analysis that uses abnormalism and linear colligation to establish causal sequences has the potential to answer this question.

    Regarding the fifth and final problem of equifinality and necessary conditions, a strict definition of necessity would imply that there are no necessary conditions for the war in the Donbas at all. Strictly speaking, any component of the causal sequence that led to the outbreak of violence could be replaced by a hypothetical alternative. Naturally, some counterfactuals of this kind are more plausible than others. In theory, it could be argued that the deployment of the Ukrainian military to the Donbas was not a necessary condition for the war because an intervention of US troops could have led to the same result. Of course, this is a highly implausible scenario, but the same logic has concrete implications for this book. In particular, it could be argued that any identified degree of Russian involvement was not a necessary condition for the war because, in its absence, local separatism could have been stronger and taken its place. This argument works the other way around as well. Russia could have stepped up its engagement if separatist activism had been weaker. What these examples show is that a discussion of necessary causation inevitably requires a discussion of counterfactuals. This is in line with Fearon (1991, 171–175), who argues that the use of counterfactuals is unavoidable and commonplace in both history and political science, despite a widespread reluctance to discuss this explicitly. Inevitably, the use of counterfactuals brings a certain degree of speculation to the analysis, but, as both Fearon (1991) and Levy (2015) convincingly argue, there is no alternative. This suggests that transparency regarding the use of counterfactuals and the assumptions and evidence they are based on is the best available option. For this reason, my definition of causal necessity in the context of the Donbas War will be based on the analysis of counterfactual scenarios that resemble the actual course of events as closely as possible while removing the causal factor in question. If there is no concrete evidence of a replacement factor, which would have been likely to lead to the same outcome in such a counterfactual scenario, I will consider the causal factor in question a necessary one.

3.4.3. Additional Limitations and Remedies

In addition to the conceptual challenges described above, digital forensic process tracing also faces two limitations of a more practical nature. Firstly, there is the issue of gaps, when no data is openly available. Secondly, there is the issue of unconscious bias, when different analysts look at the same data and come to different conclusions. Neither of these issues can be eliminated completely. However, the fact that the use of Bayesian updating forces researchers to spell out uncertainty can mitigate them to some extent. This mitigating effect can be further strengthened by two supplementary components. The first component is the contextualization of missing data (Gonzalez-Ocantos and LaPorte 2021, 1417–1421), which can draw on the philosophical principles of Occam's razor and the Sagan standard. The second component is a clear terminology to facilitate the verbalization of probabilities.

3.4.3.1. Occam's Razor and the Sagan Standard

The problem of missing data is an important challenge for process tracing theorists. On the one hand, process tracing needs evidence to assess hypotheses about cause and effect. On the other hand, it is well known that the absence of evidence is not necessarily evidence of absence. Occam's razor and the Sagan standard are two philosophical principles that can help process tracing researchers to navigate this dilemma. In the words of Pigliucci and Boudry's (2014, 493), "Occam's razor urges us to reject theoretical constructs that are 'superfluous,' in the sense that they are not strictly demanded by the evidence." The Sagan standard is related to Occam's razor and postulates that "extraordinary claims require extraordinary evidence." Although it is widely known as the Sagan standard, Pigliucci and Boudry (2014, 500) argue that it is actually based on the philosophy of David Hume.

In the absence of evidence, Occam's razor and the Sagan standard require process tracing researchers to choose the most parsimonious and least extraordinary explanation. If they assume the existence of a causal mechanism or a step within a causal mechanism even though there is no evidence of it, they must justify why existence is more parsimonious and less extraordinary than absence. The claim that someone did something without leaving traces needs circumstantial evidence that makes the assumption that no action was taken extraordinary and complicated to justify.

The application of Occam's razor and the Sagan standard means that complex and extraordinary explanations without clear evidence in their favor will be dismissed. Consequently, a hypothetical top-secret Russian operation in the Donbas that unleashed war through undercover agents without leaving any traces would remain undetected. However, this shortcoming is inevitable because the only alternative would be a descent into conspiratorial thinking. The benefits of dismissing far-fetched explanations in the absence of evidence clearly outweigh the risk of overlooking an elaborate, well-executed conspiracy.

3.4.3.2. The PHIA Probability Yardstick and Informal Bayesian Analysis

The requirement to assess the degree to which a proposed explanation is parsimonious and unextraordinary reemphasizes the problem of unconscious bias. Different researchers may have different ideas of what constitutes an extraordinary claim or a parsimonious explanation. Structuring Bayesian analysis in a concise and accessible way can mitigate this problem to some extent. Doing so cannot prevent disagreements among scholars about the extent to which a certain piece of evidence changes the probability of a hypothesis. However, it forces researchers to spell out the probabilistic weight they attach to certain pieces of evidence or to the absence of evidence. This, in turn, increases transparency and clarifies where exactly assessments converge and differ. It also encourages researchers to reflect on their own biases.

Attempts to calculate exact numerical probabilities would reduce rather than increase the clarity and accessibility of Bayesian analysis in the context of digital forensic process tracing. It would move the focus of analysis away from the discussion of sources toward calculations and the discussion of numbers. As an alternative, I propose following Barrenechea and Mahoney's (2019, 453) suggestion to use "verbal understandings of likelihood" to express the probabilistic impact of different pieces of evidence. As a system of such verbal categories, I suggest the terminology of the Professional Head of Intelligence Analysis (PHIA) Probability Yardstick.[7] This is a scale of probabilistic language widely used by UK intelligence and law enforcement agencies (UK Government 2019). It defines specific terms to describe specific margins of probability. These terms and margins are: *remote chance* ($\approx$5%), *highly unlikely* ($\approx$10-20%), *unlikely* ($\approx$25-35%), *realistic possibility* ($\approx$40-50%), *likely* ($\approx$55-75%), *highly likely* ($\approx$80-90%), and *almost certain* ($\approx$95%). Using this

---

7   I would like to thank Rupert Barrett-Taylor for drawing my attention to this particular system.

terminology allows for an explicitly probabilistic analysis and follows the general principles of Bayesian updating without creating a false impression of mathematical accuracy. I call this approach informal Bayesian analysis, in contrast to the formal Bayesian analysis discussed by Fairfield and Charman (2017) and Zaks (2021).

3.4.4. Digital Forensic Process Tracing in Practice

The remainder of this book will apply the methodology developed in this chapter to the case of the 2014 Donbas conflict. The six remaining empirical chapters will use digital forensic process tracing to investigate the causal mechanisms behind the six critical junctures of the war's escalation sequence. To obtain the results reported in each of the subsequent empirical chapters, I operationalized the principles developed in the present chapter in the following way:

The starting point of my research on each empirical chapter were the media reports on the respective critical junctures which I obtained from the extended media dataset and which I cited in chapter two. These reports provided a variety of keywords and keyword combinations to search the Internet for further information on the events in question. In turn, this search for further information provided even more keywords. My primary tools for source discovery were the search engines of Google, Yandex, and YouTube and the different search operators they provide, such as date-specific search, domain-specific search, image search, or reverse image search. In most cases, it was possible to reduce the initial multitude of search results to a relatively small set of primary sources that contained the original information about the event. Most other sources could be discarded because they merely cited or interpreted these primary sources. I then assessed the credibility of each source and the information contained within it. For written sources, I checked whether it is clear who the author was and how the author obtained the information provided. I also checked the track record of the author and the publication for potential biases and a potential tendency to publish disinformation of a certain kind. For example, a report by a correspondent of a local news outlet, which makes clear what the correspondent witnessed and what additional information they received from other local sources, is more trustworthy than a statement from a military spokesperson. Finally, I checked whether other sources confirm or dispute the information provided. For audio-visual sources, I made extensive use of Google Earth Pro to verify the location of photos and videos. I also checked whether the material showed any signs of editing and whether the timing and the context of its publication make manipulation more or less likely. For example, if a video appeared immediately after an event, it is less likely to be edited than if it appeared weeks later. Similarly, a video published by a pro-separatist source is less likely to contain fabricated evidence of Russian involvement than a video published by the Ukrainian military.

I stopped the source discovery process when multiple rounds of additional keyword searches did not yield any new events, new aspects of events, or new evidence. This approach is in line with the concept of data saturation which is widely used in qualitative research to justify the number of interviews or focus groups that a researcher conducts (Braun and Clarke 2021, 202–206). To maximize traceability and minimize the risk of data loss in relation to the selected primary sources, I cited the archived record of websites in the Internet Archive and archive.today repositories, whenever this was feasible.

For each chapter, I separated this data gathering and analysis process into two parts. The first round focused on hypothesis building. I concentrated on singling out those aspects of the critical juncture that are key for the relative importance of internal and external causes. For example, while there was hardly ever disagreement among sources that a certain armed clash had taken place, it was often controversial who had fired the first shot and how many people had died. While these controversies are important, they are secondary in the context of my investigation. For the purpose of this book, it made sense to concentrate additional source discovery and analysis efforts on the relative importance of internal and external causes. Hence, I developed competing hypotheses and causal mechanisms that explain the critical juncture in question with a focus on these aspects. I then used Occam's razor and the Sagan standard to define which hypothesis should be the default assumption. On this basis, I carried out a second round of data gathering and analysis. I searched for evidence that could either further strengthen or weaken the default hypothesis, assessed the credibility of this evidence, and updated probabilities according to the result of this assessment and the principles of informal Bayesian analysis.

3.5. Chapter Conclusion

This chapter has developed digital forensic process tracing as the methodology of choice for the further investigation of causality in the context of the six critical junctures that characterize the Donbas War's formative escalation sequence. The key characteristics of this methodology are:

- A focus on primary information from the conflict zone published by openly available online sources.
- An explicit discussion of the reliability of evidence, which takes into account the source of any evidence and the context in which it was published.
- A prioritization of causal factors according to the principle of *abnormalism*.
- A probabilistic evaluation of the available evidence using the principles of Occam's razor and the Sagan standard as well as the terminology of the PHIA Probability Yardstick for informal Bayesian analysis.

Digital forensic process tracing enables a more transparent analysis of the role of domestic factors on the one hand and Russian involvement on the other in the escalation of the Donbas War. I will use the following six chapters to demonstrate this. These chapters will use digital forensic process tracing to investigate the war's six critical junctures. This application of the methodology developed in the present chapter to the events of chapter two's escalation sequence will provide important insights into the domestic and external causal dynamics within each critical juncture. In turn, the sum of these causal dynamics will provide a compelling explanation of the war as a whole.

4. Of Arms and Barricades
Donetsk and Luhansk in Early April

This chapter will investigate the causes of the first critical juncture of the 2014 Donbas conflict — the building occupations in Donetsk and Luhansk in early April. I will start by providing an overview of the events and develop three hypotheses regarding their causes. The first hypothesis defines the events as the result of a local grassroots movement. The second hypothesis defines them as an elite-controlled insurrection. The third hypothesis defines them as the result of Russian interference. I will then discuss the available digital open source evidence in relation to each hypothesis. I will conclude that there is convincing evidence that the actions of both local elites and Russia were important auxiliary factors. However, this evidence is not sufficient to overturn the default assumption that the events in question were primarily a bottom-up uprising of local pro-Russian fringe activists.

Events unfolded as follows: On April 6, 2014, a crowd of pro-Russian protesters gathered on Lenin Square in the center of Donetsk. Similar rallies had been held in the same location on every weekend since March 1. As on previous occasions, this rally was followed by a march along Artem Street and Shevchenko Boulevard to the building of the Donetsk Oblast State Administration — the local representation of the Kyiv authorities in Donetsk Oblast. Like on previous occasions, a number of activists entered the building after local riot police refrained from using force to protect it. Unlike on previous occasions, however, they did not leave again. During the night of April 6-7, a group of several dozen men also stormed the Donetsk branch of the Security Service of Ukraine (SBU) and started searching for weapons (YouTube 2016a; 2014aa). On April 7, a news website reported first rumors that boxes with firearms had been brought to the State Administration (Ostrov 2014h; Vesti 2014b). On the same day, a meeting inside the State Administration proclaimed the independence of the Donetsk People's Republic (DNR) (YouTube 2014x). By April 8, the separatists had vacated the SBU building again (Ukrainska Pravda 2014h), but the State Administration remained under their control, and they had erected barricades around the entrance (YouTube 2014z). Inside, separatist leaders held a meeting and appointed a "Provisional Government" (YouTube 2014y). Moreover, a source in the SBU confirmed that firearms had been removed from the SBU building during its brief occupation and brought into the State Administration (62.ua 2014). Because the Kyiv authorities refrained from any attempt to liberate the State Administration by force, these firearms were not used for the time being. Nevertheless, they turned the Donetsk State Administration building into the first armed and barricaded foothold of the separatist movement in Donetsk Oblast.

Simultaneously, a second permanent and armed building seizure took place in Luhansk. On April 6, a group of people stormed the local SBU headquarters, opened the armory, and started to erect barricades around the building (YouTube 2014p; 2014v; 2014ac; Ostrov 2014i). The occupants of the building called themselves the "Army of the Southeast." They demanded an amnesty for all security forces accused of violence against Maidan protesters in Kyiv, the cancellation of the Ukrainian presidential election, and some sort of referendum for Ukraine's Southeast (Relke and Bolotov 2014). Like in Donetsk, they established a first armed foothold that Ukraine's central authorities never regained control over.

Nobody disputes that these events took place. What is contentious is whether a one-part causal mechanism is sufficient to explain them. Matveeva's (2016, 35) claim that the separatist movement in the Donbas "was leaderless and not spearheaded by [an] elite" suggests that the activists in question acted primarily of their own accord. It suggests that the causal mechanism consists only of a single component that links local sentiment in the form of grassroot activists' individual motives as a cause to the escalation of the conflict as a result. Wilson's (2016, 649) claim that the Donbas conflict was "a process catalyzed and escalated by local elites and by Russia, with local foot-soldiers," on the other hand, implies that the causal mechanism leading to conflict escalation needs to include an additional step. This step would consist of either Russia or local elites organizing and instructing the actors that occupied the buildings. In this scenario, the primary cause of the escalation are not the individual motives of those occupying the buildings but the desire of Russia or local elites to destabilize the situation and put pressure on the Kyiv authorities.

Three hypotheses can be derived from these arguments to explain the escalation of the conflict in early April 2014. Each hypothesis corresponds to a specific causal mechanism. The first hypothesis is linked to the simple one-part mechanism that defines grassroots activism as the primary cause of the present instance of conflict escalation. The second and third mechanisms consist of two parts and place the emphasis on the actions of local elites and Russia. Together, these three causal mechanisms and the hypotheses associated with them reflect the divide in the academic debate on the causes of the 2014 Donbas conflict. The first and second hypotheses are compatible with the argument that the escalation of violence was primarily a homegrown phenomenon while the third hypothesis is in line with the idea of covert Russian aggression.

H1: The building occupations of early April 2014 were carried out by a leaderless grassroots movement.

Figure 2: Causal Mechanism of Grassroots Insurrection

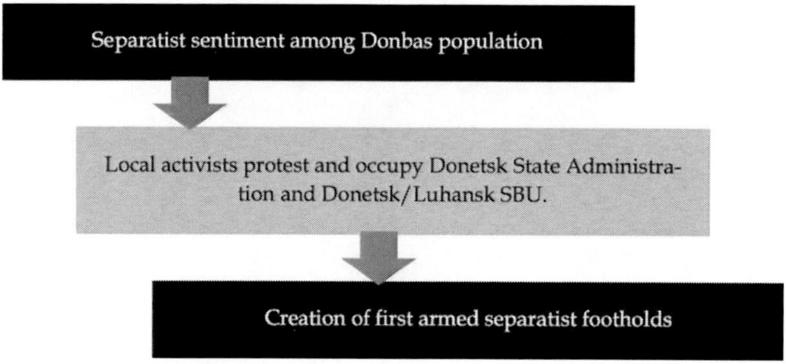

Separatist sentiment among Donbas population

↓

Local activists protest and occupy Donetsk State Administration and Donetsk/Luhansk SBU.

↓

Creation of first armed separatist footholds

Source: the author

H2: The building occupations of early April 2014 were carried out by agents of local elites.

Figure 3: Causal Mechanism of Elite-Controlled Insurrection

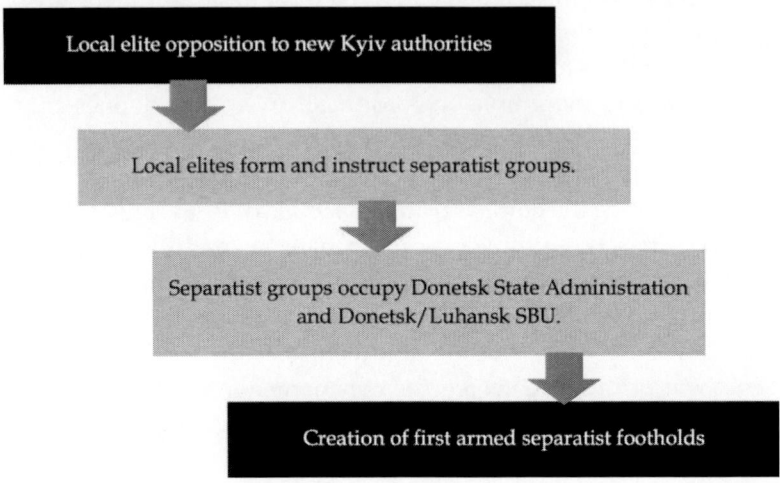

Source: the author

H3: The building occupations of early April 2014 were carried out by agents of the Russian state.

Figure 4: Causal Mechanism of Covert Russian Invasion

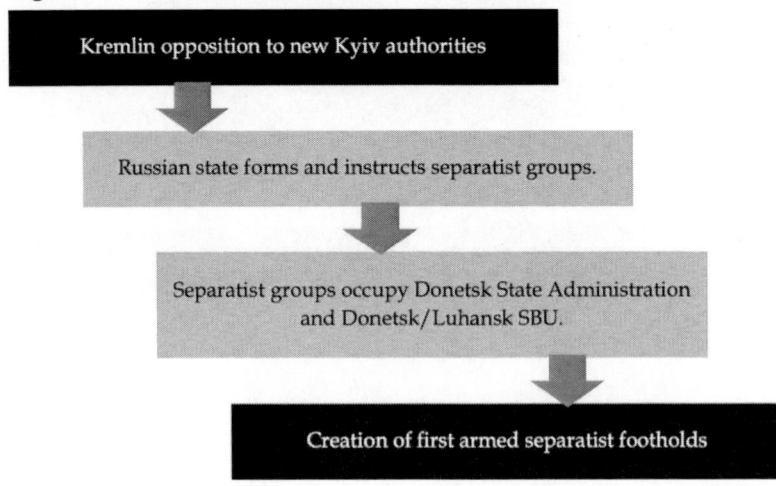

Source: the author

Naturally, all three mechanisms are simplified ideal types. In reality, they are not mutually exclusive. A hypothetical grassroots movement could receive some support from local elites or Russia. Agents of local elites or Russia could, to some extent, pursue an agenda of their own. Local elites could conspire with Russia or pursue a parallel agenda. While these nuances have to be taken into account, it makes sense to analyze the three mechanisms separately before attempting to combine them. Doing so enables a more transparent assessment of their relative weight. A discussion of caveats and combinations should follow after each hypothesis has been tested against the available digital open source evidence.

4.1. Enthusiasts or Agents?
The Role of Grassroots Activism

An obvious *smoking-gun* (see section 3.1.2.) in support of H1 would be evidence that the building occupations emanated from a mass movement which was too big, too complex, and too dynamic to be subject to top-down control. Such evidence would increase the probability of H1 considerably while decreasing the probability of H2 and H3. However, evidence of this kind is absent in the present case. As I have argued in chapter two, the events in question were not the result of a rise in general protest sentiment. Moreover, footage of the activists breaking through the police cordon into the Donetsk State Administration building suggests that most people were passive bystanders. Only a group of several dozen men are actually attacking the police and forcing their way into the building (YouTube 2014w). Finally, another video shows that most of the crowd had dispersed once it got dark (YouTube 2014u). The same was the case in Luhansk. Most people were passive bystanders while a relatively small number of activists stormed the building (YouTube 2014p; 2014v). The crowd dispersed completely by the following morning, when the building was photographed with only a few dozen people in front of it (Ostrov 2014i). Rather than being carried by a mass protest movement, the building seizures resulted from the actions of two relatively small groups of activists at a time when general protest turnout was decreasing.

4.1.1. The Burden of Proof

This finding does not automatically imply that the groups in question were acting on someone else's behalf. It remains entirely plausible that a small core of separatist activists radicalized, increased organizational cohesion, and decided to resort to more extreme measures as general protest sentiment faded. In fact, Pigliucci and Boudry's (2014) discussion of the burden of proof suggest that this explanation should be given a head start against the other two hypotheses in terms of initial probability. Occam's razor and the Sagan standard suggest that H1 should still be considered the default hypothesis in the absence of convincing evidence against it. As discussed in chapter three, Occam's razor favors parsimonious explanations. In the present case, a principal-agent-relationship between the people occupying the buildings and a leadership directing them from elsewhere clearly adds an additional layer of complexity. According to Occam's razor, this additional complexity should be rejected unless the simpler explanation that the people occupying the building acted of their own accord is incompatible with the available evidence. At the same time, the Sagan standard also suggests an imbalance of initial probabilities in favor of H1. A covert operation orchestrated by local elites or Russia is a more extraordinary event than two small groups of radical protesters occupying buildings. As a result, the starting point for informal Bayesian analysis (see sections 3.1.4. and 3.4.3.2.) should be that H1 is a *likely* explanation while H2 and H3 are *highly unlikely* explanations.

4.1.2. The Chaotic Birth of the Donetsk People's Republic

In the case of Donetsk, H1 does not have to rely on Occam's razor and the Sagan standard alone. Two observations provide additional evidence in its favor and further increase its probability. Firstly, the degree of organization and coordination among the State Administration's occupants was not above a level that could be expected from a self-organizing group of fringe activist. The situation inside the occupied building featured elements of chaos and confusion. Video footage taken on April 6, soon after the building was seized, shows a variety of people coming and going, walking around, filming, shouting slogans, or arguing. Discipline and leadership are weak. A police officer counters a separatist leader's request to vacate the building with the proposal to "wait for the guy who was here earlier and said he was another organizer" (YouTube 2014o at 2:23:00). Three other police officers ask a group of separatists for a point of contact and whether anyone is in charge of the activists surrounding them (YouTube 2014o at 2:33:00). One person claiming to be in charge has to shout through a megaphone to urge a group of others not to use violence against the police (YouTube 2014r). Another separatist suddenly barges in on an improvised press conference to voice an appeal to "mother Russia" (YouTube 2014o at 2:43:50). A high degree of improvisation is also visible during the first session of the DNR's "Provisional Government" on April 8. Some of the new "republic's" leaders do not even appear to know each other's names (YouTube 2014y).

Secondly, the available digital open source information about the people trying to take charge of the situation points at a random array of men from different backgrounds. Some have a previous history of pro-Russian activism but as members of different marginal organizations. Others appear to be new to politics. There are no obvious links between Donetsk's separatist leaders at this early stage of the conflict, apart from the fact that they are Donetsk Oblast residents or natives and share pro-Russian, anti-Western views. Their profiles are entirely consistent with the type of leadership group that a fringe grassroots coalition would be expected to have.

- *Volodymyr Makovych* was filmed announcing the formation of a "coordination council" (YouTube 2014t) and negotiating with the police (YouTube 2014s) in the State Administration building on April 6. He also read out the proclamation of the DNR on April 7 (YouTube 2014x) and participated in the meeting that appointed its "Provisional Government" on the following day (YouTube 2014y). According to Ukraine's NGO register, he created an organization called Young Patriots' Movement in Donetsk after the Orange Revolution in 2005 (Bezsonova 2015; Holovnov 2014).
- *Vadym Cherniakov* was filmed together with Makovych while negotiating with the police. He is also the person telling activists through a megaphone not to use force against the police (YouTube 2014r). He then chaired the

proclamation session and the formation of the "Provisional Government." In November 2012, he appeared in a local news report covering the demolition of a metallurgical plant in Horlivka. He was interviewed as the "technical director" of AVAKO – the construction company in charge of the demolition (06242.ua 2012). According to a CV that Cherniakov uploaded to a Ukrainian job website in February 2012, he had been working for AVAKO since 2009 and was based in Donetsk (Cherniakov 2012).

- *Denys Pushylin*, who became the leader of the DNR in 2018, was also present on April 6, 2014 and tried to coordinate events inside the occupied State Administration building. He then co-chaired the proclamation session and the formation of the "Provisional Government" together with Cherniakov. Before, he coordinated the latest Ukrainian iteration of the notorious Russian MMM Ponzi scheme (OTB TV 2013). On websites associated with the scheme, Pushylin (2013a; 2013b) described himself as an MMM "consultant" from Makiivka. In the December 2013 parliamentary byelection in a Kyiv Oblast constituency, he was the candidate of a political party founded by MMM and gained 72 votes (Pushylin 2014; Central Electoral Commission of Ukraine 2014).

- *Mykola Solntsev* interrupted Makovych's, Cherniakov's, and Pushylin's press conference after the seizure of the building (YouTube 2014o at 2:43:50). He was also eager to draw attention to himself during the "Provisional Government" meeting. Solntsev was one of the leaders of a pro-Russian organization called Eastern Front and had spoken to journalists as early as February 23. He said that he worked as an auditor in a Donetsk company (Smyrnova 2014). In another interview from early March, Solntsev said that his organization was opposed to Donetsk "People's Governor" Pavlo Hubariev[8] (Solntsev and Okopov 2014).

- *Myroslav Rudenko*, on the other hand, who can be seen standing next to Solntsev during the DNR proclamation

---

[8] Because Hubariev was a Ukrainian citizen at the time of the events, I use the Ukrainian transliteration of his name, rather than the Russian transliteration Pavel Gubarev.

and who was appointed to its "Provisional Government," was an early follower of Hubariev. On March 2, he was filmed agitating against the Kyiv authorities outside Hubariev's apartment (Matsuka 2014). In his memoirs, Hubariev (2016, 45) describes Rudenko as an old friend from university. Rudenko describes himself as a "historian and writer," who was born in the Donetsk Oblast town of Debaltseve and had lived in Donetsk since the year 2000 (Alternatio.org n.d.; Rudenko 2010). In 2010, he was a Party of Regions candidate for the Donetsk City Council (Novosti Donbassa 2010).

- *Viacheslav Ponomarov*, who told a Russian news agency that he was a key organizer of the seizure of the Donetsk SBU building during the night of April 6–7 (Ponomarov 2014), would later in April become famous as the "People's Mayor" of Sloviansk. Local residents told *Wall Street Journal* correspondent Philip Shishkin (2014), who visited Sloviansk in late April, that Ponomarov was the manager of a local soap factory. Ponomarov also showed his soap factory to British pro-Russian activist Graham Phillips (2014). According to Shishkin's sources, Ponomarov had previously run a sewing factory, managed supplies for a military hospital, and traded cars. According to Ponomarov (2014), his group decided not to stay in the SBU building and went to the State Administration with the weapons they had seized. However, he said that his group was so appalled by the chaos and lack of leadership in the State Administration building that they decided to go home after a short time.

Naturally this evidence remains patchy. Only certain moments of the relevant events have been captured on camera, there is no guarantee that all relevant actors have been recorded, and the biographies of those identified may include aspects that have not been documented in publicly available sources. Neither is it possible to verify all of Ponomarov's claims. Nevertheless, the signs of chaos and confusion in the occupied State Administration and the heterogeneity of the separatist leaders' profiles are *straw-in-the-wind* evidence (see section 3.1.2.) for a grassroots movement. Since this evidence remains relatively weak, it does not change the balance of probabilities fundamentally, and H1 should still be considered a *likely* explanation for the events in Donetsk. However, to tilt the balance of probabilities against H1, evidence for H2 and H3 would have to outweigh both the straw-in-the-wind evidence in H1's favor and H1's higher initial probability due to Occam's razor and the Sagan standard.

4.1.3. Partisans from Stakhanov? The "Army of the Southeast" in Luhansk

The evidence of grassroots activism observed in Donetsk is absent in Luhansk. The "Army of the Southeast," which occupied the Luhansk SBU building, differed from the nascent DNR in four important aspects. Firstly, there is evidence that the group had access to weapons before storming the building and had been preparing for a militarization of the situation at least since mid-March. On April 7, two of its leaders, Alexej Relke and Valerii Bolotov (2014) spoke to a journalist inside the occupied building. During this interview, Relke confirmed that their group was behind a series of YouTube video messages that had gained media attention over the previous month. The first of these messages was posted on March 16 and shows three masked men (YouTube 2014l). The eyes and the voice of the person speaking match Bolotov. The eyes and the body shape of the man to his right match Relke. The men pose with five automatic rifles and a grenade launcher. They threaten the Kyiv authorities that any actions against separatist demonstrations would be seen as a "declaration of war." The text accompanying the video features a call for donations with a link to the social media profile of Ida Relke, who later confirmed that she was Alexej Relke's mother (Ostermann and Relke 2014). On March 22, Russian state-controlled TV channel *Rossiya 24* and Russian pro-Kremlin tabloid *Komsomolskaya Pravda* published reports about the video. Both reports feature an interview with one of the masked men, whose eyes and body size match Relke (Poddubnyy 2014; Kots and Steshin 2014a; 2014b). On April 1, the same three men published another video in which they call themselves the "United Command of the Southeast" (YouTube 2014n). They demand the "cancellation of the presidential election and a concrete date for a referendum on the

Southeast." Otherwise, "the People's Army of the Southeast will be mobilized on April 6." They urge any resident of the Southeast "who is ready to make a stand for their right to life and freedom" to come to the central square of their town "on April 6 between 10-12am" and bring "a form of personal ID, water for a day, and any available weapons or protective equipment."

Secondly, the available open source evidence indicates that the "Army of the Southeast" was a hierarchical paramilitary structure that was better organized than the activists who stormed buildings in Donetsk. Luhansk investigative journalist Andrii Dikhtiarenko was allowed to visit the occupied SBU building on April 11. He noted a "strict hierarchy," not only between the protest camp in front of the building and the inside, but even within the building itself. "Not only do few people have the right to enter, only a very small number is allowed into the inner sanctum of the command unit" (Dikhtiarenko 2014). This observation is consistent with Valerii Bolotov's claim during an April 9 press conference that his group included many people with a military background – former members of the Ukrainian security forces, reserve officers, Afghan war veterans, and Cossacks (YouTube 2014ad, at 2:55).

Thirdly, there is evidence that the "Army of the Southeast" had its origin in the town of Stakhanov,[9] 50 kilometers west of Luhansk. Relke's mother told a journalist that her son emigrated with her to Germany in 1990 but struggled to fit in and returned to the family's hometown of Stakhanov in 2006 (Ostermann and Relke 2014). At the same time, one of the few undisputed facts about Bolotov's background is that he went to school in Stakhanov (Novorosinform.org 2020). Moreover, Dikhtiarenko (2014) writes that a third separatist leader he talked to in the occupied SBU building, Oleksii Kariakin, was from Stakhanov as well. Finally, Stakhanov is the hometown of Pavlo Dromov, who later became a prominent separatist commander (Khrypun 2015; Kazanskyi 2015b; Dromov and Akhmedova 2014; see also chapter seven of this book).

---

9   Until 1937 the town had been known as Kadiivka. The Ukrainian authorities reinstated this name as part of the 2016 decommunization reform. However, the self-declared Luhansk People's Republic that continues to control the town still refers to it as Stakhanov. This book uses the name Stakhanov because it was the town's official name in 2014 and used by all sides of the conflict at the time.

In a June 2014 interview, Dromov confirmed that he was from Stakhanov and had participated in the seizure of the SBU building (Dromov, Lavin, and Veselovskiy 2014 at 13:45). According to Alexej Relke, Dromov was part of a group of people who later left the occupied building in Luhansk and returned to Stakhanov after disagreements with Bolotov (Lugansk 1 TV 2017).

Fourthly, none of the people leading the occupation of the SBU building had a public profile predating the events of April. Information about their lives before the "Army of the Southeast" is limited and most of it is based on their own claims. According to his mother, Relke was planning to set up a wellness salon (Ostermann and Relke 2014). Bolotov (2014) says that he was the chairman of the Association of Luhansk Oblast Airborne Forces Veterans but there is no openly available documentation of any activity on his part in this function. When an investigative journalist analyzed Kariakin's social media profile, all she found was that he "had an active interest in the airborne forces and regularly took part in historical re-enactments" (Krykun 2014). Dromov said that he used to be a bricklayer, a factory worker, an agricultural worker, a "bandit," and a migrant worker in Russia (Dromov and Akhmedova 2014). Two other separatist representatives who gave a press conference with Bolotov on April 9 (YouTube 2014ad) had not featured in openly available sources either and described themselves as low-profile businessmen. Serhii Korsunskyi said in an interview with a Ukrainian website that he used to own mines in Luhansk Oblast (Korsunskyi and Stanko 2016). Pavlo Strubchevskyi told a Russian website that he was an entrepreneur from the Luhansk Oblast town of Sievierodonetsk, who self-identified as a Don Cossack (Strubchevskyi and Kotkalo 2015; Kuzmina 2019).

The "Army of the Southeast's" armed underground activity, its military hierarchy, its epicenter in Stakhanov, and the lack of information on its leadership's backgrounds could be seen as evidence that the group was acting on somebody else's behalf. However, this evidence remains weak and is unable to shift the balance of probabilities far enough to overcome the initial burden of proof. It remains plausible that a small group of previously unknown people formed a well-organized underground organization in Stakhanov, obtained a small number of arms on the black market, and carried out the seizure of the SBU building on their own initiative. Considering Occam's razor and the Sagan standard, this explanation still has to be considered *likely* in the absence of compelling evidence to the contrary. At the same time, the burden of proof for H2 and H3 is somewhat lower than in the case of Donetsk.

4.2. Apathetic Oligarchs: The Role of Local Elites

The previous sections of this chapter have shown that H1 is the most probable explanation for the occupation of government buildings in both Donetsk and Luhansk in the absence of compelling evidence for H2 or H3. Such evidence would need to be stronger in the case of Donetsk than Luhansk because the former case features stronger evidence for H1. On this basis, the present section will proceed to examine H2.

4.2.1. The Yanukovych "Family"

A prime suspect in the orchestration of the separatist movement in the Donbas is former Ukrainian President Viktor Yanukovych. The Ukrainian authorities and Ukrainian journalists claim that the so-called "Family" – the business network surrounding Viktor Yanukovych, his son Oleksandr, and their closest associates – was behind the events of early April 2014. However, although it is plausible that Yanukovych and his associates supported separatist activities to some extent, there is no strong evidence of "Family" control over the separatist groups.

Sources linked to the new Kyiv authorities have accused the Yanukovych "Family" of directly financing separatist activities in the Donbas from their Russian exile. In June 2014, journalist Oleksandr Paskhover published an article summarizing such claims. Andrii Parubii, then head of Ukraine's National Security Council, claimed that Yanukovch and his associates had set up a headquarters in Russia's Rostov-on-Don, from where they were financing the separatist movement. Ukrainian conflict analyst and activist Dmytro Tymchuk said that the SBU had intercepted several corresponding money transfers from Russia to Donetsk. Viktor Chumak, then head of the Ukrainian parliament's Committee for the Fight against Corruption and Organized Crime, added that

Yanukovych had accumulated significant cash reserves which he was now spending on separatism in the Donbas (Paskhover 2014). Yehor Firsov, a prominent pro-European activist from Donetsk also said in a May 2014 interview that Yanukovych was among those who financed separatism in the Donbas (Firsov and Ivanov 2014). In mid-April 2014, then Donetsk Oblast Governor Serhii Taruta said in an interview that the separatists were "not even hiding the presence of hired people around the State Administration building." The journalist interviewing Taruta replied that he had information that these people received their remunerations from the Yanukovych "Family." In response, Taruta said that he had heard the same allegation but that he did not have hard evidence for it. He also claimed that not all separatist activists were being paid (Taruta and Shlinchak 2014).

While none of the cited officials and journalists present evidence to support their claims, three pieces of circumstantial evidence give them some degree of credibility. Firstly, Yanukovych had a clear motive to finance separatism, namely revenge against those who replaced him. Secondly, Yanukovych had the capacity to provide covert financial support to separatism through the maze of his Donbas business network. Research by investigative journalist Serhii Shcherbyna (2014a; 2014c) in Ukrainian company registers illustrates the complexity and reach of this network and even discovered links to the pre-conflict business activities of Donetsk "People's Governor" Pavlo Hubariev. Thirdly, the use of middlemen and shell companies can make financial support difficult to prove, which makes the absence of concrete evidence for the above claims less surprising. These considerations suggest that, even in the absence of more direct evidence, it is likely that the Yanukovych "Family" provided some degree of financial support for separatism in the Donbas around the time of the April 2014 building occupations. It is also likely that some of this money ended up supporting activists present in the occupied Donetsk State Administration building. In Luhansk, where the SBU was occupied by a less heterogenous, more confined group and where the "Family's" business network was less developed, this is only a realistic possibility.

However, the likely presence of financial support does not suggest that the Yanukovych "Family's" activities were the key determinant of separatist activities in the Donbas at the time in question. There is no evidence to suggest that the separatist activists were dependent on Yanukovych's money. On the contrary, the following sections will show that the "Family" was far from the only potential source of financial support. However, even a hypothetical financial dependency on Yanukovych could hardly qualify as the dominant cause of separatist actions according to the principle of *abnormalism* (see section 3.4.2.). The fact that a group of local people was willing to self-organize, obtain arms, and barricade buildings would remain the factor that is most *disruptive* to the normal course of events even if this group depended on Yanukovych's money. Regardless of the degree of dependence, Yanukovych's potential use of some of his immense wealth to support separatist activities from the safety of his exile should be considered less abnormal than the separatists' activities themselves.

To become the factor that is most disruptive to the normal course of events, the "Family" would have to be more directly involved in the organization of separatist activities. Its ties to the separatist leadership would have to be close enough to define the separatist leaders as agents acting on behalf of the "Family." However, the only concrete evidence in this direction — Shcherbyna's (2014a; 2014c) investigation of business relationships between Yanukovych associates and Pavlo Hubariev — is very weak. Hubariev was not directly involved in the events of April 2014 because he was imprisoned in Kyiv at the time. Moreover, given the size of Yanukovych's business network, it is not surprising that Hubariev or other separatist leaders used to work for or cooperate with companies associated with it. Past business links of this kind are no evidence of a principal-agent relationship. Only evidence of direct employment or a close business relationship with the "Family" during the time leading up to the events of April 2014 could potentially be considered a *smoking gun* in this regard. Such evidence is currently absent for any of the separatist leaders involved in the building occupations of early April. The likely presence of some financial support is not sufficient to suggest that the actions of the Yanukovych "Family" were the primary cause of the building occupations in either Donetsk or Luhansk. As a result, the balance of probabilities between H1 and H2 remains unaltered.

4.2.2. Rinat Akhmetov

Another key suspect of orchestrating the building occupations in Donetsk is Rinat Akhmetov — then Ukraine's richest man, owner of another large business network in Donetsk Oblast, and former ally of Viktor Yanukovych. Several journalists have suggested that Akhmetov was the key person behind the events of early April 2014. However, these allegations are also based on weak evidence. Moreover, an audio recording of Akhmetov's attempts to negotiate with the separatists and his subsequent failure to act as a mediator suggest that he is even less likely to have been in control of the separatist movement than Yanukovych.

Russian journalist Yuliya Latynina (2014) concluded after a visit to Donetsk in late April that separatist leader Denys Pushylin followed Rinat Akhmetov's orders. Latynina based this conclusion on her observation that Pushylin changed his mind about meeting former Russian oligarch Mikhail Khodorkovskiy — supposedly after Akhmetov intervened. However, even if Latynina is correct and Akhmetov managed to convince Pushylin to meet Khodorkovskiy, this is only weak evidence that Akhmetov controlled Pushylin or other separatist figures. Ukrainian journalist and anti-corruption activist Serhii Leshchenko (2014) posted on his Facebook page on April 7 that a "trustworthy source" had told him that Akhmetov had met Vladimir Putin in Moscow in March or April 2014. "As far as I understand, the result is what we are seeing on the streets of Donetsk today," Leshchenko said. However, even if Leshchenko's source is, indeed, trustworthy, the fact that Akhmetov had met with Putin is no evidence that Akhmetov controlled the events. Such a meeting could have had many different purposes and outcomes. Other journalists link Akhmetov to Oleksandr Zakharchenko, who became leader of the DNR on August 8, 2014. In the early days of the conflict, Zakharchenko was the leader of Oplot, a group of activists that was present in the occupied Donetsk state administration building shortly after its seizure (Grove and Baczynska 2014; Ostrov 2014p). According to Serhii Shcherbyna's research (2014b), Zakharchenko used to be the director of a company which was tied to Rinat Akhmetov's business empire through two other intermediary enterprises. In addition, journalist Kateryna Serhatskova

(2015) cited an anonymous source in Ukraine's intelligence apparatus claiming that Zakharchenko used to be involved in the trafficking of goods across the Russian border and "began his career in a group of bandits linked to Rinat Akhmetov." However, the implications of these alleged links are the same as the implications of Pavlo Hubariev's alleged links to the Yanukovych "Family." Given the size of Akhmetov's business network, past business links of this kind are not evidence of a principal-agent relationship.

Despite their weakness, the sum of the above claims still slightly increases the probability of H2 in relation to Akhmetov. However, another piece of evidence reverses this effect. This evidence relates to a meeting during the night of April 7-8 between Akhmetov and representatives of the activists occupying the Donetsk State Administration building. The first part of the meeting took place on a street in central Donetsk and was recorded by one of the activists (YouTube 2014ab). The activists tell Akhmetov that they "need a leader" and ask if he would be willing to lead a "committee of the Donbas." In response, Akhmetov assures the activists that he shares their objective of safeguarding the interests of the Donbas and that he will do everything he can to prevent the Kyiv authorities from using force to retake the occupied building. However, he also tells them that secession is not the way forward. Instead, he urges them to formulate concrete political demands and engage in a dialogue with the new Kyiv authorities. "If we say 'Donetsk, Donbas, Ukraine!' I will be with you," Akhmetov says. The activists reject this idea and say that it is too late to give up the objective of seceding from Ukraine and joining Russia. They also doubt that there is any point in negotiating with the Kyiv authorities. Finally, Akhmetov suggests that the separatists choose a smaller group of representatives to come with him and meet Ukrainian Deputy Prime Minister Vitalii Yarema to continue negotiations. Akhmetov leaves with the representatives. The man who is recording walks back toward the occupied State Administration building. Before ending the recording, he predicts that the "movement's leaders […] will now betray everything to Rinat."

The recording is almost certainly authentic because the footage can be geolocated to a precise location on Teatralnyi Boulevard in central Donetsk and both Akhmetov and Yarema confirmed that negotiations took place that night (Ukrainska Pravda 2014j; 2014f). The recording is *smoking-gun* evidence that significantly reduces the probability of H2 because the discussion between Akhmetov and the activists does not suggest in any way that Akhmetov is in control of the situation. Rather than speaking from a position of authority, he is pleading with the activists, who respond to his arguments with skepticism. Furthermore, the fact that further negotiations did not yield any results is a failed *hoop test* (see section 3.1.2.), which rules out the counterhypothesis that Akhmetov may have staged the nightly meeting. Contrary to the prediction by the person filming, the activists occupying the building did not change their agenda according to Akhmetov's ideas. His mediation efforts, both in the immediate aftermath of the building occupation and in the weeks that followed, did not prevent the further escalation of the conflict in and around Donetsk.[10] This, in turn, had a severe negative impact on Akhmetov's influence and business assets in the Donbas (Prelovskaya 2014).

Akhmetov's failed mediation efforts dramatically reduce the probability that he controlled the group of separatists that occupied the Donetsk State Administration building on April 6. However, it does not suggest that Akhmetov was a strong opponent of the separatist movement who did everything in his power to prevent the conflict from escalating. On the contrary, according to Ukrainian journalist Denys Kazanskyi (2015a), the mere fact that the building occupations in Donetsk went ahead is evidence that their organizers had at least Akhmetov's tacit support. This is because "Akhmetov has always had complete control over the situation in Donetsk Oblast and it is a fairly open secret that all officials of any real significance in the oblast were generally appointed with his approval." Kazanskyi started his career as an anti-corruption blogger in Donetsk Oblast and was a well-known expert in local politics long before the outbreak of the war. For this reason, his assessment carries considerable weight. Moreover, Yehor Firsov, another prominent pro-European activist from Donetsk makes a similar argument. He said:

---

10 As I will argue in chapter six, Akhmetov's efforts to prevent further conflict escalation were more successful in Mariupol.

> I have lived in Donetsk all twenty-five years of my live. For the last seven years, I have been involved in politics, and I am 100 percent certain that not a single more or less significant process takes place without Akhmetov's permission (Firsov and Ivanov 2014).

Kazanskyi's news website Chetvertaya Vlast (2015) also published a detailed chronology of Akhmetov's reactions to separatist activities in the run-up to April, which suggests that he did little more than issuing vague statements. In addition, Kazanskyi (2015a) argues that Akhmetov controlled the Donetsk Oblast police, which failed to prevent or resist the building occupations. Journalist and anticorruption activist Artem Furmaniuk (2014) makes a similar argument by naming three high-ranking police officials in Donetsk who, according to his sources, used to work for companies owned by Akhmetov.

Considering these assessments as well as Akhmetov's halfhearted statements against separatism and his open attempt to co-opt the separatists' agenda, it is clear that he did not do all he could to prevent the events of early April from happening. This failure on his part does not change the conclusion that he was not in control of the situation. But it does suggest that he overestimated his ability to regain control over the events and remained confident that he could step in and use the threat of separatism to his advantage until it was too late.

4.2.3. Oleksandr Yefremov

In Luhansk, accusations of orchestrating separatism have focused on Oleksandr Yefremov, a local oligarch and former head of the Party of Regions faction in the Ukrainian Parliament. Yefremov has publicly expressed solidarity with the separatist movement. He is also the only high-profile Ukrainian politician who was detained and put on trial for supporting separatism. Nevertheless, neither the court case against Yefremov nor those who accused him in the media have revealed any convincing evidence linking him directly to the group that occupied the Luhansk SBU building on April 6.

To some extent, Yefremov has sided with the separatists in public. On March 2, he told a separatist rally in Luhansk that the regime change in Kyiv was unconstitutional (Yefremov 2014a). He then entered the Oblast Assembly building where the deputies voted for a resolution that declared the Kyiv authorities "illegitimate" and "reserved the right" to call the "brotherly nation" of Russia for help if the situation did not improve (Holenko 2014). Shortly after the occupation of the Luhansk SBU on April 6, Yefremov (2014b) told journalists that the people who occupied the building represent "the opinion of many people and want to make a stand for this opinion." As late as mid-May, he used a parliamentary hearing in Kyiv to blame the central government for the escalation of the situation. He urged interim President Turchynov, to end any military operations in the Donbas, take the result of the separatist "referenda" of May 11 seriously, and engage in negotiations (Yefremov 2014c).

The first allegations that Yefremov's support for separatism consisted of more than just rhetoric, were voiced by Luhansk investigative blogger Serhii Ivanov and former Party of Regions MP Volodymyr Landik. They claim that Yefremov financed separatist activities and collaborated with Russian intelligence to bring activists from Russia to Luhansk. They also claim that Valerii Bolotov, a leader of the "Army of the Southeast," used to oversee illegal coal mines in Luhansk Oblast on Yefremov's behalf (Ivanov and Zarovna 2014; Landik 2014; 2016). Moreover, journalistic investigations by Ukrainian journalist Stanislav Kmet (2014) and Russian journalist Yuliya Polukhina (2015) both reached the conclusion that the war of 2014 did not change the economic power structures in Luhansk Oblast. They argue that Yefremov's local business networks remained largely intact and that many of his close associates were appointed to senior positions in the self-proclaimed Luhansk People's Republic (LNR).

However, there is no concrete evidence that Yefremov controlled the separatist movement in Luhansk or that any financial support of his had reached the "Army of the Southeast" by April 2014. Yefremov's trial commenced in January 2017 (RBK-Ukraina 2017) and was still ongoing five years later without bringing to light any convincing evidence. On the contrary, the former leadership of the Luhansk SBU testified in favor of Yefremov. Former Luhansk SBU head, Oleksandr Petrulevych (2017), testified that he did not know of any evidence that links Yefremov to the creation of the "Army of the Southeast." Petrulevych's deputy Oleh Zhyvotov (2018) said that he did not have any information regarding a link between Yefremov and Bolotov, either.

This does not mean that Yefremov did not contribute to the escalation of the situation. Like Akhmetov in Donetsk, he failed to use his influence in the region to prevent separatist activities. What is more, he did not even hide the fact that he was trying to use separatism to put pressure on the Kyiv authorities. This fact and the close ties of his business network to the separatist authorities that later emerged in Luhansk make it likely that Yefremov financed separatist activities in Luhansk to some extent at some point in time. There is a realistic possibility that some of this funding reached the "Army of the Southeast." At the same time, there is no compelling evidence that the men who occupied the Luhansk SBU in April were under his control.

The conclusions regarding Akhmetov's and Yefremov's role raise the question of whether the causal mechanism accompanying H2 needs to be modified to define the inaction rather than the actions of local elites as the primary cause of the critical juncture in question. There are two reasons against such a modification. Firstly, even under the assumption that Akhmetov and Yefremov had almost complete control over the police in Donetsk and Luhansk before April 2014, it remains uncertain whether this would have been sufficient to prevent the building seizures. If Akhmetov and Yefremov had spoken out against separatism and demanded the use of force against separatist protests, the security forces may have turned against them. Secondly and more importantly, refocusing the causal mechanism on elite inaction would contradict the principle of *abnormalism*. The reasoning here is analogous to Yanukovych's potential financing of separatist activities. The fact that a group of local people was willing to self-organize, obtain arms, and barricade buildings was more *disruptive* to the normal course of events than the fact that local elites initially responded with a wait-and-see approach. Given that both Akhmetov and Yefremov used to be allies of Yanukovych, it is by no means extraordinary that they did not rush to the aid of the new Kyiv authorities but tried to exploit the situation. For this reason, their passivity should be mentioned as a supporting factor within the causal mechanism but not as its key determinant.

4.2.4. Oleksandr Bobkov

Another former Party of Regions MP from the Donbas accused of sponsoring separatism is Oleksandr Bobkov. Ukrainian journalists Denys Kazanskyi and Maryna Vorotyntseva (2020, 245–254) call Bobkov "the godfather of Donetsk separatism." They argue that Bobkov founded and financed a separatist group called Oplot. Ukrainian journalist Artem Furmaniuk (2016), Ukrainian activist Yegor Firsov (Ostrov 2014p), along with unnamed insider sources of the Russian newspaper *Novaya Gazeta* (Kanygin 2014), have voiced similar claims.

In the case of Bobkov, there is additional evidence indicating direct collaboration with Oplot. In a 2016 interview with a separatist news website, Bobkov admitted that he had met Oplot leader Oleksandr Zakharchenko at protests against the new Kyiv authorities in Donetsk in spring 2014. He also admitted that he had talked to Zakharchenko about plans to have the Donetsk City Council issue certain demands to the Kyiv authorities (Komitet 2016). On April 16, 2014, armed Oplot members entered the Donetsk City Council building. According to a correspondent of the local news website *62.ua*, Oleksandr Zakharchenko told reporters at the scene that Oplot demanded that the Kyiv authorities "pass Oleksandr Bobkov's draft law on local referenda" (Lazorenko 2014).

This episode strengthens the credibility of the sources that claim that Bobkov played a key role in the creation and operation of Oplot. It suggests that it is likely that Bobkov and Zakharchenko closely coordinated their actions around the time of the Donetsk State Administration seizure. This would mean that Bobkov's involvement in the events went beyond permissive passivity. However, it does not imply that this involvement was a necessary condition for the events of early April in Donetsk. Although Zakharchenko and Oplot were present in the Donetsk State Administration building soon after its occupation (Grove and Baczynska 2014; Ostrov 2014p), there is no evidence to suggest that they played a leading role in the events of April 6. In fact, pro-separatist journalist Aleksandr Barkov (2018), who was a Donbas correspondent of the Russian extreme-right-wing newspaper *Zavtra* at the time, writes in his memoirs that Oplot established its base in the occupied building only on April 11. In any case, even if Zakharchenko or other Oplot members helped seize the building, they were only one component of a heterogenous group of actors. There is nothing to suggest that the seizure of the building could not have taken place without them. Moreover, since Bobkov was not a major oligarch and did not have access to the same resources as the Yanukovych "Family," it is likely that Zakharchenko and his men would have simply looked for another sponsor had Bobkov withdrawn his support.

4.2.5. Other Potential Sponsors

Although accusations of orchestrating Donbas separatism mainly focus on Yanukovych, Akhmetov, Yefremov, and Bobkov, several other politicians have also been associated with it. The role of three of these actors merits a brief discussion. However, the probability that any of them controlled the building occupations in Donetsk or Luhansk is even lower than for the four actors discussed above.

Of all the members of parliament of Yanukovych's Party of Regions, *Oleh Tsarov* was the one who voiced the strongest support for the separatist movement in public. He travelled to Donetsk on 11 April, gave speeches supporting the separatists both inside and outside the occupied State Administration building, and posted videos of these speeches on his own YouTube channel (Tsarov 2014a; 2014b). On the following day, he spoke outside the occupied SBU building in Luhansk (Tsarov 2014c; 2014d). However, Tsarov was from Dnipropetrovsk Oblast and did not have a business network in the Donbas. Neither is there any other evidence that suggests that he had significant control over the separatist movement. His flying visits to the occupied buildings rather suggest that he was trying to jump on a separatist bandwagon.

The ties of Party of Regions MP *Mykola Levchenko* to the separatists are also well documented. According to Rinat Akhmetov, Levchenko was the person who informed him that activists from the State Administration building wanted to meet him on the night of April 7–8 (Ukrainska Pravda 2014j). Levchenko was present at that meeting. When Akhmetov drove off with some separatist representatives to continue negotiations, Levchenko walked with a group of activists—including the person who was secretly recording—back to the square in front of the State Administration. During the conversation, Levchenko expressed support for a united Ukraine, but he also said that Ukraine, Russia, and Belarus should ideally merge into one state (YouTube 2014ab at 36:30). Moreover, Levchenko was the person who enabled Donetsk "People's Governor" Pavlo Hubariev's first public appearance at the Donetsk City Council on February 28. According to Donbas news website Ostrov (2014c), Levchenko urged the deputies to let Hubariev speak by saying: "I have known him for a long time. He has helped us in election campaigns." However, even though this episode and the recording of April 7–8 suggest that Levchenko was on good terms with some members of the separatist movement, they do not indicate that he was in a position of authority or control. Neither was he a major oligarch with access to financial means comparable to the wealth of Akhmetov, Yefremov, or the Yanukovych "Family."

Finally, Luhansk anti-corruption activist Maksym Mykhalkov (2014) accused the Luhansk branch of the Communist Party of Ukraine and its branch leader *Spiridon Kilinkarov* of financing the separatist movement. Considering that collaboration between Ukraine's Communist Party and a separatist fringe group in the Donbas was documented as early as 2006 (Novosti Donbassa 2006), it is likely that these claims are accurate. However, as in the cases of Yanukovych and Yefremov, there is no evidence which links Kilinkarov or the Communist Party of Ukraine directly to the occupation of government buildings in April 2014 or suggests any degree of control over the people involved in them.

4.3. Cossacks, Eurasianists, and Kremlin Advisers: The Role of Russia

The findings of the previous section leave the initial balance of probabilities unaltered, which means that H2 should be discarded as a *highly unlikely* explanation for the escalation of the situation in Donetsk and Luhansk in early April. While local elites contributed to the events, evidence of their involvement is not strong enough to support the claim that they were the primary cause. The following section will determine whether the same applies to H3.

4.3.1. The Glazyev Tapes

Key evidence of direct Russian state support for separatism in Southeast Ukraine comes in the form of intercepted phone conversations between separatist activists and Russian Presidential Adviser Sergey Glazyev. Ukraine's Prosecutor General's Office (2016) first published a small collection of intercepts in August 2016. Ukraine's Military Prosecutor's Office then presented a larger collection of 35 intercepts in late 2017 and early 2018. Audio files and annotated transcripts were subsequently published by the Ukrainian news website *Tsenzor.net* (Romaliiska 2017a; 2017b; 2018a; 2018b; 2018c). According to the Ukrainian prosecutors, the intercepted calls were made between February 27 and March 6, 2014. Most of the calls are between Glazyev and Konstantin Zatulin, the head of a pro-Kremlin Russian think tank. Most of their content focuses on the political situation in Crimea. Some conversations, however, also focus on the situation in other regions. Glazyev and Zatulin discuss the financing of separatist protests in Kharkiv and Odesa. An activist from Kharkiv calls Glazyev to ask for money. And Glazyev urges pro-Russian activists from Odesa, Zaporizhzhia, and Luhansk to occupy the local oblast assemblies and force them to adopt resolutions declaring the Kyiv authorities illegitimate.

Glazyev called the recordings "nonsense created by neo-Nazi criminals" and declined to comment further (RBK 2016). Zatulin, on the other hand, claimed that the recordings were a "doctored compilation," while admitting that they were based on intercepts of actual conversations between him and Glazyev (Business FM 2016; RBK 2016). Indeed, the fact that the Ukrainian authorities only published these recordings several years after the relevant events raises some doubts regarding their authenticity. However, it is highly unlikely that the Ukrainian authorities went through the effort of fabricating more than two hours of detailed and plausible conversations without making them more incriminating. The recordings do not prove a targeted and elaborate Russian conspiracy that led to the eventual escalation of violence. All they prove is that a Kremlin adviser was trying to coordinate and finance a variety of pro-Russian separatist forces across Ukraine's Southeast in the immediate aftermath of the regime change in Kyiv. None of the key actors involved in the later escalation of violence feature in the Glazyev tapes. On the contrary, the efforts of the actors Glazyev was speaking to failed in Odesa, Kharkiv, Dnipro, and Zaporizhzhia. Moreover, the content of the intercepted conversations is entirely consistent with an article that Glazyev wrote for the Russian extreme-right-wing newspaper *Zavtra* in May 2019. In this article, he laments that Russia did not take more decisive actions in early 2014 to prevent Ukraine from becoming "occupied by pro-American neo-Fascists" (Glazyev 2019). Finally, the content of the Glazyev tapes is also in line with Donetsk "People's Governor" Pavlo Hubariev's memoirs. Hubariev writes that Glazyev called him on the evening of March 5, 2014 to express approval and moral support. Hubariev also writes that he and his associates tried to set up a Skype call with Konstantin Zatulin the same evening, which failed because of an Internet outage (Hubariev 2016, 113).

It cannot be ruled out that certain details of the Glazyev tapes were subject to manipulation. However, it is highly likely that their overall content is accurate, which means that a Kremlin adviser was communicating with separatist activists in eastern Ukraine in early March 2014. At the same time, this does not necessarily mean that Glazyev was implementing a carefully devised plan that was supported by the entirety of Russia's political elite. Although Glazyev states in one of the conversations that he has "direct instructions from the leadership" (Prosecutor General's Office of Ukraine 2016, at 5:17), this may be an exaggeration. In fact, Glazyev is known for his extreme views. Russian presidential spokesperson Dmitriy Peskov (2015; 2016; 2017; 2019) said on regular occasions that these views do not necessarily align with those of the Kremlin. Moreover, Glazyev's conversations with Zatulin suggest that their financial means were limited and that Zatulin financed some separatist activities out of his own pocket (Prosecutor General's Office of Ukraine 2016, from 3:28). Therefore, it is entirely plausible that Glazyev's contacts with separatist activists were his own initiative rather than part of a plan handed down to him from further up in the chain of command. However, this does not change the fact that Glazyev was a Russian presidential adviser and remained in this position for several years after the events in question. He did not cease to represent the state just because he may well have enjoyed a certain degree of autonomy to pursue his own initiatives. No state apparatus is entirely homogenous. On the contrary, a certain degree of autonomy is integral to many systems of governance, including Putin's Russia.[11] It is commonplace that the actions of some actors are more extreme than the actions of others while all of them represent the same state. If a state makes no meaningful effort to disassociate itself from the actions of its officials, these actions should be attributed to the state – especially if they relate to core competencies of the state such as foreign policy and security. Hence, in the absence of strong evidence that his superiors tried to prevent and reverse Glazyev's activities, it makes sense to attribute his actions to the Russian state as a fragmented yet collective entity.

The link between the Glazyev tapes and the events of April, however, remains indirect and tentative. The latest recording is dated March 6, and Donetsk and Luhansk are not discussed extensively. Nevertheless, it is unlikely that the ties of Glazyev or other Russian state actors with a similar agenda to the two oblasts with the strongest separatist sentiment were weaker than to the rest of Ukraine's Southeast. It is also unlikely that Russian state actors severed such ties as attention shifted from successfully annexed Crimea to the Ukrainian mainland in mid-March. This does not prove Kremlin control over the actors occupying the buildings in Donetsk and Luhansk. But it does suggest that it is likely that representatives of the Russian state were in contact with these actors and offered strategic and financial support.

4.3.2. Eurasianism and Its Friends in Donetsk

In addition to likely support from the Kremlin itself, the occupants of the State Administration in Donetsk almost certainly received support from Russian neo-Imperial and neo-Soviet organizations.

---

11 See my discussion of informal practices and the principle of *otmashka* in chapter five.

Their direct involvement in the events is well documented. On March 29, 2014, Kateryna Hubarieva, the wife of Donetsk "People's Governor" Pavlo Hubariev published a recorded Skype conversation between her and Russian right-wing extremist philosopher and activist Aleksandr Dugin (Dugin and Hubarieva 2014). During the call, Dugin says that his Eurasian Movement is "in permanent contact with our country's leadership" and that "the Russian state and Russian society are absolutely determined to fight for Ukraine's Southeast." Dugin criticizes separatist activists for leaving occupied buildings. He says that they must stay in the buildings, assert their authority, and appoint representatives. Finally, Dugin claims that several dozen of his activists had recently travelled to Ukraine. Many more had tried but were supposedly stopped by Ukrainian border guards.

Dugin's conversation with Hubarieva gains additional significance from the fact that the "Provisional Government" of the DNR appointed Hubarieva chairwoman of the DNR's "Committee on Foreign Political Relations" on April 10. This appointment was announced in a statement which also noted that Hubarieva was currently in Russia on an "official visit" (YouTube 2014ae). According to Hubariev's (2016, 102, 124) memoirs, his wife and children had left Donetsk on March 2 to stay with a supporter of Dugin's movement in Rostov-on-Don.[12]

Dugin's interest in the Donbas was not new. He had started to support the idea of secession already after the 2004 Orange Revolution. Anton Shekhovtsov (2016), a leading expert on Russian extreme-right ideology, and Ukrainian journalist Inna Bezsonova (2015) have collected evidence of Dugin's links with Donbas activists. According to their investigations, a key partner of Dugin's Eurasian Youth Movement (ESM) in Ukraine was the Donetsk Republic (DR) — a fringe separatist organization created in 2005. It was this organization's emblem that the DNR adopted as its "official" flag. Shekhovtsov and Bezsonova collected photographs of DR activists attending an ESM training camp in Russia in 2005, posing with DR

---

12 Hubarieva kept a relatively low profile as the conflict developed further, but she re-emerged after the invasion of 2022 as a Russia-appointed official in occupied Kherson Oblast.

and ESM flags while collecting signatures for an independence referendum in Donetsk in 2006, and participating in a conference titled "the Donbas in the Eurasian Project" together with leading ESM figures in 2012. The pictures from all three events feature DR cofounder Andrii Purhin. On the 2012 conference panel, Purhin and others were joined by Oleksandr Khriakov, another pro-Russian activist from Donetsk, who had been a vocal opponent of Ukraine's integration with the West since the Orange Revolution (Ostrov 2014p). Purhin and Khriakov were both present at the first session of the "Provisional Government" of the DNR in the occupied State Administration building on April 8. They can be seen talking to each other and leaving the room together during the session, shortly before Purhin is "elected" as one of the "Provisional Government's" first six members (YouTube 2014y).

Dugin's network was not the only Russian organization with a direct involvement in the events. On April 2, Eduard Limonov, leader of the nationalist, anti-Western Other Russia movement, wrote on Facebook that two of his movement's activists had been arrested in Donetsk. The SBU confirmed one arrest (Holos Ukrainy 2014). Another activist of Limonov's movement posted pictures of himself at separatist rallies in Donetsk in early March (Ostrov 2014f; pauluskp 2014). What is more, during the April 6 separatist rally on Donetsk's Lenin Square, one of the speakers, Artem Olkhin (2014), said that "representatives of Yevgeniy Federov's National Liberation Movement" were with him on the stage. He also said that the separatist movement in Donetsk is "collaborating with Kurginyan's Sut Vremeni." The National Liberation Movement is an organization of anti-Western activists founded and headed by Yevgeniy Federov—a Russian State Duma deputy from Vladimir Putin's United Russia party. Sut Vremeni (Essence of Time) is a Soviet restorationist movement led and founded by Russian theater producer Sergey Kurginyan. Given the confirmed presence of Dugin's and Limonov's followers in Donetsk, it is highly likely that the separatists' own claim that Federov's and Kurginyan's followers were also working with them is accurate as well.

Moreover, already in early March, there was at least one social media page that was recruiting Russian volunteers to take part in protests in Donetsk. Potential volunteers were asked to call a person named Vladimir on a Russian mobile phone number (Ukrainska Pravda 2014b). Recruitment efforts of this kind continued. On April 11, a Russian radio correspondent interviewed a volunteer from Russia inside the occupied State Administration building. The man introduced himself as Pavel Paramonov from the town of Yefremov in Tula Oblast (Russkaya Sluzhba Novostey 2014). In May, Paramonov (2014) gave another interview to a local Tula news agency and said that he had been recruited via social media by a person with the pseudonym "Russian Patriot."

The evidence above suggests that Russian organizations were directly involved in the occupation of the Donetsk State Administration, with Dugin's Eurasianist network playing a particularly important role. By staying in the occupied building and creating an institutional structure, the separatists de facto followed Dugin's advice from a week earlier. They adopted the flag of a local partner organization of Dugin's movement and appointed a local supporter of Dugin to the "Provisional Government."

However, the available evidence only links two of the people present in the occupied building to Dugin and identifies only one Russian citizen directly involved in the events. This is not sufficient to outweigh the combined evidential weight of evidence for H1 and the initial bias in favor of H1 due to Occam's razor and the Sagan standard. Together with the Glazyev tapes, the evidence discussed in this section indicates Russian support rather than Russian control. It does not prove that the Donetsk separatists were agents of the mentioned Russian actors. At the same time, the observed degree of cooperation cannot be considered abnormal for local radical separatist groups with the aim to join Russia. Hence, it remains highly unlikely that the mentioned Russian actors and organizations were the main cause of the events in Donetsk.

4.3.3. The Crimean Link

A final piece of evidence of the Russian state's involvement in the events in Donetsk is Viacheslav Ponomarov's (2014) account of the temporary seizure of the Donetsk SBU building on April 6–7. Ponomarov, who claims to be a key organizer of the Donetsk SBU seizure, openly admits that he visited annexed Crimea for consultations at an unspecified time between mid-March and April 6. This is in line with the account of an anonymous Crimean militiaman with the nom-de-guerre Trifon, who also says that Ponomarov came to Crimea in the second half of March and asked for support (Trifon and Bezsonov 2020a). Trifon was a member of an armed group that would come to the Donbas and take control of towns north of Donetsk on April 12–14. Chapter five, which discusses these events, will argue that this armed group was almost certainly acting as an organ of the Russian state and had the support of the Russian security apparatus. Other members of this group (Khokhlov 2019a, at 0:21; Anosov 2019, at 5:19) reported that two of their fellow militiamen, Igor Bezler (nom-de-guerre Bes) and Aleksandr Parkhomenko (nom-de-guerre Volk), were sent to the Donbas from Crimea early for reconnaissance purposes. Ponomarov (2014) said that these two men visited the Donetsk SBU building on the morning of April 7 while it was still occupied. The presence of Bezler, and Parkhomentko in the occupied SBU building is also confirmed by Donetsk separatist activist Serhii Tsypkalov and another activist with the nom-de-guerre Buynyy. Both men were associates of Donetsk "People's Governor" Pavlo Hubariev and their testimonies feature in Hubariev's memoirs (Hubariev 2016, 162–67). However, none of the cited accounts indicate that Bezler and Parkhomenko had a leading role in the operation. In the absence of further evidence to the contrary—and in light of Occam's razor and the Sagan standard—it remains likely that Ponomarov's claim that a local activist network was in charge of the Donetsk SBU operation is correct. However, it is almost certain that Ponomarov coordinated these actions with paramilitary forces involved in the Russian takeover of Crimea and received advise from them.

4.3.4. The Don Cossack Network

In the case of Luhansk, it was Don Cossacks from neighboring Russian regions who played the role that Dugin and other Russian extremists played in Donetsk. On March 29, Anastasiia Piaterykova, a leading figure in the Luhansk Guard, one of the main separatist organizations active in Luhansk throughout March, spoke at a Don Cossack rally in the Russian town of Voronezh and called for help.

In response, Aleksandr Agulov, a local Don Cossack leader, said that the Don Cossacks would "come to help" their "closest neighbor Luhansk," noting that they had also gone to Crimea "when the Crimeans turned to them for help" (Votinova 2014).

There is no evidence that Don Cossacks from Russia came to Luhansk already in early April. However, it is highly likely that they provided material and organizational support to local Cossacks who stormed the building together with the "Army of the Southeast."[13] More significant evidence of this than Agulov's promise is the fact that Mykola Tarasenko was filmed in the occupied SBU building on April 9 (YouTube 2014ac). Tarasenko is a former archaeologist, who became a local attraction in Luhansk Oblast after he settled on a hill near the village of Kamianka and started to build a church (Krykun 2014; YouTube 2014am). However, Tarasenko also self-identifies as a Don Cossack and is a close associate of Nikolay Kozitsyn, a Don Cossack leader from Russia's Rostov Oblast who would play an important role in the further escalation of the conflict. On April 9, Kozitsyn (2014a; 2014b) announced the creation of a "Cossack National Guard" in Ukraine and appointed "Cossack Elder" Mykola Tarasenko as the head of this organization's "Security Service." However, there is no evidence documenting the presence of other Don Cossacks with prior links to Russia in the occupied SBU building or indicating that Tarasenko had a leadership role within the "Army of the Southeast." This means that, as in the case of Dugin in Donetsk, the presence of Tarasenko in the Luhansk SBU building combined with the Glazyev tapes is evidence of Russian support, but not of the primary role of the Russian state.

4.3.5. FSB and GRU in Luhansk

Potential evidence of Russian control in Luhansk are the accounts of the city's former SBU leadership. Oleksandr Petrulevych, who

---

13 It is important to note that the actions of Cossack activists who supported separatism in 2014 are not representative of people identifying as Cossacks in the Donbas, let alone in Ukraine as a whole. The pro-Russian Don Cossack movement is only one facet of Cossack identity in eastern Ukraine. Many other people identify as Zaporizhzhian Cossacks and are strongly in favor of Ukrainian independence.

was the head of the SBU in Luhansk and present in the building when the separatists stormed it, claims that the occupation of the building was an operation by Russia's domestic intelligence service FSB. He argues that the FSB founded and controlled the "Army of the Southeast." Moreover, he claims that he was questioned by FSB officers while being held captive inside the building. These officers "introduced themselves and even showed their ID, covering their last name and rank with a finger" (Dvali and Petrulevych 2014). Petrulevych says he was smuggled out of separatist captivity by Mykola Tsukur, a separatist activist who had changed sides and worked undercover for the SBU at the time of the occupation. Tsukur subsequently confirmed this and also claimed that he saw people entering the occupied building who introduced themselves as FSB agents to separatist leaders and showed their IDs (Tsukur and Dvali 2015). Oleh Zhyvotov, who was Petrulevych's deputy at the time, also supports Petrulevych's and Tsukur's claims and argues that the group that occupied the SBU building "is not worth being called separatists — they are direct agents of the FSB and the GRU [Russia's military intelligence service]." Zhyvotov also claims that, when the SBU arrested some members of the "Army of the Southeast" on April 5, one day before the others stormed the building, they confiscated a computer and "found and documented all the evidence of their cooperation with Russian special services" (Zhyvotov and Butkevych 2016).

However, the testimonies of all three people leave doubts. Zhyvotov says that Alexej Relke was the "main coordinator of the separatist movement in all southeastern regions of Ukraine" and makes far-reaching claims about Relke's past:

> He is a career operative of Russian intelligence who worked for the German police in a unit working with Russians. He retired when he was 35 and suddenly moved to Ukraine in 2007 – after being assigned a new mission on the frontline. At the same time, he continued to receive a pension via Russia's Sberbank (Zhyvotov and Butkevych 2016).

Zhyvotov's account is not compatible with the account of Relke's mother. In Summer 2014, after Relke had been arrested by the SBU and taken to Kyiv, a journalist spoke to Ida Relke in the German town of Koblenz. According to his mother, Alexej worked in construction and had regular trouble with the police because he was "quick with his fists." He returned to Stakhanov in 2006 after losing his job in Germany but continued to rely on frequent money transfers from his mother (Ostermann and Relke 2014). Three considerations suggest that Ida Relke's account is highly likely to be closer to the truth than Zhyvotov's. Firstly, the level of Alexej Relke's German, which he demonstrated during an interview with German journalists in the occupied SBU building in April 2014 (Gathmann 2015), is unlikely to be sufficient to work in the German police force. Secondly, considering German civil service employment regulations, it is unlikely that Relke was able to retire and receive a pension in his mid-thirties. Thirdly, it is unlikely that Relke gave up a successful career in the German police to live as a sleeper agent in Stakhanov for seven years or that Russian intelligence withdrew an agent from the German police for this purpose.

Petrulevych also stresses the role of Relke and calls him a "career operative of Russia's special services" (Petrulevych and Hordon 2017). Moreover, Petrulevych's frequent interviews, in which he presents himself as one of the few Ukrainian state officials who had the integrity to make a stand against Russian aggression in 2014, also raise the possibility that his account contains exaggerations. After all, it is more beneficial for his reputation to have lost his Luhansk headquarters to a well-equipped and organized Russian intelligence operation than to a group of local separatists.

Mykola Tsukur's credibility is called into question by his turbulent career: At first, he was a separatist. Then he became an SBU mole. After that, he became the deputy commander of a pro-Ukrainian volunteer battalion (Tsukur and Dvali 2015). Finally, this battalion was disbanded, and its leadership was convicted of abduction and torture. Tsukur was sentenced to nine years in prison (Gordon 2017).

The most problematic aspect of Zhyvotov, Petrulevych, and Tsukur's statements, however, is the lack of additional supporting evidence. Tsukur and Petrulevych insist that the Russian intelligence operatives did not hide their affiliation and even carried IDs. At the same time, Zhyvotov and Petrulevych both talk about the 5

April raid and claim that the SBU not only confiscated a computer with valuable information but also arrested one of the "Army of the Southeast's" alleged handlers, "GRU Officer" Sergey Bannykh (Petrulevych and Hordon 2017; Zhyvotov and Butkevych 2016). Despite this arrest and the Russian intelligence officers' alleged openness, the SBU has published very little evidence to back up Zhyvotov, Petrulevych, and Tsukur's claims. All there is is a statement on the SBU's official website from April 7, 2014, which features a picture supposedly showing Bannykh and claims that he was "registered at Military Base 13204, which is part of the GRU" (SBU 2014b).

The SBU did not publish any documents confirming Bannykh's position or his relationship with the "Army of the Southeast," apart from a link to two intercepted phone conversations – allegedly between Bannykh and another intelligence operative in Russia. On the recording, two men can be heard talking about "two groups in Luhansk," which are "equipped" and "ready for action." One of the men asks if "the guys from Belgorod" will join. They also mention a person called "Vova" who is currently in Moscow. They then talk about organizing rallies in Donetsk and Luhansk and about flying to Crimea to get support from there. Finally, the man captioned as Bannykh says that "if all the little groups from Donetsk and Luhansk can be brought together in some way, it will be possible to form one group that is more or less combat-ready" (SBU 2014a). Although these recordings are shorter than the Glazyev Tapes, they are likely to be authentic for the same reason—they do not contain any *smoking-gun* evidence. All that can be deducted from them is that two unidentified men were trying to organize material and organizational support for separatist groups in Donetsk and Luhansk from Russia and Crimea. This is entirely consistent with the evidence of Russian support discussed so far but does not prove that Russian intelligence service activity was the primary determinant of the separatist movement's actions.

The available evidence against Zhyvotov, Petrulevych, and Tsukur's claims suggests it is likely that their accounts contain exaggerations. However, there remains a realistic possibility that their overall assessment regarding the role of Russian intelligence in Luhansk is correct. In Luhansk, there is little evidence for H1 apart from Occam's razor and the Sagan standard. The combined weight of the Glazyev tapes, the Don Cossack involvement, the SBU officers' testimony, and the SBU's intercepted phone conversation come closer to tipping the balance of probability in favor of H3 than in Donetsk. However, they still do not quite make it. There is a realistic possibility that the "Army of the Southeast" acted as an organ of the Russian state. However, there remains the other, somewhat more probable realistic possibility that the "Army of the Southeast" consisted of a network of local war veterans, Don Cossacks, and Soviet nostalgists, who acted primarily on their own accord, albeit with Russian support.

4.4. Chapter Conclusion

The analysis of the available digital open source data has not found sufficient evidence to turn the balance of probability in favor of either H2 or H3. Considering Occam's razor and the Sagan standard, it remains highly unlikely that the buildings occupations in Donetsk and Luhansk were orchestrated primarily by local elites. Russian involvement as the primary cause is *highly unlikely* in the case of Donetsk. In the case of Luhansk, H3 is a *realistic possibility*. H1 is also a *realistic possibility* in the case of Luhansk but remains the slightly more probable explanation. In the case of Donetsk, H1 remains *likely*. At the same time, the analysis in this chapter has highlighted that H1 only reflects the currently available digital open source evidence and has pointed out a number of caveats.

- The building occupations of April 2014 were the result of a fringe rather than a mass movement. Protest turnout in early April was visibly lower than in early March. What increased was not general separatist protest sentiment but the level of organization and determination on the part of a small radical core of activists.
- It is likely that some of the founders of the DNR in Donetsk received financial support from the business network surrounding former President Viktor Yanukovych. In Luhansk, financial support for the "Army of the Southeast" from Yanukovych and local oligarch Oleksandr Yefremov is a realistic possibility.

- It is almost certain that Yefremov as well as Donetsk oligarch Rinat Akhmetov did not use all the resources available to them to prevent or end the building occupations, in the hope to use separatism for their own political agenda.
- It is likely that Party of Regions MP Oleksandr Bobkov supported and coordinated the actions of one of the separatist groups involved in the aftermath of the Donetsk State Administration building occupation.
- It is almost certain that the nascent DNR received direct financial and organizational support from Russian organizations. This support came from a variety of neo-Imperial and neo-Soviet networks with Aleksandr Dugin's Eurasian Movement playing a particular important role. In Luhansk, it is highly likely that the Don Cossacks were a similar source of support for the "Army of the Southeast." Even though some of the organizations in question have an ambiguous relationship with the Russian authorities, the Kremlin has given them space to pursue their activities within Russia's tightly controlled NGO sector (Arnold and Umland 2018; Baranec 2014; Kolsto 2016; Laruelle 2014). Neither has the Kremlin made any attempts to prevent them from supporting separatism in Ukraine. For these reasons, it is appropriate to see them as informal organs of the Russian state and their activities in the Donbas as a Russian foreign policy instrument.[14]
- It is likely that Russian financial and organizational support was not limited to the above organizations but also involved Kremlin adviser Sergey Glazyev. In the case of Donetsk, it almost certainly also involved a paramilitary group that had participated in Russia's takeover of Crimea.

These caveats take account of the fact that all initial hypotheses were ideal types. It is therefore not surprising that the causal explanation most closely in line with the available evidence features elements of all three. This explanation is illustrated in Figure 5 below.

---

14 I will discuss the idea of informal state organs and their relationship with the Kremlin in greater detail in section 5.4. of this book.

Figure 5: Causal Mechanism for Juncture 1

Source: the author

A comprehensive explanation of the critical juncture investigated in this chapter should mention all the factors listed above. A reductionist approach that focuses on the element that was most *disruptive* to the normal course of events should single out the activities of small radicalized pro-Russian fringe groups as the primary cause of the escalation. However, even such a reductionist approach would have to highlight another caveat: Even though the events of April 6 marked the creation of the first armed separatist footholds in the Donbas, they did not mark the beginning of the armed conflict. The Kyiv authorities responded to the developments with negotiations rather than violence. When the first person died in armed combat a week later, it was far away from the two occupied buildings and under completely different circumstances which will be scrutinized in the following chapter. Fighting did not reach Donetsk and Luhansk for more than a month and half, and, by the time it did, the situation across the Donbas had changed fundamentally.

5. Enter Igor Girkin
The Occupation of Sloviansk and Kramatorsk

This chapter will analyze the second critical juncture of the Donbas War's escalation sequence—the occupation of the Sloviansk-Kramatorsk area by a group of armed men.[15] It will investigate two hypotheses. According to the first hypothesis, the primary cause of the armed men's action was the domestic separatist movement in the Donbas. According to the second hypothesis, the primary cause were the actions of the Russian state. I will argue that three sets of evidence enable three stages of informal Bayesian updating (see sections 3.1.4. and 3.4.3.2.). This evidence relates to the armed men's prior participation in the Russian takeover of Crimea, documented ties between the group's leader and actors in Russia, and the unwillingness of the Russian state to punish any of the involved actors. If added up, these three stages of Bayesian updating increase the probability of the second hypothesis to *almost certain* while only leaving a *remote chance* that the first hypothesis is accurate.

The events in question unfolded as follows: On the morning of April 12, 2014, a group of masked men in camouflage armed with automatic rifles occupied the police station in the town of Sloviansk, 90 km north of Donetsk, close to the border between Donetsk Oblast and Kharkiv Oblast (YouTube 2014ah). The armed men and some local helpers constructed barricades outside the building while a crowd of local residents stood by and cheered (YouTube 2014ag). On the evening of the same day, armed men of a similar appearance to those seen in Sloviansk stormed the police station in the neighboring town of Kramatorsk. They shot in the air and pushed aside a group of men who tried to explain to them that the police station had already been "taken by Afghan war veterans from Kramatorsk" who were "for the Donetsk People's Republic" and "for Russia" (YouTube 2014ai).

On the morning of April 13, 2014, Ukrainian special forces, who had been deployed to Sloviansk, were ambushed on one of the

---

15 This chapter is an expanded version of an investigation previously published in Hauter 2021c, 6–14.

major roads approaching the town. Footage from the site, which was aired by a Russian television channel and can be geolocated to a woodland area near the town's southeastern boundary, shows one dead and one injured person (LifeNews 2014b). Later that day, Ukraine's Acting President Oleksandr Turchynov reported that the dead person was an officer of the Ukrainian Security Service (SBU) and that three other members of the security forces had sustained injuries in the attack. He then officially announced the start of an "antiterrorist operation" involving the Ukrainian Armed Forces (Turchynov 2014b).

The events of April 12–13 are key to the second critical juncture of the conflict. This critical juncture is of particular importance because it encompasses the crossing of three escalation thresholds—the appearance of armed groups, the deployment of the military, and armed clashes—within a short period of time. Only the first one of these thresholds, the appearance of armed groups, had been crossed before elsewhere in the Donbas, namely during the previous week when separatist activists in Donetsk and Luhansk seized military-grade weaponry from buildings they had occupied. Outside the two regional centers, however, no armed men had been spotted so far. More importantly, the Kyiv authorities had not previously responded with force. This time, armed units were deployed to Sloviansk and met armed resistance, which led to the first battle-related casualty in the Donbas. According to the Uppsala Conflict Data Program's methodology, the first battle-related casualty marks the dividing line between peace and armed conflict (Pettersson 2020, 6). Moreover, the Sloviansk-Kramatorsk area remained the central theater of armed combat in the Donbas until the separatist forces withdrew to Donetsk in early July.

The head of the armed group that occupied the buildings was Igor Girkin (also known as Igor Strelkov or under his nom-de-guerre Strelok), a Russian citizen and resident of Moscow. Girkin is briefly visible in the first seconds of on one of the first videos showing the occupation of Sloviansk on April 12 (YouTube 2014ag). His first major media appearance took place on April 26 in a video interview with the Russian tabloid newspaper *Komsomolskaya Pravda* (Girkin, Kots, and Steshin 2014). In this interview Girkin said that his group had gathered in Crimea and that two thirds of it consisted of Ukrainian citizens—residents of Crimea and "refugees" from other regions. Subsequently, Girkin made frequent media appearances both during and after his time in the Donbas. He provided a particularly detailed account of his activities in an interview with Ukrainian journalist Dmytro Hordon, which was published in May 2020. As on previous occasions, Girkin confirmed in this interview that he was a Russian citizen and used to work for Russia's internal FSB intelligence service until 2013 (Girkin and Hordon 2020 from 13:05). However, he challenged Hordon's assertion that he and his men were Russian agents. Girkin claimed that his group mainly consisted of Ukrainian volunteers and that neither he nor any other group members were working for the Russian state (Girkin and Hordon 2020 from 58:14).

This disagreement between Girkin and his interviewer has important implications for the causal mechanism at work within this particularly important critical juncture of the conflict that crossed the dividing line between war and peace in the region. It is, therefore, not surprising that the divide between proponents of domestic and foreign causes of the 2014 Donbas War in the academic literature is also visible in different scholars' characterizations of Igor Girkin. Some portray Girkin and his men as mavericks, who were not acting on behalf of the Russian authorities (Katchanovski 2016, 479–80; Kudelia 2016, 14–17; Robinson 2016, 511). Others portray Girkin as an agent of the Russian state (Kuromiya 2019, 257–258; Mitrokhin 2014, 167–170; Wilson 2016, 648).

This divide in the characterization of the key actors leads to two contradicting hypotheses regarding the causes of the occupation of Sloviansk and Kramatorsk. Each of the two hypotheses is associated with a specific causal mechanism (Figures 6 and 7). Naturally, both causal mechanisms are simplifications. They are examples of "linear colligation," in which the "most disruptive or abnormal" conditions were selected form a large web of contributing factors (Roberts 1996, 109–10). Neither mechanism presents an exhaustive explanation. However, the two mechanisms represent the two primary causal dynamics that dominate the political and academic debate on the events in question.

H1: Igor Girkin and his men were non-state actors who participated in the conflict as part of a domestic separatist movement.

Figure 6: Sloviansk-Kramatorsk Internal Conflict Mechanism

Source: the author

H2: Igor Girkin and his men were an organ of the Russian state and their participation in the conflict was de facto a Russian invasion.

Figure 7: Sloviansk-Kramatorsk Russian Invasion Mechanism

Source: the author

These two contradicting hypotheses and the two associated causal mechanisms need to be tested against the available digital open source evidence. As a starting point for informal Bayesian analysis, it is appropriate to begin with the assumption that H1 is *likely* while H2 is *unlikely*. As in the previous chapter, this assumption is based on Occam's razor and the Sagan standard. The hypothesis that a group of volunteers decided to seize Sloviansk and Kramatorsk does not require the additional explanatory construct of state instruction or approval, unless there is evidence that demands this addition. At the same time, an act of Russian aggression against its neighbor is a more extraordinary claim than conflict escalation by a group of maverick volunteers. This means that, to overcome the initial burden of proof, H2 requires strong evidence in its support. Such evidence could come from eyewitness accounts, intercepted communications, or circumstantial observations which point at a principal-agent relationship between Girkin's group and the Russian state.

5.1. From Crimea to the Donbas: The Genesis of Girkin's Militia

Even though H2 starts off as the weaker hypothesis, the available digital open source evidence allows for three stages of informal Bayesian updating which not only flip the balance of probabilities but raise the probability of H2 to *almost certain*. The first stage is based on evidence that Girkin's group formed in Crimea and included many people who had been involved in Russia's annexation of the peninsula.[16] Girkin himself never made a secret of this and at least two journalists working for nationalist Russian websites confirmed his leading role in the Crimean events. Sergey Shargunov

---

16   Russia's illegal military takeover of Crimea started on February 27, 2014 when armed men in camouflage stormed the Crimean Parliament building and installed Sergey Aksyonov as new prime minister of the region, which is an autonomous republic within Ukraine. Over the following days, unmarked Russian troops supported by paramilitary forces took control of all important government and infrastructure facilities across the peninsula. On March 16, the occupation authorities staged a "referendum" on joining Russia. Two days later, Vladimir Putin and the Russia-appointed leaders of Crimea signed an accession treaty which was ratified by the Russian Federation Council on March 21.

said that he had met Girkin in Crimea in late February 2014 as an authority figure among the paramilitary groups which supported the Russian takeover (Girkin and Shargunov 2014). Oleg Kashin (2014a; 2014b; 2014c) also wrote that he met Girkin in Crimea in March as an influential figure. Moreover, Girkin appears in a video showing the arrest of Ukrainian businessman Hennadii Balashov in Simferopol, Crimea, on March 4, 2014 (Hromadske TV 2014a at 3:25). In the video, Girkin can be seen talking to Samvel Mardoyan, a prominent paramilitary figure at the time. In his interview with Hordon, Girkin again confirmed his involvement in the Crimean takeover (Girkin and Hordon 2020 from 30:00).

Numerous other members of Girkin's group have either spoken about their experience, feature in the accounts of their comrades-in-arms, or were identified by journalists through their social media profiles. According to Girkin, the group that gathered in Crimea and went to Sloviansk comprised a total of 54 men (Girkin and Hordon 2020 at 57:42).[17] On the basis of the available digital open source evidence, I have been able to gather information on 27 men who were highly likely members of this group. At least nine of them are Russian citizens. More importantly, many of them had also been involved in the Russian annexation of Crimea before following Girkin to Sloviansk.

- *Igor Girkin* (also known as Igor Strelkov, nom-de-guerre: "Strelok") was the leader and key public face of the group while it was in control of Sloviansk. Previously, he played an important role in Russia's annexation of Crimea.
- *Yevgeniy Skripnik* (nom-de-guerre: "Prapor") appears with Girkin in the first seconds of a video taken in Sloviansk on April 12 (YouTube 2014ag). In autumn 2014, Skripnik confirmed in an interview that he had come to Ukraine from Russia and that he had taken part in the takeover of Crimea before moving on to Sloviansk (YouTube 2014bt, from 06:48 and at 15:55). He also confirmed that he had known Girkin since their joint involvement in the Transnistrian conflict in

---

17 Many other accounts of the events speak of 52 men. In the interview with Hordon, Girkin initially admits that he is not entirely sure anymore if the group had a size of 52 or 54 but eventually goes for the latter figure.

1992 (YouTube 2014bt, at 09:35). As of autumn 2020, he runs a social media profile under his real name (Skripnik n.d.).

- *Vladimir Kollontay* (nom-de-guerre: "Ded") went missing in action near Sloviansk in June 2014 and was presumed dead. In an obituary posted on Russian social network VK, Andrey Afanasyev (2016), a well-connected supporter of Donbas separatism from Russia's Novosibirsk, wrote that Kollontay had taken part in the takeover of Crimea before moving on to Sloviansk together with Girkin. Kollontay is also mentioned in another group member's account of the trip from Crimea to Sloviansk (Trifon and Bezsonov 2020c). In a post in the forum of the Novorossiya Movement, which he founded after he returned from Ukraine to Russia, Girkin (2016c) wrote that Kollontay had served in Transnistria and both Cechen wars. In another social media post, Girkin (2016b) specified that Kollontay was a former GRU military intelligence officer and posted a picture showing himself next to Kollontay in Chechnya in 2000.

- *"Tikhiy"* is the nom-de-guerre of a member of Girkin's group who gave an extended interview to a pro-separatist YouTube channel in April 2020 (YouTube 2020a). He wore a balaclava and did not give his real name. Shortly afterward, Girkin gave an interview to the same YouTube channel. He confirmed that Tikhiy had been part of his group during the takeover of Crimea and went with him to Sloviansk. He did not identify Tikhiy by his real name but said that they had first met in 2000 in Chechnya and that Tikhiy was a former Russian GRU military intelligence officer (YouTube 2020b, at 1:30 and 27:57).

- *Igor Bezler* (nom-de-guerre: "Bes") was a member of Girkin's group who, according to the consistent accounts of two other group members (Khokhlov 2019a, at 0:21; Anosov 2019, at 4:37), was sent from Crimea to the Donbas early on a reconnaissance mission. After the rest of the group arrived, Bezler did not stay in Sloviansk but established a separatist unit in the town of Horlivka. In an interview with Russian state news agency RIA Novosti, he confirmed that he was a Russian citizen and army veteran who had taken part in the takeover of Crimea (Bezler 2014).[18]

- *Arsen Pavlov* (nom-de-guerre: "Motorola") was a Russian citizen who later became a prominent separatist commander in Donetsk. In conversations with Russian journalists, Pavlov claimed that he had served in the Russian military and fought in Chechnya (Olevskiy and Romenskiy 2014; Pavlov and Gorbachova 2015). Girkin mentioned Pavlov as one of the members of his group in a 2014 Interview (Girkin and Shargunov 2014). According to another group member's account, Pavlov arrived in Crimea in early April with a group of men who had previously taken part in separatist protests in Kharkiv (Chalenko and Saveliev 2019).
- *Aleksandr Mozhayev* (nom-de-guerre: "Babay"), a Russian citizen from the town of Belorechensk in Russia's Krasnodar Krai, identified himself by showing his passport to journalist Simon Ostrovsky (2014) in Kramatorsk on April 21. In a later interview with another journalist, Mozhayev also admitted that he had participated in the occupation of Crimea (Mozhayev and Shuster 2014).
- *Yevgeniy Ponomaryov* (nom-de-guerre: "Dingo"), also a Russian citizen from Belorechensk, told Ostrovsky (2014) that he and Mozhayev were "Terek Cossacks." He did not give his name at the time but was later identified by Ukrainian activists through his social media profile (Babiak 2014; Garmata.org 2014c).
- *Anton Morozov* is another Russian citizen who was photographed with other members of Girkin's group outside the Sloviansk City Council building during the first days of the occupation (Babiak 2014; Garmata.org 2014a). According to his social media profile, he is from Irkutsk and a supporter of Aleksandr Dugin's Eurasian Movement (Morozov 2014). Morozov also featured in a later report on events in Sloviansk by a local Irkutsk TV station (Malyshkina 2014).

---

18 See chapter seven for a more thorough analysis of Bezler´s background, his links to Russia, and his relationship to Girkin during their time in the Donbas.

- *Ihor Heorhiievskyi*,[19] a resident of Simferopol, is visible in the background of Simon Ostrovsky's (2014) video. He was also photographed together with Aleksandr Mozhayev in Sloviansk by photojournalist Maxim Dondyuk (2014). He was later identified by Ukrainian activists through his social media profile, where he posted personal information and pictures of himself among paramilitary forces in Crimea (Babiak 2014; Garmata.org 2014b). Moreover, he posted Ostrovsky's (2014) video on his social media profile and this post was subsequently shared by Anton Morozov (2014).
- *Evgen Zloy* is the social media pseudonym of another man who was photographed with other members of Girkin's group outside the Sloviansk City Council building during the first days of the occupation (Babiak 2014; Garmata.org 2014a). On his social media profile, he wrote that he was a resident of Simferopol and attended the city's School No. 3 (VK 2014). His profile also shows that he is friends with Anton Morozov.
- *Tikhon Karetnyy* is the social media pseudonym of another man who was photographed with other members of Girkin's group outside the Sloviansk City Council building during the first days of the occupation (Babiak 2014; Garmata.org 2014d). There is little additional reliable information on his background. According to Babiak (2014), his social media profile was part of the Terek Cossack community in the Russian town of Belorechensk, but this information is not visible on the archived version of Karetnyy's page.
- *Serhii Zdryliuk* (nom-de-guerre: "Abver") spoke to a journalist in early May and said that he was Girkin's deputy (Inter TV 2014). A few days later, a Ukrainian newspaper interviewed his mother and former neighbors. They said that Zdryliuk was from Ukraine's Vinnytsia Oblast but had lived in Crimea for many years (Zdryliuk and

---

19 I will use Ukrainian transliterations for the names of all group members who may have held Ukrainian citizenship before the Russian annexation of Crimea. It is possible that some of them obtained Russian citizenship before travelling from Crimea to Sloviansk, but this is difficult to verify.

Murakhovska 2014). Zdryliuk is also mentioned in another group member's account as one of Girkin's deputies on the way from Crimea to Sloviansk (Trifon and Bezsonov 2020c).

- *Andrii Saveliev* (nom-de-guerre: "Vandal") was a sixteen-year-old boy from Kyiv who took part in the Russian takeover of Crimea and travelled with Girkin's group to Sloviansk. He subsequently wrote a book about his adventures as a child soldier and presented it at public book launches in Russia and Crimea (Saveliev 2019a; 2019b; 2019c).
- *"Krot"* is the nom-de-guerre of a close friend of Saveliev's. He features prominently in Saveliev's memoirs (Chalenko and Saveliev 2019; Saveliev 2019a). According to Saveliev, Krot's first name is Sergey and both of them had been members of a pro-Russian Cossack youth group in Kyiv before travelling to Crimea, taking part in the Russian takeover, and moving on to Sloviansk as part of Girkin's group.
- *Dmytro Zhukov* (nom-de-guerre: "Kedr") took part in Saveliev's book launch in Sevastopol (Saveliev 2019b from 49:25). He described himself as a pro-Russian resident of Kyiv who went to Crimea after the Euromaidan revolution and participated in the Russian takeover under Girkin's command before following Girkin to Sloviansk. These basic facts of his personal story are consistent with an investigative article on his identity and background published by a Ukrainian journalist (Dobryi 2018).
- *Artem Razuvaiev* (nom-de-guerre: "Frits") took part in Saveliev's book launch in Moscow. During the event, Saveliev said that he had known Razuvaiev from Kyiv and met him again by chance on the ferry from Crimea to Russia when Saveliev was travelling to Sloviansk as part of Girkin's group (Saveliev 2019c from 26:45). After the meeting on the ferry, Razuvaiev spontaneously decided to join Girkin's group. In an earlier interview with a Russian news website, Razuvaiev told the same story. He said he was a Ukrainian citizen who had taken part in the annexation of Crimea as part of a pro-Russian Cossack group. When was on his way to Rostov-on-Don to look for a job in Russia, he met old friends from Kyiv on the ferry. These friends were part of

Girkin's group and Razuvaiev decided to join them (Pegov 2016).
- *Vadym Ilovchenko* (nom-de-guerre: "Terets") also participated in Saveliev's book launch in Sevastopol and described himself as a pro-Russian Cossack leader from Crimea. He said he met Igor Girkin in early March, served with him in Crimea, and followed him to Sloviansk (Saveliev 2019b from 22:50). Information from the SBU published in Ukrainian media confirms Ilovchenko's own claim that he played an important role in both the annexation of Crimea and the occupation of Sloviansk and Kramatorsk (TSN 2019b).
- *Serhii Zhurykov* (nom-de-guerre: "Romashka") was a pro-Russian resident of Kyiv. In his interview with Dmytro Hordon, Igor Girkin mentioned that he met Zhurykov during a trip to Kyiv in January 2014 (Girkin and Hordon 2020 at 21:40). Publications by Ukrainian journalists as well as Andrii Saveliev's memoirs confirm that Zhurykov joined Girkin's group during the Russian takeover of Crimea and then went on to Sloviansk, where he died in an armed clash (Butusov 2016; Dobryi 2018; Saveliev 2019d; 2019a, 89).
- *Illia Khokhlov* (nom-de-guerre: "Makhno") gave an interview to a Russian nationalist YouTube channel in spring 2019. He said he came to Sloviansk with Girkin's group and commanded a group of fighters in one of the first major clashes with the Ukrainian Armed Forces on May 5 (Khokhlov 2019a).
- *Viktor Anosov* (nom-de-guerre: "Nos") gave an interview in response to Khokhlov. He criticized various details of Khokhlov's account but confirmed that both of them were from Simferopol, took part in the takeover of Crimea, and went to Sloviansk as part of Girkin's group (Anosov 2019).
- *Denys Koval* identified himself during a heated argument with Viktor Anosov in the comments section of Khokhlov's (2019a) YouTube testimony. Anosov accused Koval of betraying Girkin by leaving Sloviansk and joining Igor Bezler in Horlivka. Koval responded by saying that he went to Horlivka after receiving an order from Bezler, who had been his commander "since the very beginning—since

Crimea." Another group member's account of the trip from Crimea to the Donbas also mentions a man called "Koval" and describes him as a resident of Crimea (Trifon and Bezsonov 2020c).

- *Oleksandr Parkhomenko* (nom-de-guerre: "Volk") died in combat on May 5 and was buried in Sloviansk two days later (Slavyansk Delovoy 2014). In their accounts of the events, both Illia Khokhlov (2019a, at 0:21) and Viktor Anosov (2019, at 4:37) confirm that Parkhomenko was part of their group. They also report that he was sent from Crimea to the Donbas early on a reconnaissance mission together with Igor Bezler.[20] It is possible that his name is a pseudonym because Aleksandr Parkhomenko is also a historical figure from the Russian Civil War and subject of a Soviet adventure film.

- *Viacheslav Rudakov* (nom-de-guerre: "Medved") died and was buried on the same day as Parkhomenko (Slavyansk Delovoy 2014). According to his comrade-in-arms Tikhiy, Rudakov was a former paratrooper but did not have any combat experience (YouTube 2020a, at 29:55). Rudakov's nom-de-guerre also features in another group member's account of the trip from Crimea to the Donbas (Trifon and Bezsonov 2020c). A journalist later discovered Rudakov's name on a photo carried by members of the "Crimean Self Defense Forces" during a memorial event for Crimeans who died in the Donbas (Veselova 2017).

- *Serhii Trifonov* (nom-de-guerre: "Trifon") provided a detailed account of the formation of Girkin's group and its trip from Crimea to Sloviansk for a Russian news website (Trifon and Bezsonov 2020b; 2020a; 2020c). Writing under his nom-de-guerre, Trifon describes himself as a former member of the Ukrainian security forces who took part in the Russian annexation of Crimea. The nom-de-guerre Trifon also appears on documents of "military tribunals" which handed down death sentences during the occupation of Sloviansk. Journalists from Radio Free

---

20 As mentioned in chapter four, Bezler and Parkhmenko visited the temporarily occupied Donetsk SBU building during their reconnaissance mission in early April.

Europe/Radio Liberty analyzed the documents and tried to establish the identity of the people responsible (Miller, Dobrynin, and Krutov 2020). They identify Trifon as Serhii Trifonov but fail to specify how they came to this conclusion. However, regardless of whether Serhii Trifonov is his real name, Trifon's account of events is consistent with the story of other group members and identifies several of them.

- *Viacheslav Apraksimov* (nom-de-guerre: "Balu") is another member of the "military tribunals" investigated by Radio Free Europe/Radio Liberty (Miller, Dobrynin, and Krutov 2020). Further evidence linking name and nom-de-guerre is a YouTube video calling for donations for the separatist cause in the Donbas. The video was published in late 2014 by an account named Viacheslav Apraksimov and features the caption "Team 'Balu'" (Apraksimov 2014). Andrii Saveliev also mentions a man with the nom-de-guerre of Balu, who arrived in Crimea from Kharkiv in early April (Chalenko and Saveliev 2019). Moreover, a man called Viacheslav Apraksimov received the medal "For the Defense of the Crimean Republic" from the Crimean occupation authorities in October 2015 (Aksyonov 2015). However, Saveliev (2019a, 120) also writes that Balu travelled to Sloviansk from Crimea via mainland Ukraine and not via Russia like the rest of the group.
- *Edvard Piterskiy* is the pseudonym of another man who, according to a portrait published by a pro-separatist YouTube channel, travelled from Kharkiv to Crimea and joined Girkin's group there (YouTube 2014au). According to the video, Piterskiy was born in Vinnytsia and lived in both Ukraine and Russia before becoming a member of the separatist movement. Aleksandr Barkov (2018), who was a correspondent of the Russian extreme-right-wing newspaper *Zavtra* at the time, also remembers meeting Piterskiy in Sloviansk in May 2014. He writes that Piterskiy had joined Girkin in Crimea coming from Kharkiv together with Arsen Pavlov.

The accounts of Trifon, Saveliev, and Russian pro-separatist activist Aleksandr Zhuchkovskiy—who arrived in Sloviansk in May and subsequently wrote a book about the events—mention 15 other noms-de-guerre of purported members of the group that went with Girkin from Crimea to Sloviansk. These noms-de-guerre are "Bolik", "Gus", "Lyolik", "Ramses", "Vasilich", and "Veter" (Trifon and Bezsonov 2020c); "Argun", "Glas", "Nemoy", "Odessa", and "Ten" (Zhuchkovskiy 2018, 20–21); and "Boroda", "Moskal", and "Piter" (Saveliev 2019a, 146, 170). However, the respective authors give little or no information on these men's backgrounds or identities. Veter is purportedly from Crimea; Bolik, Lyolik, and Vasilich are said to be from Zhytomyr; and Odessa is supposedly from Odesa. Online searches for these noms-de-guerre did not yield any useful results, either.

Even though the background information on many group members remains patchy or non-existent, the described digital open source evidence on 27 of them offers considerable insights into the group's composition. It suggests that Girkin's men were recruited primarily from the paramilitary forces which supported the Russian annexation of Crimea. These forces included Russian military and intelligence veterans as well as residents of Crimea and some pro-Russian activists from Kyiv. However, as Crimean militia member Vadym Ilovchenko openly admitted, paramilitary groups in Crimea coordinated their actions with Russia's intelligence agencies from the very beginning of the Russian takeover (Saveliev 2019b at 33:15). There is no reason to doubt his words. In a March 2015 Russian TV documentary, Vladimir Putin himself admitted that the takeover of Crimea was planned in the Kremlin and that Russia's military and security apparatus was in charge of its implementation (Rossiya 24 2015, at 1:47 and from 1:06:44). This means that it is almost certain that any paramilitary group assisting the Russian annexation was under the close supervision of Russian state structures.

The testimonies of Girkin and other group members also indicate that Girkin and his men travelled to Sloviansk via Russia. According to Girkin, his group crossed the border on foot and was met by vehicles organized by Ukrainian separatists on Ukrainian territory (Girkin and Shargunov 2014). Girkin also stated that his group spent a day preparing and stocking up on equipment in Russia before crossing the border to Ukraine. On this day, his group "received the uniforms that we should have already received in Crimea" (Girkin and Urzhumov 2016). Girkin's account is consistent with the account of his subordinate Trifon, who wrote that the group left Crimea during the night of April 8–9 and spent a day in Rostov-on-Don. During the night of April 10–11, they left Rostov. They crossed the border on foot in a rural location,[21] were met by a car and a minibus on a road, and arrived in Sloviansk on the morning of April 12 (Trifon and Bezsonov 2020c). Group members Andrii Saveliev and Artem Razuvaiev also said that the group took the ferry from Crimea to Russia before moving on to the Donbas (Saveliev 2019c from 26:45). What is more, the group carried military-grade weaponry via Russia into Ukraine. In a 2017 debate with Russian opposition leader Aleksey Navalnyy, Girkin admitted that he had obtained weapons for the Sloviansk operation in Crimea (Girkin, Navalnyy, and Zygar 2017). Girkin´s associate and group member Tikhiy also confirmed that the group carried automatic rifles across the border (YouTube 2020a, at 5:30).

This evidence that the men who occupied Sloviansk and Kramatorsk were the same people who helped the Russian state annex Crimea, and that they took military-grade weaponry from Crimea via Russia to mainland Ukraine, shifts the burden of proof. H1 becomes the *likely* default explanation. The hypothesis that Girkin's group continued to act on behalf of the Russian state after Crimea is both simpler and less extraordinary than the hypothesis that they went rogue and acted on their own. In the absence of evidence to the contrary, it is unlikely that a paramilitary group that collaborated with Russia's security services was able to travel from Crimea to the Donbas without their knowledge and approval. This does not necessarily imply that Girkin and his group were following an explicit command when they moved to the Donbas. However, this is of secondary importance, as I will discuss further below.

---

21 None of the group members has disclosed the exact location. However, Girkin stated in his interview with Hordon that he initially thought about occupying Shakhtarsk or Snizhne, which are located east of Donetsk. He said he decided to go to Sloviansk only after entering Ukraine and talking to the local separatists who met his group (Girkin and Hordon 2020 from 1:00:45). This indicates that Girkin's group may have crossed the border near Vyselky or Marynivka, southeast of Donetsk because these sections of the border are located on the most direct route between Rostov-on-Don and Shakhtarsk or Snizhne.

5.2. Girkin's Links to the Kremlin: The Oligarch and the "Prime Minister"

The second stage of informal Bayesian updating draws on a series of recordings which the SBU published on April 14, 2014, two days after the armed group first appeared in Sloviansk (SBU 2014c). According to the SBU, the recordings are phone conversations of militiamen intercepted the previous day. In one of the recordings, a person addressed as "Strelok" is told that "Aleksandr from Russia" is calling. Strelok takes the call and reports to Aleksandr that his group "repelled the first attack." In a subsequent recording, Strelok reports to a person who he addresses as "Konstantin Valeriyevich" about the same attack. He says that his group fired at three cars with Ukrainian security operatives and "eliminated" the people inside. In response, Konstantin Valeriyevich asks if Strelok has "briefed Aksyonov." After Strelok says that he has not been able to get hold of Aksyonov, Konstantin Valeriyevich tells him to keep trying, but also mentions that Aksyonov "will land here tonight" and that he "will meet with him tomorrow."

The voices in the recording almost certainly belong to Igor Girkin (nom-de-guerre Strelok), Aleksandr Boroday, and Konstantin Valeriyevich Malofeyev. Boroday is a Russian political PR consultant, who would later become head of the self-proclaimed Donetsk People's Republic. Malofeyev is a Russian oligarch and a strong advocate of conservative Russian Orthodox values. Aksyonov is the surname of Crimea's "Prime Minister" Sergey Aksyonov[22] who was installed during the Russian takeover of the peninsula. The recording is almost certainly an authentic conversation between these three people for the following reasons:

- Although Boroday and Malofeyev denied collaborating with Girkin in connection with the occupation of Sloviansk and Kramatorsk, they admitted that they knew him well. Boroday said in an interview on Russian state TV that he was Girkin's friend and had known him since the 1990s. He

---

22   Aksyonov had been a Ukrainian citizen before the annexation of Crimea. With the annexation, however, he became a Russian state official according to Russian law, which is why I transliterate the Russian version of his name.

also confirmed that Girkin had spoken to him on the phone from Sloviansk but claimed that the SBU had manipulated the contents of the recording in some unspecified way (Boroday and Maksimovskaya 2014 from 4:41). In a Russian newspaper interview, Malofeyev admitted that Girkin had travelled with him to Kyiv as part of his security personnel as recently as January 2014 (Malofeyev, Sergina, and Kozlov 2014). Girkin confirmed this and even admitted that Malofeyev had financed him during the Crimean operation, and that he had bought the combat gear for the Sloviansk operation with Malofeyev's money (Girkin and Hordon 2020 from 28:15 and from 1:20:40).

- Russian journalist Oleg Kashin (2014a; 2014b; 2014c) wrote that he had met Girkin in Crimea in early March as a senior member of Crimean "Prime Minister" Sergey Aksyonov's staff. Girkin himself confirmed that he closely collaborated with Aksyonov in Crimea (Girkin and Hordon 2020, from 28:45) and even admitted that he went to Sloviansk "with Aksyonov's direct support" (Girkin and Hordon 2020, at 52:50). Moreover, Aleksandr Boroday said that he also worked as an "unofficial adviser" for Aksyonov (Boroday and Maksimovskaya 2014 at 3:37).
- Sergey Aksyonov was participating in an event in Crimea on the morning of April 13 (KrymInform 2014). On April 14, he met Vladimir Putin in Moscow (Putin and Aksyonov 2014). This is in line with Malofeyev's description of Aksyonov's travel plans, assuming that Malofeyev was in Moscow at the time of the conversation.
- Girkin's description of the armed clash near Sloviansk matches footage from the scene that was shown by Russian TV channel LifeNews and published on YouTube on April 13, which shows three damaged cars (LifeNews 2014b).
- The SBU published its recordings on April 14. Fabricating a recording with plausible voice imitations and the observed degree of detail within a day does not seem realistic, especially given that the SBU was facing a crisis situation at the time.

The fact that Girkin reported back to Malofeyev and Aksyonov after the occupation of Sloviansk further decreases the probability that Girkin's group stopped acting on behalf of the Russian state after moving from Crimea to the Donbas. The amicable, respectful tone of the conversation between Girkin and Malofeyev, combined with Girkin's claim that Aksyonov supported his actions (Girkin and Hordon 2020, at 52:50), makes it highly unlikely that Girkin was no longer acting on behalf of the two men.

In turn, there is only a remote chance that Malofeyev and Aksyonov could not count on the approval of at least some decisionmakers within the Kremlin. Malofeyev's links to the Kremlin are corroborated by a set of leaked emails published by Ukrainian activists and attributed to Kremlin officials. According to these emails, Malofeyev had met Kremlin advisers Sergey Glazyev and Vladislav Surkov in late 2013 to discuss ways to prevent Ukraine's integration with the West (Hosaka 2018, 361; 2019, 753–55). Hosaka (2018, 322–23) reports that he examined the context, content, and metadata of sample emails and is confident that the leak is authentic. Of course, there remains a chance that he is mistaken and the emails are fabrications, but this can be considered unlikely. Hence, combined with the general proximity between oligarchs and the state in modern Russia, the emails are evidence that Malofeyev acted at least with the tacit approval of parts of the Kremlin.

Crimean "Prime Minister" Sergey Aksyonov's links to the Kremlin are even clearer. According to Russian law, Aksyonov was heading a newly incorporated Russian Federation subject. This means that a newly appointed Russian state official was directly involved in the Sloviansk operation and met Vladimir Putin one day after the first armed clash. Considering Aksyonov's dependence on the Kremlin, it is hard to imagine that he risked acting without the knowledge or against the wishes of his new superiors. For these reasons, Girkin's continuing communication with Malofeyev and Aksyonov after the start of the Sloviansk operation increases the probability of H2 to *highly likely* and make it *highly unlikely* that H1 is correct.

5.3. Actions without Consequences: Girkin's Return to Russia

The third and final stage of informal Bayesian updating draws on the absence of any actions by the Russian authorities to restrict or sanction the activities of Girkin, Boroday, Malofeyev, or Aksyonov. If Girkin's armed group and its backers acted without the knowledge and approval of the Russian authorities, it could be expected that the Russian state took actions to either stop their activities or punish them. Neither was the case. Girkin returned to Russia in August 2014 and many of his group members followed his example. In his interview with Hordon, Girkin admitted that he left the Donbas as the result of pressure from Moscow. He said he was told that the separatists would not receive the support they needed if he did not leave (Girkin and Hordon 2020 from 1:52:15). However, even though the Russian leadership decided to remove Girkin from the conflict zone, they did not take further actions against Girkin or other key actors associated with his group. In the years that followed, Girkin and Malofeyev lived in Moscow without ever facing an investigation. On the contrary, Girkin was able to create his Novorossiya Movement within Russia's strictly regulated NGO environment. Andrii Saveliev was able to publish a book on how he fought for Girkin's group at the age of 16, and to promote it in Russia and Crimea together with his former comrades-in-arms. Sergey Aksyonov remained head of Crimea. And Aleksandr Boroday became a member of parliament for the ruling United Russia party in the September 2021 State Duma elections (State Duma n.d.).

Moreover, a recent investigation by the Bellingcat research collective suggests that Girkin used the fake identity of Sergey Runov to travel around Russia after his return and was in possession of a Russian passport under this name (Bellingcat 2022). According to Bellingcat, the serial number of this passport was in close proximity to the serial numbers of at least two other cover identity passports that were used by FSB operatives identified in other investigations. The evidence presented by Bellingcat is convincing and the investigation uses the same methodology that has successfully identified several other cover identities provided by Russian intelligence services.²³ It is therefore possible to conclude that Girkin received or retained a cover identity issued by the Russian state after his return from the Donbas.

Added to the previous two stages of updating, the Russian authorities' failure to take any action against Girkin or his associates combined with their willingness to provide Girkin with a second identity further increases the probability of H2. It becomes *almost certain* that Girkin and his group acted as informal organs of the Russian state. In turn, there remains only a remote chance that they participated in the conflict as non-state actors who were part of a domestic separatist movement.

5.4. Order or Tacit Approval? On Putin's Role

Although the available digital open source evidence strongly supports H2, the explanatory power of the causal mechanism associated with this hypothesis comes with an important caveat. The causal mechanism does not specify whether the Kremlin ordered or merely approved Girkin's Donbas operation. What is more, it even leaves the possibility open that the operation was Girkin's personal initiative and that the Russian state's approval was tacit and implicit. This question is left open deliberately because conclusive evidence in relation to it is virtually impossible to find. Any official order to intervene in the Donbas would be a top-secret matter that none of those involved would consider disclosing. If any written documentation of such an order exists, it is stored in Russian intelligence archives and remains inaccessible for the foreseeable future.

At the same time, several subject matter experts argue that the informal practices of Russia's security apparatus often avoid explicit orders and make it difficult to draw a dividing line between command and approval. According to Russian journalist Oleg Kashin, Vladimir Putin may have told Konstantin Malofeyev to "do whatever" rather than giving precise instructions (Kashin, Merkulova, and Solomin 2014). This is in line with the assessment of former Kremlin consultant Gleb Pavlovsky (2016), who argues

---

23 See also the discussion of the cover identities of separatist commander Igor Bezler and GRU military intelligence officer Oleg Ivannikov in chapter seven of this book.

that the Putin regime's "governance style relies on indirection and interpretation rather than command and control." Pavlovsky highlights the importance of "*otmashka*, which can be translated as 'go-ahead,' implying not so much an order as a license to act in a desired direction." Christo Grozev (2020), lead Russia investigator of the Bellingcat investigation collective, makes a similar point, arguing that the Russian state outsources interference abroad to private actors, who offer "competing, but always deniable, solutions to the Kremlin, and enjoy significant freedom." Similarly, Galeotti (2020) calls Putin's Russia an "adhocracy" — a "de-institutionalized" system "in which the president's favor is the main asset everyone wants to earn, and formal roles and responsibilities matter less than how one can be of use today."

These interpretations appear just as plausible — if not more plausible — than the existence of an explicit order. Moreover, they allow for the possibility that Girkin's Sloviansk operation was subject to disagreements and changes of mind within the Russian elite. They are even compatible with Aleksandr Boroday's claim that, after meeting Girkin in Rostov-on-Don and providing him with the latest tranche of money from Malofeyev, he discussed the operation with five unnamed people in Moscow. According to Boroday, he advised caution and the group agreed to pause the operation and summon Girkin to Moscow. Girkin however, had anticipated this development, switched off his phone, and carried on with his plan (Zhuchkovskiy 2018, 44–45). However, even if this account is true, Boroday, Aksyonov, Malofeyev, and their contacts within the Russian leadership accepted the fact that Girkin went ahead. Girkin remained in contact, was not called back to Russia until August, and did not face punishment for his actions.

H2 allows for a spectrum of Kremlin involvement. At one end of this spectrum, someone in a position of power in Moscow gave an explicit order to prepare a covert operation in the Donbas. At the other end, the Kremlin merely provided Girkin and his associates with the autonomy to make their own plans and tacitly approved the operation by acquiescence. However, the exact location of the decision-making process on this spectrum is of secondary importance. Following the historical explanation paradigm of *abnormalism* (see section 3.4.2.), Kremlin knowledge and tacit approval of the operation is sufficient to establish Russian state responsibility as its primary cause. It is not surprising that there were some actors in Russia who were willing to intervene in Ukraine for ideological reasons. Far more abnormal, and hence more important as a cause, are the close contacts between these actors and the Russian state combined with the fact that the Kremlin was prepared to let them go ahead with their actions.

Regardless of the existence of an explicit order, the Kremlin was more than a passive bystander who failed to intervene. The three stages of informal Bayesian updating carried out above show that the role of the Russian state in Sloviansk and Kramatorsk was different from the role of the Ukrainian state and local elites in the previous critical juncture. In Donetsk and Luhansk, the Ukrainian state was too weak to prevent the building seizures through its law enforcement organs. Local elites had a conflicted relationship with the state and, according to the available evidence, remained largely passive and adopted a wait-and-see approach. There was no strong evidence of systematic and active collaboration between state organs or local elites on the one hand and the separatist actors on the other. This is entirely different in the context of the present critical juncture. Girkin's group had collaborated with the Russian state in Crimea immediately before moving to Sloviansk. They reported back to a Russian state official and a Russian oligarch after their arrival, and they returned to Russia after the end of their operation. At the same time, the Russian state had not been weakened in a way that suggested it was incapable of controlling the activity of paramilitary groups on its territory or reign in oligarchs supervising such groups.

The coordination between the Russian state and Girkin's group, along with the Kremlin's obvious power to stop them, means that the Russian state's actions were more *disruptive* to the normal course of events than the personal motives of the group members. This line of reasoning can be illustrated with the allegory of a robbery. If a person is robbed at gunpoint and a bystander fails to intervene—either because the bystander is physically incapable or cannot be bothered—the actions of the robber should be considered the primary cause of the robbery. They are more disruptive to the normal course of events than the passivity of the bystander.

However, this assessment changes if the bystander and the robber had broken into a house together the day before, after which the bystander had given the robber a gun while talking about a personal grudge against the prospective robbery victim. The assessment changes even further if the robber calls the bystander to report on the progress of the robbery and returns to the bystander's house after the bystander pressures him to leave the crime scene. In such a scenario, there can be no doubt that the bystander's actions supersede the robber's actions as the primary cause that is most disruptive to the normal course of events.

As chapter four has shown, Russian imperialist organizations also played a role in the building occupations in Donetsk and Luhansk, and it is reasonable to assume that these organizations also acted with the knowledge and approval of the Kremlin. However, the role of these organizations in the previous critical juncture was less prominent and their actions were less violent than the actions of Girkin's group in Sloviansk and Kramatorsk. As I argued in chapter four, the available evidence indicates that the activities of Russian actors were less disruptive to the normal course of events than the actions of local separatists. What local actors did was more abnormal than the fact that the Kremlin allowed Russian imperialist organizations to fan the flames of separatism and provide a certain degree of support for local pro-Russian activities. This is no longer the case in the context of the present critical juncture because Russian actors took the lead.

5.5. A Separatist Bandwagon: The Role of Locals

These considerations lead to another important caveat that has to be addressed, namely the role of local residents supporting Girkin's occupation. Girkin claims that "about 300 activists were ready and waiting when we arrived" (Girkin and Shargunov 2014). This number may be exaggerated, but the claim that a group of local separatists was ready to actively support Girkin is in line with the available evidence. Protests against the new Kyiv authorities had taken place in Sloviansk as early as February 23 (YouTube 2014a). Viacheslav Ponomarov, who became Sloviansk "People's Mayor" during Girkin's occupation, was a local resident, who, on March 30, gave an interview as the leader of a local "self-defense group," which, according to him, was helping the police to protect the town from Maidan activists (YouTube 2014ba). Video footage from April 12 does not only show cheering local bystanders but also a group of people in civilian clothing, who help Girkin's armed men guard the occupied police station (YouTube 2014ag). Moreover, Girkin stated that he had met with Ukrainian separatist activists in Russia to prepare the operation and that these people organized local support and transport from the border prior to his group's arrival (Girkin and Hordon 2020 from 59:49). In particular, he said that he had been in contact with Kateryna Hubarieva, the wife of Donetsk Oblast "People's Governor" Pavlo Hubariev who was imprisoned in Kyiv at the time (Girkin and Hordon 2020 at 1:08:08; see also Hubariev 2016, 158).[24]

However, it is undisputed that Girkin's men not only initiated the Sloviansk operation but also remained in charge of the separatist forces in the area until their forced withdrawal in early July. Local activists were the subordinates of Girkin and his men. The seizure of the Kramatorsk police station, where Girkin's men pushed aside local activists while shooting in the air, clearly illustrates this (YouTube 2014ai). The recordings intercepted by the Ukrainian Security Service also indicate that Girkin was in charge of the operation and local activists were under the command of members of his group (SBU 2014c). Moreover, after an initial period of cooperation, local "People's Mayor" Viacheslav Ponomarov was arrested on June 10 on Girkin's orders (TASS 2014c). Finally, there is no evidence that local separatist activists in Sloviansk would have been able and willing to organize an armed occupation on their own if Girkin's group had not come. At the same time, it is doubtful that the Ukrainian authorities would have responded to an occupation by locals in the same way they responded to Girkin's group.

Even though Girkin's group depended on local support, the *abnormalism* paradigm points to Girkin's actions as the primary condition for the occupation and the subsequent escalation of the

---

24 As discussed in chapter four, Hubarieva was appointed as chairwoman of the Donetsk People's Republic's "Committee on Foreign Political Relations" on April 10. She was staying in Russia at the time and was in contact with Aleksandr Dugin's Eurasian Movement.

conflict. In the context of the political situation in eastern Ukraine in April 2014, it is not surprising that there were some activists in Sloviansk and Kramatorsk who were willing to support a Russian invasion. The arrival of heavily armed men from Russia with the determination and ability to lead an insurrection is far more disruptive to the normal course of events than the fact that some locals were willing to jump on these men's bandwagon.

5.6. Chapter Conclusion

This chapter has argued that the second critical juncture in the escalation of the Donbas conflict was initiated and led by an armed group that had previously participated in Russia's takeover of Crimea. The leader of this group had close and well-documented ties to the Kremlin-appointed "prime minister" of Crimea and to a Russian oligarch with close links to the Kremlin. Neither the group's leader, nor his Russian supervisors, nor any members of his group have been sanctioned by the Russian state because of their actions in the Donbas. On this basis, I have argued that the occupation of Sloviansk and Kramatorsk was primarily the result of the actions of the Russian state. A more detailed account of the causal dynamics at play within this critical juncture should mention the difficulty of tracing decision-making processes within the Russian elite and of distinguishing between instruction and tacit approval. It should also mention the fact that Girkin and his group received local support, while stressing the secondary nature of both of these factors. A reductionist account aiming to single out the most significant factor, however, should focus on H2. The adapted causal mechanism is shown in Figure 8.

Figure 8: Sloviansk-Kramatorsk Consolidated Causal Mechanism

Source: the author

6. Mariupol
Where Separatism Failed

This chapter will investigate the third critical juncture of the Donbas War's escalation sequence, which consists of armed clashes in the port city of Mariupol in the south of Donetsk Oblast. Mariupol receives comparatively little attention in the context of the 2014 events. This is not surprising considering that violence in Mariupol at the time was less intense and more short-lived than in other parts of the region. As a result, there is a risk of overlooking the fact that the city was the second place in the Donbas that witnessed armed clashes between separatists and the Ukrainian security forces. These clashes left a legacy of violence in the city that was only superseded by the Russian offensive of 2022, which left most of Mariupol in ruins.

What is more, the fact that violence in Mariupol in 2014 was relatively short-lived while it escalated further in other places provides additional insights into the relative importance of different causal factors from a comparative perspective. For these reasons, the causal mechanism behind the brief outbreak of violence in Mariupol is worth investigating even though separatism failed in the city in 2014. As in chapter four, I investigate three hypotheses which highlight the role of grassroots activists, local elites, and Russia respectively. As in the case of Donetsk and Luhansk, I conclude that there is insufficient evidence of a leading role of either local elites or Russia. This means that the events in Mariupol in 2014 should be seen primarily as a case of grassroots separatism. However, I also conclude that the contrast between the failure of separatism in Mariupol and the further escalation in other parts of the Donbas indicates that the domestic conflict potential in the Donbas was limited.

Until mid-April, the trajectory of conflict escalation in Mariupol resembled the sequence of events in Donetsk and Luhansk with a time lag. Throughout March, Mariupol witnessed both separatist and pro-unity demonstrations which largely remained peaceful (Pratskova 2014a; Sokolova 2014a; Pratskova 2014b). Attempts to storm administrative buildings in mid-March and early April remained short-lived and inconsequential (Novosti Donbassa 2014b; Pratskova 2014c; Sokolova 2014b). In late March, separatist leader Dmytro Kuzmenko proclaimed himself "people's mayor" and was arrested by the Kyiv authorities in early April (TSN 2014a; Sokolova 2014b).[25] On April 13 — a week after the armed building occupations in Donetsk and Luhansk and one day after the appearance of Igor Girkin's armed group in Sloviansk and Kramatorsk — separatist activists successfully occupied the Mariupol City Council building and erected barricades around it (Pratskova 2014d). This day, as well as a smaller protest on April 11, also featured some violence among protesters but to a lesser extent than clashes in Donetsk a month earlier (Pratskova 2014e; Sviashchenko 2014a).

On the night of April 16–17, however, conflict escalation in Mariupol overtook events in Donetsk and Luhansk. At this time, Mariupol witnessed its first armed clashes between separatist fighters and the Ukrainian security forces. As a result, it became the second theater of armed conflict in the Donbas – shortly after the first armed clash near Sloviansk and long before fighting reached the two regional centers.

On the evening of April 16, a group of people gathered at the entrance of Military Base No. 3057 which is located not far from the city center and was home to a Ukrainian National Guard unit at the time. A video filmed at the gates shows masked men who urge the soldiers through a megaphone to rebel against their leadership and come out and join the protesters (Hromadske TV 2014c). A picture from the same location published by the Ukrainian news website *Fakty* shows that some of the men were armed with clubs (Zhychko

---

25 This chapter draws heavily on the reporting of the local news website *0629.com.ua*, a franchise of the popular City Sites network with a specific focus on developments in Mariupol. The website's correspondents provided the most comprehensive first-hand, real-time coverage of many key events that took place in Mariupol during the time period in question. They frequently illustrated their reports with photos from the respective scenes and were widely cited in other Ukrainian media. In most cases, the website's reporting did not engage in analysis or commentary, but recounted observed events that were not disputed by other sources and did not contradict the narrative of either conflict party. In line with this book's general treatment of news sources, this chapter describes such events as facts. Information that may be disputed and should not be considered a fact but rather a claim made by the website is highlighted as such.

2014). Moreover, a local TV report that aired the following day shows masked men at the same location throwing Molotov cocktails toward the base, after which gunshots can be heard (Telekanal Donbass 2014). The correspondent of another local news website who was at the scene also reported extended periods of gunfire (mnews 2014a). Another local TV news report by a different channel that was filmed on the following day shows burn marks and bullet shells around the entrance of the base (TRK Sigma 2014).

Ukrainian Interior Minister Arsen Avakov reported on the morning of April 17 that three people who attacked the base had been killed and 13 had been injured (Ostrov 2014j). A pro-separatist social media group claimed that as many as 19 people had died (Pratskova 2014g). However, over the following week, only two victims, Oleksandr Averbakh and Andrii Guzhva, were named (mnews 2014b).

Attributions of blame for the fatal shots are also contradictory. According to the *mnews* correspondent at the scene, the situation escalated when the protesters started to throw Molotov cocktails at the base, after which the soldiers opened fire on them (mnews 2014a). However, the base's deputy commander told local TV that some of the protesters had been armed and opened fire themselves, after which his soldiers only fired warning shots in the air. He claimed that any casualties among the protesters were due to friendly fire (TRK Sigma 2014). The *Fakty* report cites unnamed eyewitnesses who confirm that some of the attackers were armed. It also quotes a local resident who claims that a relative stationed at the base told her on the phone that his unit would "fight back to the last bullet" (Zhychko 2014).

It is not possible to establish from this contradictory evidence with a high degree of confidence which side opened fire and who was responsible for the fatal shots. However, given that the only confirmed deaths were on the side of the protesters, the explanation that they were killed by soldiers trying to fight back attackers appears somewhat more plausible than the friendly fire hypothesis. Regarding the number of casualties, it is unlikely that the death toll was much higher than the two confirmed cases. In light of the close media scrutiny that the events' aftermath received from all sides, it would have been difficult to conceal a large number of additional deaths.

After over two weeks of relative calm, new clashes between separatists and the Ukrainian security forces took place in early May (Pratskova 2014h; Vesti 2014d; Sviashchenko 2014b; Pratskova 2014i). Initially, violence remained below the scale of the April 16-17 events. On May 9, however, fighting suddenly intensified and reached the highest level observed in Mariupol throughout the Donbas conflict's formative phase. On this day, armed separatist activists tried to seize the city's police headquarters. Soldiers of Ukraine's National Guard, the Ukrainian Armed Forces, as well as volunteer battalion fighters came to the aid of the police. The result was intense fighting in the city center.

Interior Minister Avakov claimed on the day that about 20 "terrorists" and one member of the security forces had been killed as a result of the fighting (Vesti 2014e). The following evening, the local health service reported that a total of nine people had been killed and 42 wounded on May 9 (Ostrov 2014k). By May 15, the local news website *0629.com.ua* had gathered from official sources as well as social media the names of 13 men who had died. Six of them were members of the security forces (Sviashchenko 2014c). This is the most comprehensive and detailed list of casualties that is available.

It is not disputed by either conflict party that fighting broke out around the police headquarters, after which the military intervened and people died on both sides. According to the Ukrainian security forces, a group of separatists attacked the police headquarters with the aim of seizing weapons stored in the building, after which the local police commander called for reinforcements (Romanenko and Abroskin 2016; Zhyrokhov 2020). According to the separatist narrative, local police officers rebelled against their commander who had given them the order to dissolve pro-Russian protests in the city by force, after which the besieged commander called the military for help (Novorossia.su 2014; Sibirtsev 2014).

As in the case of the April 16–17 events, it is not possible to confirm either version with a high degree of certainty. Moreover, it is also possible that the local police commander was facing both a separatist attack and a rebellion by some officers at the same time.

However, considering the high level of restraint shown by the law enforcement authorities toward pro-Russian protesters both before and after May 9, it appears unlikely that the local police commander had given an order to dissolve protests by force.

The question which side fired the first shots and who exactly was responsible for the casualties is important and should be subject to further investigation. However, in order to assess the events in Mariupol in relation to the causes of the Donbas conflict as a whole, it is of secondary importance. The primary puzzle that needs resolving is the question who the two conflict parties were. In relation to this question, the possible hypotheses that could explain events in Mariupol are analogous to the three hypotheses examined in chapter four in the context of the building seizures in Donetsk and Luhansk.

H1: Fighting in Mariupol took place between the Ukrainian security forces and pro-Russian grassroots activists.

Figure 9: Internal Grassroots-Driven Causal Sequence

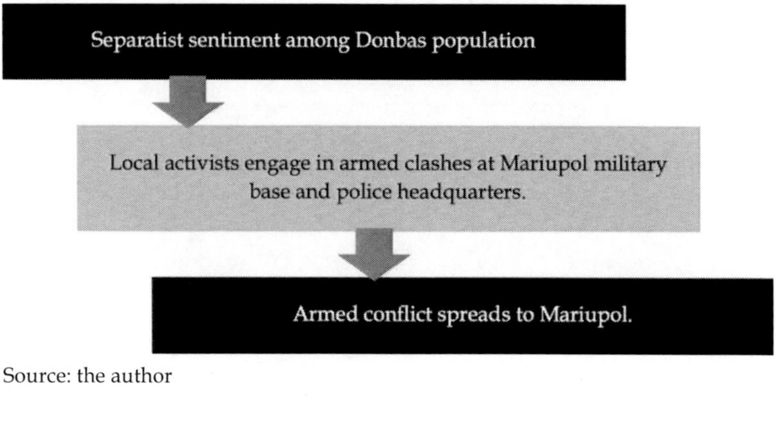

Separatist sentiment among Donbas population

↓

Local activists engage in armed clashes at Mariupol military base and police headquarters.

↓

Armed conflict spreads to Mariupol.

Source: the author

H2: Fighting in Mariupol took place between the Ukrainian security forces and agents of local elites.

Figure 10: Internal Elite-Driven Causal Sequence

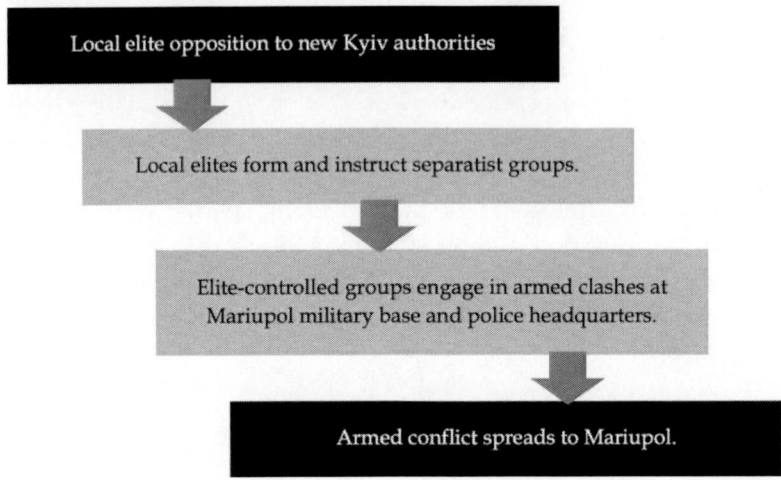

Source: the author

H3: Fighting in Mariupol took place between the Ukrainian security forces and organs of the Russian state.

Figure 11: External Causal Sequence

Source: the author

As in the case of Donetsk and Luhansk, Occam's razor and the Sagan standard suggest a probabilistic head start of H1 in relation to the other two hypotheses. Although the precedent of Igor Girkin's arrival in Sloviansk and Kramatorsk somewhat reduces this head start in relation to H3, grassroots protests remain a more parsimonious and less extraordinary explanation of events than a plot by Russia or local elites. This means that H1 should be considered a *realistic possibility,* H2 *highly unlikely,* and H3 *unlikely* to start with. The burden of proof remains with proponents of H2 or H3.

6.1. Mariupol's Separatist Movement

Similar to the case of Donetsk in chapter four, this burden of proof increases somewhat after a first round of informal Bayesian updating (see sections 3.1.4. and 3.4.3.2.) that considers evidence in favor of H1. The most important evidence in this regard comes from the Ukrainian law enforcement agencies which have not identified a single Russian citizen among those arrested or put on wanted lists after the escalation of violence in the city. Neither have they provided any evidence of ties between detained or wanted separatist activist in Mariupol and local oligarchs or the Russian state. Shortly after the April 16–17 incident, Ukraine's Deputy Interior Minister Serhii Yarovyi claimed that the group who attacked the military base mainly consisted of local minor criminals. He claimed that the security forces had arrested 77 people, 90 percent of whom were known to the law enforcement agencies because of previous criminal or administrative offenses (Espreso TV 2014). On the first anniversary of the May 9 clashes, Donetsk Oblast police chief Viacheslav Abroskin (2015a) published a statement saying that the core group of separatist activists in Mariupol in May 2014 comprised 80 people. He claimed that the law enforcement agencies had established the identity of most of them and arrested some. In the same post, Abroskin published the names and pictures of ten men who were allegedly directly involved in the violence. All the men were captioned as residents of Mariupol. Two weeks later, Abroskin (2015b) published names and photos of another 15 separatist activists who had been detained or were wanted in relation to the events in Mariupol. According to Abroskin, 11 of them were residents of Mariupol and surrounding areas, three lived in Donetsk, and one in Makiivka. In the same post, Abroskin wrote about Andrii Borysov (nom-de-guerre Chechen), the "commander of the security forces" of the Donetsk People's Republic (DNR) in Mariupol between mid-May and mid-June (YouTube 2014ap). Abroskin (2015b) described Borysov as a "typical social parasite." He claimed that Borysov had lived near Mariupol with the financial support of his parents before he started attending pro-Russian rallies in Donetsk and made up a story about having fought in Chechnya. Abroskin did not mention any connections to Russia or local oligarchs in his description of Borysov or any of the other suspects. The absence of claims or evidence in this regard from the statements of Abroskin or other law enforcement officials increases the probability of H1. At the same time, it decreases the probability of H3 in particular, because Ukraine's law enforcement agencies have absolutely no incentive to hide evidence of Russian involvement in the Mariupol events. On the contrary, fighting off a covert invasion would be more prestigious for them than struggling with a random group of locals.

Moreover, like in the case of Donetsk, the background of the different separatist leadership figures in Mariupol is consistent with what would be expected from a heterogenous grassroots movement consisting of local pro-Russian fringe activists.

- According to *0629.com.ua*, Mariupol's first "People's Mayor" *Dmytro Kuzmenko* and his brother and successor *Denys Kuzmenko* had been running a local boxing club in Mariupol (Hudilin 2020). The website published pictures of the Kuzmenko brothers at the club's opening in 2013. It also alleged that they were involved in organized crime but did not provide any evidence for this allegation.
- *Viacheslav Kuklin*, who was elected interim "people's mayor" by a group of protesters on April 14 (Pratskova 2014f) but immediately disappeared again from the limelight, was an elderly activist in a local residents association. His previous online footprint includes a speech at a March 18 Mariupol City Council hearing (YouTube 2014m) and a speech at a 2012 Victory Day celebration (GO Sovest 2012).

- *Ihor Khakimzianov*, the "first DNR defense minister," who was arrested by the Ukrainian security forces in Mariupol on May 6 and publicly interrogated by controversial Ukrainian populist politician Oleh Liashko (TSN 2014b), was a separatist activist from Donetsk. Khakimzianov made his first public appearance on April 10, when he was appointed as "commander of the People's Army" at a session of the first DNR "government" (YouTube 2014af). In a 2018 interview, Khakimzianov said that he came to Mariupol on April 16, 2014 with a group of "40-50 men to help with the seizure and disarmament of the military base" (YouTube 2017a).
- *Oleksandr Fomenko*, who announced on June 1 that he had been chosen to replace the arrested Denys Kuzmenko (Fomenko 2014), was a local entrepreneur and Communist Party of Ukraine activist. Ukrainian journalist Yuliia Dydenko interviewed the imprisoned Fomenko about his background and his version of the events in 2018 (Fomenko and Dydenko 2018).

Naturally, the openly available information on these men and their affiliations remains patchy. In the absence of additional evidence to the contrary, however, the seemingly random array of people that appeared to lead Mariupol's separatist movement at different points in time is more consistent with H1 than with the other two hypotheses. In combination with the statements of Ukraine's law enforcement authorities, it suggests that H1 becomes *likely* while both H2 and H3 lose probability and would require additional evidence to tip the balance. Such evidence would have to outweigh both H1's probabilistic head start and the additional evidence in its favor.

6.2. Oligarchic Resistance?
The Role of Rinat Akhmetov

The only plausible candidate for an elite-controlled insurrection in Mariupol would be oligarch Rinat Akhmetov, whose Metinvest group was a major local employer and driver of the local economy. However, the available open source evidence reduces rather than increases the probability that Akhmetov controlled Mariupol's separatist activists. The behavior of Metinvest after the May 9 clashes is a failed *hoop test* (see section 3.1.2.) for the hypothesis that supporters of the DNR in Mariupol acted on Akhmetov's behalf. When the Ukrainian military withdrew from the city after the May 9 violence, Metinvest issued a statement urging the authorities to refrain from any further attempts to use force in urban areas. To maintain peace and public order in Mariupol, the company promised to set up volunteer squads (*narodnyye druzhyny*) of steelworkers who would patrol the city in support of the local police (Metinvest 2014). According to a local correspondent for Ukraine's *Hromadske Radio*, these volunteer squads began their patrols over the following days (Burlakov 2014). The patrols did not enter into direct confrontation with separatist activists. DNR supporters were able to cast their votes in the May 11 "referendum on self-governance" undisturbed. However, volunteer squads and local police were not absorbed by the separatist movement, either. Neither Metinvest nor the local police subordinated themselves to the DNR. On the contrary, Rinat Akhmetov (2014) published a strongly worded video statement on May 19, in which he condemned the DNR. He said the DNR's activities were a "struggle against the people of our region" and a "genocide of the Donbas." He called for a "Donbas without weapons" and for daily lunchtime warning strikes across all enterprises in the Donbas to protest for peace. In Mariupol, the local steelworks observed this call at least for the following two days. In response, a small group of DNR supporters organized a protest calling for the "nationalization" of Akhmetov's enterprises, but there were no attempts to take any actions along these lines (Ostrov 2014m). Instead, the May 25 Ukrainian presidential election, which the DNR considered illegitimate, was able to go ahead in Mariupol, with local police and Metinvest volunteers guarding polling stations (Sokolova 2014d; Pratskova 2014j). On the day of the election, local DNR figurehead Denys Kuzmenko was arrested by a special police unit (LB.ua 2014a; Novosti Donbassa 2014g). On May 28, DNR commander Andrii Borysov published an appeal to Mariupol's mayor, the city's residents, and Rinat Akhmetov. Borysov urged them to cooperate with the DNR, complained about a lack of support, and warned of a looming Ukrainian counteroffensive (YouTube

2014as). These events clearly show that the DNR failed to establish a monopoly of violence in Mariupol despite the withdrawal of the Ukrainian military from the city. DNR activists had to share de facto control with the local authorities and Metinvest. This tense but largely peaceful coexistence continued until June 13, when the Ukrainian military returned and forced the DNR out of Mariupol (Novorosinform.org 2014a; Novosti Donbassa 2014i).

This evidence does not necessarily suggest that the actions of Metinvest were the only factor that prevented the DNR from establishing a monopoly of violence. However, it suggests that they at least contributed. After the May 9 clashes, Rinat Akhmetov and the DNR coexisted but worked against each other. If the DNR activists had been Akhmetov's agents, the expected observation would be the opposite, namely cooperation or replacement. This failed *hoop test* reduces the probability of H2 and leaves only a *remote chance* that separatist activists in Mariupol were agents of local elites.

Like in the case of Donetsk, this conclusion does not imply that Rinat Akhmetov is completely innocent. On the contrary, the timing of Metinvest's actions and Akhmetov's anti-DNR statement suggests that Akhmetov did nothing to prevent initial manifestations of separatism although he may have been able to do so. Before May 10, there is no evidence that Akhmetov was trying to rein in separatist activism in Mariupol in any way. This observation reinforces the conclusion of chapter four regarding Akhmetov's behavior in Donetsk. He did not do all he could to prevent separatist violence from happening in the first place. Instead, Akhmetov overestimated his own control over the situation and was permissive, if not supportive, toward initial manifestations of separatism, maybe because he hoped it would strengthen his position in relation to the new Kyiv authorities. At the same time, however, Akhmetov's reaction to the May 9 events in Mariupol also reinforces another conclusion of chapter four, namely that a war in the Donbas or the region's secession from Ukraine were not in Akhmetov's interest. It is almost certain that, by mid-May, Akhmetov was trying to prevent a further escalation of violence. In Mariupol, this attempt was successful, even though it took another operation by the Ukrainian military on June 13 to bring separatist activities to an end and prevent a Russian occupation of Mariupol for another eight years.

6.3. A Handshake and Some Weapons: The Role of Russia

Evidence that separatist activities in Mariupol were led by agents of the Russian state is relatively sparse and weak. The strongest evidence of Russian influence is a visit by future "People's Mayor" Dmytro Kuzmenko to Crimea in early March. On March 4, the local news website *0629.com.ua* published a scan of a letter signed by Crimea's new "Prime Minister" Sergey Aksyonov. In this letter, Aksyonov expressed his support for anti-Kyiv activism in Mariupol and promised "maximal efforts" to coordinate the actions of his forces in Crimea with the actions of Kuzmenko's forces in Mariupol. Together with the letter, the website also published a picture of Aksyonov and Kuzmenko shaking hands (Zhezhera 2014). On March 8, Kuzmenko spoke at a separatist rally in Mariupol. He was introduced as "a man who has come from Crimea" and read out the first part of Aksyonov's letter (YouTube 2014k, from 21:00). Since chapter five has demonstrated that Aksyonov was generally willing to support separatism in the Donbas, it appears plausible that he was happy to meet Kuzmenko and unlikely that Kuzmenko fabricated the letter and the photo from Crimea. However, Kuzmenko had returned to Mariupol by March 8. There is no evidence that he had been more than a brief visitor to Crimea or that he received any material assistance. Neither is there any direct evidence to suggest that the promised coordination between Mariupol's separatists and forces involved in the Crimean takeover actually took place. On the other hand, if Kuzmenko's early-March trip to Crimea is seen in conjunction with the findings of chapter five, a certain degree of Russian state support for Mariupol's separatists cannot be ruled out. Chapter five showed, that Aksyonov co-organized Igor Girkin's occupation of Sloviansk and Kramatorsk on April 12. In this context, Kuzmenko's Crimea trip suggests at least a realistic possibility that separatist activists in Mariupol also received some further advice and material support from Aksyonov.

Additional evidence of potential material support from Crimea for separatism in Mariupol comes from a Ukrainian court judgement discovered by Kudelia (2019, 291). In the judgement, a court in the town of Berdiansk, 70 kilometres southwest of

Mariupol in Ukraine's Zaporizhzhia Oblast, sentenced a resident of Mariupol to 13 years in prison for treason, creation of a terrorist group, and illegal handling of weapons (Berdiansk District Court 2015). According to the judgement, the defendant was a close associate of Denys Kuzmenko and travelled to Berdiansk on May 25, 2014 together with other local separatists to receive a shipment of weapons from Crimea. Both the weapons and the men were intercepted by Security Service of Ukraine (SBU) operatives. The defendant denied the charges but admitted that another separatist activist in Mariupol had told him in April that they were conducting negotiations about weapons deliveries from Russia. He also admitted that he joined Denys Kuzmenko on May 25 to receive the weapons and was arrested together with him. The judgement does not indicate whether any weapons deliveries from Russian-controlled territory to Mariupol took place before the failed attempt of May 25. Nevertheless, the judgement suggests that separatist forces in Mariupol continued to be in contact with the Russian state after Dmytro Kuzmenko's initial visit to Crimea. This raises the probability that separatist activists in Mariupol received at least some advice and material support from Russia to *likely*.

Other evidence of Russian involvement in the Mariupol events is weaker than Kuzmenko's Crimea trip and the court judgement. In his comments after the April 16–17 events, Deputy Interior Minister Yarovyi claimed that one of the killed attackers of the military base had served a prison sentence in Russia in the past (Espreso TV 2014). However, he did not go into further detail and did not allege any links between the Russian state and the separatists. Ukrainian populist politician Oleh Liashko claimed after his interrogation of DNR "Defense Minister" Ihor Khakimzianov that the latter had admitted to having received money from Russia's FSB intelligence agency and orders from Igor Girkin (TSN 2014b). However, Liashko is famous for controversial PR stunts and statements of dubious veracity. Moreover, given the circumstances of the interrogation, any confession by Khakimzianov would have been made under duress. Another potential link between Khakimzianov and the Russian state can be inferred from Khakimzianov's own account of his biography in a 2015 interview with a separatist YouTube channel. In the beginning of the interview,

Khakimzianov says that he was born in Makiivka but went to school in Russia's Krasnodar Krai and spent a few years at a military higher education facility there before returning to the Donbas in 2001 (YouTube 2015b, at 1:27). However, this link remains weak because of the considerable time that had passed since Khakimzianov's return to the Donbas. Another uncorroborated claim of Russian intelligence involvement was made by Ukrainian military historian Mykhailo Zhyrokhov (2020) in his analysis of the May 9, 2014 events, which draws on sources in Ukraine's law enforcement agencies. Zhyrokhov's article claims that the group that attacked the Mariupol police headquarters consisted of local separatists who had travelled to Donetsk before the attack, where they had received arms and orders form unnamed "Russian handlers" [*kuratory*]. However, Zhyrokhov does not provide further evidence regarding this purported trip to Donetsk or the identity of the alleged handlers. Similar claims of contacts between separatist activists in Mariupol and Russia's GRU military intelligence agency are made by a man with the pseudonym Ivan Bohdan in a book about the rise and fall of separatism in Mariupol (Bohdan 2016; Pyzhova 2016). In his book, Bohdan claims that he was in Mariupol at the time of events and that he has SBU insider knowledge. However, he does not provide references and does not sufficiently explain how he or his contacts know about the alleged collaboration between separatists in Mariupol and the GRU, and why they are confident that this information is correct. Finally, a more direct piece of evidence of Russian presence in Mariupol consists of pictures of an "exhibition" about Ukrainian "fascism" in front of the occupied City Council building on April 26, 2014 (Sokolova 2014c). The pictures suggest that the exhibition was organized by supporters of Sut Vremeni — a Soviet restorationist movement headed by Russian theater producer Sergey Kurginyan. However, it remains unclear whether any supporters of the movement had travelled to Mariupol from Russia, and it is possible that the organizers were local followers of Kurginyan.

To sum up, there is some *straw-in-the-wind* (see section 3.1.2.) evidence of links between Mariupol's separatists and Russia but no *smoking gun* indicating that they received more than a letter of support and a handshake. The only documented weapons delivery from Russia took place as late as May 25 and was intercepted by the SBU. The evidence for H3 discussed in this section is insufficient to significantly change the balance of probability between the different hypotheses. To do so would require more substantive evidence, such as photos or videos of Russian actors in Mariupol, intercepted phone conversations, or detailed and credible eyewitness testimony from participants suggesting instruction and coordination from Russia. In the absence of such evidence, the balance of probability remains tilted against H3. While some degree of Russian support in the form of money, weapons, or advise is likely, it remains unlikely that this support reached an extent that justifies defining Mariupol's separatists as organs of the Russian state. H1 remains the most accurate explanation for events in Mariupol, with the caveats that some degree of Russian support is likely, and that separatist activity benefited from the initial inaction of Rinat Akhmetov.

6.4. Mariupol Elsewhere: A Counterfactual Thought Experiment

The case of Mariupol indicates that there was potential for violence between the Ukrainian security forces and pro-Russian grassroots activists in the Donbas in the spring of 2014. In Mariupol, this violence resulted in armed clashes and more than a dozen confirmed deaths. At the same time, however, the case of Mariupol also indicates that domestic escalation dynamics in the Donbas were not inevitably self-perpetuating. It suggests that it was possible for separatism to fizzle out even after the military had been deployed and engaged in armed combat. Violence in Mariupol in 2014 was relatively short-lived and the situation did not escalate further after the armed clashes of May 9. Despite the temporary withdrawal of the Ukrainian military, separatist activists were unable to establish a monopoly of violence in Mariupol and did not manage to turn the city into a militarized stronghold of the DNR. As a result, they were defeated by the returning Ukrainian forces a month later in an operation that involved less violence than the earlier clashes.

It is relatively simple to apply the Mariupol scenario to other locations in a counterfactual thought experiment: Attempts by separatist activists to occupy buildings and obtain arms lead to clashes with the military. The military withdraws. Local elites give up their tacit support for separatism and step up their engagement for public order. Separatist activity does not subside completely but stagnates. Local authorities and separatist institutions coexist until the security forces regroup and eventually remove the separatists. Playing out this scenario across the Donbas would involve a certain degree of militarized violence in various locations, which may well cross 25-casualty threshold which the Uppsala Conflict Data Program defines for armed conflict. However, it is almost certain that such a counterfactual scenario would involve only a tiny fraction of the violence and destruction that the Donbas witnessed over the summer of 2014 and the years that followed.

Even though the events of spring 2014 left a legacy of violence in Mariupol, this legacy was dwarfed by what other parts of the region had to endure at the time. It was only in 2022 that war reached Mariupol in full force and with devastating consequences. The observation that militarized violence in Mariupol remained at a comparatively low level in 2014 raises the question why the conflict's escalation sequence in other parts of the Donbas followed a different path. Particularly striking in this regard is the case of Sloviansk and Kramatorsk, where the first armed clashes occurred at about the same time as in Mariupol. Why were separatist forces able to achieve a monopoly of violence and further militarize Sloviansk and Kramatorsk after the first armed clashes but failed to do so in Mariupol? A comparison of the causal mechanism identified in chapter five and the causal mechanism identified in the present chapter provides a compelling explanation. While local separatists in Mariupol were largely left to their own devices, the separatist takeover of Sloviansk and Kramatorsk was led by Igor Girkin's group of Russian and Crimean fighters with their experience, determination, and equipment. Hence, a comparison of the two cases adds additional support to the findings of the previous chapter's analysis, which identified Russian interference as the primary cause of conflict escalation in Sloviansk-Kramatorsk. The following chapter will investigate whether Russian interference is also an adequate explanation for why Donetsk, Luhansk, and other locations across the Donbas witnessed a further escalation of violence in 2014, rather than a fizzling out of separatist activity like Mariupol.

7. The Fighting Spreads

This chapter will analyze the fourth critical juncture of the Donbas War's escalation sequence—the outbreak of armed combat in several new locations across the Donbas and the resulting emergence of territorial frontlines in late May to mid-June 2014. Until the second half of May 2014, armed clashes between separatist fighters and Ukrainian forces were largely confined to two hotspots—the Sloviansk-Kramatorsk area and the city of Mariupol. In other parts of the Donbas, separatist activities remained well below this level of escalation and did not involve armed combat, except for one isolated incident in Luhansk.[26] Between late May and mid-June, however, the theater of war expanded rapidly. Within this time period, armed clashes occurred halfway between Donetsk and Mariupol, in the immediate surroundings of Donetsk and Luhansk, near the Russian-Ukrainian border in the south of Donetsk and Luhansk Oblasts, and in an urban agglomeration northwest of Luhansk. These outbreaks of fighting in various locations within a relatively short period of time were another critical juncture in the escalation of the conflict. On the one hand, they left a lasting legacy of violence in some of the affected areas. On the other hand, they were a necessary condition for further conflict escalation because they increased the geographical limits of violence. Rather than a vertical upward movement on the conflict's escalation ladder, they represent a horizontal movement which spread the highest level of escalation that the conflict had reached so far across a larger area. As a result, the conflict changed shape. Both sides demarcated their control over territory. Larger frontlines replaced insular hotspots of violence. Without this development, the war could not have escalated further in the way it did over the following months.

    I will investigate each major outbreak of fighting in a new location separately. As a result, I will divide this chapter's critical juncture into four component parts. Firstly, I will look at an attack on Ukrainian forces near Volnovakha, which can be attributed to a

---

26 On May 3, the storming of a military enlistment office in Luhansk led to a shootout and one reported death on the side of the separatists (0642.ua 2014b).

group of separatist fighters based in Horlivka and led by Igor Bezler. Secondly, I will look at fighting around Donetsk city with a particular focus on a failed attempt to seize Donetsk Airport, which led to a large number of separatist casualties. Thirdly, I will look at the consolidation of separatist control over Luhansk city and its immediate surroundings. Fourthly, I will look at fighting in the west and south of Luhansk Oblast. The digital open source information available on each of these four episodes will be tested against two hypotheses, emphasizing domestic and external causes respectively. I will argue that, in the case of all four components, there is convincing evidence that the actions of the Russian state were the primary cause of the outbreak of fighting.

Neither the separatists nor the Ukrainian side dispute that any of the armed clashes in question took place. What is more, they do not even disagree on the basic sequence of events in each case. The key difference between their narratives does not concern the events as such but their normative justification. The Ukrainian side argues that it had the right to advance on separatist positions and defend its facilities from separatist attempts to seize them because the new Kyiv authorities had to maintain their monopoly of violence over Ukrainian territory. The separatists, on the other hand, argue that they had the right to attack advancing Ukrainian forces and seize Ukrainian military facilities because the new Kyiv authorities did not have any legitimate claim to the Donbas. While I would argue that the Ukrainian justification narrative is far more convincing than the separatist one, this normative dispute is not of central importance in the context of this book. I investigate whether the use of violence against representatives of the Kyiv authorities during the incidents in question should be attributed primarily to local or Russian actors. Whether or not these actors had the moral or legal right to use violence is an important question but has no impact on the causal sequence itself. Regarding the basic sequence of events, only two hypotheses have to be tested. Each of them can be visualized as a simple single-component causal mechanism.

H1: The units that engaged Ukrainian forces in combat in various parts of Donetsk and Luhansk Oblasts between late May and mid-June were primarily local actors.

Figure 12: Internal Conflict Mechanism

Source: the author

H2: *The units that engaged Ukrainian forces in combat in various parts of Donetsk and Luhansk Oblasts between late May and mid-June were organs of the Russian state.*

Figure 13: Russian Invasion Mechanism

Source: the author

The remainder of this chapter will now test these two hypotheses against the four conflict escalation clusters included in the critical juncture investigated in this chapter. Like in the previous chapters, an explanation focusing on local factors will be given a probabilistic head start in line with Occams razor and the Sagan standard. This means that, as a starting point for the evaluation of evidence, I will consider H1 *likely* and H2 a *realistic possibility*.

7.1. The Volnovakha Attack: A "Demon" from Russia

On the morning of May 22, 2014, a group of armed men attacked a Ukrainian Armed Forces checkpoint near the town of Volnovakha, about 45 km southwest of Donetsk. This attack was the deadliest armed clash of the conflict so far. Sixteen Ukrainian servicemen lost their lives and 32 were injured (Memorybook.org.ua n.d.b; Ostrov 2014n). Moreover, the attack took place in a region of the Donbas that had not witnessed armed separatist activity before. There is no footage of the actual attack available. However, a video reportedly taken on May 21 shows the checkpoint intact. It also shows men in civilian clothing telling the soldiers that they are "occupiers," who have been "zombified" by the Ukrainian authorities. The conversations in the video suggest that the soldiers are unable to advance because the road ahead has been blocked by local residents (YouTube 2019a).

Videos from May 22 show the destruction caused by the separatist ambush (YouTube 2019b; ICTV 2014). They also show what appears to be friendly fire by Ukrainian helicopters, which arrived after the original attackers had retreated (YouTube 2014aq). Russian state television used the footage of the helicopters to portray the entire event as a punitive operation by the Ukrainian authorities against their own unit – supposedly because this unit had refused to fire at civilians and asked to return to its base (Channel 1 2014; NTV 2014). This narrative contradicts the later eyewitness accounts of surviving Ukrainian servicemen collected by military historian Mykhaylo Zhyrokhov (2016b). According to these accounts, the initial attack was carried out by separatist fighters. The subsequent friendly fire, which only injured one soldier, occurred because the helicopter pilots mistook burning vehicles for separatist positions.

What is more, the Russian propaganda account also contradicts the narrative of the separatist group that carried out the attack. On May 23, the BBC's Russian Service published an interview with a masked man captioned as the "leader of the rebels in Horlivka," who claimed responsibility for the attack and showed his interviewers a large quantity of seized weapons (BBC News 2014b). The voice and eyes of this man match Horlivka separatist leader Igor Bezler (nom-de-guerre: "Bes" — which translates as "Demon"). This observation is consistent with a statement reaffirming his group's responsibility, which Bezler (2017) posted on his social media profile on the third anniversary of the attack. In light of this evidence, it can be considered a fact that a separatist unit from Horlivka under Igor Bezler's command was responsible for the May 22 ambush against the Ukrainian checkpoint near Volnovakha. In turn, Bezler's background and affiliation are key to answering the question whether the attack can be attributed primarily to local separatism or the Russian state.

Bezler first caught the attention of a wider media audience when he led the seizure of the Horlivka police headquarters on April 14. In a video published on this day, he addressed a group of local police officers and introduced himself as a "lieutenant colonel of the Russian Army" (YouTube 2014aj). Shortly afterward, the Security Service of Ukraine (SBU) claimed that Bezler was an agent of Russia's GRU military intelligence agency (Ukrainska Pravda 2014l). It published a scan of a Russian passport issued to Bezler in 2002 in the town of Mirnyy in Russia's Arkhangelsk Oblast which was, at the time, home to a base of Russia's Strategic Missile Forces (serg_slavorum 2015). The SBU claimed that Bezler finished his active military service in 2002 and "was sent to Ukraine," where the GRU "re-established contact" with him in February 2014 and instructed him to take part in the occupation of Crimea (Ukrainska Pravda 2014l). In an interview with Russian state news agency RIA Novosti, Bezler (2014) denied links to Russian intelligence agencies but confirmed the SBU's remaining claims. He said that he was a Russian citizen with a Ukrainian residence permit, that he had served in the Russian Armed Forces until the early 2000s, and that he had played an active role in Russia's takeover of Crimea. Hence, similar to the case of Igor Girkin, the key point of contention is not Bezler's identity or biography but the question whether or not he acted on behalf of the Russian state in spring 2014.

7.1.1. The Origins of Igor Bezler and His Group

Like in Igor Girkin's case (see chapter five), there is convincing evidence linking Igor Bezler to the Russian security apparatus. This evidence consists of three parts, each of which increases the probability of H2 in relation to Bezler's group. The first part relates to the fact that the core of Bezler's group consisted of men who had come to Ukraine from Crimea with Igor Girkin. The accounts of Bezler's comrades-in-arms indicate that he participated in the takeover of Crimea and prepared his activity in the Donbas as part of the same paramilitary group as Girkin. This has been confirmed by Girkin (2016a) and two other group members—Illia Khokhlov (2019a, at 0:21) and Viktor Anosov (2019, at 4:37). All three report that Bezler was sent from Crimea to the Donbas on a reconnaissance mission before the rest of them entered mainland Ukraine. Further confirmation of their accounts comes from Sloviansk "People's Mayor" Viacheslav Ponomarov (2014), who said that Bezler visited the temporarily occupied Donetsk SBU building on April 7.

After Girkin's arrival in Sloviansk, Bezler formed a separate base in Horlivka, where he was joined by some of Girkin's men. Girkin (2016a) and Khokhlov (2019b, from 1:43) report that Bezler re-joined their group after its arrival in Sloviansk on April 12, but that he almost immediately left again and went to Horlivka on his own. This is consistent with the account of another member of Girkin's group with the nom-de-guerre Trifon. According to him, Bezler came to Sloviansk on April 13 but got into an argument with Girkin and left the town (Trifon and Bezsonov 2020c). However, Bezler did not cut all ties with his counterparts in Sloviansk. On the contrary, Girkin (2016a) says that he sent "a detachment of 40 armed fighters" to Horlivka in May, which helped Bezler to gain "complete control" over the town. Khokhlov (2019b, from 4:05) and Anosov (2019, at 34:38) both confirm that members of Girkin's group joined Bezler in Horlivka in late May but suggest that these fighters did not leave Sloviansk on friendly terms. The comments sections of their YouTube testimonies (Khokhlov 2019a; Anosov 2019) also feature posts by other group members who enter a heated argument about whether those who joined Bezler in Horlivka betrayed Girkin.

These testimonies suggest that several fighters who had been involved in the occupation of Sloviansk and Kramatorsk joined Bezler in Horlivka near the time of the Volnovakha attack. They also prove that, despite their disagreements, both Bezler and Girkin participated in the Russian takeover of Crimea and moved on to the

Donbas as part of the same network. As I discussed in chapter five, this network was coordinated by Crimean "Prime Minister" Sergey Aksyonov and Russian oligarch Konstantin Malofeyev with at least the knowledge and tacit approval of Russia's intelligence services and the Kremlin.

Hence, it is almost certain that the people in charge of the attack near Volnovakha came from the same Russian-led network of men that was responsible for the occupation of Sloviansk and Kramatorsk. Starting from the default assumption that H2 is a realistic possibility, this first round of informal Bayesian updating (see sections 3.1.4. and 3.4.3.2.) makes it now *likely* that Bezler and those members of Girkin's group that joined him in Horlivka continued to act on the Russian state's behalf. At the same time, the apparent tensions between Girkin's and Bezler's groups also leave a *realistic possibility* that Bezler severed his ties with Russia. However, the probability that this was the case is reduced significantly by additional evidence.

7.1.2. Bezler's Second Passport

The second stage of updating considers evidence that Russian intelligence services provided Bezler with a cover identity. When the Bellingcat (2019) research collective obtained and analyzed a leaked database of Russian flight passenger information, it discovered that a passport issued to Igor Nikolayevich Beregovoy was used to travel from Krasnodar to Simferopol on October 27, 2014. On October 28, Igor Nikolayevich Bezler—whose date and place of birth are identical to those on Beregovoy's passport—called his associates in Horlivka and told them that he had left the Donbas for good (Gorlovka.ua 2014). Moreover, Bellingcat checked Beregovoy's passport details against a database of Russian taxpayer identification numbers and did not find any entry, which further increases the likelihood that Igor Beregovoy is a fake identity. Finally, Bellingcat found that there is only a 28-digit difference between the serial number of Beregovoy's passport and the serial number of a passport issued to Andrey Ivanovich Laptev. According to Bellingcat, the latter name is the cover identity of Oleg Ivannikov, a GRU agent active in the Donbas in 2014 (Rakuszitzky et al. 2018).[27] Bellingcat (2019) argues that the serial number proximity suggests that the two passports were part of the same batch. This argument is consistent with the findings of Bellingcat's (2018a) initial investigation of Russia's 2018 chemical weapons attack in Salisbury in the United Kingdom. In this investigation, Bellingcat also discovered that several GRU agents held second identity passports with serial numbers in close proximity of each other.

Naturally, this evidence stands or falls on the authenticity of the flight passenger information database obtained by Bellingcat. However, Bellingcat has extensive experience of working with leaked databases sold on the Russian Internet. For example, such information also helped Bellingcat to identify the Russian agents responsible for the Salisbury poisonings (Bellingcat 2018a; 2018b; 2018c). In this case, evidence from a variety of other sources proved to be consistent with the evidence from leaked databases. Against this backdrop, it can be considered highly likely that Bellingcat's assessment of the obtained flight passenger data's authenticity is correct. As a result, it is highly likely that Russian intelligence services issued Igor Bezler with a cover identity either before or during his activities in the Donbas. This finding, in turn, increases the probability of H2 in relation to Bezler's group to *highly likely* as well.

7.1.3. Bezler's Handler: Introducing Vasiliy Geranin

The third and final stage of informal Bayesian updating refers to evidence that Bezler was cooperating with a Russian intelligence officer before, during, and after his activities in the Donbas. On July 17, 2014, only hours after Malaysian Airlines flight MH17 had been shot down over the conflict zone, the SBU (2014d) published an excerpt of an intercepted phone conversation between Bezler and "Russian GRU Colonel Vasiliy Nikolayevich Geranin."[28] On July

---

27 I will discuss Ivannikov in further detail below in the context of the events in Luhansk city.
28 The main topic of the present section is the interaction between Bezler and Geranin rather than the story of MH17. Neither Bezler nor Geranin have been indicted for the downing of the airliner, and the available evidence suggests that they were not actively involved but only discussed second-hand information about the incident. I will discuss MH17 further in chapter eight.

18, Russian pro-Kremlin media quoted Bezler as saying that this conversation had taken place but that it was not about MH17 but a different plane (Lenta.ru 2014; MK.ru 2014). Bezler (2016; 2020) later repeated this claim on his social media account. He argued that the SBU had faked the recording's timestamp and that he had been discussing a downed Ukrainian military aircraft rather than MH17. However, Bezler did not dispute the authenticity of the conversation itself. Moreover, shortly after the recording was published, Russian journalist Ilya Barabanov (2014) reported that he had called the number displayed in the SBU intercept and reached a man who responded when addressed as Vasiliy Nikolayevich Geranin. According to Barabanov, the man denied having discussed an airplane with anyone, but his voice sounded similar to the voice in the SBU's conversation excerpt.

A recording of the full conversation between Bezler and Geranin surfaced in 2020 in the context of the Dutch MH17 trial. First, additional excerpts were published by Ukrainian video blogger Anatolii Sharii (2020a from 5:35), who claimed that he had got the file from an anonymous source. Sharii is a strong critic of Ukraine's post-Maidan administrations and promotes pro-Russian political messaging. He presented the additional excerpts as proof that the SBU had taken the initial excerpts out of context. Subsequently, Bellingcat (2020b; 2020c) published and analyzed the complete audio recording of the conversation. It said it had obtained the audio file from a leaked email sent by Bezler to a Russian intelligence officer. Bellingcat's analysis of the contents contradicts Sharii's. Bellingcat argues that the full recording is even less compatible with Bezler's claim that the conversation with Geranin did not refer to MH17. However, regardless of this dispute and the implications for the MH17 case, both Sharii and Bellingcat agree that they are talking about the same recording and do not question its authenticity (Sharii 2020b).

This recording of the full conversation between Bezler and Geranin (Bellingcat 2020b) suggests that Geranin was Bezler's superior and that they discussed the operations of Bezler's group in great detail on a regular basis. Bezler addresses Geranin as Vasiliy Nikolayevich and uses the formal second person plural whereas Geranin addresses Bezler only by his first name Igor and uses the informal second person singular. Geranin starts the call by asking for an update on what happened to the body of a killed fighter. Then Bezler reports that his men downed a Ukrainian fighter jet "thirty minutes ago" and are now attacking Ukrainian positions near the town of Rozivka.[29] Geranin asks Bezler to send him photos via MMS and wants to know whether Bezler's men are using anti-tank missiles. Bezler then mentions that his men have seized Ukrainian RK-2 missiles. Geranin reminds Bezler that he has already told him to send these missiles to an unspecified location where unspecified people are waiting for them. Bezler replies that he needs three or four vehicles to transport all the missiles because his group seized a whole factory, but he also says that they are still looking for a launcher. Geranin tells Bezler to send only sample missiles and keep the rest. At the end of the call, Geranin asks if Bezler has made any progress commissioning propaganda banners.

There is convincing digital open source evidence to confirm Geranin's identity and corroborate the SBU's claim that he is a Russian intelligence officer. At the time the initial excerpt of the conversation was published by the SBU, the only verified photo of a "Colonel Vasily Geranin" was taken in April 2013 in Moscow at a roundtable titled "The War in Syria—Lessons for Russia." The roundtable was organized by the Russian military news weekly *Nezavisimoye Voyennoye Obozreniye* (NVO). Geranin gave a talk on effective combat strategies against organized armed groups and his photo accompanied a writeup of his presentation in the newspaper's print edition (NVO 2013, 6). A scan is available via the commercial online database PressReader. The photo's caption did not specify in which military branch or agency Geranin was serving. The only tentative link to the events in the Donbas was the fact that Igor Girkin participated in the same roundtable.

However, more evidence corroborating Geranin's identity and his ties to Igor Bezler appeared in January 2020. This evidence was provided by Russian journalist Vyacheslav Nemyshev (2020), who published a video showing himself with Igor Bezler and

---

29 The SBU and Bellingcat argue that this part of the conversation is referring to MH17. Bellingcat (2020c) suspects that Bezler had incomplete information. As a result, he incorrectly assumed that the downed plane was a Ukrainian fighter jet, and he also assumed that his men were responsible for the downing.

another man captioned as "military consultant Vasiliy Makagonov" on a yacht in Crimea. In the video, Makagonov is wearing a T-Shirt with the caption "Syria" and looks strikingly similar to NVO's 2013 photo of Geranin. Additional evidence that Geranin and Makagonov are the same person comes from participants in Russia's takeover of Crimea. On March 10, 2014, a Ukrainian Ministry of Defense spokesperson reported that a group of armed men, "who, according to our sources, are under the command of Russian Federation Colonel Makagonov," had entered a Ukrainian military base in the Crimean town of Bakhchysarai (Ukrainska Pravda 2014d). Ukrainian journalist Levko Stek (2020, from 17:55) showed the footage of Makagonov on the yacht to a Ukrainian officer who was stationed at this Bakhchysarai base in March 2014. The officer confirmed that the man on the yacht and the man leading the Russian occupation of the base were the same person. Moreover, he confirmed that Igor Bezler also participated in the occupation under Makagonov's command. Confirmation that the leader of the Bakhchysarai base occupation also used the surname Geranin comes from one of his own militiamen. Vadym Ilovchenko — a pro-Russian Cossack who would later join Igor Girkin in the occupation of Sloviansk and Kramatorsk (see chapter five) — gave a short TV interview at the Bakhchysarai base a few days after its occupation (ITV 2014). A more in-depth interview with Ilovchenko features in a book published in 2019 by Andrii Saveliev, one of Illovchenko and Girkin's comrades-in-arms (AiF 2019; Saveliev 2019a, 102). In this longer interview, Ilovchenko says that he joined a paramilitary group under the command of "Colonel Geranin" in Simferopol on March 7, 2014 at the recommendation of Girkin.[30] According to Ilovchenko, Geranin's nom-de-guerre at the time was "Kanaris".

The pseudonym Kanaris leads to yet another piece of evidence confirming Geranin's identity and his links to Bezler. In a public

---

30 Ilovchenko also claims that Geranin was not on active duty. However, Geranin's formal employment status is of secondary importance if he played a leading role in the Russian annexation of Crimea. As I have argued in chapter five, the paramilitary forces that supported the Russian takeover should be considered informal state organs because they were under the control of the Russian security apparatus. Moreover, the fact that Geranin was able to enjoy himself on a yacht in Crimea in the winter of 2019-2020 is additional evidence that the Russian state approved his activities in relation to the Donbas conflict.

post on his social media page, Igor Girkin (2019) identified Kanaris in a video from 2019, which shows Vasiliy Makagonov/Geranin and Bezler on another boat trip. In this post, Girkin describes Makagonov/Geranin as a retired Russian intelligence service colonel who received three Orders of Courage for serving in Chechnya. In response to another user's comment, Girkin adds that Geranin's credentials as a "military professional" are significantly stronger than his own because Geranin had been a "career special forces officer 'from an early age.'"

Taken together, these pieces of evidence suggest that it is almost certain that Kanaris, Vasiliy Makagonov, and Vasiliy Geranin are the same person – a colonel with a long service record in Russia's intelligence apparatus. Furthermore, it is almost certain that Kanaris/Makagonov/Geranin was Bezler's commander during the occupation of Crimea, that Bezler continued to report to him and to receive orders from him during his time in the Donbas, and that they remained on friendly terms after Bezler left the Donbas and returned to Crimea.

Bezler's links to Girkin's group, his second identity provided by the Russian authorities, and his close contacts to senior Russian intelligence officer Vasiliy Geranin are cumulative evidence that Bezler acted in the Donbas on behalf of the Russian state. These three stages of informal Bayesian updating increase the probability of H2 in relation to Bezler to *almost certain*. As a result, the same reasoning that applied to Girkin's group in chapter five also applies to Bezler and his men. Although Bezler may have enjoyed some degree of operational autonomy and relied on local recruits, the evidence discussed above suggests that Bezler's group was an informal organ of the Russian state. Therefore, it is almost certain that the actions of the Russian state were the primary cause of the attack on the Ukrainian Armed Forces near Volnovakha on May 22, 2014.

7.2. Donetsk and Surroundings: Boroday's "Volunteers"

The death toll of the Volnovakha attack was surpassed on May 26 when a failed attempt to seize Donetsk Airport led to serious losses on the separatist side. Separatist forces briefly managed to occupy one of the terminal buildings but were forced into a chaotic retreat when the Ukrainian units that were holding the other terminal building opened fire and received air support. During the retreat, a truck carrying separatist fighters was destroyed by friendly fire, which considerably increased the number of casualties.

7.2.1. Russian Fighters in Donetsk

There is considerable evidence that the group which attacked Donetsk Airport included many fighters from Russia. One day before the events, trucks with heavily armed men gathered for a separatist rally in central Donetsk. During this rally, a CNN (2014) correspondent spoke to two men who said that they were "volunteers" from Chechnya and confirmed that they had been "Kadyrovtsi" [militants under the command of Chechen Republic Head Ramzan Kadyrov] in the past. A few days after the operation, on May 29, the Donetsk People's Republic (DNR) openly acknowledged that a major part of the casualties of May 26 were, in fact, Russian citizens. DNR "Prime Minister" Aleksandr Boroday said in a press conference that about 60 separatist fighters had died and that 34 bodies of killed Russian citizens had been returned to Russia (Boroday and Pushylin 2014 at 17:53 and 13:25).

Further evidence of Russian involvement emerged when fighters who had joined the Donetsk separatists from Russia and taken part in the May 26 operation talked about the events. One detailed account was published by Radio Free Europe/Radio Liberty (Gasparyan and Shakirov 2014) and another one by pro-separatist blogger El-Murid (2014). Although these two sources hold diametrically opposed views on the conflict, both eyewitness accounts are largely consistent. According to both, a group of 100–120 "volunteers," who had been recruited on social media, gathered in mid-May in an undisclosed location in Russia's Rostov Oblast. They received about two weeks of military training from unidentified instructors and entered Ukraine a few days before the battle, led by a man with the nom-de-guerre *Iskra*.

There is additional evidence that the presence of fighters from Russia in and around Donetsk was not limited to the case of the Iskra Detachment. In his May 29 press conference, Boroday stated that the number of Russian "volunteers" in the ranks of the DNR "as of today" was "at least 200" (Boroday and Pushylin 2014 at 16:40). Subsequent first-hand reports by journalists suggest that at least some of these fighters were from Russia's North Caucasus and had significant previous combat experience. On June 1, the DNR's Vostok Battalion allowed a group of journalists to visit their training camp near Donetsk. Vostok was the dominant separatist unit in Donetsk at the time. Its commander was former Ukrainian special forces officer Oleksandr Khodakovskyi, who had also played a coordinating role in the Donetsk Airport operation. Following the visit to Vostok's training camp, journalist Max Avdeev (2014) reported that there were "far more locals" than foreign fighters at the camp but that "the foreigners are worth ten local volunteers." He further reported that the foreign fighters he met were Ossetians who had fought in the 2008 war between Russia and Georgia. This is consistent with the report of journalist Kateryna Serhatskova, who took part in the same visit. She reported that a leading figure in the Vostok Battalion was an Ossetian with the nom-de-guerre Mamay, who showed the journalists around the camp. Mamay was happy to pose for a photograph with eight other Ossetian "volunteers" (Serhatskova 2014). Mamay is also mentioned by journalist Mark Franchetti, who accompanied the Vostok Battalion on June 5 during a failed attack on the Marynivka border checkpoint 80 km southeast of Donetsk. According to Franchetti (2014), Mamay "rarely leaves Khodakovskyi's side." More information on Mamay became available when he died at the frontline near Donetsk on May 17, 2018. A day after his death, the DNR "Information Ministry" published a video captioned as "the last interview with Oleg Mamiyev (nom-de-guerre Mamay)" (Mamiyev 2018). In this interview, Mamay confirmed that he was from Vladikavkaz in Russia's Republic of North Ossetia and that he had fought in the 2008 war with Georgia. He said he had left Vladikavkaz for Donetsk on April 28, 2014 after meeting three unidentified men from Donetsk, who were travelling Russia's Caucasus republics in search for volunteers.

The evidence cited above suggests that it is highly likely that irregular fighters from Russia, many of whom came from Russia's Caucasus republics, arrived in Donetsk from late April or early May onward. It is also highly likely that at least some of these fighters had gained combat experience during the recent wars in Chechnya and Georgia. Moreover, it is almost certain that more Russian fighters arrived with the Iskra Detachment in late May, which had received combat training on Russian territory before entering Ukraine. It is also almost certain that the failed May 26 attack on Donetsk Airport was mainly carried out by this detachment and highly likely that the number of Russian fighters in Donetsk still exceeded 200 by the end of the month. At the same time, it is highly likely that the leading role of Russian fighters in DNR units also extended to combat operations other than the Donetsk Airport attack. The most important examples from the time period in question are the Vostok Battalion's May 23 clash with the pro-Ukrainian Donbas Battalion in the town of Karlivka (Semenchenko 2014) and Vostok's June 5 attack on the Marynivka border checkpoint (Franchetti 2014). Even if Russian fighters were outnumbered by locals during these operations, their superior average combat experience highly likely meant that they were in a position of authority. After all, the most recent opportunity for Ukrainian citizens to engage in armed combat was the Soviet Union's war in Afghanistan.

The central role of fighters from Russia in the separatist units fighting Ukrainian forces around Donetsk raises the question to what extent Russian volunteers can be considered state organs. The same question arose in chapter five as the result of Igor Girkin's claim that he had planned the Sloviansk operation himself and nobody had forced him to go. Similarly, there is no evidence to suggest that the Russian citizens fighting in Donetsk in May were deployed to the Donbas as regular members of the Russian security apparatus. As a result, it should be assumed that their own personal motives were a necessary condition for their involvement in the war. However, it is entirely possible to be a volunteer with great enthusiasm for a war's cause and a state actor at the same time. Many regular soldiers choose to serve rather than being conscripted. Like in the case of Girkin's group, the key question is not whether the Russian volunteers in Donetsk had been forced to go but whether the Russian state's actions can be considered the primary cause of their presence. The reasoning here is similar to the reasoning in chapter five, and it leads to the same conclusion. Even under the assumption that the recruitment and training of volunteers in Russia was conducted by private actors like veteran organizations, it can be considered almost certain that the Russian state was aware of these activities and could have stopped them. Recruiting a large number of Russian citizens, providing them with combat training, and sending them across the border would not have been possible without the approval of the authorities. Throughout the 2000s, the Kremlin increased the effectiveness of its security apparatus and successfully restricted civil society activity that it considered incompatible with its policy objectives. The current Russian regime neither lacks the capacity nor the determination to take action against undesirable paramilitary activity on its territory. Against this backdrop, the Kremlin's permissiveness toward paramilitary recruitment of Russian citizens to fight in Ukraine is more *disruptive* to the normal course of events than the fact that volunteers were found.

Therefore, the evidence discussed so far turns the burden of proof in relation to the Donetsk area against H1. It increases the probability of H2 to *likely* and reduces the probability of H1 to *unlikely*. An important remaining source of uncertainty, however, is the question to what extent the Russian state maintained its control over the fighters once they had crossed the border. In the following section, I will discuss evidence that reduces this uncertainty.

7.2.2. Boroday and Surkov

Russian involvement in the armed clashes around Donetsk in late May 2014 was not limited to the presence of experienced Russian paramilitary foot soldiers. It also extended to the command structures in charge of the separatist units. *Smoking-gun* evidence (see section 3.1.2.) for this is an October 2017 speech by Aleksandr Boroday[31] at a gathering of the "Union of Donbas Volunteers" in Moscow (Boroday 2017; Butusov 2019). In this speech, Boroday identified the leader of the Iskra Detachment—which had arrived in Donetsk from Russia in late May 2014 and played a leading role in the

---

31 Boroday himself is a Russian citizen with links to Russian oligarch Konstantin Malofeyev (see chapter five). He assumed the role of DNR "prime minister" on May 16, 2014 and returned to Russia in August.

May 26 attack of Donetsk Airport—as Boris Sysenko. According to Boroday, Sysenko was a "retired intelligence officer" with the rank of lieutenant colonel, who died during the battle at the airport. Boroday said that he himself had instructed Sysenko with the formation of the Iskra Detachment before leaving Russia to become DNR "prime minister." In addition to Sysenko, the detachment's leadership included two other "retired intelligence officers," called Yura and Sergey.

Moreover, Boroday blamed Vostok Battalion Commander Oleksandr Khodakovskyi for the separatists' defeat at Donetsk Airport. Boroday claimed that Khodakovskyi had carried out the operation against his will:

> Already back then, Aleksandr Sergeyevich [Khodakovskyi] was well connected. I'll be frank, he contacted my superiors in the leadership of the Russian Spring. Don't get any ideas, this was not the Presidential Administration, not [Russian Presidential Adviser] Vladislav Surkov, not Russian Federation state officials. I can't [inaudible]. Nevertheless, he received approval for this operation (Boroday 2017 at 12:00).

Boroday admits that, even though he was the "prime minister" of a self-proclaimed republic, the combat operations of this republic's units were subject to the approval of unnamed "superiors." Considering the Kremlin's official denial of its participation in the 2014 Donbas conflict, it is a matter of course that Boroday denies any affiliation of these superiors with the Russian state. However, five considerations suggest that this denial is not credible. Firstly, before he came to the Donbas as DNR "prime minister," Boroday had played a coordinating role in the April 12 occupation of Sloviansk and Kramatorsk—almost certainly on behalf of the Russian state (see chapter five). Secondly, leaked emails sent to an account belonging to Russian Presidential Adviser Vladislav Surkov, which are highly likely authentic, contain a message from May 13, 2014 with a list of suggested members for a new DNR "Government" (Digital Forensic Research Lab 2016; Hosaka 2019, 758; Shandra and Seely 2019, 26). The field for the post of "prime minister" was left blank. Three days later, a new DNR "Government" was formed –

under the leadership of Boroday and with eight of the 11 people from the list in the suggested positions (Ostrov 2014l). Thirdly, on June 16, 2014, a Russian news website quoted Boroday as saying that he has "known Presidential Adviser Vladislav Surkov for a long time" (Aktualnyye Kommentarii 2014). Fourthly, an unnamed separatist activist from Donetsk told Russian sociologist Maksim Aljukov that Boroday introduced himself as Surkov's envoy upon his arrival in Donetsk (Aljukov 2019, 127). Fifthly, the MH17 Joint Investigation Team (JIT 2019a; 2019b) verified and published two intercepted phone conversations between Boroday and Surkov from early July 2014. The cordial tone of these conversations suggests that the two men know each other well. Moreover, their detailed discussion of various aspects of the situation in the Donbas suggests that they talked about DNR affairs on a regular basis. In June 2021, Boroday and Surkov gave a joint YouTube interview, in which they gave the impression that they were good friends. During this interview, Surkov refused to confirm the authenticity of the intercepted conversations published by the JIT but confirmed that he and Boroday had been in contact in summer 2014 (Surkov and Boroday 2021 from 15:50).

Added to the evidence regarding the presence of Russian fighters, Boroday's (2017) statement and his documented links to Surkov further increase the probability of H2 in relation to the escalation of fighting around Donetsk in late May 2014. It suggests that men with a history of working for Russian intelligence agencies were leading one of the key detachments of Russian fighters in the region at the time. It also suggests that the separatist actions around the time of the Donetsk Airport operation were subject to one or more chains of command that reached far into the Russian state apparatus. At least one of these command chains included Presidential Adviser Vladislav Surkov and had been in place at least since Boroday's appointment as DNR "prime minister" on May 16.

In turn, this implies that the Russian state did not only permit the influx of trained irregular fighters from Russia to Donetsk, but, at least from mid-May onward, also coordinated the actions of their units. It can be assumed that this applies not only to the May 26 Donetsk Airport operation but to all combat activity of Donetsk-based separatist forces in late May and early June 2014. As a result, the probability of H2 in relation to these events increases to *highly likely* while the probability of H1 decreases to *highly unlikely*.

7.3. Luhansk City: Where Wagner Meets Orion

Parallel to the escalation of fighting in Donetsk Oblast, the city of Luhansk also witnessed separatist attempts to consolidate control over its surroundings by attacking facilities of Ukraine's security apparatus. From the separatists' perspective, these operations were a success. Ukrainian forces either withdrew, were disarmed and demobilized, or joined the separatists. On May 28, 2014, separatist forces stormed a base of the Ukrainian National Guard in a southeastern suburb of Luhansk. It came to a shootout in which one Ukrainian serviceman died. The Ukrainian authorities also claimed that several separatist fighters were killed (LB.ua 2014b; Memorybook.org.ua n.d.c). A Russian state TV correspondent reported from the scene that "there is at least one death on either side" (LifeNews 2014c). On May 29, separatist forces attacked a National Guard depot in Oleksandrivsk, a northwestern suburb of Luhansk. The depot caught fire and both sides had to withdraw. No casualties were reported. Separatist forces claimed that they detained several Ukrainian servicemen, which the National Guard denied (Bozhko 2014; LifeNews 2014d). More serious fighting occurred during the first four days of June when separatist forces besieged the Luhansk headquarters of the Ukrainian Border Service in a southwestern suburb of the city. Ukrainian forces withdrew on June 4, with four injured servicemen. They claimed that about ten separatist fighters had died (Zhyrokhov 2016c). The separatists admitted six losses (yadocent 2014).

The events of early June also affected Luhansk's civilian population and included potential violations of international humanitarian law. Russian state TV footage of the separatists' siege of the border service headquarters clearly shows that separatist forces were attacking the base from adjacent residential areas (YouTube 2014at). On the other hand, the Oblast State Administration building in central Luhansk and the park in front of it were hit by missiles on June 2. No military units were present at the site of the attack at the time. According to separatist sources, eight people died and 28 were injured (yadocent 2014). Although the Ukrainian authorities denied responsibility, there is consensus among both pro-Ukrainian and pro-separatist open source investigators that the attack was carried out by a Ukrainian Mi-25 aircraft, which was filmed launching missiles over Luhansk on the same day (Stopfake.org 2014; Giuretis 2014; Putin@war 2014; ds_mok 2014).

Fighting escalated further toward mid-June. A first separatist attempt to attack Ukrainian paratroopers holding Luhansk Airport failed on June 10. Sources in the Ukrainian Military claimed that one separatist was killed and 14 injured (TSN 2014c). Four days later, however, the separatists shot down a Ukrainian IL-76 cargo plane that was approaching the airport, carrying 40 soldiers and nine crew members, all of whom died (Memorybook.org.ua n.d.d). This incident was the largest loss of life in a single day for the Ukrainian Armed Forces in the conflict so far. On June 17, the Ukrainian Armed Forces sustained additional casualties while trying to advance toward Luhansk from the north and clashing with separatists between Shchastia and Metalist (Memorybook.org.ua n.d.e; Novosti Donbassa 2014j). These events of early to mid-June consolidated separatist control over the city of Luhansk and defined the airport, located 17 km south of the city center, and the area north of Luhansk toward the Siverskyi Donets river, as battlefields for the coming months.

7.3.1. The Wagner Group in Luhansk

Like in the case of Donetsk, there is evidence that paramilitary fighters from Russia were present in Luhansk in late May to early June 2014. In autumn 2017, the SBU published a presentation claiming that it had established the identities of 72 Russian mercenaries who had entered Luhansk Oblast on May 29, 2014 and were responsible for the downing of the Ukrainian IL-76 on June 14. It claimed that these men acted on behalf of Russia's intelligence agencies and that they were part of the Wagner Group—a Russian military company (SBU 2017). This group's operations in Syria and several African countries gained global media attention in recent years (Hauer 2018; Lee 2020; Sukhankin 2020a; 2020b). Nevertheless, Kremlin spokesperson Dmitriy Peskov (2020), still claimed not to know anything whatsoever about the Wagner Group as recently as July 2020. What is more, the group's owner, Yevgeniy Prigozhin, denied any links between him and the "non-existent Wagner Group" as recently as mid-February 2022. He even filed a claim with the European General Court demanding that the EU remove corresponding assertions from official documents (Interfax 2022).

This Russian denial narrative in relation to the Wagner Group completely unraveled after the full-scale invasion of 2022. The group became increasingly open about the fact that it was fighting alongside the regular Russian military in Ukraine and that it was actively recruiting new members for this purpose. In mid-September 2022, Yevgeniy Prigozhin himself implicitly confirmed that Wagner Group members were currently present near Bakhmut in Donetsk Oblast and that he was recruiting inmates from Russian prisons to join the group and fight in Ukraine (Prigozhin 2022a). At the end of September, he went a step further and explicitly admitted his own involvement in the creation of the group as well as the group's involvement in fighting at Luhansk Airport in 2014:

> I cleaned old weapons, sorted out bulletproof vests, and found specialists who could help me. From this moment, May 1, 2014, the group of patriots was born that subsequently acquired the name 'Battalion Tactical Group Wagner.' Only because of their bravery and courage, it became possible to liberate Luhansk Airport and many other territories, and the fate of the LNR and the DNR changed dramatically (Prigozhin 2022b).

However, even before Prigozhin's admission, the SBU's claims regarding the Wagner Group's presence in Luhansk in 2014 were corroborated by at least three other sources.[32] The first source is Yevstafiy Botvinyev, a Russian mercenary who gave an interview to a Russian news website in May 2018. Botvinyev claimed that he came to Donetsk on May 23, 2014 and later moved on to Luhansk,

---

[32] I would like to thank Sergey Sukhankin for drawing my attention to these three sources. I was made aware of them through his Jamestown Foundation report on the activity of Russian private military companies in Ukraine (Sukhankin 2019).

where he met the Wagner Group's leader, Dmitriy Utkin (nom-de-guerre Wagner), who arrived in June with a group of 80 men (Botvinyev and Dolgareva 2018). Secondly, an article by Radio Free Europe/Radio Liberty from March 2018 cites three anonymous Wagner commanders, who say that two groups of mercenaries consisting of "up to 250 men" gathered in Rostov-on-Don and moved on to the Donbas in June 2014. One of the groups was led by Dmitriy Utkin and later adopted Utkin's nom-de-guerre, "Wagner" (Khasov-Kassiya 2018). Finally, a blogger with the username Mikhail Utov (2019) found several social media profiles under the names of Wagner mercenaries, who, according to the SBU, died in Luhansk Oblast in July and August 2014. Some of the screenshots of their accounts feature pictures posted by the men's relatives with the characteristic black-cross medals that the Wagner Group sends to the families of mercenaries who died abroad (Leviev 2017a; 2017b; Nazarova and Barabanov 2018; Utov 2019). Moreover, the funeral of Vladimir Kalmanov, one of the men on the SBU's list, was covered in a local TV news report in his hometown of Krymsk in Russia's Krasnodar Krai. In this report, the presenter mentioned that Kalmanov had fought in Syria before joining the separatists in Ukraine (Elektron-Media 2014).

In addition to the Wagner Group's reported activities, the identity of two other Russian "volunteers" who played a leading role in the fighting north of Luhansk on June 17 has been established in a Russian courtroom. The two men appeared as witnesses for the prosecution during the trial against Ukrainian volunteer battalion member Nadiia Savchenko, who had been captured by separatist forces near the town of Metalist on June 17. Subsequently, Savchenko was brought to Russia and put on trial for the alleged killing of a Russian war correspondent. Shortly after her arrest on the battlefield on June 17, she was filmed by Yegor Russkiy, who later testified against her in court (Russkiy 2018; Russkiy and LifeNews 2018; Mediazona 2015a). Between his involvement in Ukraine and his court appearance, Russkiy featured in a local TV report in his hometown of Ukhta in Russia's Komi Republic. In this report, the presenter disclosed that Russkiy was a Russian Army veteran who fought in the 2008 war against Georgia (Planeta Novostey 2014). The other man who testified in court against

Savchenko was Sergey Moiseyev. There is no further information about his background on openly available sources, but he confirmed during the trial that he was a Russian citizen, who fought with the Luhansk separatists on June 17, 2014 (Mediazona 2015b).

In sum, the evidence discussed above suggests that it is almost certain that more than 100 paramilitary fighters from Russia, many of whom were mercenaries associated with the Wagner Group, joined the separatist forces in Luhansk Oblast in June 2014. It is highly likely that these fighters used their superior combat experience to play a leading role in the combat operations at Luhansk Airport on June 14 and north of Luhansk on June 17. Moreover, considering that Russian paramilitary fighters with combat experience started to arrive in Donetsk already between late April and early May, it is likely that at least some of their Luhansk counterparts were already present for the first smaller combat operations in Luhansk in late May. Analogous to the case of Donetsk, this evidence flips the balance of probability between H1 and H2, which means that the former becomes *unlikely* while the latter becomes *likely* – at least for the events of mid-June. In the case of the first series of armed clashes in Luhansk in late May and early June, both H1 and H2 could be a *realistic possibility* at this stage.

7.3.2. Orion, Elbrus, and Pavel Karpov

There is evidence that separatist militias in and around Luhansk were supervised by two Russian intelligence officers and a political consultant from Moscow. As in the case of Donetsk, this evidence of links between irregular fighters and Russian state structures further increases the probability of H2. In his May 2018 interview, Russian mercenary Yevstafiy Botvinyev said that his group, as well as the Wagner Group mercenaries who he met in Luhansk, were not under the command of the local separatist leadership. Instead, he claimed that the mercenaries and Luhansk People's Republic (LNR) "Defense Minister" Ihor Plotnytskyi both reported to the same superior – a man with the codename "Andrey Ivanovich" (Botvinyev and Dolgareva 2018). A variant of the same codename also features in the writing of an anonymous Russian "volunteer," who says that he offered logistical support for the Luhansk separatists from the very beginning of the conflict. According to this person's account, a Russian intelligence officer called "Andrey Ivanych," who was known for his "high-pitched voice," approved Plotnytskyi's appointment as LNR "defense minister" in late May in the first place (Nemezida-LNR 2016).

A person captioned as "Andrey Ivanovich" with a distinct high-pitched voice also features in an SBU (2014e) phone intercept and a JIT (2016d) call for witnesses in the context of the downing of Malaysian Airlines flight MH17. According to the SBU and the JIT, the person in question was a Russian intelligence officer, who used "Andrey Ivanovich" as well as "Orion" as pseudonyms. In 2018, the Bellingcat research collective succeeded in establishing Andrey Ivanovich Orion's identity. After analysing the openly available information on Andrey Ivanovich Orion, Bellingcat searched for additional clues in leaked Russian telephone, car registration, and residential address databases. On the basis of this research, Bellingcat concluded "with a very high degree of certainty" that Orion is, in fact, Oleg Vladimirovich Ivannikov, a Russian GRU officer who also used the fake identity of Andrey Ivanovich Laptev (Rakuszitzky et al. 2018). While it is not possible to verify the origin and reliability of the leaked data used, the report thoroughly explains every step of the investigation in a transparent manner. At the same time, Bellingcat has an impressive track record of conducting high-quality investigations. For these reasons, it is reasonable to assume that their identification of Andrey Ivanonich Orion as Oleg Vladimirovich Ivannikov is highly likely correct.

In addition to Ivannikov, the presence of two other men in Luhansk in early to mid-June points at Russian state control over the LNR leadership and its military. In both cases, the initial lead is the case of Nadiia Savchenko. Firstly, during the trial against Savchenko, a separatist fighter with the nom-de-guerre Ilim presented his account of the June 17 events to Russian journalist Ilya Azar (2016). In this interview, Ilim mentions in passing that, after Savchenko had been arrested, her belongings were handed over to a person with the codename Elbrus, who was an "FSB adviser to the LNR authorities." In April 2020, Bellingcat (2020a) published a report on Elbrus, drawing on open source material as well as leaked Russian databases. The report concluded that Elbrus was the codename of Russian Federal Security Service (FSB) Colonel Igor Anatolyevich Yegorov, who was the FSB counterpart of GRU officer Ivannikov in Luhansk in summer 2014. The report's findings are highly likely to be correct for the same reasons that apply in the case of Ivannikov.

Secondly, Nadiia Savchenko said during her trial that a Russian political consultant called Pavel Karpov had organized her transfer from Luhansk to Russia. Karpov's presence is also remembered by local Luhansk journalists, who say that he summoned them to the Luhansk Oblast State Administration on June 10, 2014 to demand their loyalty to the LNR authorities (Dobrov 2015). After Savchenko's allegation, the Russian news magazine *Kommersant Vlast* contacted Karpov, who denied any involvement in the Savchenko case but confirmed that he had spent time in Luhansk in Summer 2014 (Tumanov 2016). Additional research by *Kommersant Vlast* and Luhansk anti-separatist newspaper *Realnaya Gazeta* revealed that Karpov was well-connected in Russian nationalist circles (Dobrov 2015; Tumanov 2016). In 2012, for example, he appeared with future DNR "Prime Minister" Aleksandr Boroday at a roundtable discussion hosted by the extreme-right-wing newspaper *Zavtra* (Karpov and Boroday 2012). Moreover, *Realnaya Gazeta* found evidence in publicly available Russian databases that Karpov was a board member of a pro-Kremlin youth organization that received a total of 10 million rubles of government grants in 2012 (Dobrov 2015). Until at least Autumn 2018, he was also a member of the Moscow Public Chamber – an advisory organ for the Moscow City authorities consisting of selected state-approved civil society representatives (Moscow Public Chamber 2018).

The evidence cited above suggests that it is highly likely that Russian GRU officer Oleg Ivannikov was in a position of authority in relation to the military units of the LNR in Luhansk by mid-June 2014. It is likely that Ivannikov had been in this position at least since late May and approved the appointment of Ihor Plotnytskyi as LNR "defense minister." Furthermore, it is highly likely that, by mid-June, FSB officer Igor Yegorov and political consultant Pavel Karpov – an associate of DNR "Prime Minister" Boroday – had joined Ivannikov. Although there is no evidence of Yegorov's and

Karpov's presence in Luhansk before mid-June, it is a realistic possibility that they assumed their respective roles earlier.

7.3.3. Yevgeniy Prigozhin: Putin's Chef

Another important connection between separatist fighters in Luhansk Oblast and the Russian state is Wagner Group owner Yevgeniy Prigozhin. There is ample evidence of personal links between Prigozhin and Vladimir Putin. Prigozhin developed a major restaurant and catering business network in St. Petersburg in the 1990s. In an interview with a local newspaper, Prigozhin (2011) said that he first met Vladimir Putin in the early 2000s when Putin dined at one of his restaurants. According to research by the *Forbes Russia* magazine and Aleksey Navalny's Anti-Corruption Foundation, Prigozhin's businesses soon became a major service provider for the Kemlin and the Russian military (Navalnyy 2016; Zhegulev 2013). In a 2018 interview, Putin denied that he was friends with Prigozhin but admitted that he knew him (Putin and Kelly 2018).

Regardless of whether or not they were personal friends, it is undisputed that Prigozhin and his business empire had close and longstanding ties with the Russian state leadership and with Vladimir Putin himself. If Prigozhin's involvement in the Donbas was against the Russian state's interests and wishes, it could be expected that the Russian state leadership and Putin would severe these ties. However, there is no evidence that Prigozhin's creation of the Wagner Group and its deployment to the Donbas in 2014 had a negative impact on his function as a service provider for the Russian state in any way. It is therefore reasonable to conclude that Prigozhin acted with the knowledge and approval of the Russian state and in the spirit of his public-private partnership with the Kremlin when sending his fighters to the Donbas.

Added to the evidence regarding Russian mercenaries, the evidence relating to Orion (Ivannikov), Elbrus (Yegorov), Karpov, and Prigozhin further increases the probability of H2 in relation to the events in Luhansk. As a result, it is *highly likely* that the actions of the Russian state were the primary cause of the June 14 IL-76 downing at Luhansk Airport and the June 17 fighting north of Luhansk. The evidence of Russian involvement prior to mid-June remains weaker. Nevertheless, it is now *likely* that the same causal mechanism applies to the first series of armed clashes in Luhansk in late May and early June.

7.4. Luhansk Oblast: The Don Cossack Invasion

Luhansk and its immediate surroundings were not the first part of Luhansk Oblast to experience larger armed clashes. On May 22, separatist units blocked the advance of Ukrainian forces at a bridge across the Siverskyi Donets river near the town of Rubizhne, 80 km northwest of Luhansk. The Ukrainian soldiers were moving toward the town of Lysychansk but were unable to cross the bridge and also found the way back blocked with felled trees and angry local residents. What followed were hours of armed clashes alternating with negotiations. In the end, the Ukrainian units were allowed to retreat the way they came. By then, three Ukrainian soldiers were dead and at least two injured (Memorybook.org.ua n.d.b; Zhyrokhov 2016b). The separatists admitted the death of ten fighters (Shapovalov 2014).

In early June, a third hotspot of fighting appeared in the far south of Luhansk Oblast near the Russian border. The Border Service of Ukraine reported attacks on its units near the village of Diakove on May 30 and June 4. According to the Ukrainian authorities, two attackers died and one was injured in the June 4 attack (LB.ua 2014c; 2014d). The local mayor reported further intense armed clashes near the village on June 12–13 (Glavkom 2014).

7.4.1. Ataman Nikolay Kozitsyn and the "Cossack National Guard"

While some uncertainty remains about Russia's role in the armed clashes near Rubizhne, there is clear evidence linking the clashes in the south of Luhansk Oblast to the Russian state. The repeated attacks on the Russian-Ukrainian border near Diakove can be attributed to Russian Don Cossack leader Nikolay Kozitsyn. According to Kozitsyn's (2016) own account published on the website of his "Cossack National Guard," he led a group of Don Cossacks that went to Ukraine on April 27 and took control of the town of Antratsyt, 18 km north of Diakove. Russian historian and Cossack expert Yuriy Soshin (2017), on the other hand, writes that Kozitsyn and his men entered Ukraine on May 3 on two trucks "armed with light weapons and a ZU-23-2 antiaircraft cannon." Either way, it is undisputed that Kozitsyn and his men had arrived by May 5, when videos showing three trucks driving past cheering locals in the center of Antratsyt appeared on YouTube. Two of the trucks were carrying armed men wearing papakhas – fur hats characteristic of Cossack warriors (YouTube 2014an; 2014ao). On May 31, a YouTube channel linked to Kozitsyn's "Cossack National Guard" posted a video captioned "Shelling of the Diakove Border Detachment" (KazakTV 2014). Moreover, members of the "Cossack National Guard" gathered in Diakove to commemorate the 5-year anniversary of the battle on June 12, 2019 (Antel-Plus Antratsit 2019).

Even though their "Cossack National Guard" was not officially registered with the Russian authorities, it is appropriate to consider Kozitsyn and his subordinates informal Russian state organs. The same reasoning that applies to the Russian fighters around Donetsk city and Luhansk city also applies to Kozitsyn and his men. His paramilitary group was allowed to operate within Russia's tightly regulated NGO environment. After publicly declaring his support for separatism in Luhansk in early April (see chapter four), he was able to obtain military grade weaponry and travel to the Donbas undisturbed. Moreover, Kozitsyn's "voluntary" paramilitary intervention in the Donbas, followed by a "voluntary" withdrawal to a quiet life in Russia, strongly resembles the stories of Igor Girkin, Igor Bezler, and Aleksandr Boroday. All three are Russian citizens who claim to have come to the Donbas on their own initiative. However, chapter five and the present chapter have shown that all three have documented ties to Russian political elites and intelligence services. Given these precedents in Donetsk Oblast, it is likely that similar schemes were behind Kozitsyn's activities in rural Luhansk. For these reasons, the probability of H2 in relation to Kozitsyn's group should be considered *likely* as well.

7.4.2. Pavlo Dromov and Oleksii Mozghovyi

Regarding the earlier armed clashes northwest of Luhansk, the evidence is more ambiguous. There is some evidence suggesting that some of the separatist fighters present in the so-called "triangle" — the urban agglomeration encompassing Rubizhne, Lysychansk, and Sievierodonetsk — were linked to Kozitsyn. On May 26, Kozitsyn told a Russian newspaper that ten Cossacks had died in armed clashes in Luhansk Oblast. According to Kozitsyn all of these Cossacks were local residents and some were from Rubizhne, Lysychansk, and Sievierodonetsk (Shapovalov 2014). Moreover, there is evidence that some of the men fighting in Rubizhne were under the command of Pavlo Dromov, who affiliated himself with the pro-Russian Don Cossack movement. The funeral of five separatist fighters who died in Rubizhne on May 22 took place on May 24 in the town of Stakhanov, 50 km south of Rubizhne (YouTube 2014ar). Pavlo Dromov was present at the funeral as one of Stakhanov's separatist leaders.[33] A week later, Dromov appeared in Sievierodonetsk and introduced himself as the commander of the town's separatist forces. He was wearing a papakha (Dromov 2014). Two weeks later, on June 16, Dromov gave another interview and said that he had just returned from a trip to the south of Luhansk Oblast, where he and his men had assisted Kozitsyn in the attack on the Diakove border checkpoint (Dromov, Lavin, and Veselovskiy 2014).

Another group of fighters with some documented links to Russia that was present in the area northwest of Luhansk on May 22 was the battalion of Oleksii Mozghovyi. This group arrived in Lysychansk on May 20 and established a base at a local manufacturing plant (Polemika 2014). Previously, it had undergone combat training at a camp which can be geolocated to the south of Luhansk Oblast near the area of operation of Kozitsyn's Cossacks. On May 19, the BBC aired an interview with Mozghovyi, recorded at a "secret training base not far from the Russian border" (BBC News 2014a). The report includes footage of separatist fighters bathing in a lake. In a 2020 interview, Mozghovyi's former bodyguard mentioned in passing that the training base in question was located at a holiday camp in "Yaseny" in "Sverdlovsk District" (Girkin and

---

[33] Dromov had participated in the seizure of the SBU building in Luhansk in early April and returned to Stakhanov after disagreements with other separatists (see chapter four).

Tavr 2020 at 3:03). A "Yaseny holiday camp" next to a lake in Luhansk Oblast's southern Sverdlovsk District can be found on the cartographical platform Wikimapia (n.d.). It is located just over a kilometer away from the Russian border near the Dovzhanskyi checkpoint. There is evidence that this location had been chosen to facilitate military supplies. When the BBC journalist asked Mozghovyi where his men had got their weapons from, Mozghovyi evaded the question and replied that they had been supplied by Barack Obama (BBC News 2014a at 1:42). Moreover, the BBC journalist noted that he had first met Mozghovyi a month earlier, when the latter "had just returned from meetings with officials in Moscow" (BBC News 2014a at 1:30). Given the proximity of his camp to the Russian border, his evasiveness regarding the origin of his weapons, and his recent trip to Moscow, it is almost certain that Mozghovyi received weapons supplies from the Russian state.

Nevertheless, the evidence of connections of Dromov and Mozghovyi's groups with the Russian state is less clear than in the other cases examined in this chapter. Dromov's identification with the pro-Russian Don Cossack movement and his mid-June trip to Diakove suggest that he cooperated with Nikolay Kozitsyn. However, even though it is likely that Kozitsyn acted on behalf of the Russian state, Dromov was one step removed from him. There is no direct evidence that he was under the command of Kozitsyn or other Russian actors at the time his fighters established footholds northwest of Luhansk. The same is the case for Oleksii Mozghovyi. Even though it is almost certain that his group received weapons from Russia before moving to Lysychansk, there is no direct evidence that he and his fighters were controlled by Russian actors.

However, it is reasonable to argue that the evidence of Russian involvement discussed in the previous sections of this chapter, combined with the evidence discussed in chapter five, has shifted the initial burden of proof. In light of the strong evidence of Russian interference in other places, the claim that Dromov and Mozghovyi's groups included fighters from Russia, and reported to Russian state actors, can no longer be considered particularly extraordinary. At the same time, the assumption that Dromov and Mozghovyi's groups were more independent from Russia than other groups fighting the Ukrainian Armed Forces in the region at the same time is no longer the most parsimonious explanation of events. Hence, the initial distribution of probabilities between H1 and H2 in relation to Dromov and Mozghovyi's groups should be considered even, if not slightly tilted toward H2. Dromov's ties to Kozitsyn and the location of Mozghovyi's training base combined with his trips to Russia are *straw-in-the-wind* evidence (see section 3.1.2.) that increases this tilt further. However, because all evidence remains relatively weak and circumstantial, both H1 and H2 should be considered *realistic possibilities* in relation to Dromov and Mozghovyi's groups.

7.5. The Role of Locals and Kremlin Infighting

While the available evidence overall clearly supports H2, it also highlights two important caveats to Russia's role in the spread of fighting across the Donbas during the time period in question. Firstly, local actors did play an important auxiliary role in the escalation of violence. It is a fact that at least a vocal minority of local residents supported the separatist cause, which meant that Ukrainian units often had to operate in a hostile environment. What is more, it is highly likely that most separatist fighters were, in fact, locals. Although these local fighters were ultimately subject to Russian decisions and commands, and most of them had less combat experience than their Russian peers, they provided crucial support for Russia's actions. As in the case of Sloviansk and Kramatorsk (see chapter five), this local support was an important, albeit secondary, condition for the course of events.

Secondly, the findings of the present chapter do not imply Russian control in the sense of one single consolidated chain of command. Instead, the available evidence suggests that different actors within the Russian state apparatus entered separate and sometimes even competing relationships with agents on the ground. Strong evidence of this is one of the intercepted phone conversations between DNR "Prime Minister" Boroday and Russian Presidential Adviser Surkov. In this conversation, Boroday says that he needs "a solution to the problem with Bezler" who is allegedly destabilizing the DNR. Surkov promises to try but says that there is another person in an influential position who disagrees with Boroday's assessment of the situation (JIT 2019b from 13:35). However, the fact that no open in-fighting broke out, even though Bezler stayed in Horlivka until November, suggests that Boroday, Bezler, and their respective superiors in Moscow came to some sort of agreement. Moreover, the fact that the influx of fighters from Russia and the activity of separatist groups intensified at around the same time in the different places described in this chapter suggests a certain degree of coordination. It is plausible that the Russian authorities gave the go-ahead for further conflict escalation to destabilize the situation in Ukraine around the May 25 presidential election. However, this does not necessarily mean that the Kremlin was following a coherent long-term plan.

Nevertheless, the findings of the present chapter suggest that the Kremlin signaled to the intelligence agencies and other actors in its orbit that they had permission to proceed with their destabilization projects in the Donbas. This would be in line with the principle of *otmashka*, which I discussed in chapter five (Galeotti 2020; Grozev 2020; Kashin, Merkulova, and Solomin 2014; Pavlovsky 2016). The informality and implicitness that comes with this outsourcing of violence is supposed to create deniability and make the role of the Russian state more difficult to prove. However, the present chapter has shown that this practice did not erase all traces of Kremlin involvement. Neither does it reduce Moscow's responsibility for the spread of fighting across the Donbas in late May to mid-June 2014.

7.6. Chapter Conclusion

This chapter has shown that the fourth critical juncture of the Donbas conflict—the spread of fighting beyond the conflict's two initial hotspots in late May and early to mid-June 2014—was primarily the result of Russia's actions. It has illustrated that the critical juncture in question comprised four local episodes of conflict escalation, all of which left a legacy of violence and contributed to the emergence of territorial frontlines in the region. In all four cases, H2—the hypothesis that the Russian state's actions were the primary cause of conflict escalation—is the most suitable explanation.

The May 22 attack on Ukrainian forces near Volnovakha was carried out by separatist fighters under the command of Russian citizen Igor Bezler, the leader of the separatists in Horlivka. Bezler was part of the same network of Russian state agents that was responsible for the occupation of Sloviansk and Kramatorsk on April 12. Moreover, Russian state institutions provided him with a fake identity before or during his activities in the Donbas. In addition, Bezler was in close contact with Russian intelligence officer Vasiliy Geranin before, during, and after his activities in the Donbas. The evidence in support of these three findings increases the probability of H2 in relation to Bezler to *almost certain*.

The May 26 attack on Donetsk Airport was carried out by a detachment of Russian paramilitary fighters who had gathered and trained on Russian territory before moving to the Donbas. It can also be assumed that experienced paramilitary fighters from Russia played a leading role in the armed clashes in Karlivka on May 23 and the attack on the Marynivka border checkpoint on June 5. There is evidence that all these operations were subject to chains of command, which led into the Russian state apparatus. One command chain is clearly documented in openly available sources and involved the DNR's Russian "Prime Minister" Aleksandr Boroday and Russian Presidential Adviser Vladislav Surkov. In sum, the available evidence increases the probability of H2 in the context of the events in and around Donetsk to *highly likely*.

Russian paramilitary fighters, some of whom belonged to a group which would later become known as the Wagner military company, played a leading role in conflict escalation around the city of Luhansk in mid-June. This episode included the June 14 downing of a Ukrainian military transport aircraft at Luhansk Airport and the June 17 battle north of Luhansk and led to unprecedented losses on the Ukrainian side. Moreover, at least two Russian intelligence operatives—Oleg Ivannikov and Igor Yegorov—and one political consultant from Moscow—Pavel Karpov—were in positions of authority in Luhansk at the time. All this increases the probability of H2 in relation to the mid-June events to *highly likely*. Regarding earlier incidents of conflict escalation around Luhansk in late May and early June, it is *likely* that at least some fighters from

Russia as well as Ivannikov were already present and that H2 is the more accurate explanation.

Fighting in early June near the village of Diakove at the Russian-Ukrainian border in the south of Luhansk Oblast was led by Russian Cossacks under the command of Nikolay Kozitsyn, who was *likely* acting on behalf of the Russian state. Fighting on May 22 in the town of Rubizhne northwest of Luhansk involved separatist units under the command of Pavlo Dromov and Oleksii Mozghovyi. The former had links to Kozitsyn's Cossacks while the latter had received arms supplies from Russia. It is a *realistic possibility* that Dromov and Mozghovyi's groups were informal organs of the Russian state because the large body of evidence demonstrating Russian involvement across the Donbas has shifted the burden of proof. However, the lack of direct evidence of Russian control in the cases of Dromov and Mozghovyi suggests that there also remains a slightly less probable *realistic possibility* that they acted primarily independently.

These findings lead to the overall conclusion that H2 is more closely in line with the available evidence in the context of all four components of the conflict's fourth critical juncture. The only case in which the likelihood of H1 comes close to H2 is the case of the outbreak of fighting northwest of Luhansk. However, this was also the location with the weakest level of separatist control. Ukrainian forces retook Rubizhne, Sievierodonetsk, and Lysychansk in late July 2014 (Svetikov 2017) and remained in control of the area until 2022, when Russia's all-out invasion led to intense fighting and massive destruction in all three cities.

The present chapter leaves the possibility open that the events of the conflict's fourth critical juncture were the result of ad hoc decisions in Moscow and not part of a sustained commitment to escalating violence in the Donbas. The following chapter will investigate whether the Kremlin stepped back and let the conflict evolve locally over the summer, or whether it further intensified its involvement. I will find that the latter was the case. Rather than leaving its informal troops to their own devices, Moscow supplied them with the heavy arms they required to turn the Donbas conflict into a full-scale war.

8. The Calibers Grow

This chapter investigates the fifth critical juncture of the Donbas War—the appearance of tanks and heavy artillery across the conflict zone between mid-June and mid-July 2014. After the armed clashes discussed in chapter seven had established relatively clear frontlines between separatist-controlled areas and areas controlled by Kyiv, the emergence of heavy weapons along these frontlines marked the further transformation toward regular warfare. This development had devastating consequences for the region and its inhabitants. The destructive potential of these weapons dramatically increased the number of military and civilian casualties and the damage to the region's infrastructure.

Much of the political messaging focusing on this phase of the conflict is aimed at blaming the opposing sides for civilian casualties. The separatists accused Ukrainian forces of shelling residential areas, and the Ukrainian leadership accused separatist forces of using civilians as human shields by placing artillery systems in precisely those areas. While the investigation of potential war crimes related to the use of heavy artillery in the Donbas in 2014 is important, it is not the primary focus of this chapter. Like this book as a whole, the present chapter investigates the relative importance of domestic and external factors. It focuses primarily on the origin of tanks and heavy artillery on the separatist side as the key factor determining the relative importance of domestic and external causes of the present critical juncture.

I will start by discussing the general probability of separatists seizing heavy arms from the Ukrainian military compared to the general probability of arms supplies from Russia. I will then assess the available digital open source evidence surrounding the different instances in which tanks and heavy artillery in separatist hands first appeared across the different battlefields. I will conclude that it is *highly likely* that Russia supplied the vast majority of heavy arms used by the separatists, which means that Russia's role continued to be of primary importance during the critical juncture investigated in this chapter.

The key point of contention that I investigate in the present chapter can be captured in two opposing hypotheses. The first hypothesis assumes that Russia did not step up its involvement in the conflict beyond the level described in the previous chapter. This would not necessarily imply that Russia stopped sending fighters to the Donbas, or that the Russian state cut its ties with the separatist leadership. However, it would leave this possibility open by suggesting that the Russian state refused to get more deeply involved and left its irregular fighters in the Donbas to their own devices. The second hypothesis, on the other hand, would reaffirm the ties between the Russian state and the separatists documented in the previous chapters. It suggests that, rather than distancing itself from the paramilitaries fighting on its behalf, the Russian State took its involvement to the next level by dramatically increasing their military capabilities. As a result, the primary actors responsible for the conflict's further escalation in the context of the present critical juncture would be the Ukrainian military, on the one hand, and the Russian military, on the other.

H1: Separatist forces in the Donbas gained access to tanks and heavy artillery as the result of an internal conflict dynamic because they captured these arms from the Ukrainian military.

Figure 14: Internal Escalation Mechanism

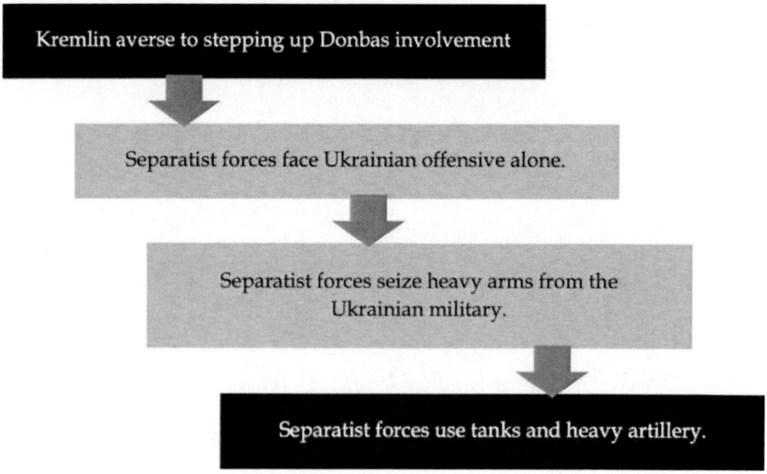

```
Kremlin averse to stepping up Donbas involvement
                        ↓
     Separatist forces face Ukrainian offensive alone.
                        ↓
     Separatist forces seize heavy arms from the
                 Ukrainian military.
                        ↓
     Separatist forces use tanks and heavy artillery.
```

Source: the author

H2: *Separatist forces in the Donbas gained access to tanks and heavy artillery as the result of Russian arms deliveries.*

Figure 15: External Escalation Mechanism

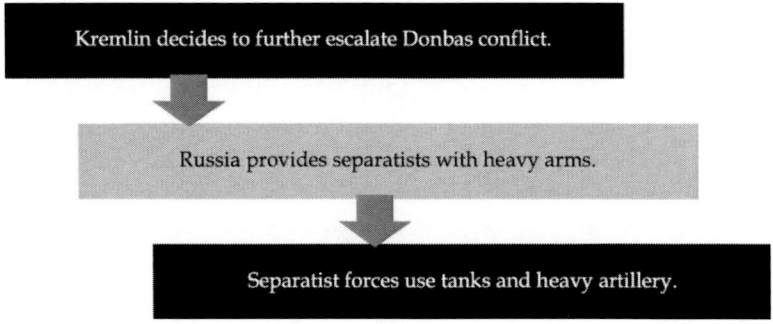

Source: the author

8.1. From Russia to the Donbas: The First Convoys of Heavy Arms

On first sight, Occam's razor and the Sagan standard suggest that H1 is the more likely hypothesis. Separatist forces seizing heavy arms from military facilities in areas under their control or from advancing Ukrainian forces appears like a more parsimonious and less extraordinary explanation than heavy arms deliveries from Russia. Moreover, H1 receives an additional initial boost from a report by the ARES arms and munitions consultancy (Ferguson and Jenzen-Jones 2014). This report found that the heavy arms observed in the hands of Donbas separatists in early summer 2014 comprised Soviet-era models that were part of both the Russian and the Ukrainian arsenal. While this observation does not rule out the possibility that the separatists received this military hardware from Russia, it is a passed *hoop test* (see section 3.1.2.) for H1 and strengthens the initial plausibility of this hypothesis.

8.1.1. Few Places to Rob: The Unavailability of Ukrainian Heavy Arms

However, three other pieces of circumstantial evidence cancel out this head start for H1 and create an even balance of probabilities between the two hypotheses. The first piece consists of media reports on the geographical distribution of Ukraine's military units before the conflict. Maps produced by both Ukrainian and Russian media outlets indicate that the presence of the Ukrainian Armed Forces in the Donbas was weak. In March 2014, in response to Russia's annexation of Crimea, Harvard University Russia analyst Dmitry Gorenburg (2014) published two maps showing the locations where Ukrainian military units were stationed. He took these maps from a Russian military blog, but their inscriptions suggest that they were originally published by Russian daily newspaper *Kommersant* and its weekly sister publication *Kommersant Vlast*. The maps show that the units of the Ukrainian Armed Forces were generally concentrated in the west and center of the country. What is more, they do not show any tank or artillery units in the Donbas at all. Similarly, a map published by *The Ukrainian Week* (2014) illustrates the geographical distribution of Ukrainian military units in 2012 and shows an air defense artillery regiment as the sole unit stationed in the Donbas. Of course, it must be kept in mind that these maps were created by media sources and are not exhaustive. For example, they do not include the Artemivsk[34] tank depot which was a potential source of heavy arms for the separatists and will be discussed in further detail below. Nevertheless, the maps indicate that the number of potential sources for separatist tanks and heavy artillery within the territories under their control was limited to start with.[35]

The second piece of evidence is the lack of media reports on heavy arms in separatist hands prior to June 2014. Any seizure of military bases and heavy equipment would have been a great success for the separatist movement. Pictures or videos of seized military facilities and Ukrainian tanks under separatist control would have been an important propaganda opportunity. Footage of this kind would have had the potential to boost public confidence in the

---

34 A town north of Donetsk that was renamed Bakhmut during the Ukrainian authorities' 2016 decommunization initiative. Because, in 2014, all key actors still referred to the town as Artemivsk, I will do so as well to avoid confusion.
35 The relative lack of military facilities in the Donbas also reflects the fact that Ukraine inherited its military structures from the Soviet Union, which was naturally more concerned with its western border than with the border region between the Russian and Ukrainian Soviet Republics.

separatist movement and damage the morale of the Ukrainian Armed Forces. However, before early June, reports of seized Ukrainian equipment were rare. The only notable exception was the seizure of five armored vehicles and one Nona artillery gun from a Ukrainian military unit in the Sloviansk-Kramatorsk area on April 15 (Zhuchkovskiy 2018, 68). In this case, the separatists paraded the captured vehicles through Kramatorsk and Sloviansk and numerous videos showing these vehicles are available online (YouTube 2014ak; 2014al; 2014bs; 2017b). As I argued in the previous chapter, the further escalation of fighting across the region and the seizure of additional Ukrainian military facilities around Luhansk in late May to early June was also subject to intensive media coverage. Keeping the capture of Ukrainian tanks and heavy artillery on these occasions a secret would have been not only undesirable from a propaganda perspective but also difficult in practice. Nevertheless, no additional footage of seized Ukrainian heavy arms emerged in the aftermath of these clashes. This lack of documented instances reduces the probability that separatist forces had seized tanks and heavy artillery from the Ukrainian Armed Forces before mid-June. Moreover, reports on Russian state-controlled media also concluded that, as of early June, the Donbas separatists were not in possession of tanks or heavy artillery. Pro-Kremlin newspaper *Izvestiya* reported that, as of May 31, the separatists' arsenal included only a single heavy artillery gun—presumably the Nona shown in the footage from Kramatorsk and Sloviansk from mid-April—and about ten armored vehicles (Petelin and Raskin 2014). Russian state news agency *RIA Novosti* (2014a) reported on June 6 that the separatists were trying to restore an old Soviet tank from a World War Two monument. The report claimed that this was the first tank of the separatists, who had previously only captured armored vehicles from the Ukrainian military.

The third piece of evidence is the military situation in the conflict zone at the time when tanks and heavy artillery first appeared. By early June, the territory in which separatist units could operate freely had reached its all-time maximum. During the course of the month, the Ukrainian response to separatism in the Donbas became more determined. The Kyiv authorities deployed additional forces and pushed the separatists into a defensive position. This became particularly evident in the key hotbed of fighting around Sloviansk. On June 6, the Ukrainian Armed Forces first confirmed that they had deployed tanks to the Sloviansk area (Segodnya 2014d). On June 19, Russian tabloid *Komsomolskaya Pravda* published a video appeal by Sloviansk separatist commander Igor Girkin. Looking tired and disillusioned, Girkin said that Ukrainian forces were attacking Sloviansk from all sides and that his forces were outnumbered and insufficiently equipped to withstand the attack. He finished by appealing to the Russian authorities to step in (Girkin 2014). On July 5, Girkin's forces withdrew from the Sloviansk area to Donetsk. The fact that the military tide began to turn in this way from early June onward decreases the probability that the separatists were able to seize additional Ukrainian military assets in the Donbas. It also reduces the probability that they were able to overrun Ukrainian positions and seize the tanks and heavy artillery that Kyiv deployed to the region in June.

These three pieces of evidence consist of general, high-level observations. For this reason, they cannot increase the probability of H2 far enough to justify the conclusion that most heavy arms under separatist control came from Russia. However, they neutralize the initial probabilistic advantage of H1 and shift the burden of proof into a more balanced position. This means that, when it comes to the investigation of the origins of particular tanks or heavy artillery under separatist control, neither H1 nor H2 has a head start in terms of the burden of proof. In turn, the following sections will demonstrate that the available evidence relating to such individual items strongly tilts the balance of probabilities toward H2.

8.1.2. From Siberia to the Donbas: The June 12 Tank Convoy

The first evidence of operational tanks under the control of separatist forces in eastern Ukraine emerged on June 12. On this day, two videos appeared on YouTube. Both videos show the same convoy of three tanks and two trucks carrying people in camouflage. One of the trucks is towing an artillery gun. The first video's caption says that it was filmed in the town of Torez,[36] 60 km east of

---

[36] Before 1964, this town was known as Chystiakove. The Kyiv authorities restored this name during their 2016 decommunization initiative.

Donetsk (YouTube 2014ax). This can be verified by geolocating the visible array of buildings and trees, which matches Google Earth satellite imagery of a square in the town's center between Tytova and Nikolaeva Streets. The convoy is driving along the H21 highway from east to west toward Donetsk. The second video's caption points at Makiivka, a town adjacent to the northeast of Donetsk (YouTube 2014aw). The distinctive buildings visible in this video make it possible to geolocate it to the intersection between the H21 Highway and Sverdlova Street in the town center. The convoy continues to drive west toward Donetsk.

The fact that the three tanks are approaching Donetsk from the east is a first *straw-in-the-wind* indicator (see section 3.1.2.) for their Russian origins. As of early June, the only reports of Ukrainian tank deployments referred to the Sloviansk area north of Donetsk. The only Ukrainian tank depot in the conflict zone that is documented in openly available sources was in Artemivsk, which is also north of Donetsk. Hence, the convoy could only be of Ukrainian origin if it had driven around Donetsk in a giant loop, or if the Ukrainian military had deployed and lost tanks much further east without either side reporting on it. A second piece of *straw-in-the-wind* evidence is the separatists' failure to provide a coherent explanation for the three tanks' origin. On June 9, a fringe Russian news website cited unspecified social media posts by Luhansk separatists who allegedly reported the capture of three Ukrainian tanks "in a suburb of Luhansk" after "a serious armed clash" with Ukrainian forces (Rossiiskiy Mirotvorets 2014). However, there are no other reports and no footage of armed clashes involving tanks near Luhansk from June 9 or the preceding days. Neither did the separatists provide additional information on the tanks' origins in the days that followed. On June 12, a separatist spokesperson merely confirmed that the Donetsk People's Republic (DNR) had "received" three tanks without providing any further details (RIA Novosti 2014b). Specifying the time and place of their capture and providing evidence of the tanks' origins would have been an easy and effective way to counter allegations of Russian meddling if the tanks had, indeed, been captured from Ukrainian forces.

Smoking-gun evidence (see section 3.1.2.) for the tanks' Russian origin are a series of pictures and a video discovered by pro-

Ukrainian investigative bloggers (Koshkin and Sobachkin 2016). The pictures were posted on June 12, 2014 on the social media account of a separatist fighter with the social media pseudonym "Georgiy Krymskiy". This account was active and publicly available until at least 2020. It features numerous pictures of Krymskiy with separatist fighters in 2014 — one picture shows him next to Igor Girkin and Aleksandr Boroday (Krymskiy 2014e). However, it also features newer pictures in different contexts. Some show Krymskiy in the company of what appear to be family members. Others show him partying with friends (Krymskiy n.d.). One picture shows him with Crimean "Prime Minister" Sergey Aksyonov (Krymskiy 2018). Another one shows him wearing a Russian military uniform and the medal "For the Defense of Crimea" (Krymskiy 2015; Nagrady Rossiyskoy Federatsii n.d.). Although Georgiy Krymskiy is probably a pseudonym, the diversity and level of detail of the posted pictures leave only a remote chance that they are fake. The four pictures that are important for the present chapter were posted on July 12, 2014 and show Krimskiy and other separatist fighters on a tank (Krymskiy 2014a; 2014b; 2014c; 2014d). One of the pictures has a geolocation tag from the Donetsk Oblast town of Snizhne (Krymskiy 2014b), which is located just to the east of Torez. The picture also features a building with a distinct yellow façade. The blogger who discovered the pictures identified a similar yellow façade next to a little square on Lenin Street in the center of Snizhne. Moreover, other group photos posted by Krymskiy show features of a nearby industrial plant (Koshkin and Sobachkin 2016). This geolocation is convincing and verifiable through Google Earth.

Krymskiy's photos are important because a video posted on YouTube in autumn 2014 suggests that the tank in question was provided by the Russian Armed Forces. The video shows a tank being loaded onto an An-124 transport aircraft. The caption says that the video was filmed on May 31, 2014 in Russia's Krasnoyarsk Krai. It was posted by an account whose content focuses on aviation and parachuting events in this region (YouTube 2014br). Ukrainian blogger Askai (2014) argues that the terminal and hangar buildings in the video, indeed, match the Yemelyanovo Airfield in Krasnoyarsk Krai. Google Earth imagery of this airfield suggests that this assessment is correct. In addition, Koshkin and Sobachkin (2016) argue that the Yemelyanovo tank features the same stain marks as the tank on Georgiy Krymskiy's pictures from Snizhne. This assessment is convincing as well. Both the video from Yemelyanovo and Georgiy Krymskiy's pictures provide a close-up view of the armor plates on the left-hand side of the tank's body. In both cases, the armor plates feature the same random patterns of stains. There is only a remote chance that the same level of similarity could feature on two different tanks. At the same time, it would require significant video editing efforts to seamlessly insert the complex staining pattern from the photos into the video of the tank. There is only a remote chance that pro-Ukrainian activists went to such lengths in autumn 2014, then managed to sneak the video into a YouTube account focusing on niche aviation-related content from Krasnoyarsk Krai, but then waited until 2016 to reveal the similarity. It is therefore almost certain that a tank that had been loaded onto a transport aircraft in Siberia was photographed in Ukraine's Snizhne on June 12, 2014.

It remains unclear whether this tank is one of the three tanks that were filmed driving through neighboring Torez or whether it is a fourth tank that went elsewhere. Either way, however, this tank's Russian origin, combined with the *straw-in-the-wind* evidence discussed above, suggests that it is highly likely that the three tanks and the howitzer that were filmed on the move to Donetsk on June 12 were all Russian.

8.1.3. Burning Vegetables: The June 13 Grad Attack on Dobropillia

Evidence that the first Russian heavy arms deliveries to the Donbas in mid-June were not limited to tanks appeared in the aftermath of a rocket attack on the town of Dobropillia, 55 km southwest of Sloviansk. On the morning of June 13, a local news website reported that rockets had hit a vegetable market in Dobropillia and killed a security guard (Salnychenko 2014). This report is consistent with Google Earth satellite imagery from early July 2014, which shows four holes in the roof of a building in an industrial area at the southwestern end of town. On the crowdsourced annotated cartographic platform Wikimapia, this building is marked as the "Perspektiva vegetable market." Moreover, the Google Earth imagery shows a burned-down side building and at least 19 impact craters in fields to the south and west of the site. The news report from June 13 also cites local residents who report ongoing fighting between Ukrainian and separatist forces near Nykanorivka, about 15 km east of the impact site. According to these residents, the separatist forces had approached the area from the northeast (Salnychenko 2014). In the early afternoon of June 13, another news website published pictures of a damaged Grad multiple rocket launcher that is missing 26 of its 40 rockets (Segodnya 2014e). The array of buildings visible in one of the pictures makes it possible to geolocate it to the northeastern corner of the clay storage site at the Mertsalove railway station, just west of Nykanorivka. The same Grad launcher at the same location is visible in a video published on the same day. In this video, a Ukrainian serviceman tells a journalist that two separatist Grad launchers opened fire from this location, presumably targeting a Ukrainian checkpoint on the road between Dobropillia and Sviatohorivka, but hitting the vegetable market instead. One of the launchers was withdrawn from the area while the other one broke down and was abandoned (YouTube 2014ay). This narrative is consistent with another video posted on YouTube on the following day, which can be geolocated to a location near the southwestern corner of the main building complex at the Mertsalove railway station. Two salvos of rocket fire can be heard on the footage and, during the second salvo, at least twenty rockets can be seen flying from the direction of the alleged launch site toward the west (YouTube 2014az). On the basis of this evidence, it can be considered a fact that the Grad rocket launcher on the pictures had fired at Dobropillia as part of a failed separatist advance into the area.

Pictures supposed to prove the Russian origin of the abandoned Grad launcher were posted by the Ukrainian activist group Information Resistance (2014) on June 14. In particular, one photo shows the cover page of a set of vehicle documents, which features a stamp with the Russian language inscription "Military Base 27777." Another photo shows a faint symbol in the shape of a sliced rhombus inside a square on the launcher's right door. According to Information Resistance, this symbol is an example of "poorly painted over insignia" which point at the launcher's original

Russian owners. An Internet search of "Military Base 27777" reveals that it is located in Chechnya and, in 2014, was the home of Russia's 18th Guards Motor Rifle Brigade (Voyskovye Chasti Rossii n.d.). A long blog post on this brigade, published by a Russian military enthusiast in 2011, features pictures of trucks with rhombus-square insignia on their doors. It also features pictures of Grad launchers with a similar camouflage pattern to the launcher that attacked Dobropillia (Mokrushin 2011). Nevertheless, in the absence of additional material, the pictures of the document and the faded sign on the launcher's door would only be *straw-in-the-wind* evidence of the launcher's Russian origin because both are relatively easy to fabricate. The document could have been taken from elsewhere, the camouflage pattern similarity could be a coincidence, and the symbol on the door could have been added after the launcher had been seized by the Ukrainian Armed Forces.

In the present case, however, there is additional evidence that only leaves a remote chance that the pictures are fabricated. This evidence consists of a video that was published on June 11, 2014 (YouTube 2014av) but does not feature prominently in the media discussion of the Dobropillia incident. It can be found through a reverse image search of pictures of the Grad launcher near Dobropillia. One of the search results leads to the Lost Armour project — a website documenting pictures of destroyed or damaged military hardware in the Donbas. A user comment on this page from October 2015 contains the link to the video and suggests that it might show the same Grad launcher (Lost Armour 2015). The video shows three trucks driving through a location captioned as Luhansk (YouTube 2014av). The slope and bend in the road in combination with the fence and the buildings next to it, make it possible to geolocate the footage to 1st Keramichna Street. The trucks are bypassing the city center on its southern side while driving in an east-west direction. This would be part of a logical route from the Russian border near Krasnodon[37] to the separatist-controlled areas north of Donetsk. The trucks' backs are covered by tarpaulins, so it is not

---

37 Now renamed Sorokyne as part the Ukrainian authorities' decommunization initiative. The Luhansk People's Republic (LNR), which controls the town, still refers to it as Krasnodon.

possible to see what they carry. However, the camouflage pattern on the driver's cabin of the middle truck is identical to the driver's cabin of the Grad launcher that attacked Dobropillia. Moreover, the truck in Luhansk is missing its right rear light and has a towing hitch with two protruding pieces of metal—one silver and one white. These features are also visible on the Grad launcher near Dobropillia. The right-hand door of the middle truck is not visible on the footage from Luhansk, but the left-hand door of the rear truck is marked with a red rhombus-square symbol. It is plausible that the middle truck carried the same symbol on its right-hand door and that an unsuccessful attempt to erase it left it grey and faint as it appears in the picture of the Grad launcher near Dobropillia.

The video from Luhansk turns the footage from Dobropillia into *smoking-gun* evidence. There is only a remote chance that Ukrainian forces altered footage of a captured Grad launcher within a day to match a video published two days earlier but then failed to point out the video's existence to the media sources covering the story. It is therefore highly likely that the Grad launcher that fired at Dobropillia and the middle truck of the Luhansk convoy are the same vehicle. What is almost certain is that both vehicles are part of the same delivery of military hardware which comprised at least three vehicles that used to belong to Russia's 18th Guards Motor Rifle Brigade.

8.1.4. Armor Patterns on a Russian Highway: The June 19–21 Tank Convoys

More evidence of additional Russian tank deliveries to the separatists appeared just over a week later. It consists of a series of four videos which were discovered by Ukrainian blogger Askai (2014). The first video was posted on June 20 and shows two tanks, two armored vehicles, and three trucks driving past an uncompleted building in a residential area. The video's description specifies its location as Horlivka Division Street in the town of Horlivka, 35 km northeast of Donetsk (YouTube 2014bc). A matching array of an uncompleted building between two residential buildings is clearly visible on Google Earth imagery of Horlivka Division Street between the intersections with Yaroslavska Street and Zaporizkyi

Lane. The video shows a distinct pattern of armor plates on the left-hand side of the tanks' bodies. The first tank features a line of plates which does not fully extend to the tank's rear. The first three plates are placed further apart and lower than the rest. Two single protruding plates are visible above the main row. The second tank has fewer armor plates. They are arranged in a straight line that has a gap toward the rear and only covers a small portion of the tank's side. The same patterns of armor plates are visible on two tanks photographed by Associated Press journalist Dmitry Lovetsky (2014) on June 20. According to Lovetsky, the picture was taken near the town of Yenakiieve, just southeast of Horlivka. This picture is important because it shows that the front tank has a blue number seven painted on its searchlight cover.

The second video shows two different tanks, three armored vehicles, and three trucks, one of which is towing an artillery gun. The original account which posted the video had been deleted by the time of writing but reposts from June 21, 2014 and from February 2015 are still available (YouTube 2014bd; 2015a). The video's caption claims that it was filmed in Torez on June 21, 2014. The buildings visible on the footage are not specific enough to geolocate the video. However, the video also features a red van with a Donetsk Oblast numberplate. Moreover, the military vehicles do not carry numberplates or visible insignia, apart from one of the tanks, which is flying an orange and black St. George's flag — a separatist symbol. It also has a blue number "10" painted on its searchlight cover, which is similar to the separatist tank observed in Yenakiieve and Horlivka. It can therefore be assumed that the second video was taken in Donetsk Oblast and shows military vehicles under separatist control. The tank which is flying the flag has four rows of armor plates which do not fully extend to the front and rear but cover most of its left-hand side. The second tank only features three lone armor plates near the front of its left-hand side.

The third video was posted on June 20, and shows a convoy of six trucks carrying five tanks next to a major highway. The convoy is accompanied by a police van in the back and a police car and a silver 4x4 vehicle in the front (YouTube 2014bb). Despite the low video quality, it is clearly visible that the amor plates on the two rear tanks are a perfect match for the two tanks filmed in Horlivka and Yenakiieve. The armor plate patterns on the two front tanks, on the other hand, are a perfect match for the tanks in the second video. As Askai (2014) points out, the blue stripe on the accompanying police vehicles matches the markings of Russia's Military Transport Police. This claim can be verified through a simple Google Image search of the term.

The fourth video shows the first three tank-carrying trucks of the same convoy as well as the 4x4 vehicle and the police car at the convoy's front (YouTube 2014bk). The video was posted on July 11, but its description says that it was filmed on June 19 on the M4 highway in Russia's Rostov Oblast. This geolocation can be verified through a road sign indicating a highway exit toward the Rostov Oblast town of Gornyy that is visible in the video. The road lane layout, the patterns of trees and fields, and the service station next to the highway match Google Earth satellite imagery of the M4 highway exit two kilometers northwest of Gornyy. Moreover, the vehicles' numberplates match the layout of Russian numberplates and the letters RF (Russian Federation) are visible on the police car in front of the convoy. Although this fourth and final video was posted a few weeks after the event, the described level of detail only leaves a remote chance that it is fake.

Hence, the four videos discussed suggest that it is almost certain that four tanks transported along a highway in Russia's Rostov Oblast under the supervision of Russian military police were filmed under separatist control in the Donbas, on June 20 and 21. In turn, it is highly likely that the fifth tank of the Rostov Oblast convoy ended up in Ukraine as well and that the armored vehicles, the trucks, and the artillery gun that accompanied the tanks in Ukraine also came from Russia.

8.1.5. The Artemivsk Tank Depot: An Implausible Source

The appearance of the June 20–21 tank convoys coincided with a more specific attempt by the Donbas separatists to explain their possession of heavy arms. This attempt focused on a Ukrainian military base in the town of Artemivsk that acted as a storage facility for tanks. The tanks had been out of service for many years and their exact condition remains unclear, but it makes sense to assume that many of them were either still operational or easy to repair. On 19–20 June, several pro-separatist media outlets claimed that separatist forces had captured the base (Novyy Den 2014; colonelcassad 2014a; Vesti.ru 2014). Although a separatist spokesperson soon denied these reports (Vesti.ru 2014), the Artemivsk tank base continued to feature as a supposed key source of captured tanks and heavy artillery in the separatist narrative over the following years (Interfax 2019).

However, the Ukrainian Armed Forces deny that the separatists ever gained control of the base. Ukrainian military historian Mykhailo Zhyrokhov (2016a) spoke to several soldiers present at the base, who told him about several failed seizure attempts between mid-April and late June. The account of Zhyrokhov's sources is in line with reports published on a local Artemivsk news website on June 20 and 27 in the immediate aftermath of separatist attacks on the tank depot (Pyvovarova 2014a; 2014b). The website's correspondents published pictures of damage to adjacent buildings but reported that the base continued to be under the control of the Ukrainian Armed Forces. Moreover, Sloviansk separatist commander Igor Girkin (2015) also confirmed in an interview that separatist forces never captured the Artemivsk base. He claimed that his own men made a first unsuccessful attempt shortly after they first seized Sloviansk. Girkin then said that subsequent attempts to seize the depot were made not by him but by Horlivka separatist commander Igor Bezler, who, rather than capturing any Ukrainian tanks, lost one of his own tanks in the process. Girkin did not specify the origin of Bezler's lost tank, but, given that two tanks of Russian origin were filmed in Horlivka on June 20, his account is plausible. In any case, the consistent accounts of Ukrainian servicemen, local journalists, and Igor Girkin, combined with the absence of additional evidence to the contrary, leave only a remote chance that separatist forces seized any heavy arms from the Artemivsk depot.

8.2. Losing Territory, but Gaining Tanks: The Separatists in July 2014

In early July, the military pressure on the separatists increased further, which made the seizure of tanks and heavy artillery from the

Ukrainian Armed Forces even more difficult. On July 6, the separatists' window of opportunity to seize tanks in Artemivsk closed once and for all. On this day, Ukrainian forces took complete control over the town and the surrounding area (Ukrainska Pravda 2014n). A day earlier, Igor Girkin's forces had abandoned the Sloviansk-Kramatorsk area north of Artemivsk and withdrawn to Donetsk (Interfax 2014). At the same time, Ukrainian forces advanced along the Russian-Ukrainian border south of Donetsk and reached the southeast of Luhansk Oblast (Zhyrokhov 2017). In the west of Luhansk Oblast, preparations began for an offensive that would force separatist units to withdraw from Sievierodonetsk and Lysychansk in the second half of July (Svetikov 2017).

However, as the military pressure on the separatists increased across the battlefields, so did their arsenal of heavy arms. Three videos posted on YouTube on July 4 show a convoy of five tanks passing through a residential neighborhood in the northeast of the Luhansk Oblast town of Krasnodon, about 15 km away from the Izvaryne border crossing (YouTube 2014be; 2014bg; 2014bf). A precise geolocation is possible because of a distinct little church in a field next to a roundabout with overhead wires for trolleybuses. On July 13, a video was posted showing a large separatist convoy driving along Oboronna Street in Luhansk toward the north (YouTube 2014bl). Distinct buildings on the footage make a precise geolocation possible. The convoy consisted of five tanks, seven armored vehicles, one Grad multiple rocket launcher, one truck-mounted antiaircraft gun, and five towed artillery guns. On July 15, a video was posted showing three tanks, three Gvozdika self-propelled howitzers, and one armored vehicle near a petrol station north of Yenakiieve (YouTube 2014bm). The tanks have the numbers 35, 38, and 36 painted in white on their searchlight covers. On July 16, Russian state TV aired a report from a Vostok Battalion base at an undisclosed location "a few kilometres away from Donetsk" (YouTube 2014bn). The footage shows tanks with the numbers "30", "40", and "41" painted on their searchlight covers. It also shows a fourth tank with an illegible number as well as two Nona self-propelled artillery guns. It is possible that the July 4 footage from Krasnodon, the July 13 footage from Luhansk, and the July 15–16 footage from near Donetsk show the same tanks. However, the videos from near Donetsk alone show six distinct tanks. The armor plate patterns of these tanks and the numbers painted on them are different from the tanks filmed in late June. Moreover, it is likely that the tanks' numbers were added by the separatists. Neither the Ukrainian nor the Russian armed forces are known to number their tanks in this way. Hence, it is likely that, by mid-July, the separatists had at least 41 tanks at their disposal. In addition, they possessed heavy artillery systems, including at least three Gvozdika howitzers.

There is no *smoking-gun* evidence that links the military hardware of early July to Russia. However, the clear evidence of Russian arms deliveries in mid- and late June and the unfavorable military situation of the separatists in early July have shifted the burden of proof. In the absence of evidence of a Ukrainian origin of separatist hardware, it must be considered likely that the separatists obtained their new arms of early July from Russia as well.

Moreover, there is additional circumstantial evidence that speaks for a continuation and intensification of Russian arms deliveries in early to mid-July. This evidence tilts the overall balance of probabilities even further toward H2. It is presented in the final section of this chapter.

8.3. Russia's Envoys and the Downing of MH17

In early to mid-July, three Russian citizens with links to state structures appeared in Donetsk and Luhansk. One of them admitted on camera that Russia was supplying heavy arms to the separatists. The other two stayed to become senior separatist officials. Their appearance not only coincided with the sightings of military hardware described in the previous section but also with the downing of Malaysian Airlines flight MH17 by a Russian missile launcher.

8.3.1. Civil Society's Tanks: Sergey Kurginyan in Donetsk

On July 7, Sergey Kurginyan, leader of the Russian Soviet restorationist movement Sut Vremeny visited Donetsk. His visit featured a press conference during which he entered a heated argument with Donetsk "People's Governor" Pavlo Hubariev and two members of Igor Girkin's group, who had left Sloviansk two days earlier. A recording of the exchange is available on YouTube (2014bh). The separatists complain about a lack of supplies from Russia. Kurginyan argues that such criticism is only partly justified. He admits that heavy arms deliveries organized by "Russian civil society"[38] were initially rare and of poor quality but that "the situation improved significantly over the last two-three weeks" (YouTube 2014bh at 37:40). One of the separatists responds by saying that Girkin's group only received three tanks and three armored vehicles while holding Sloviansk (YouTube 2014bh at 38:30). Kurginyan concedes that Russian support for the separatist cause is still insufficient and promises additional arms supplies (YouTube 2014bh at 43:00).

It remains unclear to what extent Kurginyan was personally involved in the organization of Russian weapons deliveries and to what extent he was able to lobby the Kremlin in this regard. However, it is appropriate to assume that both he and the separatists he talks to possess a certain degree of insider knowledge.[39] At the same time, they agree that Russian weapons deliveries picked up speed in June but need to be increased further in light of the dire military situation. Hence, their discussion further increases the burden of proof for those who argue that supplies of heavy weapons for separatist units in early July did not come from Russia. The hypothesis that Russia acted in line with the separatists' pleas and Kurginyan's predictions is a more plausible explanation than the hypothesis that Russia suddenly stopped its deliveries while the separatists suddenly started to succeed in seizing Ukrainian weapons.

8.3.2. Appoint More Russians: The Separatist Administrations in Early July

Additional evidence that Russia increased rather than decreased its involvement in the Donbas after the withdrawal from Sloviansk were the successive appointments of two Russian citizens to senior

---

38 This is an obvious euphemism. The idea that Russian non-state actors were able to send heavy weapons to Ukraine without the knowledge and approval of the state is ridiculous and does not merit further discussion.
39 Some Sut Vremeni activists had been collaborating with separatist activists in Donetsk as early as April (see chapter four), and some were fighting in leading positions in the Vostok Battalion (YouTube 2014bj).

positions in both the DNR and the Luhansk People's Republic (LNR). In Donetsk, "Prime Minister" Boroday introduced Vladimir Antyufeyev, at a July 10 press conference, as his new "first deputy prime minister." During the press conference, Antyufeyev confirmed that he had just arrived from Russia, and that he would be responsible for "state security, internal affairs, customs, and the courts" (YouTube 2014bi from 14:15). Antyufeyev's imminent arrival was also mentioned in an intercepted phone conversation between Boroday and Russian Presidential Adviser Vladislav Surkov from July 3 (JIT 2019b from 10:16). Antyufeyev is a Russian citizen and a former Soviet riot police officer, who was "state security minister" of the Moldovan breakaway region of Transnistria between 1992 and 2012. According to the Russian news website *Nakanune.ru*, Antufeyev also admitted during an interview on DNR television on July 16, 2014 that he had participated in the Russian takeover of Crimea in March (Chernyshev 2014). This is consistent with information which the Moldovan investigative journalist collective RISE Moldova obtained from the Ukrainian authorities. According to this information, Antyufeyev travelled to Simferopol on March 7, 2014 (RISE Moldova 2019 at 5:30). Moreover, the journalists found an entry in a Russian companies register, which suggests that, since 2013, Antyufeyev had been deputy general director of ODK – a company producing engine parts for the Russian Air Force and Navy (RISE Moldova 2019 from 10:07). Information published by the Russian Aviation Industry Workers Union (2017) confirms this. A report on the union's website on a March 2017 meeting between union officials and the ODK leadership lists Antyufeyev as an ODR deputy director. The report also includes a photo of Antyufeyev, which proves that the ODR deputy director and the former DNR "first deputy prime minister" are the same person.

In Luhansk, another Russian citizen, Marat Bashirov, was appointed LNR "prime minister." According to the Russian news website *Gazeta.ru*, Bashirov worked as a senior manager in the company empire of oligarch Viktor Vekselberg and specialized in political communication before his appointment in the Donbas (Dergachev 2014). Like Antyufeyev, Bashirov returned to Russia before the end of 2014 and continued to pursue a career in the orbit of state institutions. As of late 2020, he frequently appeared as a political analyst and commentator on Russian state-controlled media (RIA Novosti n.d.; Radio Komsomolskaya Pravda n.d.).

Antyufeyev's and Bashirov's appointment to leading positions in the separatist "republics" was almost certainly approved by the Russian authorities. Evidence of this is their work for businesses with close links to the Russian state before their time in the Donbas and their successful careers in the orbit of the Russian state after their return. In turn, this further increase in Russian involvement in the DNR and LNR's administrations is more compatible with a simultaneous increase in Russian weapons deliveries than with a sudden stop of such deliveries in July.

8.3.3. MH17

Shortly after Kurginyan's visit and Antyufeyev's and Bashirov's appointments, a Russian BUK missile launcher shot down Malaysian Airlines flight MH17 over the conflict zone. This war crime is arguably the most scrutinized episode of the 2014 Donbas War. The death of 298 civilians led to a surge in political and media attention. At the same time, the case contributed greatly to the rise of journalistic digital open source investigations. In particular, it brought to fame the Bellingcat research collective, which, long before the results of any official investigation, presented evidence that a BUK missile launcher that had entered the region from Russia was responsible for the downing of the aircraft (Allen et al. 2014; Bellingcat 2015d; Allen et al. 2016). Later, the Joint Investigation Committee (JIT), consisting of law enforcement officials and forensic experts from the Netherlands, Australia, Malaysia, and Ukraine, published several reports that confirmed Bellingcat's conclusions beyond reasonable doubt. It established that flight MH17 had been shot down by a BUK missile launcher belonging to Russia's 53rd Antiaircraft Missile Brigade. The launcher left the brigade's home base near Kursk on June 23 and was brought to a location near the Russian-Ukrainian border near the town of Millerovo. It probably entered Ukraine during the night of July 16–17 and was brought to Donetsk. On July 17, it drove to a field near Snizhne where it fired the missile that downed the airliner. After the incident, the missile launcher was quickly evacuated back to Russia (JIT 2016a; 2016b; 2016c; 2018).

It is neither necessary nor appropriate to reassess the large volume of videos showing the missile launcher on its way to and from the launch site in clearly identifiable locations on both Russian and Ukrainian territory in this chapter. The same is the case for the large number of intercepted phone calls discussing the event. There is not even a remote chance that this extensive and diverse body of consistent and unequivocal evidence has been fabricated and that Bellingcat and the JIT did not notice this or actively participated in it. At the same time, a BUK is a more sophisticated weapons system than the tanks and artillery systems observed in the Donbas in mid- and late June. For this reason, the BUK missile launcher that destroyed MH17 is additional *smoking-gun* evidence that Russia had stepped up rather than scaled down its arms deliveries to the Donbas by mid-July.

8.4. Chapter Conclusion

This chapter has found overwhelming evidence that the Russian authorities were the key driving force behind the appearance of tanks and heavy artillery under separatist control between June and July 2014. It has established that it is *almost certain* that:

- A tank that was photographed in the Donbas town of Snizhne on June 12 had previously been filmed while being loaded onto a Russian military cargo plane in Krasnoyarsk Krai.
- A Grad multiple rocket launcher belonging to Russia's 18th Guards Motor Rifle Brigade fired at a vegetable market in Dobropillia on June 13.
- Four tanks that feature in footage from the Donbas that was published on June 20–21 were previously filmed while being carried along a highway in Russia's Rostov Oblast with a Russian Military Transport Police escort.
- A BUK missile launcher belonging to Russia's 53rd Antiaircraft Missile Brigade shot down Malaysian Airlines flight MH17 over the conflict zone on July 17.

In addition to these vehicles, footage from the Donbas from mid-June to mid-July features at least eight tanks, seven towed artillery guns, three Gvozdika self-propelled howitzers, one Grad multiple rocket launcher, and one truck-mounted antiaircraft gun. Although there is no direct evidence linking these vehicles to Russia, the cumulation of the following pieces of circumstantial evidence makes it *highly likely* that most if not all of them originated from Russia as well:

- The additional items appeared in the same time period as the vehicles that could be traced back to Russia.
- Although the separatists had a clear incentive to use the seizure of Ukrainian equipment for propaganda purposes, they did not provide any plausible explanation, let alone convincing evidence, for the origin of their military hardware. Their only elaborate justification attempt—the supposed seizure of hardware from the Artemivsk tank depot—is almost certainly false.
- Tanks and heavy artillery under separatist control appeared in the Donbas at a time when the Ukrainian military was starting to operate against the separatist forces in a more coordinated manner and pushed them into a defensive position. In these circumstances, the likelihood of separatist forces being able to overrun Ukrainian military units and seizing their equipment was lower than in April or May. And even in April and May, such equipment seizures had been rare and included only one Nona artillery gun and no tanks.
- Russian pro-separatist activist Sergey Kurginyan and separatist fighters openly discussed Russian heavy arms deliveries in Donetsk in early July.
- Russia further increased its direct involvement in the DNR and LNR's administrations in early July through the appointment of Vladimir Antyufeyev and Marat Bashirov—Russian citizens with links to Russia's defense industry and state-controlled media—to senior positions.

At the same time, the separatist forces also had a clear incentive to hide the true scale of their heavy arms supplies from Russia in order to maintain the image of a poorly equipped local insurrection. For this reason, it is likely that only a fraction of the supplied tanks and heavy artillery were caught on camera and that supply levels far exceeded the items listed above. One possible indicator of the scale of Russian arms deliveries are the numbers painted on tanks filmed in Donetsk in mid-July (YouTube 2014bn). The number "41" on one of the tanks suggests that, by mid-July, the separatists had received at least 41 tanks. However, this number, as well as the number of heavy artillery items, remains difficult to verify. But whatever the true number may be, for the reasons outlined above, it is *highly likely* that Russia supplied the overwhelming majority of tanks and heavy artillery guns used by separatist forces in the Donbas in summer 2014. This means that, in the context of the critical juncture examined in this chapter, H2 can be considered confirmed while H1 should be discarded.

However, Russia's role in the escalation of the Donbas War did not end with the supply of tanks and heavy artillery to its own irregular forces. Throughout the course of July, Russia intensified its involvement further. First, it began to shell Ukrainian positions from across the border. Later, it sent regular military units to the Donbas to end the Ukrainian advance. But these events are part of another critical juncture and will be the subject of this book's final empirical chapter.

9. The Tide Turns
The Ukrainian Defeat of August 2014

This chapter will investigate the final critical juncture in the Donbas War's formative escalation sequence—the defeat of the advancing Ukrainian forces in late August 2014. In particular, I will investigate to what extent Russia further intensified its involvement in the conflict during this critical juncture by deploying its regular armed forces to the Donbas. I will address claims of Russian cross-border shelling and the alleged deployment of paratroopers from Pskov to Luhansk in mid-August, before focusing on the three key battles lost by Ukrainian forces in late August. I will argue that there is overwhelming evidence of the presence of regular Russian forces in the Donbas at the time in question. Furthermore, I will argue that these regular Russian forces played more than just an auxiliary role in support of the Russian-led separatists.[40] Instead, the available evidence indicates that the involvement of regular Russian forces was the primary cause of the Ukrainian defeat.

Ukrainian forces continued to increase the pressure on the Russian-led separatists over the summer of 2014. By mid-August, the position of the two self-proclaimed republics looked precarious. In Luhansk Oblast, Ukrainian forces had not only retaken Sievierodonetsk and Lysychansk but also Lutuhyne just south of Luhansk city (Svetikov 2017; informator.lg.ua 2014; colonelcassad 2014b). This meant that Luhansk was close to being surrounded, with Ukrainian forces positioned in its immediate surroundings to the north, west, and south. In Donetsk Oblast, Ukrainian forces were attacking Ilovaisk from the south and gained a foothold in the town's western part on August 18 (Donbas Battalion 2014). Taking Ilovaisk would have been an important step toward the encirclement of the Donetsk metropolitan area, and toward cutting off the supply chains from Russia.

---

40 The cumulative evidence of Russian involvement outlined in chapters five, seven, and eight suggests that it is appropriate to describe the separatist forces that were fighting the Ukrainian military in summer 2014 as Russian-led.

Two weeks later, however, the situation had changed completely. By early September, Ukrainian forces had been forced to abandon their positions south and west of Luhansk. At Ilovaisk, Ukraine had suffered the most devastating defeat of the entire conflict so far. Its forces had been encircled in the town's southwestern surroundings. More than 350 soldiers and volunteer battalion members died[41] during the siege and the unsuccessful attempt to break out of it.[42] As a result, Ukrainian forces no longer controlled the southern and southeastern surroundings of Donetsk. In addition, a new front had opened on the southern coast, where Ukrainian forces had lost control of the border and the town of Novoazovsk and the enemy was advancing toward Mariupol. Against the backdrop of this dramatic military turnaround, Ukraine agreed to the terms of the First Minsk Agreement on September 5.

The Ukrainian military claimed that its resounding defeat in late August was the result of a large-scale invasion by Russia's regular armed forces (Ostrov 2014r; Segodnya 2014g) — a claim which Russia denied and continues to deny. Against the backdrop of these claims and the findings of the previous chapters, a process tracing analysis of the Ukrainian defeat in late August 2014 should test three hypotheses.

---

41 For a thorough discussion of different casualty estimates, see Teslenko and Tynchenko (2019). Yaroslav Tynchenko is the deputy director of Ukraine's National Military History Museum and a co-founder of the Memory Book for Ukraine's Fallen volunteer project — the most authoritative source on Ukraine's losses in the Donbas up to 2022. According to Tynchenko, a total of 366 Ukrainian soldiers and volunteer battalion members died in the Ilovaisk area from August 7–31, 2014. Most of them, a total of 254, died during the failed attempt to leave the area on August 29.

42 The exact circumstances of the withdrawal attempt on August 29 continue to be a contentious topic. Two participants of the events — journalist Rostyslav Shaposhnikov and Ukrainian officer Serhii Naselevets — blame the commander of Ukraine's forces around Ilovaisk — General Ruslan Khomchak — for the tragedy (Shaposhnikov 2014). They argue that Khomchak ordered his forces to break out of the encirclement while negotiations with the enemy regarding a safe passage corridor were still ongoing. Khomchak refuses to publicly comment on the details of the events. However, he confirmed that the Russian military demanded that his forces surrender all weapons before withdrawing, which, according to him, was unacceptable (Khomchak 2019 from 23:12).

H1: Irregular Russian-led separatists defeated the advancing Ukrainian forces without involvement from Russia beyond the level described in the previous chapters.

Figure 16: No Involvement of Regular Russian Forces

Source: the author

H2: Russia stepped up its involvement by sending some regular troops to Ukraine, which played an auxiliary role in the Ukrainian defeat.

Figure 17: Limited Involvement of Regular Russian Forces

Source: the author

H3: Russia stepped up its involvement and engaged its regular armed forces to an extent that was decisive for the Ukrainian defeat.

Figure 18: Decisive Involvement of Regular Russian Forces

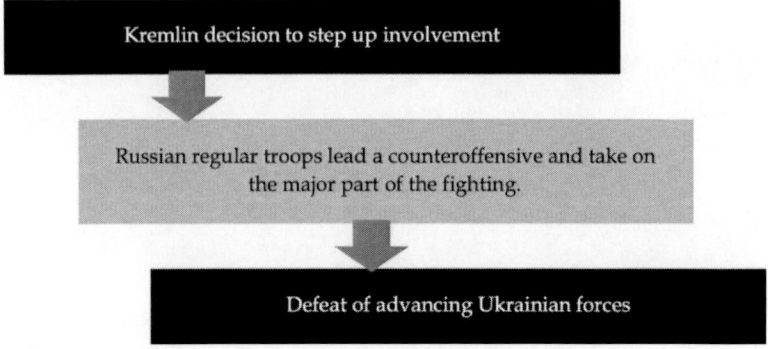

Source: the author

9.1. Prologue I: Cross-Border Shelling

Allegations that Ukrainian forces became the target of artillery shelling from Russian territory throughout July and August are a first *hoop test* (see section 3.1.2.) for H1. Regardless of the degree to which they contributed to the Ukrainian defeat in late August, attacks on Ukrainian positions by units operating from Russian territory would represent an escalation of the conflict beyond its previous limits. Also, cross-border combat operations of this kind would almost certainly involve regular Russian forces.

The first major instance of an alleged cross-border artillery attack was the shelling of Ukrainian positions near the Luhansk Oblast village of Zelenopillia on July 11 (Ukrainska Pravda 2014o). This attack killed 36 Ukrainian servicemen – the second largest loss of the Ukrainian Armed Forces in a single incident during the conflict so far.[43] In January 2015, pro-Ukrainian conflict analyst Dajey-Petros published a blog post in which he wrote that the origin of

---

[43] Up to July 11, the only single incident with a higher death toll had been the downing of a Ukrainian IL-76 military transport plane near Luhansk Airport on June 14, in which 49 servicemen died. The casualty data for both incidents was taken from the Memory Book for Ukraine's Fallen project (Memorybook.org.ua n.d.a).

the Zelenopillia attack was visible on Google Earth satellite imagery (Ukraine@war 2015). He correctly pointed out that, on satellite imagery from mid-August, burn marks are visible in a field south of the village of Klunykove, just a few hundred meters inside Ukrainian territory. Moreover, several vehicle tracks are visible in the field between these burn marks and the Russian border. The marks on the ground are arranged in a row and their shape is compatible with the traces left by fire from Grad multiple rocket launchers or similar systems. The marks' shape, with a narrower end in the northeast and a wider end in the southwest, suggests that the missiles were fired toward the northeast. Moreover, an imaginary line that extends the burn marks' approximate axis of symmetry to the northeast points directly at the destroyed military camp near Zelenopillia.

Additional investigations suggest that the Zelenopillia attack was followed by hundreds of other incidents of cross-border shelling. Bellingcat (2015c, 19–21) confirmed DajeyPetros' findings regarding the Zelenopillia attack in a report that focused on cross-border vehicle tracks on satellite imagery of the conflict zone. In addition, it also published two separate reports dedicated exclusively to the analysis of Russian artillery shelling of Ukrainian positions along the border (Bellingcat 2015b; Case and Anders 2016). In these reports, Bellingcat analyzed the shape and location of impact craters on satellite imagery to match them with "likely firing positions." In total, the researchers identified 279 such positions, 262 of which were located on Russian territory and 17 on Ukrainian territory within 2 km of the border (Case and Anders 2016, 16). Bellingcat then visualized these findings, using the carto mapping tool to link likely firing positions and targets on a map (Bellingcat n.d.b). This visualization shows that cross-border artillery attacks focused on two areas southeast of Donetsk—around Amvrosiivka and Marynivka. A smaller number of attacks took place in the southeastern corner of Luhansk Oblast near the town of Dovzhansk. This was the area in which the Ukrainian attempt to secure the entirety of the border by advancing along it ground to a halt (Zhyrokhov 2017).

There is no reason to doubt Bellingcat's findings. Due to space and time constraints, it was not possible to use Google Earth to check the accuracy of all their assessments in this book. However, considering the group's elaborate description of its methodology and internal peer review process as well as its record of providing high-quality digital open source investigations, it is appropriate to have a high degree of confidence in the reports' findings. Moreover, even if Bellingcat was wrong more than 50 percent of the time, this would still leave more than 100 cases of cross-border artillery attacks. It is therefore appropriate to conclude that the artillery of the Russian Armed Forces almost certainly attacked Ukrainian forces from across or just within the border in a regular and systematic manner from mid-July onward.

The presented evidence of Russian artillery attacks means that H1 can be discarded. It suggests that, even before the battles of late August, Russia had stepped up its involvement beyond the level described in the previous chapters. By doing so, it inflicted damage on Ukrainian positions and made it more difficult for Ukrainian forces to establish control over strategically important areas along the border. There can be no doubt that this contributed to the eventual Ukrainian defeat, at least to a certain extent. However, it was not the decisive factor because most fighting in late August took place further away from the border. For this reason, the presented evidence of cross-border shelling does not affect the balance of probability between H2 and H3.

9.2. Prologue II: The Pskov Paratroopers

The first convincing evidence of systematic Russian troop deployments deeper into Ukrainian territory relates to armed clashes south of Luhansk on August 19–20. On the morning of August 22, 2014, the Ukrainian news website *Espreso TV* reposted images from the Facebook page of Ukrainian war correspondent Roman Bochkala (Ostafiichuk 2014). The images show an armored vehicle, Russian bank cards and identity documents, a personnel list with 60 names and ranks, as well as other equipment. Bochkala wrote that these items had been left behind after an armed clash near the village of Heorhiivka, located between Lutuhyne and Luhansk Airport. He also claimed that the vehicle and the documents belonged to a paratrooper unit from the Russian town of Pskov. The *Espreso*

TV report further specified that the unit in question was Russia's 76th Guards Air Assault Division based in Pskov. It also claimed that it had found the social media profiles of 17 soldiers whose names featured on the lists and documents found in Heorhiivka.

These claims from Ukrainian sources were subsequently confirmed by Russian journalists. On August 25, correspondents of the Russian newspapers *Pskovskaya Guberniya* and *Novaya Gazeta* visited the cemetery in the village of Vybuty near Pskov (Petlyanova 2014; Semenov 2014). They wanted to investigate rumors that Russian soldiers who had died in Ukraine would be buried there. The journalists saw numerous soldiers gathered for a memorial service and found the fresh graves of two men — Leonid Yuryevich Kichatkin and Aleksandr Osipov. The photos of Kichatkin's grave published by the journalists feature a picture of a young man in military uniform. According to the inscription on the grave, he died on August 19. The photos of Osipov's grave feature a wreath with a dedication from his fellow paratroopers. His date of death is given as August 20. Osipov's name does not seem to feature in the documents published in Ukraine several days earlier. The name Leonid Yuryevich Kichatkin, however, features as number "15" on the personnel list published by Roman Bochkala after the armed clash near Heorhiivka.

The claims were also confirmed by Russian journalists' sources in the Russian Armed Forces. *Pskovskaya Guberniya* editor in chief Lev Shlosberg (2014) was told by sources in the Russian military that Kichatkin and several of his comrades had left for Ukraine on August 15–16. According to Shlosberg's sources, they had terminated their contract with the Russian military "by mutual agreement" and signed a new contract with an unknown third party before setting off.[44] Research by Russian opposition TV channel *Dozhd* (2014) over the following weeks established the identities

---

44 Regardless of its veracity, this claim does not affect the categorization of the men in question as regular Russian soldiers. Even under the assumption that they signed corresponding paperwork and went to the Donbas of their own free will, the Russian military still tolerated the fact that its regular soldiers went to Ukraine on a combat mission. The argument that Russian servicemen "took leave" or "resigned" just before their deployment to the Donbas War should be rejected as a legalistic attempt to cover up state responsibility.

of four other servicemen of the 76th Guards Air Assault Division who had died in unknown circumstances. *Dozhd* also found three other servicemen of the same division, who had stopped responding to relatives and friends in mid-August and only got back in touch after rumors started that they had died in Ukraine. In addition, in early September, *Pskovskaya Guberniya* (2014) published transcripts of what it claimed were recorded conversations between members of the Russian military after the events. The newspaper said it had no reason to doubt the veracity of these transcripts. The transcripts refer to rumors that 90 Russian soldiers fought in Heorhiivka, but that only ten survived. However, the people speaking do not seem to be sure about the exact figures, so they may well be exaggerations even if the transcripts are authentic.

The sum of this confirmatory evidence from Russian media sources suggests that there is less than a remote chance that the Ukrainian military fabricated the evidence featured in the August 22 *Espreso TV* report. In turn, it is almost certain that several soldiers serving in Russia's 76th Guards Air Assault Division were fighting against Ukrainian forces at Heorhiivka on August 19–20, and it is likely that their actual number amounted to several dozen. Like the evidence of cross-border artillery shelling, this evidence is incompatible with H1 because it indicates a degree of Russian involvement that had not been observed previously. However, since this initial deployment of paratroopers turned out to be unsuccessful, it cannot affect the balance of probability between H2 and H3, either.

9.3. The Battle of Ilovaisk

The first convincing evidence for H3 and against H2 emerges in the context of the Battle of Ilovaisk. As the most devastating defeat of Ukraine's armed forces and its volunteer battalions, this battle is the most important component of the critical juncture investigated in this chapter. At the same time, it is also the part of the critical juncture that has been subject to highest level of public interest and journalistic scrutiny. As a result, a large quantity of information on this battle is available online.

This evidence has been gathered, verified, and visualized in 2018-2019 by the Forensic Architecture research agency as part of a project that documented the course of the battle and Russia's role in it (Forensic Architecture 2019b). I was one of two Ukraine specialists who worked on the project and who were responsible for gathering, cross-checking, and geolocating evidence. Our final catalogue included just over 200 primary pieces of evidence in the form of videos, photos, and eyewitness testimony. We then linked these sources to a series of 135 events. Forensic Architecture's software developers placed these events and the underlying source material on an interactive online platform, which features a map, a timeline, and the opportunity to filter the evidence in line with certain themes (Forensic Architecture 2019a). By locating these events in time and space, the platform turns a lose conglomerate of claims into an interconnected grid. The links between the different points on this grid strengthen the credibility of the underlying evidence and create a clear picture of Russia's involvement in the battle.

Due to space constraints, it is not possible to describe the whole dataset of evidence and events in the present chapter. However, the key takeaways of Forensic Architecture's Ilovaisk project are the following:

- Video and photo material showed several damaged or destroyed tanks in the surroundings of Ilovaisk after the battle. Forensic Architecture's visual modelling specialists used a 3-D computer model to identify four of these tanks as T-72B3s — a recent modification of the T-72, which, at the time of the battle, was used exclusively by the Russian Armed Forces. Moreover, independent military experts identified another two destroyed tanks as T-72BA or T-72B Obr.1989 — previous modifications of the T-72, which had never been exported to Ukraine, either.
- During the Battle of Ilovaisk, Ukrainian forces captured 17 servicemen, who said they were members of the Russian Armed Forces. Russia's military leadership claimed that some of these soldiers had lost their way and entered Ukraine by accident while others had supposedly left the armed forces and fought in Ukraine as volunteers. However, the soldiers' own testimony, their social media profiles, as well as reports on Russian media, contradict this

claim and suggest that several of them resumed their military service after their return to Russia.
- Ukrainian forces advanced toward Ilovaisk from the south and established a foothold on the western edge of the town. Positions of the self-proclaimed Donetsk People's Republic (DNR) were located toward the north and in the town itself. On August 24, 2014, Ukrainian forces around Ilovaisk were attacked from the rear and encircled. All territory in this direction had previously been under Ukrainian control — right up to the nearby Russian border. After Ukrainian forces suddenly lost control over this territory, Google Earth satellite imagery caught pictures of military convoys moving between the area south of the line of encirclement and a remote stretch of the Russian-Ukrainian border. Additional vehicles as well as traces of camps were visible directly across the border on Russian territory.

Given that the Battle of Ilovaisk involved several thousand soldiers and several hundred pieces of armor, the presence of six destroyed or damaged Russian tanks and 17 captured Russian servicemen would theoretically be compatible with both H2 and H3. However, the overall losses that Ukrainian forces managed to inflict on the enemy during the Battle were relatively small. In addition to the six Russian tanks, only a handful of destroyed armored vehicles which did not belong to Ukrainian forces were documented around Ilovaisk, and there were no reports of captured or killed separatist fighters of Ukrainian origin in the area. Hence, H2 could only be true if regular Russian forces lost a far higher share of their men and hardware than the Russian-led separatists they supported. In light of Russia's military superiority at the time, and the defeats separatist forces had suffered over the weeks preceding the battle, this appears highly unlikely. In terms of informal Bayesian analysis (see sections 3.1.4. and 3.4.3.2.), this consideration shifts the overall balance of probabilities toward H3, but not to an extent that renders H2 entirely implausible.

However, the satellite imagery of troop movements between the Russian border and the battlefield is *smoking-gun* evidence (see section 3.1.2.) that shifts the balance of probabilities even further toward H3. The Russian cross-border supply line is clearly visible on Google Earth, even though the imagery's coverage of the relevant time window is patchy. There are three available snapshots of the area south of Ilovaisk — one from August 26, one from August 31, and one from September 3. The September 3 footage alone, however, shows two large convoys comprising a total of 138 vehicles moving through Ukrainian territory toward the Russian border. Considering the patchiness of the footage, it is highly likely that the Russian invasion force was considerably larger than these two convoys and that most Russian troop movements were not caught on Google Earth. This suggests that the total size of the Russian invasion force comprised several hundred vehicles and far outnumbered both Ukrainian and DNR forces in the area. As a result, the probability of H2 decreases to a *remote chance*. At the same time, it becomes *almost certain* that it was the actions of regular units of the Russian Armed Forces, which crossed the border in large numbers and attacked Ukrainian positions from the rear, that led to the Ukrainian defeat at Ilovaisk.

9.4. The Battle of Luhansk

The evidence of Russia's role in the defeat of Ukrainian forces south of Luhansk is similar to the evidence found around Ilovaisk. Even though no Russian servicemen were captured around Luhansk, social media footage indicates that tank units of the Russian Armed Forces were present in the area. In October 2014, a VK account under the name Vitalek Marakasov posted a photo of a man in camouflage pointing at a road sign. At the time of writing, the account is no longer publicly available. However, screenshots of the account and a thorough analysis of the posted content have been published by the Ukrainian investigative blogger Askai (2015) and by the Ukrainian open source research collective Inform Napalm (2014). Askai points out that, in the foreground of the picture, the loading device of the antiaircraft machine gun of a T-90A battle tank can be seen. Indeed, the components on the picture are an exact match for the components on the T-90A, as photographed by military blogger Vitaliy Kuzmin (2014) during a Russian arms exhibition. The T-90A is a Russian tank model that entered service during the 1990s and was not used by the Ukrainian Armed Forces. At the same time, the road sign in the background proves that the picture was taken in Ukraine, near a junction of the M04 highway south of Luhansk. It features the letters M04 and indicates two highway exits—one to the right, going north toward Luhansk, and another to the left, going south toward Krasnyy Luch. In addition, Askai and Inform Napalm present other screenshots from Marakasov's profile, which suggest that he is, in fact, a tankist from Russia's 136 Motor Rifle Brigade—a unit that is equipped with T-90As. This evidence is consistent with a video that appeared on YouTube in November 2016 and shows three tanks, at least one of which can be clearly identified as a T-90A (YouTube 2016b). The video's description says that it was filmed near the village of Lyse, southeast of Luhansk, on August 25, 2014. As Askai (2016) points out, the video features several geolocation markers—masts, pipework, trees, pollards, and a railway crossing—that are a perfect match for Google Earth satellite imagery of a location just southeast of Lyse.

On its own, this evidence is not able to shift the balance of probability decisively toward H3. The material in question was published long after the events and lacks clear indicators of the time the footage was taken. This somewhat decreases its credibility, even though late August 2014 remains the most plausible time and it remains highly unlikely that detailed and consistent evidence of this kind has been fabricated. More importantly, however, the presence of a few Russian T-90A tanks and their crew around Luhansk is not sufficient to prove that Russia played the decisive role in the Ukrainian defeat.

In the case of Luhansk, the *smoking-gun* evidence that shifts the balance of probability decisively toward H3 consists of two videos of military convoys. On September 2, a video filmed by a trolleybus passenger driving past a large military convoy appeared on Youtube (2014bp). The convoy includes at least 116 military vehicles—13 tanks, one self-propelled artillery gun, 47 armored vehicles and 55 trucks. Several tanks in the convoy can be identified as either T-72BA, T-72 Obr.1989, or T-72B3—the same newer Russian tank models that were identified near Ilovaisk. The convoy also includes tanker trucks with Russian-language fire hazard warnings. The video's description on YouTube says that it was filmed on the road between Krasnodon and Molodohvardiisk in Luhansk Oblast and points out a road sign that is visible 40 seconds into the video. This road sign features the number "M04" against a blue background above the number "E40" against a green background. The latter number designates the European Route E40 leading from Calais in France to Ridder in Kazakhstan. The only place where this international route follows a national highway numbered M04 is in the Donbas between Debaltseve and the Russian border east of Krasnodon. Moreover, the long straight stretch of road in the video with trolleybus masts and trees on both sides, followed by fields, trees in the distance, and a gentle bend, matches Google Earth imagery of the M04/E40 highway directly southeast of Molodohvardiisk. This location suggests that the convoy was driving back from Luhansk toward the Russian border after Ukrainian forces had been defeated and forced to abandon their positions south of the city. Given that the video was published shortly after the events in question, there is only a remote chance that it is an elaborate fabrication.

The same is the case for another video filmed by a car dashcam and showing a convoy of 24 military vehicles – two tanks, 13 armored vehicles and nine trucks (YouTube 2014bq). Again, the two tanks can be identified as either T-72BA, T-72 Obr.1989, or T-72B3. The dashcam footage shows the exact time and coordinates of the recording—September 3, 2014 on a small road between the Luhansk Oblast villages of Pidhirne and Sievero Hundorivskyi. The long straight road with trees on both sides is consistent with Google Earth footage of the location. The convoy is driving south toward the Russian border, which is less than five kilometers away. The road used by the convoy is part of an alternative, more rural route from the battlefield south of Luhansk to the Russian border.

As in the case of Ilovaisk, general probabilistic considerations suggest that it is highly unlikely that the Russian invasion force only consisted of two convoys both of which happened to be caught on videos that were then uploaded to YouTube. In turn, this suggests that, in the case of Luhansk, the Russian invasion force also consisted of several hundred vehicles. This updates the probability of H3 in the case of Luhansk—as in the case of Ilovaisk—to *almost certain*.

9.5. The Battle of Novoazovsk

A third, smaller battle in which Ukrainian forces suffered a defeat around the same time took place near the southern coast around the town of Novoazovsk. On August 25, a resident of Novoazovsk told a *Reuters* correspondent that a military convoy including at least seven tanks was attacking the town (Lowe and Tsvetkova 2014). A day later, a *Vice News* camera team visited Novoazovsk (VICE News 2014, from 5:09). It filmed smoke plumes and machine gun salvos in its eastern surroundings as well as damaged buildings. The journalists also spoke to Ukrainian soldiers stationed in Novoazovsk. The soldiers confirmed that the area was being attacked by tanks and heavy artillery. On August 27, the journalists returned and found that Ukrainian forces had left Novoazovsk (VICE News 2014, from 10:21). On September 5, the Ukrainian military acknowledged that its forces had been pushed back as far as Shyrokyne, ten kilometers east of Mariupol (Liga.Novosti 2014b).

Like in the cases of Ilovaisk and Luhansk, there is clear evidence that a Russian invasion force was responsible for the Ukrainian defeat in the Novoazovsk area. This evidence can be divided into three parts. The first part focuses on a piece of military hardware, identified and geolocated on both sides of the border by Bellingcat (Case et al. 2015, 53–54; Higgins 2015). The vehicle in question is a Msta-S self-propelled 152 mm howitzer. This howitzer features two distinct stains on its left side as well as the number N2200, painted in a specific way. It first appears in a video uploaded to YouTube on July 30, 2014. The account that posted this video was subsequently deleted, but Bellingcat (2015a) saved a copy of the original. Because of the Rostov Oblast numberplates of the cars and the shops in the background, Bellingcat was able to geolocate the video to the intersection of the Taganrog-Mariupol highway and Solovyinaya Street in the northwest of Rostov-on-Don. As of 2021, the same shops were still visible on Google Street View (2021). An Msta-S with the same distinct features appears in a September 5 *Al Jazeera* (2014 at 0:24) report from Novoazovsk. In this report, the howitzer drives past a blue single-story building with a damaged façade and a pole in front of it. The same building is visible on a 2012 dashcam video which filmed the entire section of the Taganrog-Mariupol highway between the Russian border and Mariupol (YouTube 2012, at 11:44). This video proves that the Msta-S in the *Al Jazeera* report was filmed at the northern edge of Novoazovsk, just east of the intersection between the Taganrog-Mariupol highway and the road from Novoazovsk to Telmanove. It was driving westward. The exact location of the footage is important because there is no major road from the north between the intersection in question and the Russian border. At the same time, there is no plausible reason for hypothetical DNR reinforcements from the north to use dirt tracks near the Russian border rather than the Telmanove-Novoazovsk road on September 5, given that Ukrainian forces had already retreated from the area. It is therefore highly unlikely that the Msta-S in question was filmed in Rostov-on-Don, taken north, and handed over to Russian-led separatist forces which then took it back south. In turn, it is highly likely that the Msta-S in question was part of a Russian invasion force that entered the Novoazovsk area directly from Russia. This finding is incompatible with H1 but equally compatible with H2 and H3 because it does not specify the size of the Russian invasion force. Neither does it prove that the initial assault that started on August 25 and drove the Ukrainian forces out of Novoazovsk had come from Russia.

The second part of the evidence consists of cross-border vehicle tracks in the area northeast of Novoazovsk near the villages of Shcherbak and Markyne discovered by Bellingcat on openly available satellite imagery (Case et al. 2015, 33–35). These tracks are also visible on images from Google Earth Pro's historical satellite database, which contains images of the area taken in October 2013 and October 2014. The tracks are absent on the former and clearly visible on the latter image before they slowly fade on images from subsequent years. The same is the case for another major cross-border track further south, which is highlighted in another report (Bellingcat 2015c, 46–49). This track was located just 600 meters north of the official border checkpoint on the Taganrog-Mariupol highway in a location that is hidden from the main road by a line of trees. The prominence of the tracks suggests that it is highly likely that a major cross-border incursion directly into territory controlled by Ukrainian forces took place in the area. Even though the time of the first incursion cannot be determined by the satellite imagery, it is likely that it happened on August 25, when a local resident and Ukrainian soldiers reported the sudden appearance of tanks in the area. In the absence of evidence to the contrary that would indicate significant separatist troop movements toward the south on August 24-25, the cross-border vehicle tracks tilt the balance of probabilities in favor of H3.

The third part of the evidence in the Novoazovsk case consists of the area's geographic location almost 90 km south of the nearest previous separatist positions around Donetsk. Not only is there no evidence of separatist troop movements toward the south but such movements would not have made any strategic sense, either. Novoazovsk is located less than 15 km west of the Russian border and around 65 km south of the Russian line of encirclement near Ilovaisk. The area was therefore far more accessible to invading Russian troops than to separatist forces. This finding further increases the probability of H3 and makes it *almost certain* that Russian troops were the key driving force of the Ukrainian defeat on this battlefield as well.

9.6. Chapter Conclusion

This chapter has shown that the decisive Ukrainian defeat of late August 2014 was primarily caused by a large-scale invasion of Russia's regular army. This invasion was preceded by more than a month of Russian artillery attacks on Ukrainian positions from Russian territory or from locations inside Ukraine in the immediate vicinity of the border. The invasion of late August took place in three different theaters simultaneously. In the east of Donetsk Oblast, Russian forces invaded from the south and attacked the rear of the Ukrainian forces that were trying to seize Ilovaisk. In Luhansk Oblast, Russian units approached Luhansk from the southeast and ended Ukrainian attempts to encircle the city. In the south of Donetsk Oblast, Russian troops crossed the border and drove Ukrainian forces back along the coast toward Mariupol.

With this invasion of regular forces, Russia escalated the conflict further beyond the confines that had previously defined it – and to the highest level of violence observed until February 24,

2022. Throughout the previous stages of the conflict, Russia had delegated the war to irregular formations which it controlled and which it equipped with old military hardware. In late August, it sent its regular armed forces on modern military hardware to save these irregular units from looming defeat. By doing so, Russia paved the way for the First Minsk Agreement and for the conflict that continued to simmer in the Donbas. The level of violence decreased over the following years, and, until 2022, the frontline was no longer subject to major changes. Nevertheless, the fact that there still was a frontline, and that people continued to die fighting along this frontline, was the direct result of the critical juncture analyzed in this chapter.

10. Conclusion

This book has shown that the escalation of violence in Ukraine's Donbas in April–August 2014 was primarily the result of the Russian state's actions. Domestic factors played a secondary, auxiliary role. I proceeded in four steps. Firstly, I highlighted the importance of research on the causes of individual wars as an essential component of research on the causes of war in general and explained the importance of the 2014 Donbas War as a case study. Secondly, I used escalation theory and the concept of critical junctures to construct an escalation sequence model of the Donbas War's formative phase. Thirdly, I proposed digital forensic process tracing as the methodology of choice for further empirical research on the escalation of war in the social media age. Fourthly, and most importantly, I investigated the causes of the Donbas conflict through a digital forensic process tracing analysis of the six critical junctures comprising its formative escalation sequence.

10.1. Russia's Invasion in Disguise

The empirical chapters of this book have assessed the two opposing standpoints that divide the political and academic debate on the war's causes against the extent to which they can explain the war's escalation sequence. For each of the six critical junctures, I have evaluated whether the available evidence supports the hypothesis that events were primarily the result of a domestic dynamic or the hypothesis that they were primarily the result of Russia's actions. This step-by-step analysis of the six critical junctures in the conflict's escalation sequence showed that Russian state-actors played the dominant role in four of them. Moreover, the two critical junctures that do not feature convincing evidence of a primary role of the Russian state are also the ones that featured the least violence. All key developments that turned the Donbas conflict in 2014 into a full-scale war with thousands of casualties feature Russian state organs as the key opponent of Ukrainian forces.

10.1.1. Donetsk and Luhansk in early April

Chapter four has shown that the conflict's first critical juncture was still primarily a domestic phenomenon. It is likely that the key actors behind the armed and permanent building occupations in Donetsk and Luhansk in early April were local pro-Russian activists. Even though it is almost certain that these activists received some support from the Russian state, there is not enough evidence to conclude that Russian state actors were in control of events or the key driving force behind them. The available evidence suggests that the Kremlin and groups acting on its behalf were only one of several actors supporting the separatist movement at this initial stage. It is likely that the local activists behind the building occupations also received support from business networks surrounding Ukraine's former President Viktor Yanukovych. Moreover, the region's most influential oligarchs—Rinat Akhmetov and Oleksandr Yefremov—played at least an enabling role by refusing to take action against separatism. In this context, the degree of Russian involvement that can be deduced from the available evidence does not stand out as a factor that was more *disruptive* to the normal course of events than the actions of locals. Hence, it is appropriate to speak of Russian-backed or pro-Russian separatism in the Donbas when referring to the events of early April. However, it is important to note that these events did not yet involve any armed clashes. Two buildings had been occupied and barricaded, but the Ukrainian Armed Forces had not yet been deployed to the Donbas and, so far, nobody had died because of militarized violence.

10.1.2. Sloviansk and Kramatorsk

Chapter five has shown that the initial crossing of the threshold between peace and armed conflict in the Donbas, entailing the conflict's first battle-related casualty, was the direct result of an incursion by irregular Russian forces. Igor Girkin and his group of armed men had assisted the Russian state in the takeover of Crimea before they moved to the Donbas and turned the Sloviansk-Kramatorsk area into the conflict's first battlefield. Their incursion was financed and supervised by Russian oligarch and Kremlin ally Konstantin Malofeyev and Crimean "Prime Minister" Sergey Aksyonov who, according to Russian law, was a Russian state official. Igor Girkin and many members of his group returned to Russia after their engagement in the Donbas. Neither they nor their Russian sponsors were punished by the Russian state for their actions. In the context of this evidence, it is almost certain that Igor Girkin's group acted as an informal organ of the Russian state and carried out an incursion into Ukrainian territory on the Kremlin's behalf. The actions of Girkin's group almost certainly depended on the Kremlin's knowledge and approval. It is of secondary importance whether this knowledge and approval came in the shape of a formal order or in the shape of implicit signals. Either way, the Kremlin's willingness to let the armed paramilitaries that supported its annexation of Crimea attack mainland Ukraine was more disruptive to the normal course of events than the fact that Girkin and his men were happy to continue fighting. It was also more disruptive than the fact that Girkin's group received a certain degree of local support.

10.1.3. Mariupol

Chapter six has shown that, in the southern port city of Mariupol, the domestic resource and support base of the separatist movement was sufficient to cause some militarized violence but insufficient to cause a full-scale war. Evidence of Russian involvement in the Mariupol events is limited. Even though it is likely that the city's separatists received a certain degree of Russian support, it is unlikely that they were controlled by Russia to an extent that justifies characterizing them as organs of the Russian state. However, these local separatists failed to consolidate their control over the city, despite the Ukrainian military's withdrawal after the armed clashes of May 9. Separatist forces faced competition from the local police and volunteer squads of workers from the steelworks of oligarch Rinat Akhmetov. These forces did not actively oppose the separatists but did not subordinate themselves, either. As a result, the separatists failed to establish a monopoly of violence over the city and were removed by the returning military in a relatively bloodless operation in mid-June. The events in Mariupol illustrate how the Donbas conflict could have developed if Russia had limited itself to supporting a domestic separatist movement rather than taking the lead and assuming control over it. However, in other parts of the region, Russia chose to play a more active role and did exactly that.

10.1.4. The Fighting Spreads

Chapter seven has shown how armed conflict spread from the initial two hotspots of Sloviansk-Kramatorsk and Mariupol to other parts of the Donbas in late May and early to mid-June. It argued that, in at least four of the five new theatres of armed conflict, the Ukrainian military was facing forces under Russian control. Near Volnovakha, the Ukrainian military clashed with Igor Bezler and the Horlivka-based group of fighters under his command. Bezler was a Russian military veteran, who had lived in Ukraine for many years. However, his participation in the annexation of Crimea, his second identity provided by the Russian authorities, and his documented communication with Russian intelligence officer Vasiliy Geranin suggest that he was almost certainly an agent of the Russian state. In Donetsk, a unit of fighters that was almost certainly recruited and trained in Russia unsuccessfully tried to seize the city's airport. Moreover, the battle-hardened core of the Vostok Battalion, which was the key opponent of Ukrainian forces in other clashes in the Donetsk area, highly likely consisted of Russian citizens from Ossetia. At the same time, it is almost certain that the new "prime minister" of the Donetsk People's Republic, Aleksandr Boroday—a Russian citizen himself—closely coordinated his actions with Russian Presidential Adviser Vladislav Surkov. In Luhansk, it is highly likely that Russia's Wagner Group played a leading role in attacks on Ukrainian military facilities and that separatist fighters in the city were supervised by Russian intelligence officer Oleg Ivannikov (call-sign Orion). In the south of Luhansk Oblast, forces led by Russian Cossack commander Nikolay Kozitsyn, who was likely acting as an informal organ of the Russian state, were engaging the Ukrainian border forces. The only theater of armed conflict in which Russia's leading role is merely a realistic possibility is the northwest of Luhansk Oblast, where armed men under the command of Pavlo Dromov and Oleksii Mozghovyi blocked the advance of the Ukrainian military. Although it is almost certain that Dromov and Mozghovyi enjoyed Russian support, there is not enough evidence to establish with a high degree of confidence that they acted as informal organs of the Russian state. However, the probability of this explanation is still slightly higher than the probability of them acting primarily independently. Moreover, along the frontlines that emerged in late May and early to mid-June, the northwest of Luhansk Oblast was the area that witnessed the least violence, and, in late July, Dromov and Mozghovyi were forced to retreat.

10.1.5. Tanks and Heavy Artillery

Chapter eight has argued that Russian deliveries of tanks and heavy artillery to the Donbas from mid-June onward indicate continued Russian control over the separatist movement. There is strong photo and video evidence from this time period, which shows the same individual tanks first in Russia and then in the Donbas. At the same time, there is no evidence of large-scale seizures of Ukrainian heavy arms by separatist forces. As a result, it is highly likely that Russia supplied most if not all of the separatists' heavy arms. By doing so, Russia reaffirmed that the Russian fighters and commanders in the Donbas were acting on its behalf. Rather than distancing itself from these fighters, the Russian military dramatically increased their capabilities by providing them with more powerful weaponry.

10.1.6. Ukraine Defeated

Chapter nine has shown that the involvement of Russia's regular armed forces was decisive in the final critical juncture in the conflict's initial escalation sequence. This critical juncture was of particular importance because it paved the way for the static, low-level violence that continued in the Donbas in the years that followed. After cross-border shelling had slowed the Ukrainian advance throughout July and August, Ukrainian forces were decisively defeated in three battles at the end of August. They had to abandon the siege of Luhansk, lost control over all areas southeast of Donetsk, and faced a new enemy offensive along the southern coast. In all three cases, there is convincing evidence of the involvement of Russian regular forces. This evidence consists of photos and videos of new Russian tank models and Russian servicemen on Ukrainian territory. Additional evidence of the size of the invasion force are videos and satellite imagery showing large military convoys on the move between the battlefields and the Russian border. Based on this evidence, it can be concluded that it is almost certain that an invasion by Russia's regular armed forces was the primary cause of the Ukrainian defeat in late August 2014.

10.1.7. Counterfactual Scenarios

Organs of the Russian state were the key drivers behind four of the six critical junctures that define the genesis of the Donbas War in 2014. Removing these critical junctures from the escalation sequence would leave a number of armed men occupying administrative buildings in Donetsk and Luhansk and a short period of fighting in Mariupol. In this counterfactual domestic conflict scenario, the building occupations in Donetsk may or may not have ended peacefully and the situation in Mariupol may or may not have developed in the same way without the Sloviansk precedent. The Ukrainian government may have refrained from launching an "antiterrorist operation" and may have been able to come to an agreement with local elites and separatist activists.

However, even in a worst-case counterfactual scenario, in which militarized violence would still have occurred, there is no plausible way in which this violence could have got anywhere near the level that the region experienced in reality. It is almost certain that a domestic insurgency by pro-Russian rebels with limited support from Russia would have been defeated by early summer. It is also almost certain that such an insurgency would have involved only a tiny fraction of the death and destruction that Ukraine witnessed in 2014 and the years that followed. The lion's share of violence in the Donbas before 2022 would not have been possible without people like Bezler, Boroday, Girkin, Kozitsyn, Mamiyev, and Utkin and the irregular Russian forces under their command. Neither would it have been possible without the supplies of tanks and heavy artillery from Russia; without cross-border artillery shelling; and without the invasion of Russia's regular armed forces in late August.

All this means that Russia should be seen as a primary rather than secondary conflict party in the Donbas in 2014. Russia's actions proved to be far more disruptive to the normal course of events than local manifestations of separatism. Its involvement goes far beyond the internationalization of an internal conflict. Rather than supporting local rebels, Russia used a local fringe movement with negligible military capabilities as a cover for its own military actions against Ukraine with its own irregular and regular troops. This means that the Donbas conflict of 2014 was no civil war but a delegated interstate war (Hauter 2019) between Russia and Ukraine.

10.2. New Ways to Study War

Beyond its analysis of the Donbas, this book has made two other important contributions that could improve research on armed conflict anywhere in the world. In terms of theory and concepts, I have proposed a new way to model a war's escalation sequence by using escalation theory and the concept of critical junctures. In terms of methodology, I have improved process tracing by making it fit for the social media age through the incorporation of DOSI analysis.

10.2.1. Reviving Escalation Theory

This book has contributed to the theoretical foundations of social science research on war by combining conflict escalation theory and the concept of critical junctures to create an escalation sequence model of the Donbas War.[45] This model specified the targets of the digital forensic process tracing analysis that followed in the empirical chapters. As far as possible, the escalation sequence model remains agnostic about the war's causes. Based on a large dataset of media reports containing both pro-Western and pro-Russian sources, it does not rule out hypothetical explanations of the war. Instead, it acts as a benchmark. Whether an explanation focuses on grievances within the local population, the actions of local elites, or Russian interference, its suitability can be measured by the extent to which it can explain the events in the escalation sequence model.

45　For a previous version of this section, see Hauter 2021b, 161–163.

An escalation sequence model of this kind forces researchers investigating the war's causes to focus on the process of conflict escalation instead of second-guessing the conflict's nature by analyzing circumstantial conditions like the region's history, local public opinion, or geopolitical constellations. It also prevents researchers from choosing a theoretical framework that avoids the question or predetermines the result. For these reasons, the model can facilitate an explanation of the Donbas conflict that is transparent, comprehensive, and theory-guided. As a result, an explanation based on it can feed into a higher-level discourse and inform both comparative research and policymaking.

These advantages are by no means limited to the specific controversy surrounding the case of the Donbas. They can be easily transferred to other cases because the roadmap that I use to create the escalation sequence model is universally applicable. The creation of an escalation ladder containing the different thresholds which crossed conflict-defining limits of violence and the subsequent identification of critical junctures among these thresholds can be repeated for any other war. This applies to contemporary conflicts as well as historical cases. A detailed escalation sequence model could, for example, shed additional light on the role of different rebel groups, government forces, and either side's foreign sponsors during the war in Syria. It could also structure further investigations of Russian strategy, Ukrainian resistance, and Western support before and after the dramatic escalation of 2022. At the same time, a model like the one proposed in this book could also be used to revisit the age-old debate on the causes of World War One.

Moreover, the present escalation model can translate different methods of data collection into a common framework. Depending on the information environment that surrounds a particular conflict, a variety of data sources can be used to identify escalation thresholds and critical junctures. This book uses DOSI by exploiting a dataset of online news media as well as videos of relevant events uploaded to social media. Other studies may create an escalation sequence model on the basis of eyewitness interviews, archival documents, secondary accounts of historians, or a combination of different sources.

As a result, the creation of escalation sequence models for a number of different conflicts could create promising new opportunities for comparative research on the causes of war. Even though every case of conflict escalation has its own case-specific nuances, it is possible that the comparison of different conflict escalation models will show certain similarities between them. To use Dessler's (1991, 342–344) thunderstorm metaphor, each conflict escalation model provides an insight into the processes inside gathering storm clouds during the formation of a specific storm. Although the processes at work in the escalation of armed conflict hardly follow laws of nature in a way that is comparable to thunderstorm formation, certain patterns and common features may still become apparent. Potentially, a comparison of these processes could reveal certain commonalities that could feed into something resembling Dessler's (1991) idea of a "causal theory of war." Naturally, the case-specific conflict escalation sequence model proposed in this book is only a small step in this direction. Nevertheless, it is an avenue worth pursuing.

Even if its application to other cases does not directly lead to generalizable findings regarding the causes of war, the theoretical framework I proposed will remain an important case-focused supplement to comparative research. It builds a bridge between the focus on case-specific circumstances, which characterizes the work of most historians and area studies specialists, and the need for generalization and streamlining in comparative social science research. In addition to building this bridge between the specific and the general, the proposed model facilitates comparison and communication among scholars who focus on the relative importance of and the interactions between different explanatory factors within casestudies. Research on the causes of war can only benefit from a common frame of reference of this kind.

10.2.2. Digital Forensic Process Tracing

The methodological part of this book has demonstrated how social scientists can use online media to gain a better understanding of the causes of war.[46] It has argued that the Internet is a treasure trove of

---

46   For a previous version of this section, see Hauter 2021c, 14–15.

information rather than just a propaganda dump. Online sources have provided conflict studies researchers with access to valuable primary data from conflict zones at an unprecedented scale. This information has the potential to greatly improve case-study research on the causes of war. Harnessing this potential, however, requires methodological rigor and argumentative transparency. This means that process tracing research on armed conflict needs to pay additional attention to source criticism and probabilistic reasoning.

For this purpose, this book has proposed a forensic approach to process tracing that incorporates DOSI analysis into the methodology. This incorporation shifts the investigative focus of process tracing to source criticism and probabilistic reasoning. Furthermore, my approach uses Occam's razor, the Sagan standard, and abnormalism as guiding principles that can further strengthen the methodology, as well as the PHIA Probability Yardstick as a system to verbalize approximate probabilities. The result is digital forensic process tracing—a methodological innovation that enables transparent and methodologically rigorous case study research and can deliver reliable findings even in murky information environments. It sheds light on causal processes while making use of the Internet's full potential as an access route to primary information from conflict zones.

The forensic methodology proposed in this book has potential far beyond the case of the Donbas. It can be used to research causal processes in any conflict that has been subject to extensive firsthand coverage on the Internet. An obvious example is the war in Syria, where digital forensic process tracing could be used for a variety of purposes: to identify shifts in the composition and strategy of different rebel groups, to evaluate the impact of foreign involvement on the course of the conflict, or to track the use of chemical weapons. A large quantity of potentially useful DOSI has already been gathered and catalogued by the Syrian Archive (n.d.) and could form a useful empirical basis for such research. Another recent case is the escalation of violence in Nagorno-Karabakh in autumn 2020, which was subject to intense media scrutiny while Armenia and Azerbaijan and their respective allies were pushing contradicting accounts of events. Moreover, digital forensic process tracing could be used to investigate the war's further escalation in

2022 and help answer a number of important questions related to it: What were the reasons for the miserable failure of Russia's assault on Kyiv in February and March 2022? What was the impact of different Western weapons system deliveries to Ukraine? How did the conflict parties' strategies evolve as events unfolded? This list of potential cases and questions is by no means exhaustive.

Finally, the use of elements of digital forensic process tracing at the data gathering stage of a research project may also benefit scholars who use frequentist approaches. Treating data points as mini case studies would enable more precise coding and the inclusion of a wider range of sources in conflict datasets. Naturally, this would also increase the workload involved in the creation of such datasets. However, the combination of abundance and murkiness that characterizes information on armed conflict in the social media age could make this effort worthwhile.

Naturally, the online information space surrounding armed conflict is subject to continuous change. The emergence of so-called deepfakes has decreased the prima facie credibility of video evidence in recent years. At the same time, improved mobile Internet coverage and phone camera capabilities have improved livestreaming opportunities and video quality while the quality and availability of satellite imagery has improved as well. In reaction to the multitude of online media reports exposing Russian soldiers' involvement in Ukraine in 2014–2015, the Russian Armed Forces imposed social media bans, and an increasing number of social media users restrict access to their profiles. Following the 2022 escalation, the Ukrainian authorities warned residents not to provide open source intelligence to the enemy and imposed a ban on posting information about Ukrainian units and the consequences of Russian attacks on social media without approval. At the same time, new platforms such as TikTok and Telegram have led to a new surge in openly available video content. Adapting to these changes and staying on top of the ongoing transformation of modern information technology is a key challenge for the further development of digital forensic process tracing. However, the Internet's dominance over the information environment in which armed conflict takes place will not disappear, which means that the importance of digital forensic process tracing for research on war will only grow.

10.3. Academic Implications

The findings of this book confirm the arguments of scholars who have previously expressed support for the invasion hypothesis.[47] They confirm Wilson's (2016) argument that the domestic situation in the Donbas in 2014 could explain a certain degree of "civil conflict," but not a "civil war." They confirm Laryš and Suleimanov's (2021) argument that Russian involvement ruined the attempts of local elites to keep separatist activity contained and use it for political bargaining. They confirm Kuromiya's (2019) argument that the regional history of the Donbas does not provide a suitable explanation for the outbreak of war. They confirm Hosaka's (2021, 107–109) argument that the labelling of the self-proclaimed Donetsk and Luhansk People's Republics (DNR and LNR) as non-state actors is misleading. And they confirm Mitrokhin's (2015) argument that the conflict was a Russian attack that proceeded in phases. Russia increased its involvement when there were signs that its previous measures were insufficient to keep the conflict going. This book underpins the conclusions of these scholars and others who explicitly support the invasion hypothesis with solid methodological, conceptual, and empirical foundations. It also adds additional nuances by outlining how Russian involvement varied not only over time but also across different theatres of the conflict. Moreover, this book vindicates the numerous works that implicitly support the invasion hypothesis by focusing on Russia's role or by using terminology that suggests an interstate conflict.

In turn, the findings of this book disprove the hypothesis that, in 2014, Russia still played a secondary role in a primarily internal conflict. They contradict the findings of scholars who explicitly make this argument (Davies 2016; Katchanovski 2016; Kudelia 2016; Loshkariov and Sushentsov 2016; Matsuzato 2017; Matveeva 2016; 2018; Nitsova 2021; Robinson 2016; Sakwa 2015; 2017; Tsygankov 2015). Kudelia (2016, 5) sums up his argument by saying that Russia "exploited" domestic developments in the Donbas, "but did not play a determining role in them." I have shown that the

---

47 They are also in line with a recent decision of the European Court of Human Rights, which ruled that, by mid-May 2014, the Russian state exerted "effective control" over separatist forces in the Donbas (ECtHR 2022).

exact opposite is the case. Russia did play the determining role in turning separatist unrest into militarized violence and then into full-scale war. For this reason, the findings of this book contradict the way in which the conflict between 2014 and 2022 is currently coded by the Uppsala Conflict Data Program and the Correlates of War project (Pettersson and Öberg 2020, 608; Dixon and Sarkees 2020; Palmer et al. 2020). At the same time, my findings call into question the use of the Donbas War before 2022 as an internal conflict case study by Rauta (2016), Schram (2021), and Sambanis et al. (2020). They also challenge Boyd-Barrett (2017) and Barthel and Bürkner's (2020) claims regarding an alleged anti-Russian bias in Western media coverage. Moreover, my findings contradict Schneckener's (2021, 46–47) suggestion that the 2014 war developed an internal momentum that led to a "fragmentation of violent actors" who, at least for some time, escaped Russian control. A similar claim is made in Arel and Driscoll's (2023) recent book, which argues that, during the initial stage of "Ukraine's unnamed war" in 2014, Russia was mainly reacting to events beyond its control. My book, on the contrary, suggests that Russia successfully adjusted its actions to steer events in the desired direction, and I did not find evidence of Russia losing control at any point.

However, this finding comes with an important caveat. It does not suggest that Russia followed a carefully devised masterplan all the way from the aftermath of the Maidan revolution to the full-scale invasion of 2022. It is entirely consistent with the idea that the Russian leadership acted in an ad hoc manner without a coherent long-term strategy.

Neither does my book invalidate the findings of the numerous works that implicitly support the civil war hypothesis by focusing on domestic causes of the war or by using terminology that suggests an internal conflict. There can be no doubt that domestic causes contributed to the escalation of violence in the region. As my book has pointed out, there was a certain degree of domestic support for separatism and Russia's actions, and many of the separatist fighters were locals. Researching these aspects of the conflict and their causes remains an important objective as long as this research is framed in an appropriate way. It simply has to make clear that what is being investigated are auxiliary causes that enabled an interstate conflict and not the primary causes of a civil war. Other potentially misleading terminology should be changed accordingly. For example, speaking of "Russian-led separatists" or "separatist forces controlled by Russia" instead of "pro-Russian separatists" or "Russian-backed separatists" would go a long way toward changing the framing of many research projects without compromising their findings.

Regarding the way forward, the findings of this book suggest that future comparative and quantitative research should not treat the 2014 Donbas conflict as a Ukrainian civil war, but as the first stage of an interstate war between Russia and Ukraine that escalated further in 2022. They also suggest that further research into the primary causes of the 2014 Donbas War should focus on Russia's foreign and security policy. Russia turned into an aggressor and a threat to European security long before 2022. The events of 2014 were Russia's first attempt to destroy the modern Ukrainian state by military means. They were the prelude to the all-out invasion of 2022 rather than a fundamentally different phenomenon.

This does not mean that societal divisions within Ukraine and its domestic politics do not merit further research. On the contrary, such research can offer important additional insights into why the Russian-Ukrainian war started in the Donbas in 2014 and why certain parts of the local population were willing to fight in the ranks of irregular Russian forces. The primary reason why such forces appeared in the first place, however, can only be found in Moscow. Consequently, future research should not treat pre-2022 Ukraine as a case of state failure and interethnic conflict but as a country that resisted an attempt by its neighbor to break it into pieces by military means. The resilience shown by the Ukrainian state and Ukrainian society in the face of the full-scale invasion of 2022 should be seen as a continuation of this resistance rather than a new phenomenon.

At the same time, the findings of this book suggest that future research should investigate why the dramatic escalation of 2022 was not foreseen by more people. Why did the narrative of Russia as a restrained actor, who—if involved at all—played a secondary role in the conflict, gain so much traction in politics, media, and academia? Why were so many still preoccupied with downplaying

Russia's military involvement in Ukraine while the Kremlin was already planning the next stage of its armed aggression?

Another question that requires additional attention are the exact decision-making processes within Russia's political elite. This book has not been able to establish to what extent the actions of Russian state actors in the Donbas were the result of explicit orders from the Kremlin. It leaves open the possibility that the relevant actors instead responded to informal signaling which indicated that they were free to act or expected to act in a certain way. Neither does this book address the motivation and reasoning behind Russia's actions or potential disagreements within the state's inner leadership circle regarding the right course of action. Due to their secretive nature, both the decision-making processes within the Russian elite and the motivations that underly these processes are challenging research topics that cannot be addressed through digital forensic process tracing alone. Nevertheless, as far as data availability permits, these topics are worth pursuing. Better insights into Kremlin decision-making processes and motivations are important to understand why Russia decided to launch the disguised invasion of 2014. Like the all-out invasion of 2022, the initial decision to use military force in 2014 appears irrational. Even though the West was reluctant to recognize the Donbas War of 2014 as an act of Russian aggression and only imposed relatively minor sanctions in response, Russia's international reputation and soft power did suffer. More importantly, Russia's actions in the Donbas alienated many pro-Russian residents of Ukraine and increased national unity both in the unoccupied part of the Donbas and across the country. By using military force, Russia robbed itself of the opportunity to nurture a new pro-Russian political movement with the potential to regain widespread support. Such a movement could have exploited the resentment felt by opponents of the post-Maidan government after the change of power in Kyiv and the inevitable disillusionment soon to be felt by many Maidan supporters. This would have been a more promising and less costly way to retain influence and power in Ukraine. Russia, however, chose war, and the question why the Russian leadership made this choice deserves additional attention.

At the same time, in 2014, Russia's willingness to escalate still remained within certain limits. The Russian state kept the costs low by sending irregular forces to the Donbas and only sent the regular army when these irregular troops were faced with imminent defeat. After it had turned the tide of the war, Russia settled for a semi-frozen conflict along a static contact line rather than trying to seize the whole of the Donbas, or even larger parts of Ukraine. In 2022, Russia decided to drop this remaining restraint and escalated the conflict dramatically. For the second time in less than a decade, the Russian leadership made a seemingly irrational decision. What is more, the dominance of deluded military adventurism over rational cost-benefit analysis seemed to be even stronger in 2022 than in 2014. Rather than learning from the mistake of 2014, the Russian leadership doubled down on it. What factors made the Kremlin take its destructive strategy of conflict escalation even further instead of changing course after the experience of 2014? This question summarizes an extremely important puzzle for further research. Pursuing this question has the potential to shed additional light on the motivations and decision-making processes behind the escalation of the war in both 2014 and 2022. In turn, it could help both researchers and policymakers to better assess the risk of the Russian leadership taking additional, seemingly irrational, escalatory steps in the future and identify ways to reduce this risk. Against the backdrop of Russia's sizeable nuclear arsenal, this risk assessment and measures to prevent further escalation are of crucial importance.

10.4. How the West Failed Ukraine

Looking back at the invasion of 2014, the findings of this book suggest that the West's response was woefully inadequate. Instead of focusing its efforts on pressuring Russia to end its armed aggression and return the entire Donbas to Ukraine, Western countries essentially bought into the Russian narrative that the Donbas conflict was primarily a civil war. They accepted Russia's assertion that it was not a conflict party and agreed to pursue conflict regulation within a framework that defined the self-proclaimed republics as independent actors and Russia as a mediator. As a result, much time and energy was wasted discussing local elections in the

Donbas and Ukrainian constitutional reform. Neither of these were viable roads to peace while parts of the Donbas were de facto controlled by the Russian state. On the contrary, avoiding the elephant in the room created the impression that the West was weak and unwilling to confront Russia. At the same time, it diverted the West's attention away from the military dimension of the conflict and the possibility of a new Russian escalation.

This does not mean that the full-scale invasion was easily predictable. Even in January 2022, it was not unreasonable to assume that the decisionmakers in the Kremlin were assessing the military and political situation in Ukraine correctly and knew that starting a full-scale war could only end in disaster. However, if the correct lessons had been learned from 2014, the West would have known that the probability of further escalation was by no means low enough to justify unpreparedness. On the contrary, the devastating consequences of war require major efforts to reduce its probability as well as contingency plans in case it occurs anyway, even if the probability is considered to be low. The outbreak of war or the sudden escalation of a simmering conflict can only be disregarded as a scenario to prepare for if the risk is negligible. In Ukraine, the experience of 2014 clearly showed that this was not the case.

Some countries understood this better than others. Following the events of 2014, the United States, Canada, and the UK became key providers of military assistance to Ukraine (Gramer and Detsch 2022; I. King 2019; Reuters 2022; Sabbagh 2022). Their support package included training, equipment, and light weaponry. There can be no doubt that this assistance contributed to Ukraine's ability to withstand Russia's all-out invasion of 2022. However, it was clearly not enough to deter Russia from launching this invasion in the first place. Moreover, military assistance programs were undermined by other countries' continued pursuit of a Russia policy that prioritized outreach and engagement. Italy, France, and Germany were among those who continued to see Russia as a potential partner rather than a systemic rival and security threat (Marange and Steward 2021; Siddi 2019). Germany played a particularly unfortunate role in this context. The launch of the Nord Stream 2 project in 2015 essentially rewarded Russia's invasion with the construction of a pipeline that had only one recognizable purpose—diminishing

Ukraine's importance as a transit country for Russian gas deliveries to Western Europe. By supporting the construction of this pipeline, Germany sent a powerful signal to Russia, indicating that at least some Western countries were happy to disregard the fate of Ukraine when their key economic interests were at stake.

Overall, the West failed to adopt a firm and united stance toward Russia. It failed to underpin negotiations with deterrence and solid support for Ukraine's independence and territorial integrity. This failure could only fuel Russian hopes that at least some western countries would eventually also acquiesce to a Russian-controlled puppet government after the Russian military had swiftly and decisively overrun Ukraine's defenses and taken Kyiv.

Of course, it is not possible to say for certain that more military support and less willingness to turn a blind eye to what Russia was doing in the Donbas would have prevented the invasion of 2022. However, it would have made the prospect of a swift victory and western acquiescence look less realistic from the Kremlin's point of view. This would not have eradicated the possibility but at least decreased the probability of Russia acting in the way it did in 2022. Moreover, better military support from the West would have enabled Ukraine to respond to a full-scale invasion even more effectively had it occurred nevertheless. Potentially, this could have prevented the atrocities Russia committed in Bucha, Mariupol, Izyum, Kherson, and other places.

10.5. Lessons to Be Learned

More could have and should have been done to support and protect Ukraine during and after the initial outbreak of war in 2014. However, there is no point in dwelling too much on past mistakes and wondering whether additional support could have prevented further escalation. What is important, however, is making sure that the mistakes of the past are not repeated. Even though the motives and processes of Kremlin decision-making require additional research, the findings of this book offer important pointers for Western military and diplomatic decision-making in the context of the invasion of 2022.

Firstly, this book has shown that the events of 2014 are aggravating rather than mitigating circumstances in any assessment of Russia's actions in 2022. The Russian regime's claim that it had to intervene after watching eight years of civil war is not only twisting but completely inverting the truth. It is true that the war started in 2014 rather than in 2022, but—already back then—it was Russia who started it. The invasion of 2022 is already Russia's second attempt to destroy Ukraine as an independent, westward looking state by military means. It was not a one-off overreaction that developed a life of its own but part of a long-term agenda. This must be kept in mind when considering any kind of negotiations or agreements with Russia. It is key that Russian efforts to destroy Ukraine come to an end once and for all. Russia must never get a third opportunity to attack. Western weapons deliveries and Western training for Ukrainian soldiers are not an obstacle preventing negotiations. They are a prerequisite for any meaningful peace talks. Lasting peace cannot be based on trust and declarations of goodwill but only on deterrence. Another deal like the Minsk Agreements, which leaves Russia in control over Ukrainian territory while it leaves Ukraine vulnerable to a new offensive some years down the line, is not an option. Ukraine must either receive security guarantees on par with NATO's collective security obligations, or it must be armed to an extent that prevents any decisionmaker in Moscow from even toying with the idea to finish what was started in 2014.

Secondly, this book has shown that Putin's Russia can and should be viewed as a collective, even though it is not a monolith. The invasion of 2014 was not the work of Vladimir Putin alone, and neither was the invasion of 2022. Both iterations of Russian aggression featured the same array of heterogeneous and sometimes competing actors under the common umbrella of the Russian state: the regular Russian Armed Forces, the personal armies of Yevgeny Prigozhin's Wagner Group and Ramzan Kadyrov's Chechen units, as well as Ukrainian collaborators. This means that decision making procedures and power structures within the Russian security apparatus are less straightforward than many assume. It also means that the interests of the various actors involved need to be taken into account when assessing the likelihood of further conflict escalation or potential willingness to deescalate. However, it does not mean that the events are any less of Russia's making. It is important to understand that the various groups involved are by no means acting independently from the state. On the contrary, as informal state organs, they are an integral part of Putin's Russia and its foreign and security policy.

Thirdly, this book has shown that there is not even a shred of legitimacy to Moscow's claims over the territory of the so-called people's republics in the Donbas. Discussions on the restoration of Ukraine's pre-war borders cannot refer to the territory controlled by Kyiv on February 23, 2022. The DNR and LNR are occupied by Russia, just like those areas of Ukraine that the Russian military seized in 2022. Recognizing any Russian claim over these territories would mean recognizing a violent landgrab. This does not necessarily mean that reconquering the whole of the Donbas by military means is feasible or advisable—especially if the Russian regime raises the stakes further and resorts to open nuclear blackmail. However, this is a decision for the Ukrainian authorities and the Ukrainian military to make. After all the country has been through, it is not up to the West to tell Ukraine how much of its own territory it is allowed to liberate and what risks it is allowed to take.

10.6. On Multicausality: Concluding Remarks

This book has investigated questions of causality throughout all its sections. Any study of causality has to deal with fundamental questions that go deep into the philosophy of science. Chapter three has discussed these questions in depth and some of the empirical chapters have revisited them. However, to better illustrate and summarize my findings, it is worth revisiting a question of particular importance once more here at the very end, namely the question how to rank simultaneously occurring necessary causes according to their importance. If both domestic separatism and Russian interference were necessary conditions for the escalation of violence in 2014, how can one be more important than the other? And how is it possible to decide whether the people at the heart of the separatist formations were acting on behalf of the Russian state if both their personal motivation and the state's approval were necessary conditions for their actions?

This book has used the philosophical paradigm of *abnormalism* as summarized by Roberts (1996, 95–99) to tackle this challenge. In his summary, Roberts uses the example of different outbreaks of fire to explain the necessity and appropriateness of ranking different necessary conditions according to the extent to which they *disrupt* the normal course of events. These examples can be developed further and turned into an allegory for the escalation of the Donbas War in 2014. Of course, this allegory is far from perfect, but it summarizes my book's key argument in a concise and accessible way.

My allegory consists of two scenarios. In the first scenario, large parts of a half-timbered house burn down after one of its inhabitants deliberately set fire to a curtain. The person in question did not like their new landlord and thought that a fire would enable the owner of the neighboring property to buy the house cheaply. The owner of the neighboring property, who is known for his unscrupulousness and also holds a personal grudge against the new landlord, encouraged the arsonist and secretly fanned the flames once the fire got going.

In this first scenario, it makes sense to emphasize the arsonist as the main cause of the damage to the house. It is the action of this person that is most *disruptive* to the normal course of events. The neighbor plays an important role that should be mentioned in any comprehensive account of events. However, even if the arsonist would not have set fire to the curtain without the neighbor's encouragement and even if the house would not have burned properly without the neighbor fanning the flames, the neighbor's role remains secondary. The arsonist's act of setting fire to their own home is more abnormal and disruptive than the neighbor's act of taking advantage of the situation, especially in light of what is known about the neighbor's character. Finally, the house's structural features could be mentioned as a contributing condition if space and time permit, but this is optional. While the house may not have burned if it had not been constructed with a timber frame, it would be inappropriate to single out this feature as the fire's primary cause. After all, many other half-timbered houses do not catch fire.

In the second scenario, the initial conditions are mostly the same, but the house is constructed in a way that prevents the curtain fire from reaching the timber frame. Instead, the initial fire causes only superficial damage. The neighbor reacts by handing several Molotov cocktails to a pyromaniac with a history of arsonism and says that it would be a shame if anything happened to the semi-timbered house next door. The pyromaniac throws a Molotov cocktail. One of the rooms catches fire while the resident of the house causes further superficial damage to another room by lighting another curtain. When the poorly equipped and inexperienced fire brigade arrives, the pyromaniac throws his remaining Molotov cocktails into several other rooms and orders the resident to join him in fanning the flames. While the fire brigade tries to attend to the multitude of burning rooms, the neighbor personally adds gasoline to all fires. When the fire brigade is about to contain them anyway, the neighbor personally cuts the fire brigade's water supply and destroys most of its equipment.

In this second scenario, it would no longer be appropriate to designate the resident's behavior as the main cause of the fire. This conclusion holds even under the assumption that the neighbor would not have acted without the resident's initial arson attempt and that the damage would have been smaller had the resident not obeyed the command to fan the flames. Either of these actions by the resident are clearly less disruptive and abnormal than what the neighbor did. At the same time, the actions of the pyromaniac in this scenario are also less disruptive and abnormal than the fact that the neighbor enabled a known arsonist to set fire to a house. Hence, any credible account of the fire would have to start with the neighbor's actions. Investigations of the resident or the pyromaniac and their motives would have to emphasize that their actions represented secondary, auxiliary causes. Finally, the structure of the house merits even less attention than in the first scenario. It withstood the initial arson attempts, whereas a variety of other building types would also have succumbed to the combined power of Molotov cocktails, gasoline, and sabotage of the fire brigade's efforts.

This allegory provides a simplified illustration of this book's approach and its findings. The first scenario is the civil war hypothesis, and the second scenario is the invasion hypothesis. This book has shown that, according to the available DOSI evidence, events in the Donbas in April–August 2014 resembled the latter scenario rather than the former. The house is the Donbas, the building structure is the region's history and society, the fire is armed separatism, the resident represents local pro-Russian activists and their local supporters, and the neighbor is the Russian state. The two burned curtains are the initial building occupations of early April and the events in Mariupol. The pyromaniac represents irregular Russian fighters, the Molotov cocktails are these fighters' armed incursions into Ukraine, the gasoline represents Russian tanks and heavy artillery, and the fire brigade is the Ukrainian military.[48] I have argued that it was the interplay of all these components that was necessary for events to unfold in the way they did. However, the presence of such a multitude of necessary conditions does not mean that all these conditions are of equal importance. This book has found that, according to the *abnormalism* paradigm, the most important cause of the war in the Donbas in 2014 were the actions of the Russian state. This does not mean that other conditions do not deserve scrutiny. However, it does mean that the Donbas War was not an internal Ukrainian conflict before 2022 but has been a war between Russia and Ukraine since its beginning in 2014.

---

48   For simplicity's sake, I refrained from introducing local elites as a separate actor in this allegory. However, they could be depicted as a corrupt property management company that underestimates the destructive potential of the fire and does little to stop it because it hopes to profit from refurbishment works.

References

62.ua. 2014. "U separatistov v zdanii Donetskogo oblsoveta nakhoditsia oruzhie, zakhvachennoe v SBU." April 8, 2014. bit.ly/3mlLV0a, also archived at archive.vn/XJYmi.

0642.ua. 2014a. "Luganskie «UDARovtsy» s palkami i v kaskakh otvoevali sebe ploshchad' u Tarasa Shevchenko." February 22, 2014. bit.ly/3xII6Hp, also archived at archive.vn/OIfwM.

— — —. 2014b. "Odin Prorossiiskii Aktivist Pogib v Perestrelke Okolo Voenkomata." May 4, 2014. bit.ly/3a6po1q, also archived at archive.vn/aqEo8.

06242.ua. 2012. "Vzryv NikitRtut'." YouTube. November 24, 2012. youtube.com/watch?v=iZNVolCUHLw.

Abroskin, Viacheslav. 2015a. "Untitled Facebook Post." May 6, 2015. bit.ly/3Ei3Lc4, archived at archive.vn/H2BDF.

— — —. 2015b. "Untitled Facebook Post." May 22, 2015. bit.ly/3xVMNy1, archived at archive.vn/U8erB.

Afanasyev, Andrey. 2016. "Pamyatnoye Slovo o Voine-Rodnovere." VK. July 13, 2016. bit.ly/3FjpeSH, archived at archive.vn/k8QwW.

AiF. 2019. "Iz Kadetov v Diversanty." Argumenty i Fakty. March 15, 2019. archive.vn/E6e5B.

Akhmetov, Rinat. 2014. "Ekstrennoe Zaiavlenie Prezidenta Kompanii SKM Rinata Akhmetova." Telekanal Donbas on YouTube. May 19, 2014. youtube.com/watch?v=OoKEjA-uLPY.

Aksenov, Sergey. 2015. "Ukaz Glavy Respubliki Krym. O Nagrazhdenii Gosudarstvennymi Nagradami Respubliki Krym." Government of the Republic of Crimea. October 29, 2015. bit.ly/2YilQqi.

Aktualnyye Kommentarii. 2014. "Borodai: Surkov — Nash Chelovek v Kremle." June 16, 2014. bit.ly/3DdE1N3, also archived at archive.vn/ihERr.

Al Jazeera. 2014. "Ukraine Rebels Advance towards Mariupol." YouTube. September 5, 2014. youtube.com/watch?v=ocfxP-lerAY.

Aljukov, Maksim. 2019. "Von Moskaus Gnaden. Genese Und Geist Der „Volksrepublik Donezk"." *Osteuropa* 69 (3–4): 123–31.

Allen, Timmi, Andrew Haggard, Eliot Higgins, Veli-Pekka Kivimaki, Iggy Ostanin, and Aric Toler. 2014. "MH17: Source of the Separatists' Buk." Bellingcat. November 8, 2014. bit.ly/3oa1ZTa.

Allen, Timmi, Daniel Romein, Klement Anders, Eliot Higgins, and Aric Toler. 2016. "The Lost Digit - Buk 3x2." Bellingcat. May 3, 2016. bit.ly/3DchXST.

Alternatio.org. n.d. "Author Page Miroslav Rudenko." Accessed April 3, 2020. bit.ly/3iymgQR, also archived at archive.ph/rPo3t.

Althaus, Scott L., Nathaniel Swigger, Svitlana Chernykh, David J. Hendry, Sergio C. Wals, and Christopher Tiwald. 2011. "Assumed Transmission in Political Science: A Call for Bringing Description Back In." *The Journal of Politics* 73 (4): 1065–1080. doi.org/10.1017/S0022381611000788.

Andrukhovych, Yurii. 2005. "Shukaiuchy Dreamland: Ese pro Vybory v Ukraini." *Krytyka* 9 (1–2): 2.

— — —. 2006. "Atlas. Medytatsii." *Krytyka* 10 (1–2): 9–12.

Angstrom, Jan, and Magnus Petersson. 2019. "Weak Party Escalation: An Underestimated Strategy for Small States?" *Journal of Strategic Studies* 42 (2): 282–300. doi.org/10.1080/01402390.2018.1559154.

Anosov, Viktor. 2019. "Viktor Anosov. Pravda i Bayki Oborony Slavyanska." Yuri Kotenok on YouTube. April 4, 2019. youtube.com/watch?v=G7Lvn3frgQM.

Antel-Plus Antratsit. 2019. "Den' Pamiati Zashchitnikov Sela D'iakovo." YouTube. June 12, 2019. youtube.com/watch?v=5ceZC8JxS_s.

Apraksimov, Vyacheslav. 2014. "Vstavai Strana Ogromnaia!!!!!" YouTube. December 5, 2014. youtube.com/watch?v=Fs9z8J5VbaU.

Arel, Dominique, and Jesse Driscoll. 2023. *Ukraine's Unnamed War: Before the Russian Invasion of 2022*. Cambridge: Cambridge University Press.

Arnold, Richard, and Andreas Umland. 2018. "The Radical Right in Post-Soviet Russia." In *The Oxford Handbook of the Radical Right*, edited by Jens Rydgren, 582–607. Oxford: Oxford University Press. doi.org/10.1093/oxfordhb/9780190274559.013.29.

Ash, Lucy. 2015. "How Russia Outfoxes Its Enemies." BBC News. January 28, 2015. bit.ly/3x0Ixxa.

Askai. 2014. "Rossiiskaia Bronetekhnika v Voine Na Donbasse ch.2." LiveJournal. December 15, 2014. bit.ly/3ixOYkJ, also archived at archive.vn/HI8VZ.

— — —. 2015. "T-90 Na Donbasse." August 14, 2015. bit.ly/3iAaK7j, also archived at archive.vn/BY19d.

— — —. 2016. "Untitled Twitter Post." November 21, 2016. bit.ly/3AdPH0e, also archived at archive.vn/x0udj.

Avdeev, Max. 2014. "Vse, Chto Vy Khoteli Znat' Pro Batal'on Vostok." Twitter. June 1, 2014. bit.ly/3AikEkg, also archived at archive.ph/SJl8k.

Azar, Ilya. 2016. "'Ya Yee Vzial i Lichno Peredal Plotnitskomu' Boets LNR Rasskazal 'Meduze,' Kak Zaderzhivali Nadezhdu Savchenko." Meduza. March 21, 2016. bit.ly/3iAQanw, also archived at archive.ph/NUckg.

Babiak, Mat. 2014. "Insurgents Identified: The Green Men of VKontakte." Euromaidan PR. April 23, 2014. bit.ly/3Bg459C, also archived at archive.ph/y08Ny.

Barabanov, Ilya. 2014. "Untitled Twitter Post." July 17, 2014. bit.ly/2YeI7W2.

Baranec, Tomáš. 2014. "Russian Cossacks in Service of the Kremlin: Recent Developments and Lessons from Ukraine." Russian Analytical Digest No. 153. bit.ly/3l8TRCw.

Barkov, Aleksandr. 2018. "Novorossiia v moem serdtse." 2018. bit.ly/30meH9I.

Barrenechea, Rodrigo, and James Mahoney. 2019. "A Set-Theoretic Approach to Bayesian Process Tracing." *Sociological Methods & Research* 48 (3): 451–84. doi.org/10.1177/0049124117701489.

Barthel, Martin, and Hans-Joachim Bürkner. 2020. "Ukraine and the Big Moral Divide: What Biased Media Coverage Means to East European Borders." *Geopolitics* 25 (3): 633–657. doi.org/10.1080/14650045.2018.1561437.

BBC News. 2014a. "Secret Training Base for Ukraine's Militias." YouTube. May 19, 2014. youtube.com/watch?v=plclJv-V2Z0.

— — —. 2014b. "Kto Atakoval Blokpost Pod Volnovakhoi." YouTube. May 23, 2014. youtube.com/watch?v=7cYC8yhdLaE.

— — —. 2020. "Nebesna Sotnia: Karta Rozstriliv Na Maidani." February 18, 2020. bit.ly/3YxzS1Z, also archived at archive.vn/fjnum.

Beach, Derek. 2017. "Process-Tracing Methods in Social Science." *Oxford Research Encyclopedia of Politics*. doi.org/10.1093/acrefore/9780190228637.013.176.

Beach, Derek, and Rasmus Brun Pedersen. 2013. *Process-Tracing Methods: Foundations and Guidelines*. Ann Arbor: The University of Michigan Press.

Befani, Barbara, and Gavin Stedman-Bryce. 2017. "Process Tracing and Bayesian Updating for Impact Evaluation." *Evaluation* 23 (1): 42–60. doi.org/10.1177/1356389016654584.

Bellingcat. 2015a. "[1071] Rostov, Voenved. Bronetekhnika Na Taganrogskom Shosse." YouTube. February 6, 2015. youtube.com/watch?v=fqL_yZBMtAQ.

— — —. 2015b. "Origin of Artillery Attacks on Ukrainian Military Positions in Eastern Ukraine between 14 July 2014 and 8 August 2014." February 17, 2015. bit.ly/2Wi5XMk.

———. 2015c. "Russia's Path(s) to War. A Bellingcat Investigation." bit.ly/3Bg6yko.

———. 2015d. "MH17 – The Open Source Evidence." October 8, 2015. bit.ly/3Bc6OBb.

———. 2018a. "Skripal Suspects Confirmed as GRU Operatives: Prior European Operations Disclosed." September 20, 2018. bit.ly/3iB7kkL.

———. 2018b. "Skripal Suspect Boshirov Identified as GRU Colonel Anatoliy Chepiga." September 26, 2018. bit.ly/3Aadrm3.

———. 2018c. "Full Report: Skripal Poisoning Suspect Dr. Alexander Mishkin, Hero of Russia." October 9, 2018. bit.ly/3lba7mz.

———. 2019. "How Russia Issues Fake Passports to Its Operatives in Ukraine." November 7, 2019. bit.ly/3AfBZdk.

———. 2020a. "Identifying FSB's Elusive 'Elbrus': From MH17 To Assassinations in Europe." April 24, 2020. bit.ly/3a8E0xs.

———. 2020b. "Bezler–Geranin." YouTube. October 17, 2020. youtube.com/watch?v=XfQaCyVr6WI.

———. 2020c. "The MH17 Trial Part 2: The Bezler Tapes, a Case of Red Herrings?" October 17, 2020. bit.ly/3AbyDYX.

———. 2022. "Donbas Doubles: The Search for Girkin and Plotnitsky's Cover Identiti...." July 18, 2022. bit.ly/3Vt3kUX, archived at archive.ph/UbuhM.

———. n.d.a. "Bellingcat's Online Investigation Toolkit." Accessed May 13, 2021. Public Document. Google Docs. bit.ly/bcattools.

———. n.d.b. "Russian Artillery Attacks on Ukraine 2014." Accessed May 5, 2021. Carto. bit.ly/3Ds47w7.

Bennett, Andrew. 2009. "Process Tracing: A Bayesian Perspective." In *The Oxford Handbook of Political Methodology*, edited by Janet M. Box-Steffensmeier, Henry E. Brady, and David Collier. Oxford Handbooks Online. Oxford University Press. doi.org/10.1093/oxfordhb/9780199286546.003.0030.

Bennett, Andrew, and Jeffrey T. Checkel. 2015. "Process Tracing: From Philosophical Roots to Best Practices." In *Process Tracing: From Metaphor to Analytic Tool*, edited by Andrew Bennett and Jeffrey T. Checkel, 3–37. Cambridge and New York: Cambridge University Press.

Berdiansk District Court. 2015. "Judgement No. 310/6513/14-k." Court Decision Register of Ukraine. April 7, 2015. bit.ly/3uIBQOt, also archived at archive.vn/99lf1.

Bezler, Igor. 2014. "Igor' (Bes) Bezler: Nachnem Nastuplenie, Kogda Protivnik Vydokhnetsia." RIA Novosti. July 16, 2014. bit.ly/3y7bgzL, also archived at archive.vn/u5QTU.

— — —. 2016. "Untitled Social Media Post." VK. September 28, 2016. bit.ly/3FmbfLU, also archived at archive.vn/CU2pL.

— — —. 2017. "Untitled Social Media Post." VK. May 22, 2017. vk.com/wall283528124_304; archived at archive.vn/P1PE4.

— — —. 2020. "Untitled Social Media Post." VK. March 9, 2020. bit.ly/3aghcvy, also archived at archive.vn/R0C9O.

Bezsonova, Inna. 2015. "Otkuda Vzialas' 'DNR' - Proekt 'DNR': 'Respublika' Desiat' Let Nazad." 112 Ukraina. April 23, 2015. bit.ly/3adzPAC, also archived at archive.ph/EsdZ1.

Bohdan, Ivan. 2016. *Mariupol' 2014*. Mariupol. bit.ly/3lcGktG.

Bojanowska, Edyta. 2022. "Putin's Anti-Colonial Agenda?" NYU Jordan Center for the Advanced Study of Russia. December 13, 2022. bit.ly/3DG83Mc.

Bolotov, Valerii. 2014. "Srochno! Luganskie Partizany Pokazali Litso i Skoro Pokazhut Zuby, Obrashchenie!" YouTube. April 5, 2014. youtube.com/watch?v=N27vV0xoMLU.

Boroday, Aleksandr. 2017. "Kommentarii A.BORODAI o Sobytiiakh 26.5.2014g. v Aeroportu 'DONYeTsK.'" YouTube. October 18, 2017. youtube.com/watch?v=EpGMrCyoSww.

Boroday, Aleksandr, and Marianna Maksimovskaya. 2014. "Pervoe Interv'iu Prem'era DNR Aleksandra Borodaia: «Nedelia» s Mariannoi Maksimovskoi." REN TV on YouTube. May 24, 2014. youtube.com/watch?v=K8IKkVG5kAs.

Boroday, Aleksandr, and Denys Pushylin. 2014. "Press-Konferentsiia Predstavitelei VS DNR 29.05.2014." YouTube. May 29, 2014. youtube.com/watch?v=nZgfs3C4PpY.

Botvinyev, Yevstafiy, and Anna Dolgareva. 2018. "«U Nas Za Eto Sazhaiut»: Interv'iu s Byvshim Soratnikom Dmitriia Vagnera. Ridus." Ridus. May 15, 2018. bit.ly/3DfLvzg, also archived at archive.vn/PjuIX.

Bowen, Andrew S. 2019. "Coercive Diplomacy and the Donbas: Explaining Russian Strategy in Eastern Ukraine." *Journal of Strategic Studies* 42 (3–4): 312–343. doi.org/10.1080/01402390.2017.1413550.

Boyd-Barrett, Oliver. 2017. "Ukraine, Mainstream Media and Conflict Propaganda." *Journalism Studies* 18 (8): 1016–1034. doi.org/10.1080/1461670X.2015.1099461.

Bozhko, Yurii. 2014. "Boitsy Natsgvardii v Aleksandrovske Ne Popadali v Plen k Terroristam - NGU." UNN. May 30, 2014. bit.ly/3Fi1cI5, also archived at archive.ph/fkSQo.

Braun, Virginia, and Victoria Clarke. 2021. "To Saturate or Not to Saturate? Questioning Data Saturation as a Useful Concept for Thematic Analysis and Sample-Size Rationales." *Qualitative Research in Sport, Exercise and Health* 13 (2): 201–216. doi.org/10.1080/2159676X.2019.1704846.

Brik, Tymofii. 2021. "The Donbas and Social Science: Terra Incognita?" In *Civil War? Interstate War? Hybrid War? Dimensions and Interpretations of the Donbas Conflict in 2014–2020*, edited by Jakob Hauter, 191–214. Stuttgart: ibidem-Verlag.

Burlakov, Oleksii. 2014. "U Mariupoli Vyishly Na Patruliuvannia DND 'Metinvest.'" Hromadske Radio. May 12, 2014. soundcloud.com/hromadske-radio/12-05-2014.

Business FM. 2016. "Uchastnik «proslushki» Glaz'eva: «Eto Kompiliatsiia i Podtasovka»." August 24, 2016. bit.ly/3DgdEWR, also archived at archive.vn/5NDJR.

Butusov, Yurii. 2016. "Pervyi Boi ATO 13 Aprelia 14-go - Boeviki Moskovskogo Patriarkhata v Otriade FSB Girkina Otkryvaiut Ogon'." Tsenzor.Net. July 17, 2016. bit.ly/3mvOc8S, also archived at archive.vn/cBfcA.

— — —. 2019. "Pochemu proizoshel boi 26 maia 2014 goda v Donetskom aeroportu." Tsenzor.net. May 27, 2019. bit.ly/3iCSiLh, also archived at archive.ph/smS3V.

Capoccia, Giovanni, and R. Daniel Kelemen. 2007. "The Study of Critical Junctures: Theory, Narrative, and Counterfactuals in Historical Institutionalism." *World Politics* 59 (3): 341–369. doi.org/10.1017/S0043887100020852.

Case, Sean, and Klement Anders. 2016. "Putin's Undeclared War. Summer 2014. Russian Artillery Strikes Against Ukraine." Bellingcat. December 21, 2016. bit.ly/3oYoDgi.

Case, Sean, Klement Anders, Aric Toler, and Eliot Higgins. 2015. "The Burning Road to Mariupol. Attacks from Russia during the Novoazovs'k Offensive of August 2014." Bellingcat. December 3, 2015. bit.ly/3mtq9rh.

Cederman, Lars-Erik, and Manuel Vogt. 2017. "Dynamics and Logics of Civil War." *Journal of Conflict Resolution* 61 (9): 1992–2016. doi.org/10.1177/0022002717721385.

Central Electoral Commission of Ukraine. 2014. "Povtorni Vybory Narodnykh Deputativ Ukrainy v Odnomandatnykh Vyborchykh Okruhakh No. 94, 132, 194, 197, 223." 2014. bit.ly/2Yn9Ljy, also archived at archive.vn/uc6Bm.

Chalenko, Aleksandr, and Andrii Saveliev. 2019. "Uchastnik Oborony Slavianska: Motorola Byl Tak Silen Dukhom, Chto Yemu Ne Protivilis' Drugie Komandiry." Ukraina.ru. February 21, 2019. bit.ly/3oArr6m, also archived at archive.vn/Sxkue.

Channel 1. 2014. "Liudei Rasstrelivali Iz Granatometov — Zhertvami Provokatsii Stali Voennosluzhashchie Ukrainskoi Armii." May 22, 2014. bit.ly/3oCHcK0, also archived at archive.vn/ScjRj.

Cherniakov, Vadym. 2012. "Resume from February 22, 2012." Work.ua. February 22, 2012. bit.ly/3lfhiu0, also archived at archive.ph/Yh2EK.

Chernyshev, Yevgeniy. 2014. "Novyi Vitse-Prem'er DNR Vladimir Antiufeev: Ya Pribyl v DNR Na Stol'ko, Na Skol'ko Budet Nuzhno. Terroristy Budut Unichtozhat'sia Na Meste." Nakanune.ru. July 16, 2014. bit.ly/3DcTpJF, also archived at archive.vn/CcORB.

Chetvertaya Vlast. 2015. "Akhmetov i DNR. Kak Donetskii Oligarkh Reagiroval Na Deistviia Separatistov - Chetvertaia Vlast'." April 21, 2015. bit.ly/2Ys0wio, also archived at archive.vn/rNh2w.

Clem, Ralph S. 2017. "Clearing the Fog of War: Public versus Official Sources and Geopolitical Storylines in the Russia-Ukraine Conflict." *Eurasian Geography and Economics* 58 (6): 592–612. doi.org/10.1080/15387216.2018.1424006.

CNN. 2014. "Kadyrovtsy v Donetske (CNN, 26.05.14)." YouTube. May 26, 2014. youtube.com/watch?v=VEtaBm0LFek.

Collier, David, and Gerardo L. Munck. 2017. "Building Blocks and Methodological Challenges: A Framework for Studying Critical Junctures." *Qualitative & Multi-Method Research* 15 (1): 2–9. doi.org/10.5281/zenodo.1145401.

colonelcassad. 2014a. "Sklad v Artemovske." LiveJournal. June 20, 2014. bit.ly/3mrX9A8, also archived at archive.vn/9AtdE.

— — —. 2014b. "Situatsiia u Lutugino." LiveJournal. July 31, 2014. bit.ly/3owPZxg, also archived at archive.vn/3r4iA.

Davies, Lance. 2016. "Russia's 'Governance' Approach: Intervention and the Conflict in the Donbas." *Europe-Asia Studies* 68 (4): 726–749. doi.org/10.1080/09668136.2016.1173652.

Dergachev, Vladimir. 2014. "Novyi Prem'er LNR Marat Bashirov Zanimalsia GR, Rabotal v «Renove» Veksel'berga i Byl Polittekhnologom v «Imidzh-Kontakte»." Gazeta.ru. July 4, 2014. bit.ly/3a94KOk, also archived at archive.vn/qONa4.

Dessler, David. 1991. "Beyond Correlations: Toward a Causal Theory of War." *International Studies Quarterly* 35 (3): 337–355. doi.org/10.2307/2600703.

Digital Forensic Research Lab. 2016. "Breaking Down the Surkov Leaks." Atlantic Council on Medium. October 26, 2016. bit.ly/3AhQIo2.

Dikhtiarenko, Andrii. 2014. "Kto Vy, «zelenye Chelovechki»?" Realnaya Gazeta. April 16, 2014. bit.ly/3FlGY04, also archived at archive.vn/GFvNu.

Dixon, Jeffrey. 2009. "What Causes Civil Wars? Integrating Quantitative Research Findings." *International Studies Review* 11 (4): 707–735. doi.org/10.1111/j.1468-2486.2009.00892.x.

Dixon, Jeffrey, and Meredith Reid Sarkees. 2015. *A Guide to Intra-State Wars. An Examination of Civil, Regional, and Intercommunal Wars, 1816-2014.* Washington DC: CQ Press.

— — —. 2020. "Intra-State War Data (v5.1)." The Correlates of War Project. April 6, 2020. bit.ly/3aeeirg.

Dobrov, Oleksii. 2015. "'Chelovek Surkova' u Istokov 'LNR.'" Realnaya Gazeta. July 30, 2015. bit.ly/3uLIZxA, also archived at archive.vn/IQV3F.

Dobryi, Dmytro. 2018. "Kak Kiyevo-Pecherskaya Lavra Vospityvala Boyevikov Dlya Girkina." Espreso. May 2, 2018. bit.ly/3odSUZl, also archived at archive.vn/SrLbe.

Donbas Battalion. 2014. "Untitled Facebook Post." August 18, 2014. bit.ly/3AjCjrw, also archived at archive.vn/4EXus.

Dondyuk, Maxim. 2014. "V Slavyanske Nochyu Zamecheny Russkiye Diversanty." Ukrainska Pravda. April 22, 2014. bit.ly/3oa6JYY, also archived at archive.vn/Z0u6p.

Dozhd. 2014. "Nashi Soldaty. Grazhdanskoe Rassledovanie. Spisok Pogibshikh, Ranenykh i Plennykh." September 11, 2014. bit.ly/3oyQYwU, also archived at archive.vn/lPpy2.

Dromov, Pavlo. 2014. "Severodonetsk 30 05 2014. Ofitsial'noe Interv'iu Shtaba Armii Yugo-Vostoka." YouTube. June 1, 2014. youtube.com/watch?v=QEDC5KC_z0c.

Dromov, Pavlo, and Marina Akhmedova. 2014. "Ataman Dremov Mezhdu Smekhom i Strakhom." Expert Online. December 30, 2014. bit.ly/3AdkJp7, also archived at archive.ph/ZIANJ.

Dromov, Pavlo, Andrii Lavin, and Sergey Veselovskiy. 2014. "Legendarnyi Batia Pavel Dremov!" Anna News on YouTube. June 16, 2014. youtube.com/watch?v=y59PGI5Mez4.

ds_mok. 2014. "2 Iiunia 2014 Goda, Lugansk. Razbor Proisshestviia." LiveJournal. July 23, 2014. bit.ly/3Bh6gtI, also archived at archive.vn/S7eeS.

Dugin, Aleksandr, and Kateryna Hubarieva. 2014. "A.Dugin i Ye.Gubareva Obsudili Budushchee Donbassa i Ukrainy." YouTube. March 29, 2014. youtube.com/watch?v=-jP0yebodlM.

Dvali, Natalia, and Oleksandr Petrulevych. 2014. "Eks-Nachal'nik Luganskoi SBU Petrulevich: Terroristicheskie Gruppy GRU Rossii Uzhe v Kieve i Zhdut Signala." Gordon. July 2, 2014. bit.ly/3ld130s, also archived at archive.vn/B1YlV.

Dyer, Sophie, and Gabriela Ivens. 2020. "What Would a Feminist Open Source Investigation Look Like?" *Digital War* 1 (1): 5–17. doi.org/10.1057/s42984-020-00008-9.

ECtHR. 2022. Ukraine and the Netherlands v. Russia (Decision). European Court of Human Rights (Grand Chamber). November 30, 2022. bit.ly/41rYMSg.

Elektron-Media. 2014. "11 Sentiabria v Krymske Provozhali v Poslednii Put' Vladimira Kal'manova." YouTube. September 11, 2014. youtube.com/watch?v=wWWhXXiLqJ4.

El-Murid. 2014. "El' Miurid—Donetsk. 26 Maia. Aeroport. Otchet Uchastnika." July 2, 2014. bit.ly/2ZRzpxE, also archived at archive.ph/8SauT.

Espreso TV. 2014. "Komentar Serhiia Yarovoho Shchodo Zatrymanykh v Mariupoli." YouTube. April 18, 2014. youtube.com/watch?v=BWet-Jmd1Vk.

Evera, Stephen van. 1997. *Guide to Methods for Students of Political Science.* Ithaca and London: Cornell University Press.

———. 1999. *Causes of War.* Ithaca and London: Cornell University Press. jstor.org/stable/10.7591/j.ctt24hg70.

Fairfield, Tasha, and Andrew E. Charman. 2017. "Explicit Bayesian Analysis for Process Tracing: Guidelines, Opportunities, and Caveats." *Political Analysis* 25 (3): 363–380. doi.org/10.1017/pan.2017.14.

Fearon, James D. 1991. "Counterfactuals and Hypothesis Testing in Political Science." *World Politics* 43 (2): 169–195.

Fearon, James D. 1995. "Rationalist Explanations for War." *International Organization* 49 (3): 379–414. doi.org/10.1017/S0020818300033324.

Ferguson, Jonathan, and N. R. Jenzen-Jones. 2014. *Raising Red Flags: An Examination of Arms & Munitions in the Ongoing Conflict in Ukraine.* Armament Research Services (ARES). bit.ly/3izJ4PS.

Firsov, Yehor, and Oleksandr Ivanov. 2014. "«Liudi Slovno Pod Gipnozom…»." Ostrov. May 14, 2014. bit.ly/3oyHVfv, also archived at archive.ph/BmUkJ.

Fomenko, Oleksandr. 2014. "Aleksandr Fomenko o Svoem Izbranii 'Narodnym Merom' Mariupolia 01.06.2014." YouTube. June 1, 2014. youtube.com/watch?v=z4GlzMg6Ef8.

Fomenko, Oleksandr, and Yuliia Dydenko. 2018. "Interv'iu v SIZO: "Tretii Narodnyi Mer 'DNR.'" YouTube. March 2, 2018. youtube.com/watch?v=1Dd9YTb74_g.

Forensic Architecture. 2019a. "The Battle of Ilovaisk. Mapping Russian Military Presence in Eastern Ukraine." August 19, 2019. bit.ly/3Dd1WMH.

— — —. 2019b. "The Battle Of Ilovaisk. Project Description." August 19, 2019. bit.ly/3uNuZ6E.

Franchetti, Mark. 2014. "Pinned to the Ground by Blizzard of Bullets." The Times. June 8, 2014. bit.ly/2YzZzoF.

Furmaniuk, Artem. 2014. "'Oprichniki' Akhmetova na strazhe mestnogo kriminaliteta i interesov Kremlia." sled.net.ua. April 8, 2014. bit.ly/3ABhLv2, also archived at archive.vn/bR3I0.

— — —. 2016. "Vostochnyi Tupik. Chto Povlekut Za Soboi Novye Rasklady v 'DNR'?" ORD. March 21, 2016. bit.ly/3bVayfj, also archived at archive.vn/osPS1.

Galeotti, Mark. 2020. "Russia's Murderous Adhocracy." The Moscow Times. August 22, 2020. bit.ly/3sUcBJI, also archived at archive.ph/Ic9UN.

Garmata.org. 2014a. "Evgen Zloy." April 23, 2014. bit.ly/3oOpmDY.

— — —. 2014b. "Ihor Heorhiievskyi." April 23, 2014. bit.ly/2RS9CkR.

— — —. 2014c. "Yevgeniy Ponomaryov." April 23, 2014. bit.ly/3aowWwX.

— — —. 2014d. "Tikhon Karetnyy – Terrorist Osobogo Naznacheniya." July 13, 2014. bit.ly/3uY9Oi0.

Gasparyan, Artur, and Mumin Shakirov. 2014. "DNR – Fiktsiia. Resheniia Prinimaiut Drugie." Radio Free Europe/Radio Liberty. July 10, 2014. bit.ly/3v0MK27, also archived at archive.vn/T2l6k.

Gathmann, Moritz. 2015. "Alexej Relke, Der 'Deutsche' von Lugansk." March 19, 2015. youtube.com/watch?v=iPPIGUnJYUk.

Gentile, Michael. 2020. "Diabolical Suggestions: Disinformation and the Curious Scale of Nationalism in Ukrainian Geopolitical Fault-Line Cities." *Geopolitics* Advance Online Publication (November 1, 2020). doi.org/10.1080/14650045.2020.1830766.

Gerring, John. 2007. *Case Study Research. Principles and Practices*. New York: Cambridge University Press.

Gibson, Stevyn D. 2013. "Open Source Intelligence." In *Routledge Companion to Intelligence Studies*, edited by Robert Dover, Michael S. Goodman, and Claudia Hillebrand, 123–131. London and New York: Routledge. doi.org/10.4324/9780203762721.ch12.

Girkin, Igor. 2014. "Igor' Strelkov: Slaviansk v Operativnom Okruzhenii." YouTube. June 19, 2014. youtube.com/watch?v=6_wwEsFaSqQ.

———. 2015. "Strelkov I.: Pochemu Ne Byli Zakhvacheny Artemovsk i Sklady Oruzhiia v Soledare." YouTube. September 10, 2015. youtube.com/watch?v=_cdlmG1U4XI.

———. 2016a. "Voprosy k Igoryu Strelkovu." Forum of Igor Strelkov's Novorossiya Movement. March 7, 2016. bit.ly/3AA1OF3, also archived at archive.vn/kwEAA#selection-1713.0-1713.1951.

———. 2016b. "VK Social Network Post." April 6, 2016. bit.ly/30miEv2, also archived at archive.vn/UIOz9.

———. 2016c. "Voprosy k Igoryu Strelkovu." Forum of Igor Strelkov's Novorossiya Movement. June 13, 2016. bit.ly/3p4RbZ9, also archived at archive.vn/Jj2QI#selection-689.0-735.113.

———. 2019. "VK Social Network Post." October 28, 2019. bit.ly/3BHECGs, also archived at archive.vn/RQs7v.

Girkin, Igor, and Dmytro Hordon. 2020. "Girkin (Strelkov). Donbass, MH17, Gaaga, FSB, Poludokhlyi Putin, Surkov, Bozhii Sud." May 18, 2020. youtube.com/watch?v=hf6K6pjK_Yw.

Girkin, Igor, Aleksandr Kots, and Dmitriy Steshin. 2014. "Komanduyushchiy samooboronoy Slavyanska Igor Strelkov: Zaderzhannyye nablyudateli — kadrovyye razvedchiki." Komsomolskaya Pravda. April 26, 2014. bit.ly/3AEIhDD, also archived at archive.is/uOsMA.

Girkin, Igor, Aleksey Navalnyy, and Mikhail Zygar. 2017. "Debaty: Aleksei Naval'nyi vs. Igor' Girkin (Strelkov)." Ekho Moskvy. July 20, 2017. bit.ly/2oH9q9J, also archived at archive.vn/bvmKD.

Girkin, Igor, and Sergey Shargunov. 2014. "Semnadtsat kilometrov my shli marshem cherez granitsu." Svobodnaya Pressa. November 11, 2014. bit.ly/3tS94cp, also archived at archive.vn/WFrBY.

Girkin, Igor, and Tavr. 2020. "Strelkov o 'Dele' Mozgovogo." YouTube. March 5, 2020. youtube.com/watch?v=nl3CpjHHApA.

Giuliano, Elise. 2018. "Who Supported Separatism in Donbas? Ethnicity and Popular Opinion at the Start of the Ukraine Crisis." *Post-Soviet Affairs* 34 (2–3): 158–78. doi.org/10.1080/1060586X.2018.1447769.

Giuretis, Tom. 2014. "An Assessment of the June 2 Luhansk Administration Building Attacks." June 3, 2014. bit.ly/3v5kwUd, also archived at archive.vn/PTVva.

Gladun, Andrii. 2020. "Protesting That Is Fit to Be Published: Issue Attention Cycle and Nationalist Bias in Coverage of Protests in Ukraine after Maidan." *Post-Soviet Affairs* 36 (3): 1–22. doi.org/10.1080/1060586X.2020.1753428.

Glavkom. 2014. "V Prigranichnom Sele Na Luganshchine Ozhestochennyi Boi. Terroristy Pytaiutsia Vyvezti Sotniu Trupov v Rossiiu." June 13, 2014. bit.ly/37oRapC, also archived at archive.vn/pxzEt.

Glazyev, Sergey. 2019. "Okkupatsiia." *Zavtra*. May 6, 2019. bit.ly/3AA57fK, also archived at archive.vn/SdfwB.

Gleditsch, Nils Petter, Peter Wallensteen, Mikael Eriksson, Margareta Sollenberg, and Håvard Strand. 2002. "Armed Conflict 1946-2001: A New Dataset." *Journal of Peace Research* 39 (5): 615–37. doi.org/10.1177/0022343302039005007.

GO Sovest. 2012. "Pozdravliaem Vsekh s Prazdnikom Velikoi Pobedy!" May 9, 2012. bit.ly/3mHLQUs, also archived at archive.vn/ViJ2I.

Gonzalez-Ocantos, Ezequiel, and Jody LaPorte. 2021. "Process Tracing and the Problem of Missing Data." *Sociological Methods & Research* 50 (3): 1407–35. doi.org/10.1177/0049124119826153.

Google Street View. 2021. "Intersection of Taganrog-Mariupol Highway and Solovyinaya Street in the Northwest of Rostov-on-Don." April 30, 2021. archive.vn/5ZVR1.

Gordon. 2017. "Obolonskii Sud Kieva Prigovoril Komandira 'Tornado' Onishchenko k 11 Godam Tiur'my, Yego Zama Tsukura – k Deviati." April 7, 2017. bit.ly/3lInYRH, also archived at archive.ph/FKY2z.

Gorenburg, Dmitry. 2014. "Maps of Russian and Ukrainian Military Forces." PONARS Eurasia. March 10, 2014. bit.ly/3Ax8d3T.

Gorlovka.ua. 2014. "Proshchal'nye Slova Besa: «Ya Bol'she v Gorlovku i DNR Nikogda Ne Vernus'»." November 4, 2014. bit.ly/2YMX7eg, also archived at archive.ph/fwcuv.

Gramer, Robbie, and Jack Detsch. 2022. "Britain, Canada Flex Hard-Power Muscles in Showdown with Russia." *Foreign Policy*. January 25, 2022. bit.ly/3XB1KSe, archived at archive.ph/lIhd9.

Grove, Thomas, and Gabriela Baczynska. 2014. "Separatists Tighten Grip on East Ukraine, EU Agrees More Sanctions on Moscow." Reuters. April 14, 2014. bit.ly/2YJm3D2, also archived at archive.vn/bljPg.

Grozev, Christo. 2020. "Russian Spying Is Privatized and Competitive. Counterespionage Should Be Too." *Newsweek*. July 27, 2020. bit.ly/3obLmXf.

Hauer, Neil. 2018. "Russia's Favorite Mercenaries." *The Atlantic*. August 27, 2018. bit.ly/3mHTBd2.

Hauter, Jakob. 2019. "Delegated Interstate War: Introducing an Addition to Armed Conflict Typologies." *Journal of Strategic Security* 12 (4): 90–103. doi.org/10.5038/1944-0472.12.4.1756.

———. 2021a. "Conclusion: Making Sense of Multicausality." In *Civil War? Interstate War? Hybrid War? Dimensions and Interpretations of the Donbas Conflict in 2014–2020*, edited by Jakob Hauter, 215–224. Stuttgart: ibidem-Verlag.

― ― ―. 2021b. "How the War Began: Conceptualizing Conflict Escalation in Ukraine's Donbas." *The Soviet and Post-Soviet Review* 48 (2): 135–163. doi.org/10.30965/18763324-20201380.

― ― ―. 2021c. "Forensic Conflict Studies: Making Sense of War in the Social Media Age." *Media, War & Conflict* Advance Online Publication (August 4, 2021). doi.org/10.1177/17506352211037325.

― ― ―. 2022. "A Digital Open Source Investigation of How War Begins: Ukraine's Donbas in 2014." PhD Thesis, London: UCL. discovery.ucl.ac.uk/id/eprint/10145765.

Hayes, Darren R., and Francesco Cappa. 2018. "Open-Source Intelligence for Risk Assessment." *Business Horizons* 61 (5): 689–697. doi.org/10.1016/j.bushor.2018.02.001.

Hedström, Peter, and Petri Ylikoski. 2010. "Causal Mechanisms in the Social Sciences." *Annual Review of Sociology* 36 (1): 49–67. doi.org/10.1146/annurev.soc.012809.102632.

Higgins, Eliot. 2015. "Confirming the Location of the Same Msta-S in Russia and Ukraine." Bellingcat. May 29, 2015. bit.ly/2X7TG0Z.

Hodgson, Geoffrey M. 2006. "What Are Institutions?" *Journal of Economic Issues* 40 (1): 1–25. doi.org/10.1080/00213624.2006.11506879.

Holenko, Valerii. 2014. "Rezoliutsiia Sessii Luganskogo Oblastnogo Soveta 2 Marta 2014." YouTube. March 2, 2014. youtube.com/watch?v=b6vO2DGpNnE.

Holos Ukrainy. 2014. "U Donetsku Zatrymaly Aktyvista 'Drugoy Rossii.'" April 2, 2014. bit.ly/3lDSagJ, also archived at archive.ph/m5NaC.

Holovnov, Serhii. 2014. "Litsa Separatizma." Insider. May 16, 2014. bit.ly/3BEZaiH, also archived at archive.vn/YCeUq.

Hosaka, Sanshiro. 2018. "The Kremlin's 'Active Measures' Failed in 2013: That's When Russia Remembered It's Last Resort - Crimea." *Demokratizatsiya: The Journal of Post-Soviet Democratization* 26 (3): 321–64.

― ― ―. 2019. "Welcome to Surkov's Theater: Russian Political Technology in the Donbas War." *Nationalities Papers* 47 (5): 750–773. doi.org/10.1017/nps.2019.70.

― ― ―. 2021. "Enough with Donbas 'Civil War' Narratives? Identifying the Main Combatant Leading 'the Bulk of the Fighting.'" In *Civil War? Interstate War? Hybrid War? Dimensions and Interpretations of the Donbas Conflict in 2014-2020*, edited by Jakob Hauter, 89–112. Stuttgart: ibidem-Verlag.

Hromadske TV. 2014a. "Zatrymannia z Hennadiia Balashova u Krymu. Girkin-Strelkov u Simferopoli. 4 Bereznia." YouTube. March 4, 2014. youtube.com/watch?v=XTlnSKglsQQ.

———. 2014b. "Sloviansk. Mistse Boiu." YouTube. April 13, 2014. youtube.com/watch?v=iwqD7sEpxDE.

———. 2014c. "Mariupol, 21:30, Liudi v Maskakh Shturmuiut Viiskovu Chastynu Vnutrishnikh Viisk (No. 3057)." YouTube. April 16, 2014. youtube.com/watch?v=EQz3RaQIWaM.

Hubariev, Pavlo. 2016. *Fakel Novorossii*. St. Petersburg: Piter.

Hudilin, Oleksandr. 2020. "Ot Separatistov Do Natsionalistov. Chto Seichas Proiskhodit Za Zakrytymi Dver'mi Izvestnogo Kluba 'Tor.'" 0629.com.ua. June 24, 2020. bit.ly/3ACEsyH, also archived at archive.vn/QYcg4.

ICTV. 2014. "Video Samogo Tragicheskogo Dnia ATO Pod Volnovakhoi." YouTube. May 23, 2014. youtube.com/watch?v=_z33SIC9TjY.

Inform Napalm. 2014. "Rossiiskie Tanki 'T-90' 136-i Motostrelkovoi Brigady v Luganskoi Oblasti." October 26, 2014. bit.ly/3oXPBrV, also archived at archive.vn/4Bs0Q.

Information Resistance. 2014. "Khroniki rossiisko-ukrainskoi voiny: rossiiskii «Grad» pod Dobropol'em." sprotyv.info. June 14, 2014. bit.ly/3oZmWlZ, also archived at archive.vn/pEyj9.

informator.lg.ua. 2014. "Ukrainskie Tanki v Lutugino." July 30, 2014. bit.ly/3awcjif, also archived at archive.vn/2nFJj.

Inter TV. 2014. "Agent 'Abver': Ni Ya, Ni Igor' Girkin Ne Imeiut Sviazei s FSB Rossii." YouTube. May 5, 2014. youtube.com/watch?v=tevKY_N3WU4.

Interfax. 2014. "Strelkov Podgotovit Donetsk k Aktivnoi Oborone." July 6, 2014. bit.ly/2YPQLef, also archived at archive.vn/ZKKll.

———. 2019. "V DNR zaiavili o primenenii pod Ilovaiskom tol'ko trofeinoi ukrainskoi tekhniki." August 19, 2019. bit.ly/3pcADOX, also archived at archive.vn/lgFnt.

———. 2022. "Prigozhin Potreboval Udalit' Zaiavleniia YeS o Yego Sviazi s 'Gruppoi Vagnera' Cherez Sud." February 12, 2022. bit.ly/3XQU2Ud, also archived at archive.ph/nxmfw.

ITV. 2014. "Priniali Prisiagu. Kak v Bakhchisarae Voennye Dali Kliatvu Na Vernost' Narodu Kryma?" YouTube. March 13, 2014. youtube.com/watch?v=RLRESEcWuXM.

Ivanov, Serhii, and Tetiana Zarovna. 2014. "Luganskii Eks-Nalogovik: Yefremov Do Sikh Por Na Svobode Iz-Za Khalatnosti Pravookhranitel'nykh Organov." Obozrevatel. July 16, 2014. bit.ly/3lAGVWc, also archived at archive.vn/cUnbQ.

JIT. 2016a. "1. Animation: The Weapon." MH17 Joint Investigation Team on YouTube. September 28, 2016. youtube.com/watch?v=dz6CUI-fTRI.

— — —. 2016b. "2. Forensic Investigation MH17." MH17 Joint Investigation Team on YouTube. September 28, 2016. youtube.com/watch?v=nMS3yVJ2h3Y.

— — —. 2016c. "3. MH17 Animation Regarding the Transport Route and the Launch Site." MH17 Joint Investigation Team on YouTube. September 28, 2016. youtube.com/watch?v=Sf6gJ8NDhYA.

— — —. 2016d. "MH17 - Call for Witnesses (V2)." MH17 Joint Investigation Team on YouTube. September 28, 2016. youtube.com/watch?v=0a6nMJyZ1JU.

— — —. 2018. "JIT MH17 Witness Appeal about 53rd Brigade." MH17 Joint Investigation Team on YouTube. May 24, 2018. youtube.com/watch?v=rhyd875Qtlg.

— — —. 2019a. "Witness Appeal June 2019: Chain of Responsibility in the Russian Federation." MH17 Joint Investigation Team on YouTube. June 18, 2019. youtube.com/watch?v=hPGmFJH2ZO8.

— — —. 2019b. "Witness Appeal November 2019 - Conversation Surkov and Borodai; Reinforcements from Russia." MH17 Joint Investigation Team on YouTube. November 13, 2019. youtube.com/watch?v=RpE0YMivLu0.

Johnson, Dominic D.P., and Dominic Tierney. 2011. "The Rubicon Theory of War: How the Path to Conflict Reaches the Point of No Return." *International Security* 36 (1): 7–40. doi.org/10.1162/ISEC_a_00043.

Kahn, Herman. 1965. *On Escalation. Metaphors and Scenarios*. London: Pall Mall Press.

Kalyvas, Stathis N. 2006. *The Logic of Violence in Civil War*. New York, NY: Cambridge University Press.

Kanygin, Pavel. 2014. "Upravliaemaia Vesna." *Novaya Gazeta*. December 8, 2014. bit.ly/3BW6FkO, also archived at archive.vn/knI5g.

Karpov, Oleg, and Aleksandr Boroday. 2012. "Zavtra.Live. 'Chetyre Mitinga.'" ZavtraTV on YouTube. February 3, 2012. youtube.com/watch?v=oguDx9txuFU.

Kashin, Oleg. 2014a. "Oleg Kashin: Vtoroy Reportazh Iz Kryma." *Sputnik i Pogrom*. March 2, 2014. bit.ly/3hoj7Ds, also archived at archive.vn/3170K.

— — —. 2014b. "Reportazh Iz Sevastopolya: Kak Glavkom VMS Ukrainy Pereprisyagal Narodu Kryma." *Sputnik i Pogrom*. March 3, 2014. bit.ly/2R7nW9v, also archived at archive.vn/rPkwS.

— — —. 2014c. "'Eto GRUshnik, Rossiyskiy, Deystvuyushchiy:' Oleg Kashin o Svoyem Znakomstve s Rekonstruktorom, Za-Voyevavshim Pol-Ukrainy." *Sputnik i Pogrom*. April 30, 2014. bit.ly/3w3LZEQ, also archived at archive.vn/bKJPi.

Kashin, Oleg, Irina Merkulova, and Aleksey Solomin. 2014. "Intervyu - V Gostyakh: Oleg Kashin." Ekho Moskvy. May 19, 2014. bit.ly/3f1PzJQ, also archived at archive.vn/HzcGN.

Katchanovski, Ivan. 2016. "The Separatist War in Donbas: A Violent Break-up of Ukraine?" *European Politics and Society* 17 (4): 473–489. doi.org/10.1080/23745118.2016.1154131.

KazakTV. 2014. "Obstrel Pogranzastavy s.D'iakovo 30.05.2014." YouTube. June 1, 2014. youtube.com/watch?v=40e2fqSllAc.

Kazanskyi, Denys. 2015a. "Akhmetov's Losing Bet. The Donbas Master's Current Clout in Politics, Economy and War." The Ukrainian Week. May 18, 2015. bit.ly/3aBkpWZ, also archived at archive.vn/JnmkY.

———. 2015b. "Put' Dremova. Ot 'Pashi Lokatora' Do 'Legendarnogo Bati.'" Chetvertaya Vlast. December 13, 2015. bit.ly/3ayXjQE, also archived at archive.vn/COFcs.

Kazanskyi, Denys, and Maryna Vorotyntseva. 2020. *Yak Ukraina Vtrachala Donbas*. Kyiv: Knyzhkove vydavnytstvo Chorna hora.

Khasov-Kassiya, Sergey. 2018. "Proekt 'Miasorubka'. Rasskazyvaiut Tri Komandira 'ChVK Vagnera.'" Radio Free Europe/Radio Liberty. March 7, 2018. bit.ly/3ABmPzw, also archived at archive.vn/Uihn1.

Khokhlov, Illia. 2019a. "Voyna Vzvodnogo 'Makhno,.'" Yuri Kotenok on YouTube. March 26, 2019. youtube.com/watch?v=ud2uQExBDE4.

———. 2019b. "Tri s Minusom. Pochemu Ne Uderzhali Karachun." Yuri Kotenok on YouTube. March 28, 2019. youtube.com/watch?v=zhsyodBxlLg.

Khomchak, Ruslan. 2019. "Novii Nachal'nik Genshtabu Ruslan Khomchak - Yekskliuzivne Interv'iu VVS." BBC Ukraine Service on YouTube. June 13, 2019. youtube.com/watch?v=IWd_jr57Tks.

Khrypun, Viacheslav. 2015. "Ataman Ne Doekhal Do Banketa." Insider. December 15, 2015. bit.ly/2YQm60f /, also archived at archive.ph/Flb5P.

KIIS. 2014a. "The Views and Opinions of South-Eastern Regions Residents of Ukraine: April 2014." Kyiv International Institute of Sociology. April 20, 2014. bit.ly/3ANQvcR, archived at archive.is/JWsQg.

———. 2014b. "Attitude to the Unitary State and Separatism in Ukraine." Kyiv International Institute of Sociology. May 22, 2014. bit.ly/3mI5UGs, archived at archive.vn/AfMFF.

King, Gary, Robert O. Keohane, and Sidney Verba. 1994. *Designing Social Inquiry*. Princeton, N.J.: Princeton University Press.

King, Ian. 2019. "Not Contributing Enough? A Summary of European Military and Developme…." Center for Strategic & International Studies. September 26, 2019. bit.ly/3UaEmIC, also archived at archive.ph/s8Kyp.

Kmet, Stanislav. 2014. "Ten' Yefremova Nad '"LNR."'" Ukrainska Pravda. December 24, 2014. bit.ly/3iXOR1T, also archived at archive.vn/7Wggx.

Kolsto, Pal. 2016. "Crimea vs. Donbas: How Putin Won Russian Nationalist Support - and Lost It Again." *Slavic Review* 75 (3): 702–725. doi.org/10.5612/slavicreview.75.3.0702.

Komitet. 2016. "Aleksandr Bobkov: «O Zakharchenko, Akhmetove i Yanukoviche»." August 1, 2016. bit.ly/3qdEPyi, also archived at archive.vn/Pcsgr.

Korsunskyi, Serhii, and Nastia Stanko. 2016. "Interviu z Serhiiem Korsunskym, Prava Ruka Bolotova v 'LNR.'" Hromadske TV. November 15, 2016. bit.ly/3ayYQX2, also archived at archive.vn/ibsxF.

Koshkin, Andrey, and Dmitriy Sobachkin. 2016. "Siniaia Desiatka." LiveJournal. May 8, 2016. bit.ly/3mPq5lR, also archived at archive.vn/QiXAv.

Kots, Aleksandr, and Dmitriy Steshin. 2014a. "Luganskie Partizany: 20 Tysiach Shtykov My Vam Garantiruem." Komsomolskaya Pravda. March 22, 2014. bit.ly/3BDyyyK, also archived at archive.vn/CbB5b.

———. 2014b. "Luganskie Partizany: 20 Tysiach Shtykov My Vam Garantiruem." Komsomolskaya Pravda on YouTube. March 22, 2014. youtube.com/watch?v=n3sTRj9SLls.

Kozitsyn, Nikolay. 2014a. "Prikaz Atamana Mezhdunarodnogo Soiuza Obshchestvennykh Ob"edinenii «Vsevelikoe Voisko Donskoe» No. 36." April 9, 2014. bit.ly/3ADfcIw, also archived at archive.vn/V8uBs.

———. 2014b. "Prikaz Atamana Mezhdunarodnogo Soiuza Obshchestvennykh Ob"edinenii «Vsevelikoe Voisko Donskoe» No. 38." April 9, 2014. bit.ly/2X5w1hE, also archived at archive.vn/a2tPw.

———. 2016. "Istoriia Kazach'ei Natsional'noi Gvardii." Cossack National Guard. January 13, 2016. bit.ly/2X83ZlH, also archived at archive.vn/cooKH.

Krykun, Yevheniia. 2014. "Kto Vozglavil Protesty v Luganske. Aktivisty Yugo-Vostoka v Litsakh." Polemika. April 23, 2014. bit.ly/3DBZM9z, also archived at archive.vn/0SPjQ.

KrymInform. 2014. "V Simferopole prokhodyat torzhestva, posvyashchennyye 70-letiyu osvobozhdeniya." April 13, 2014. bit.ly/33EtzOP, also archived at archive.vn/BPg6D.

Krymskiy, Georgiy. 2014a. "Georgy Krymskiy's Photos - Snizhne Tank 1." VK. June 12, 2014. bit.ly/3lANYOE, archived at archive.vn/MDRoU.

— — —. 2014b. "Georgy Krymskiy's Photos - Snizhne Tank 2." VK. June 12, 2014. bit.ly/3AChLL2, archived at archive.vn/AspN2.

— — —. 2014c. "Georgy Krymskiy's Photos - Snizhne Tank 3." VK. June 12, 2014. bit.ly/2X5xNPQ, archived at archive.vn/2xkfk.

— — —. 2014d. "Georgy Krymskiy's Photos - Snizhne Tank 4." VK. June 12, 2014. bit.ly/3AHc4vf, archived at archive.vn/kR1zP.

— — —. 2014e. "Georgiy Krymskiy's Photos – Girkin." VK. August 17, 2014. bit.ly/3FFQpY9, archived at archive.vn/HSrLL.

— — —. 2015. "Georgiy Krymskiy's Photos – Medal." VK. July 13, 2015. bit.ly/3AwygIE, archived at archive.vn/0z71c.

— — —. 2018. "Georgiy Krymskiy's Photos – Aksyonov." VK. May 2, 2018. bit.ly/3awk5sz, archived at archive.vn/YdQoy.

— — —. n.d. "Georgiy Krymskiy's Photos – All Pictures." VK. Accessed August 28, 2020. bit.ly/3oU03AB, archived at archive.vn/lb96U.

Kudelia, Serhiy. 2016. "The Donbas Rift." *Russian Politics & Law* 54 (1): 5–27. doi.org/10.1080/10611940.2015.1160707.

— — —. 2019. "How They Joined? Militants and Informers in the Armed Conflict in Donbas." *Small Wars & Insurgencies* 30 (2): 279–306. doi.org/10.1080/09592318.2018.1546361.

Kulchytskyi, Stanislav, and Larysa Yakubova. 2016. *Trista Rokiv Samotnosti: Ukrainskyi Donbas u Poshukakh Smysliv i Batkivshchyny*. Kyiv: Klio.

Kuromiya, Hiroaki. 1998. *Freedom and Terror in the Donbas. A Ukrainian-Russian Borderland 1870s-1990s*. Cambridge and New York: Cambridge University Press.

— — —. 2019. "The War in the Donbas in Historical Perspective." *The Soviet and Post-Soviet Review* 46 (3): 245–62. doi.org/10.1163/18763324-04603003.

Kuzio, Taras. 2017. *Putin's War Against Ukraine: Revolution, Nationalism, and Crime*. CreateSpace.

Kuzmin, Vitaliy. 2014. "Gonka Geroev Chast' 1 - Vystavka Voennoi Tekhniki." Military Blog Vitaly Kuzmin. June 11, 2014. bit.ly/3mV4AQO, also archived at archive.vn/2O3TF.

Kuzmina, Nika. 2019. "«Kazachestvo – Eto Sostoianie Dushi!» Opolchenets Pavel Strubchevskii." KIATs. January 29, 2019. bit.ly/3oZyNR1, also archived at archive.vn/ZOoP3.

Landik, Volodymyr. 2014. "Bolotov Buv 'Smotriashchym' Kopanok Yefremova." Espreso TV on YouTube. August 20, 2014. youtube.com/watch?v=98q4DV67Ih0.

— — —. 2016. "Landik Rasskazal o Roli Yefremova v Zakhvate Luganska Rossiianami." Liga Novosti. June 1, 2016. bit.ly/3DMDIsH, also archived at archive.vn/LMPlX.

Laruelle, Marlene. 2014. "Novorossiya: A Launching Pad for Russian Nationalists." PONARS Eurasia - Policy Memo No. 357. September 2014. bit.ly/3DAFhdo.

Laryš, Martin, and Emil A. Souleimanov. 2021. "Delegated Rebellions as an Unwanted Byproduct of Subnational Elites' Miscalculation: A Case Study of the Donbas." *Problems of Post-Communism* Advance Online Publication (July 19, 2021). doi.org/10.1080/10758216.2021.1943449.

Latynina, Yuliya. 2014. "Test MBKh." Novaya Gazeta. April 28, 2014. bit.ly/3DKHOBS, also archived at archive.vn/NgHeD.

Lazorenko, Roman. 2014. "V Donetske Liudi s Oruzhiem Zakhvatili Zdanie Gorodskogo Soveta." 62.ua. April 16, 2014. bit.ly/3o6WW6l, also archived at archive.vn/cSWr2.

LB.ua. 2014a. "Zaderzhan Odin Iz Rukovoditelei Mariupol'skikh Separatistov, Yego Okhrannik Pogib." May 25, 2014. bit.ly/3DHAsPs, also archived at archive.vn/jPpek.

— — —. 2014b. "V Luganske Boeviki Zakhvatili Zdaniia Batal'ona Natsgvardii Vmeste s Oruzhiem." May 29, 2014. bit.ly/3vgZtht, also archived at archive.vn/v68Is.

— — —. 2014c. "Terroristy Shturmuiut Pogranotdel v Luganskoi Oblasti." May 30, 2014. bit.ly/3vhxr5f, also archived at archive.vn/K07Ww.

— — —. 2014d. "MVD Podtverzhdaet Gibel' Dvukh Terroristov u Pogranotdela 'D'iakovo.'" June 5, 2014. bit.ly/3p4IzS5, also archived at archive.vn/cJMng.

Lee, Rob. 2020. "Untitled Twitter Thread." July 29, 2020. bit.ly/3j7sOpA.

Lenta.ru. 2014. "Bes Otverg Obvineniia v Unichtozhenii «Boinga»." July 18, 2014. bit.ly/3lJOfPf, also archived at archive.vn/qACOd.

Leshchenko, Serhii. 2014. "Dzherelo: Nynishnia Sytuatsiia v Donetsku - Resultat Zustrichei Akhmetova z Putinym." Tyzhden.ua. April 7, 2014. bit.ly/2XfVO6V, also archived at archive.vn/8xmRo.

Leviev, Ruslan. 2017a. "They Fought for Palmyra… Again: Russian Mercenaries Killed in Battle with ISIS." Conflict Intelligence Team. March 22, 2017. bit.ly/2XiKO8Y, also archived at archive.vn/ATYKq.

———. 2017b. "List of Russian Mercenary Losses in Syria Grows." Conflict Intelligence Team. October 16, 2017. bit.ly/3BLWpMO, also archived at archive.vn/ef9zw.

Levy, Jack S. 1998. "The Causes of War and the Conditions of Peace." *Annual Review of Political Science* 1 (1): 139–165. doi.org/10.1146/annurev.polisci.1.1.139.

———. 2015. "Counterfactuals, Causal Inference, and Historical Analysis." *Security Studies* 24 (3): 378–402. doi.org/10.1080/09636412.2015.1070602.

Levy, Jack S., and William R. Thompson. 2010. *Causes of War*. Chichester: Wiley-Blackwell.

LifeNews. 2014a. "Life News o Boe 13 Aprelia 2014 g. Vozle Pos. Semenovka." YouTube. April 13, 2014. youtube.com/watch?v=R805C4MydPw.

———. 2014b. "Video posle perestrelki pod Slavianskom ostorozhno, v kadre yest' ubitye." YouTube. April 13, 2014. youtube.com/watch?v=UIh22MxCvc0.

———. 2014c. "Shturm Voinskoi Chasti v Luganske - 28 Maia 2014 Goda." YouTube. May 28, 2014. youtube.com/watch?v=_PhQwizKigs.

———. 2014d. "V Aleksandrovske Vzorvali Sklad s Oruzhiem Pri Boiakh Riadom s Voennoi Chast'iu." YouTube. May 29, 2014. youtube.com/watch?v=P6JBq9GJirw.

Liga.Novosti. 2014a. "Terroristy ne smogut vernut'sia v Mariupol'." June 13, 2014. bit.ly/3EW0XSg, also archived at archive.vn/pqRjW.

———. 2014b. "Ukrainskie siloviki kontratakuiut vozle Shirokino - Sovbez." September 5, 2014. bit.ly/3n0r2rF, also archived at archive.vn/dp8UJ.

Loshkariov, Ivan D., and Andrey A. Sushentsov. 2016. "Radicalization of Russians in Ukraine: From 'Accidental' Diaspora to Rebel Movement." *Southeast European and Black Sea Studies* 16 (1): 71–90. doi.org/10.1080/14683857.2016.1149349.

Lost Armour. 2015. "ID 3374 - BM-21-1 - 2014-06-13." October 31, 2015. bit.ly/3vsJZqV, archived at archive.vn/0ndIM.

Lovetsky, Dmitry. 2014. "Separatist Tanks." Associated Press. June 20, 2014. bit.ly/3jp7vjN, also archived at archive.vn/7adjf.

Lowe, Christian, and Maria Tsvetkova. 2014. "Exclusive: In Ukraine, an Armored Column Appears out of Nowhere." Reuters. August 26, 2014. bit.ly/3DE5Pua, also archived at archive.vn/Kl8RC.

Lugansk 1 TV. 2017. "«Nam Ne Ostavili Vybora» Dokumental'nyi Fil'm o Pervykh Shagakh Stanovleniia Luganska"." YouTube. January 28, 2017. youtube.com/watch?v=6waEaimKh6o.

Mahoney, James. 2008. "Toward a Unified Theory of Causality." *Comparative Political Studies* 41 (4–5): 412–436. doi.org/10.1177/0010414007313115.

— — —. 2015. "Process Tracing and Historical Explanation." *Security Studies* 24 (2): 200–218. doi.org/10.1080/09636412.2015.1036610.

Malofeyev, Konstantin, Yelizaveta Sergina, and Petr Kozlov. 2014. "Intervyu - Konstantin Malofeyev, osnovatel Marshal kapitala." *Vedomosti*. November 13, 2014. bit.ly/3obNPki, also archived at archive.vn/VUIQ0.

Malyshkina, Yelena. 2014. "Yeshche 2 Tonny Gumanitarnogo Gruza Sobrali Irkutyane Dlya Donbassa." *Vesti Irkutsk*. June 27, 2014. bit.ly/3FNobLh, also archived at archive.vn/y1lxC.

Mamiyev, Oleg. 2018. "Poslednee Interv'iu s Olegom Mamievym (Pozyvnoi 'Mamai')." DNR "Information Ministry" on YouTube. May 18, 2018. youtube.com/watch?v=T-Qlbu7v4uE.

Maoz, Zeev, Paul L. Johnson, Jasper Kaplan, Fiona Ogunkoya, and Aaron P. Shreve. 2019. "The Dyadic Militarized Interstate Disputes (MIDs) Dataset Version 3.0: Logic, Characteristics, and Comparisons to Alternative Datasets." *Journal of Conflict Resolution* 63 (3): 811–835. doi.org/10.1177/0022002718784158.

Marange, Celine, and Susan Steward. 2021. "French and German Approaches to Russia." Chatham House. November 2021. bit.ly/3AO8pyR.

Matsuka, Oleksii. 2014. "Doma u Gubareva v Donetske 2 Marta 2014 g. Rudenko." YouTube. March 2, 2014. youtube.com/watch?v=yAlyAToDjzY.

Matsuzato, Kimitaka. 2017. "The Donbass War: Outbreak and Deadlock." *Demokratizatsiya: The Journal of Post-Soviet Democratization* 25 (2): 175–201.

Matveeva, Anna. 2016. "No Moscow Stooges: Identity Polarization and Guerrilla Movements in Donbass." *Southeast European and Black Sea Studies* 16 (1): 25–50. doi.org/10.1080/14683857.2016.1148415.

— — —. 2018. *Through Times of Trouble: Conflict in Southeastern Ukraine Explained from Within*. Lanham, MA: Lexington Books.

McDermott, Yvonne, Alexa Koenig, and Daragh Murray. 2021. "Open Source Information's Blind Spot." *Journal of International Criminal Justice* 19 (1): 85–105. doi.org/10.1093/jicj/mqab006.

Mediazona. 2015a. "Protsess Savchenko. Dopros Russkogo." October 15, 2015. bit.ly/3vdyHXn, also archived at archive.vn/jcQZg.

— — —. 2015b. "Protsess Savchenko.Svideteli Obvineniia-6." October 19, 2015. bit.ly/3AELKCh, also archived at archive.vn/ZeTpV.

Melnyk, Oleksandr. 2020. "From the 'Russian Spring' to the Armed Insurrection: Russia, Ukraine and Political Communities in the Donbas and Southern Ukraine." *The Soviet and Post-Soviet Review* 47 (1): 3–38. doi.org/10.1163/18763324-04603009.

Memorybook.org.ua. n.d.a. "Full Data in Spreadsheet Format." Accessed June 23, 2020. Memory Book for Ukraine's Fallen. bit.ly/3BK2usY.

— — —. n.d.b. "Zahybli 22 Travnia." Accessed July 7, 2020. Memory Book for Ukraine's Fallen. bit.ly/3DHuwpF.

— — —. n.d.c. "Shelemin Dmytro Mykhailovych." Accessed July 16, 2020. Memory Book for Ukraine's Fallen. bit.ly/3aDOiFV.

— — —. n.d.d. "Zahybli 14 Chervnia." Accessed August 3, 2020. Memory Book for Ukraine's Fallen. bit.ly/3BOqDP2.

— — —. n.d.e. "Zahybli 17 Chervnia." Accessed August 3, 2020. Memory Book for Ukraine's Fallen. bit.ly/3lIYwv9.

Metinvest. 2014. "Gruppa Metinvest Prizyvaet Otkazat'sia Ot Krovavykh Metodov «zachistki» Mariupolia i Drugikh Gorodov Donbassa." May 10, 2014. bit.ly/3G0jTjV, also archived at archive.vn/2ua8k.

Midlarsky, Manus I. 1990. "Systemic Wars and Dyadic Wars: No Single Theory." *International Interactions* 16 (3): 171–181. doi.org/10.1080/03050629008434754.

Miller, Christopher, Sergei Dobrynin, and Mark Krutov. 2020. "The Executioners Of Slovyansk: RFE/RL Puts Names, Faces To Death Squad." Radio Free Europe/Radio Liberty. July 23, 2020. bit.ly/3vdfMM4, also archived at archive.vn/x1q2i.

Mitrokhin, Nikolay. 2014. "Transnationale Provokation. Russische Nationalisten Und Geheimdienstler in Der Ukraine." *Osteuropa* 64 (5–6): 157–174.

— — —. 2015. "Infiltration, Instruction, Invasion: Russia's War in the Donbass." *Journal of Soviet and Post-Soviet Politics and Society* 1 (1): 219–49.

MK.ru. 2014. "Bes: Obnarodovannyi Ukrainoi Razgovor Opolchentsev Byl, No On Ne o «Boinge»." Moskovskiy Komsomolets. July 18, 2014. bit.ly/3ne0Jyr, also archived at archive.vn/FpYLz.

mnews. 2014a. "V Raione Mariupol'skoi Voinskoi Chasti Nespokoino, Yest' Postradavshie." April 16, 2014. bit.ly/3j57sJB, also archived at archive.vn/jxq1s.

— — —. 2014b. "Mitingi v Mariupole: U Gorsoveta Pominaiut Pogibshikh Vo Vremia Shturma Voinskoi Chasti, a u Dramteatra Sobralis' Storonniki Yedinoi Ukrainy." April 23, 2014. bit.ly/3AVQ9Rv, also archived at archive.vn/iptBt.

Mokrushin, Denis. 2011. "18-ia Motostrelkovaia Brigada. Boevaia Tekhnika." LiveJournal. October 16, 2011. bit.ly/3DHvJNJ, also archived at archive.vn/kdU6j.

Morozov, Anton. 2014. "VK Public Social Media Profile Snapshot." April 30, 2014. bit.ly/3BK4PEg, also archived at archive.vn/yPkNN.

Moscow Public Chamber. 2018. "Obshchestvennaia Palata Goroda Moskvy: Sostav Palaty." October 18, 2018. bit.ly/3p7In4y, also archived at archive.vn/zRZOu.

Mozhayev, Aleksandr, and Simon Shuster. 2014. "Exclusive: Meet the Pro-Russian Separatists of Eastern Ukraine." Time Magazine. April 23, 2014. bit.ly/3uM7klU, also archived at archive.vn/LrtTO.

Myers, Paul. 2020. "How to Conduct Discovery Using Open Source Methods." In *Digital Witness: Using Open Source Information for Human Rights Investigation, Documentation, and Accountability*, edited by Sam Dubberley, Alexa Koenig, and Daragh Murray, 107–142. Oxford: Oxford University Press.

Mykhalkov, Maksym. 2014. "Narodnye Deputaty Ot Luganshchiny: Knopkodavstvo i Separatizm." LB.ua. June 4, 2014. bit.ly/3p5DDfV, also archived at archive.vn/HaCTl.

Mykhnenko, Vlad. 2020. "Causes and Consequences of the War in Eastern Ukraine: An Economic Geography Perspective." *Europe-Asia Studies* 72 (3): 528–560. doi.org/10.1080/09668136.2019.1684447.

Nagrady Rossiyskoy Federatsii. n.d. "Medal' 'Za Zashchitu Kryma.'" Accessed August 28, 2020. bit.ly/3BKxuJz, also archived at archive.vn/JmFfg.

Navalnyy, Aleksey. 2016. "On Povar Putina. On Troll' Putina. On Milliarder." October 4, 2016. navalny.com/p/5086/, archived at archive.ph/eZKHI.

Nazarova, Nina, and Ilya Barabanov. 2018. "'Chem Moi Syn Khuzhe': Mat' Ubitogo v Sirii Boitsa ChVK Boretsia Za Yego Priznanie Soldatom." BBC Russian Service. February 19, 2018. bit.ly/3AKhENE, also archived at archive.vn/Bl7UO.

Nemezida-LNR. 2016. "Lugansk. Chast' 3. Rossiiskie Kuratory Donbassa." October 14, 2016. bit.ly/3lJ1JuI, also archived at archive.vn/81o5f.

Nemyshev, Vyacheslav. 2020. "Tekhnika Bezopasnost Pri Zakupke Oruzhiia." YouTube. January 22, 2020. youtube.com/watch?v=s_tU0SKrwu4.

Nitsova, Silviya. 2021. "Why the Difference? Donbas, Kharkiv and Dnipropetrovsk After Ukraine's Euromaidan Revolution." *Europe-Asia Studies* Advance Online Publication (April 23, 2021). doi.org/10.1080/09668136.2021.1912297.

North, Douglas C. 1991. "Institutions." *Journal of Economic Perspectives* 5 (1): 97–112. doi.org/10.1257/jep.5.1.97.

Novorosinform.org. 2014a. "Boi v Mariupole: Svedeniia Obeikh Storon." June 13, 2014. bit.ly/3FMg8OK, also archived at archive.vn/g2Y65.

— — —. 2014b. "Karateli ustroili v Mariupole zachistku." June 13, 2014. novorosinform.org/300467, archived at archive.vn/KTxGw.

— — —. 2014c. "Opolchentsy sdali Slaviansk, chtoby spasti mirnykh grazhdan." July 5, 2014. novorosinform.org/302066.

— — —. 2020. "Zhiteli Stakhanova Pochtili Pamiat' Pervogo Glavy LNR Valeriia Bolotova." February 14, 2020. bit.ly/3mU9760, also archived at archive.vn/vRfuA.

Novorossia.su. 2014. "Chto Proizoshlo v Mariupole?" May 10, 2014. bit.ly/3aIaBKF, also archived at archive.vn/kOSsP.

Novosti Donbassa. 2006. "Vlasti Donetska Otkryto Podderzhivaiut Separatizm i Slaviano-Fashizm." November 15, 2006. bit.ly/3vfbWCg, also archived at archive.vn/z6xHm.

— — —. 2010. "Spisok Kandidatov v Deputaty Ot Partii Regionov v Donetskii Oblsovet, Donetskii Gorsovet v Raisovety: Nichego Novogo." September 28, 2010. bit.ly/3DGleu7, also archived at archive.vn/GMYHn.

— — —. 2014a. "V Donetske neskol'ko chelovek otkryli 'Vostochnyi front.'" February 22, 2014. bit.ly/3p6Bgte, also archived at archive.vn/FLmkf.

— — —. 2014b. "V Mariupole Prorossiiskie Aktivisty Razmestili Flag RF Okolo Gorsoveta." March 1, 2014. bit.ly/3FOun5I, also archived at archive.vn/zCUBH.

— — —. 2014c. "Ofitsial'no. Lidera donetskikh separatistov Gubareva zaderzhala SBU." March 6, 2014. bit.ly/3FNDUtN, also archived at archive.vn/EX2pZ.

— — —. 2014d. "7 ubitykh, 39 ranenykh v Mariupole 9 maia." May 9, 2014. bit.ly/3FTDulM, also archived at archive.vn/h8ee5.

— — —. 2014e. "Na blokposte v Donetskoi oblasti voennye otbili ataku terroristov." May 19, 2014. bit.ly/3p7UFtI, also archived at archive.vn/hNJHD.

— — —. 2014f. "Chislo zhertv boia pod Karlovkoi bol'she, chem soobshchaiut ofitsial'nye istochniki." May 24, 2014. bit.ly/3mU8Akh, also archived at archive.vn/Ei44U.

— — —. 2014g. "Mariupol'skie Terroristy Trebuiut Osvobodit' Brata «narodnogo Mera Mariupolia» v Obmen Na Zalozhnika." May 30, 2014. bit.ly/3n32qP8, also archived at archive.vn/mXogp.

———. 2014h. "V Luganske prodolzhaetsia boi pogranichnikov s terroristami." June 2, 2014. bit.ly/3p7qYsz, also archived at archive.vn/rbGNS.

———. 2014i. "4 Boitsa Natsgvardii Raneny v Khode Provedeniia Antiterroristicheskoi Operatsii v Mariupole." June 13, 2014. bit.ly/3vffHYo, also archived at archive.vn/y3xrZ.

———. 2014j. "V Techenie Sutok Obstreliano 5 Blok-Postov Ukrainskikh Silovikov." June 18, 2014. bit.ly/3aGaCyR, also archived at archive.vn/oErPK.

Novyy Den. 2014. "Novorossiia Formiruet Pervuiu Tankovuiu Diviziiu." June 19, 2014. bit.ly/3aGv0zV, also archived at archive.vn/LsL94.

NTV. 2014. "V «PrivatBanke» Oligarkha Kolomoiskogo Zaiavili, Chto Voennye Ukrali Bronemashiny." May 22, 2014. bit.ly/3vt69cp, also archived at archive.vn/44cb9.

NVO. 2013. "Voyna v Sirii - Uroki Dlya Rossii." Nezavisimoye Voyennoye Obozreniye. May 24, 2013. No. 17 (758), pages 1 and 4-7.

OHCHR. 2022. "Conflict-Related Civilian Casualties in Ukraine." January 27, 2022. bit.ly/3ahkDpl.

Olevskiy, Timur, and Vladimir Romenskiy. 2014. "Motorola (Arsenii Pavlov) — Komandir Odnogo Iz Podrazdelenii Armii DNR." Ekho Moskvy. October 4, 2014. bit.ly/3G6SYTx, also archived at archive.vn/OCQr9.

Olkhin, Artem. 2014. "Rossiiskie Organizatsii Rabotaiut s Donetskimi Separatistami." YouTube. April 6, 2014. youtube.com/watch?v=WuU5YvMNKsI.

OSCE. 2014. "Protocol on the Results of Consultations of the Trilateral Contact Group, Signed in Minsk, 5 September 2014." September 5, 2014. osce.org/home/123257.

———. 2015. "Package of Measures for the Implementation of the Minsk Agreements." February 12, 2015. osce.org/cio/140156.

Ostafiichuk, Viktor. 2014. "V Spiskakh Razbitogo Pod Luganskom Vzvoda 76 GV DShD Znachatsia..." Espreso TV. August 22, 2014. bit.ly/3pkDq8L, also archived at archive.vn/L37Fx.

Ostermann, Dietmar, and Ida Relke. 2014. "Deutscher hat für pro-russische Separatisten gekämpft." Badische Zeitung. July 3, 2014. bit.ly/30JLl5b.

Ostrov. 2014a. "V Luganske okolo 19-00 proizoshla popytka shturma OGA. 4-kh chelovek uvezla 'skoraia.'" February 22, 2014. bit.ly/3nbmMFL, also archived at archive.vn/kUg4E.

———. 2014b. "Zhiteli Donetska ne speshat zapisyvat'sia v 'Vostochnyi front.'" February 25, 2014. bit.ly/3jh79eY, also archived at archive.vn/ISiIL.

―――. 2014c. "Narodnoe Opolchenie Donbassa Pred''iavilo Ul'timatum Donetskomu Gorsovetu." February 28, 2014. bit.ly/3AZ4lZG, also archived at archive.vn/npCmb.

―――. 2014d. "Miting v Donetske izbral 'narodnogo gubernatora.'" March 1, 2014. bit.ly/2XzXjgA, also archived at archive.vn/wExxm.

―――. 2014e. "Segodnia v tsentre Luganska sobralsia 'Narodnyi sovet Luganshchiny.'" March 1, 2014. bit.ly/2Z5R2JM, also archived at archive.vn/zMwzr.

―――. 2014f. "Rossiiskii aktivist priznalsia, chto prinimal uchastie v shturme Donetskogo oblastnogo soveta i podderzhivaet Gubareva — OstroV." March 7, 2014. bit.ly/3G8tCES, also archived at archive.vn/Tqu3y.

―――. 2014g. "Odin pogib i 26 postradali posle mitinga v Donetske." March 14, 2014. bit.ly/3pjyQra, also archived at archive.vn/vhmfo.

―――. 2014h. "Zakhvatchiki Donetskoi OGA vooruzheny avtomatami i granatometami — OstroV." April 7, 2014. bit.ly/3AXgpec, also archived at archive.vn/zVyuv.

―――. 2014i. "Zakhvatchiki zdaniia SBU v Luganske vozveli barrikady." April 7, 2014. bit.ly/3AZ0YCa, also archived at archive.vn/6ZrEU.

―――. 2014j. "Troe Napadavshikh Ubity Pri Atake Voinskoi Chasti v Mariupole – Avakov." April 17, 2014. bit.ly/3lW1D32, also archived at archive.vn/OVZoF.

―――. 2014k. "Deviat' Chelovek Pogibli i 42 Poluchili Raneniia v Mariupole 9 Maia – Utochnennye Dannye Medikov." May 10, 2014. bit.ly/3B08CvS, also archived at archive.vn/AFvsL.

―――. 2014l. "Rossiiane, Siloviki, 'Regionaly'. Kto Yest' Kto v Pravitel'stve DNR." May 16, 2014. bit.ly/3vw6ZFl, also archived at archive.vn/N5jfb.

―――. 2014m. "DNR Prizyvaet Metallurgov Akhmetova Pereiti Na Ikh Storonu." May 22, 2014. bit.ly/3E1UF2r, also archived at archive.vn/dzraa.

―――. 2014n. "Utochnennye dannye. V boiu pod Volnovakhoi pogibli 16 chelovek." May 22, 2014. bit.ly/2Xssiee, also archived at archive.vn/jHjDq.

―――. 2014o. "V Slavianske i Kramatorske polnomasshtabnaia ATO. Rabotaet aviatsiia i artilleriia." May 29, 2014. bit.ly/3naOOkT, also archived at archive.vn/d4Ueo.

―――. 2014p. "Novaia Elita Donbassa: Neudachniki, Predateli, Romantiki, Avantiuristy, Marionetki… Prodolzhenie." June 25, 2014. bit.ly/3aUSQbf, also archived at archive.vn/GjIDP.

— — —. 2014q. "Yeshche shest' luganchan postradali ot artilleriiskoi strel'by. Odna devushka pogibla." July 4, 2014. bit.ly/3vus7vv, also archived at archive.vn/YpAnh.

— — —. 2014r. "V Ukraine zafiksirovano minimum 1600 rossiiskikh voennykh, bol'shoe kolichestvo artillerii i sredstv PVO." September 1, 2014. bit.ly/3AXi0AI, also archived at archive.vn/LMiYl.

Ostrovsky, Simon. 2014. "First Video Evidence of Russians Among Ukrainian Separatists." VICE News. April 21, 2014. youtube.com/watch?v=-QP6sM5VnUQ.

OTB TV. 2013. "MMM - Piket v Khar'kove. Siuzhet Telekanala OTB." YouTube. June 25, 2013. youtube.com/watch?v=amuJBkjom1Q.

Palmer, Glenn, Roseanne W McManus, Vito D'Orazio, Michael R Kenwick, Mikaela Karstens, Chase Bloch, Nick Dietrich, Kayla Kahn, Kellan Ritter, and Michael J Soules. 2020. "MID-Level and Incident-Level Data 5.0." The Correlates of War Project. November 9, 2020. bit.ly/3lUPM5g.

— — —. 2021. "The MID5 Dataset, 2011–2014: Procedures, Coding Rules, and Description." *Conflict Management and Peace Science* Advance Online Publication (February 26, 2021). doi.org/10.1177/0738894221995743.

Paramonov, Pavel. 2014. "Narodnyi Opolchenets v Donetske: 'Menia Nikto Siuda Ne Prisylal - Ya Sam Priekhal.'" YouTube. May 14, 2014. youtube.com/watch?v=pXpMooWk48w.

Paskhover, Oleksandr. 2014. "Operatsiia Donbass: Kak Yanukovich i Yego Okruzhenie Seiut Khaos Na Vostoke Ukrainy." Novoye Vremya. June 2, 2014. bit.ly/3jjqb4h, also archived at archive.vn/4MbXk.

Pastor-Galindo, Javier, Pantaleone Nespoli, Félix Gómez Mármol, and Gregorio Martínez Pérez. 2020. "The Not Yet Exploited Goldmine of OSINT: Opportunities, Open Challenges and Future Trends." *IEEE Access* 8: 10282–304. doi.org/10.1109/ACCESS.2020.2965257.

pauluskp. 2014. "Ocherednoi Rossiiskii Turist Spalilsia v Donetske." March 6, 2014. bit.ly/3lXTGKE, also archived at archive.vn/j5p6d.

Pavlov, Arsen, and Yelena Gorbachova. 2015. "Motorola: «Prosto Ne Bylo Prikaza Na Zakhvat Aeroporta Donetska»." Russkaya Planeta. May 18, 2015. bit.ly/3nfRsG5, also archived at archive.vn/87X3B.

Pavlovsky, Gleb. 2016. "Russian Politics Under Putin." Foreign Affairs. June 2016. fam.ag/3blmxD6.

Pegov, Semyon. 2016. "Kak ostavliali Slaviansk. Chast' II. Frits." Life. July 9, 2016. bit.ly/3AXjHy4, also archived at archive.vn/5UulR.

Peskov, Dmitriy. 2015. "Peskov: Predlozheniia Glaz'eva Ne Vsegda Sovpadaiut s Pozitsiei Kremlia." RIA Novosti. September 8, 2015. bit.ly/3IaOfAD, also archived at archive.vn/3BxMN.

———. 2016. "Peskov: V Kremle Ne Soglasny So Slovami Ob 'Ekonomicheskoi Katastrofe.'" RIA Novosti. April 6, 2016. bit.ly/34Xp1HF, also archived at archive.vn/7MbPz.

———. 2017. "Putin Ne Razdeliaet 'Spornuiu' Pozitsiiu Glaz'eva Po Novomu Prezidentu Germanii." RIA Novosti. February 17, 2017. bit.ly/33DURIN, also archived at archive.vn/Axvg0.

———. 2019. "V Kremle Nazvali Slova Glaz'eva o 'Pereselentsakh' v Donbass Lichnym Mneniem." RIA Novosti. May 7, 2019. bit.ly/35gCGJx, also archived at archive.vn/CCPio.

———. 2020. "Peskov Zaiavil Ob Otsutstvii v Rossii De-Yure Poniatiia ChVK." Interfax. July 30, 2020. bit.ly/3B72NzS, also archived at archive.ph/uueL7.

Petelin, Aleksandr, and German Raskin. 2014. "Odin Den' Voiny Na Yugo-Vostoke Ukrainy Stoit $3 Mln." Izvestiya. May 30, 2014. bit.ly/3jjsxQF, also archived at archive.vn/IKuiU.

Petlyanova, Nina. 2014. "Desant." Novaya Gazeta. August 26, 2014. bit.ly/3ncfGRp, also archived at archive.vn/72EM2.

Petrulevych, Oleksandr. 2017. "V Dokumentakh Luganskoi SBU Yefremov Ne Upominalsia – Eks-Glava Upravleniia Petrulevich." June 7, 2017. bit.ly/30Ef2V7, also archived at archive.vn/ANYet.

Petrulevych, Oleksandr, and Dmytro Hordon. 2017. "Eks-Glava Donetskoi i Luganskoi SBU Petrulevich: Bez Sanktsii Syna Yanukovicha Po Klichke Sasha-Stomatolog Na Dolzhnost' v SBU Ne Naznachalsia Nikto." Gordon. March 29, 2017. bit.ly/3G5v8qX, also archived at archive.vn/KbVkI.

Pettersson, Thérése. 2020. "UCDP/PRIO Armed Conflict Dataset Codebook Version 20.1." Uppsala Conflict Data Program (UCDP). 2020. ucdp.uu.se/downloads/ucdpprio/ucdp-prio-acd-201.pdf.

Pettersson, Thérése, and Magnus Öberg. 2020. "Organized Violence, 1989–2019." *Journal of Peace Research* 57 (4): 597–613. doi.org/10.1177/0022343320934986.

Phillips, Graham. 2014. "'People's Mayor' of Sloviansk - Tour of His Soap Factory." YouTube. April 26, 2014. youtube.com/watch?v=W00KkYIMU_8.

Pigliucci, Massimo, and Maarten Boudry. 2014. "Prove It! The Burden of Proof Game in Science vs. Pseudoscience Disputes." *Philosophia* 42 (2): 487–502. doi.org/10.1007/s11406-013-9500-z.

Planeta Novostey. 2014. "Yegor Russkii Vstrecha s Kadetami 1.10.14 g." October 3, 2014. youtube.com/watch?v=dAlEhYPe-yI.

Poddubnyy, Yevgeniy. 2014. "Na Yugo-Vostoke Ukrainy Formiruiutsia Partizanskie Otriady." Rossiya 24. March 22, 2014. bit.ly/2Z4OxHR, also archived at archive.vn/2Mzqk.

Polemika. 2014. "Opolchenie Luganshchiny Vzialo Pod Kontrol' Zavod 'Proletarii.'" May 21, 2014. bit.ly/3G8D7nw, also archived at archive.vn/zar7B.

Polukhina, Yuliya. 2015. "Vse Poshlo Po Klanu." Novaya Gazeta. October 3, 2015. bit.ly/30A2EW6, also archived at archive.vn/tDOXf.

Ponomarov, Viacheslav. 2014. "Narodnyi Mer Slavianska: «My Ne Dumali, Chto Doidet Do Voiny, Tak Kak Nadeialis' Na Pomoshch' Rossii»." IA Regnum. October 20, 2014. bit.ly/3aX9Zks, also archived at archive.vn/pgZiY.

Pratskova, Anna. 2014a. "Net Voine! Pod Stenami Gorsoveta Sobralis' Sotni Mariupol'tsev Za Yedinuiu Ukrainu." 0629.com.ua. March 5, 2014. bit.ly/3B3YWR3, also archived at archive.vn/yxTN2.

— — —. 2014b. "V Mariupole Predstaviteli Prorossiiskogo Dvizheniia Razognali Miting Za Yedinuiu Ukrainu." 0629.com.ua. March 15, 2014. bit.ly/2Z82Yup, also archived at archive.vn/nvPyo.

— — —. 2014c. "V Mariupole Mitinguiushchie Vybili Dver' v Gorsovet." 0629.com.ua. March 18, 2014. bit.ly/3nfBP1h, also archived at archive.vn/00ua7.

— — —. 2014d. "V Mariupole Zakhvacheno Zdanie Gorodskogo Soveta." 0629.com.ua. April 13, 2014. bit.ly/3jk9sxT, also archived at archive.vn/4gW0P.

— — —. 2014e. "V Mariupole Pod Stenami GU Militsii Izbity 9 Mitinguiushchikh Za Yedinstvo Ukrainy." 0629.com.ua. April 13, 2014. bit.ly/3Gf68Om, also archived at archive.vn/YiNBT.

— — —. 2014f. "V Mariupole Vybrali Novogo «Narodnogo Mera» — Viacheslava Kuklina." 0629.com.ua. April 14, 2014. bit.ly/3aSLbKH, also archived at archive.vn/YgLoH.

— — —. 2014g. "Zakhvatchiki Mariupol'skogo Gorsoveta Schitaiut, Chto Pod Voinskoi Chast'iu Pogibli Bolee 10 Chelovek." 0629.com.ua. April 19, 2014. bit.ly/3vsJInA, also archived at archive.vn/PN3SU.

— — —. 2014h. "V Mariupole Militsiia Osvobodila Iz Donetskoi Narodnoi Respubliki Piaterykh Plenniykh Voennykh." 0629.com.ua. May 4, 2014. bit.ly/2Xvd9c9, also archived at archive.vn/CrI77.

— — —. 2014i. "V Mariupole Gorsovet Otseplen Voennymi. Yest' Ranenyi." 0629.com.ua. May 8, 2014. bit.ly/3DYoZLE, also archived at archive.vn/meuzM.

— — —. 2014j. "V Mariupole Obrabotano Bolee 80% Protokolov. Lidiruet Poroshenko." 0629.com.ua. May 27, 2014. bit.ly/3aV6uva, also archived at archive.vn/ed4Hd.

Prelovskaya, Vera. 2014. "Kak «khoziain Donbassa» Rinat Akhmetov Vedet Biznes v Usloviiakh Voiny." RBK. September 29, 2014. bit.ly/3jgiBY4, also archived at archive.vn/KzBgv.

Prigozhin, Yevgeniy. 2011. "Yevgenii Prigozhin: «Ya Poshel k Beglovu, On k Medvedevu, Tot k Putinu» ·...." Gorod 812. February 28, 2011. bit.ly/3OWkEPK, also archived at archive.ph/jxQJW.

— — —. 2022a. "Zapros Ot Redaktsii Radio «Komsomol'skaia Pravda» i Otvet." Concord Management and Consulting on VK. September 15, 2022. bit.ly/3XQRsxF, also archived at archive.ph/3dSDG.

— — —. 2022b. "Zapros Ot Redaktsii Izdaniia «Bloknot» i Otvet." Concord Management and Consulting on VK. September 26, 2022. bit.ly/3GQx1Lk, also archived at archive.ph/InC5c.

Prosecutor General's Office of Ukraine. 2016. "Dokazy Prychetnosti Vlady RF Do Posiahannia Na Terytorialnu Tsilistnist Ukrainy." YouTube. August 22, 2016. youtube.com/watch?v=l6K1_vHrJPU.

Pskovskaya Guberniya. 2014. "Vsiu Rotu Polozhili." September 2, 2014. bit.ly/3jkMR40, also archived at archive.vn/l1eIm.

Pushylin, Denys. 2013a. "Registratsiia v MMM Pushilin Denis Vladimirovich Donetskaia Oblast', Makeevka, Ukraina." Keymmm.com. October 10, 2013. bit.ly/3jljoai, also archived at archive.vn/dPEv7.

— — —. 2013b. "MMM Volonter: Avtobiografiia. Pushilin Denis." MMM Volonter. November 25, 2013. bit.ly/30K5nwp, also archived at archive.vn/FyiWR.

— — —. 2014. "Denis Pushilin Agitiruet Za Partiiu MMM Sergeia Mavrodi." YouTube. June 17, 2014. youtube.com/watch?v=DAHQ4FA5Tas.

Putin, Vladimir. 2022a. "Obrashchenie Prezidenta Rossiiskoi Federatsii." Kremlin.ru. February 21, 2022. bit.ly/3XVWZCF.

— — —. 2022b. "Transcript: Vladimir Putin's Televised Address on Ukraine." Bloomberg. February 24, 2022. bit.ly/3zh1azv, also archived at archive.ph/oxtBy.

Putin, Vladimir, and Sergey Aksyonov. 2014. "Vstrecha s Sergeyem Aksyonovym." Kremlin.ru. April 14, 2014. bit.ly/3vXA0sk, also archived at archive.vn/7Izz9.

Putin, Vladimir, and Megyn Kelly. 2018. "Interv'iu Amerikanskomu Telekanalu NBC." President of Russia. March 10, 2018. bit.ly/3gYdPQY, also archived at archive.ph/JOzR1.

Putin@war. 2014. "A Second More Detailed Look into the Flight Path of the Jet in Lugansk." Blogspot. June 3, 2014. bit.ly/3E2pNii, also archived at archive.vn/O43ZJ.

Pyvovarova, Oksana. 2014a. "Posledstviia Shturma Tankovoi Bazy v Artemovske 20 Iiunia: Razbitye Dorogi, Gil'zy i Pozhar." 06274.com.ua. June 20, 2014. bit.ly/3vw4EKk, also archived at archive.vn/iTtss.

— — —. 2014b. "Posledstviia Piatogo Napadeniia Na Tankovuiu Bazu v Artemovske: Razbili KPP." 06274.com.ua. June 27, 2014. bit.ly/2Z4MwM9, also archived at archive.vn/c6tJn.

Pyzhova, Oksana. 2016. "Prezentovana Kniga «Mariupol' 2014» Ob Istorii Goroda Glazami Ochevidtsa." Guru.ua. December 5, 2016. bit.ly/3BZboTy, also archived at archive.vn/C4MPr.

Radio Komsomolskaya Pravda. n.d. "Marat Bashirov." Accessed January 11, 2021. bit.ly/2Z9I2UA, also archived at archive.vn/12B9b.

Rakuszitzky, Moritz, Daniel Romein, Roman Dobrokhotov, Aric Toler, and Klement Anders. 2018. "MH17 — Russian GRU Commander 'Orion' Identified as Oleg Ivannikov." Bellingcat. May 25, 2018. bit.ly/3joD5y0.

Rauta, Vladimir. 2016. "Proxy Agents, Auxiliary Forces, and Sovereign Defection: Assessing the Outcomes of Using Non-State Actors in Civil Conflicts." *Southeast European and Black Sea Studies* 16 (1): 91–111. doi.org/10.1080/14683857.2016.1148416.

RBK. 2016. "Glaz'ev i Zatulin Otvetili Na Publikatsiiu Proslushki Ikh Razgovorov o Kryme." August 23, 2016. bit.ly/3neYZou, also archived at archive.vn/0Ige5.

RBK-Ukraina. 2017. "Delo Yefremova Nachnut Rassmatrivat' v Starobel'ske 16 Yanvaria, - GPU." January 14, 2017. bit.ly/2Zac2PA, also archived at archive.vn/LCghc.

Relke, Alexej, and Valerii Bolotov. 2014. "Interv'iu s Armiei Yugo-Vostoka 07.04.14." YouTube. April 7, 2014. youtube.com/watch?v=oh3m7GaQPQY.

Reuters. 2022. "U.S. Plane Brings Javelin Missiles and Launchers to Ukraine." Reuters. January 25, 2022. bit.ly/3U9Zgr1, also archived at archive.ph/o21zp.

RIA Novosti. 2014a. "Opolchentsy DNR Zaveli Tank Vremen Vtoroi Mirovoi Voiny." June 6, 2014. bit.ly/3E6wBvI, also archived at archive.vn/aKb6J.

— — —. 2014b. "Opolchenie DNR Priznalo, Chto Poluchilo Na Vooruzhenie Tri Tanka." June 12, 2014. bit.ly/3GcoFur, also archived at archive.vn/Rj8LJ.

— — —. n.d. "Marat Bashirov, Novosti o Persone, Poslednie Sobytiia Segodnia." Accessed January 11, 2021. bit.ly/3vwuspK, also archived at archive.vn/F8IUC.

RISE Moldova. 2019. "Generaly Bez Granits." YouTube. July 30, 2019. youtube.com/watch?v=ukQM88Whjwg.

Roberts, Clayton. 1996. *The Logic of Historical Explanation*. University Park, PA: Pennsylvania State University Press.

Robinson, Paul. 2016. "Russia's Role in the War in Donbass, and the Threat to European Security." *European Politics and Society* 17 (4): 506–21. doi.org/10.1080/23745118.2016.1154229.

Romaliiska, Iryna. 2017a. "Khronika zakhvata Kryma. Proslushka sovetnika Putina. Chast' 1." Tsenzor.net. December 21, 2017. bit.ly/30EJ9M7, archived at archive.vn/gEUtQ.

— — —. 2017b. "'Yanukovicha narod, bl#d', vy#bet v etom Sevastopole!' Proslushka sovetnika Putina. Chast' 2." Tsenzor.net. December 28, 2017. bit.ly/3m1H8C6, archived at archive.vn/jCEfc.

— — —. 2018a. "'V Khar'kove vziali uzhe oblsovet, v Donetske vziali. Nuzhno brat' v Odesse'. Proslushka sovetnika Putina. Chast' 3." Tsenzor.net. January 18, 2018. bit.ly/3CaHFHq, archived at archive.vn/Ykc9l.

— — —. 2018b. "'Yesli my zablokiruem Zaporozh'e, my vyigraem. Eto plotina, mosty i energetika. Bez energetiki Krym nezhiznesposoben'. Plenki Glaz'eva. Chast' 4." Tsenzor.net. January 30, 2018. bit.ly/3B9jtns, archived at archive.vn/ZmR92.

— — —. 2018c. "'Oni otmobilizuiut na Zapadnoi Ukraine otmorozkov, vooruzhat ikh. Eto ser'eznuiu ugrozu predstavliaet'. Plenki Glaz'eva. Chast' 5." Tsenzor.net. February 6, 2018. bit.ly/3C8f7y6, archived at archive.vn/p2Rz5.

Romanenko, Anna, and Viacheslav Abroskin. 2016. "Mangust Gotov Byl Sdat'sia. Yesli By Ne Odurachennye Mariupol'tsy, Terroristy Byli By Arestovany." 0629.com.ua. May 9, 2016. bit.ly/3b16F87, also archived at archive.vn/tDsHu.

Rossiiskiy Mirotvorets. 2014. "Opolchentsy Pod Luganskom Zakhvatili Tri Tanka T-64 Ukrainskikh VS." June 9, 2014. bit.ly/3C7VGWb, also archived at archive.vn/y18q2.

Rossiya 24. 2015. "Crimea. The Way Home. Documentary by Andrey Kondrashev." YouTube. March 15, 2015. youtube.com/watch?v=t42-71RpRgI.

Rudenko, Miroslav. 2010. "Uchastnik No.22. Rudenko Miroslav - Raboty Konkursantov - Tsvetaevskaia Osen' 2010." October 5, 2010. bit.ly/30RPsfB, also archived at archive.vn/QpRBo.

Russian Aviation Industry Workers Union. 2017. "Profsoiuz i ODK Obsuzhdaiut Osnovnye Itogi Raboty i Prioritetnye Napravleniia Na Predstoiashchii Period." March 15, 2017. bit.ly/2Z9yyIn, also archived at archive.vn/bTS8m.

Russkaya Sluzhba Novostey. 2014. "Koordinator Zakhvata OGA v Donetske Podtverdil Grazhdanstvo Rossii." YouTube. April 12, 2014. youtube.com/watch?v=cv1Qv9z0zdY.

Russkiy, Yegor. 2018. "Posle Boia Pod Luganskom u p. Metallist 17.06.2014 g." November 2, 2018. vk.com/video141474692_170788764.

Russkiy, Yegor, and LifeNews. 2018. "Razgrom Karatel'nogo Batal'ona 'Aidar.'" November 18, 2018. vk.com/video141474692_170788764.

Sabbagh, Dan. 2022. "UK Supplying Ukraine with Anti-Tank Weapons, MPs Told." The Guardian. January 17, 2022. bit.ly/3VasasE, also archived at archive.ph/e7a4j.

Sakwa, Richard. 2015. *Frontline Ukraine: Crisis in the Borderlands*. London: I.B. Tauris.

— — —. 2017. "The Ukraine Syndrome and Europe: Between Norms and Space." *The Soviet and Post-Soviet Review* 44 (1): 9–31. doi.org/10.1163/18763324-04401003.

Salnychenko, Anastasiia. 2014. "V Dobropol'skom Raione Idet Boi Opolchentsev i Natsgvardii." 06239.com.ua. June 13, 2014. bit.ly/3nox3Pc, also archived at archive.vn/ciwrn.

Sambanis, Nicholas. 2002. "A Review of Recent Advances and Future Directions in the Quantitative Literature on Civil War." *Defence and Peace Economics* 13 (3): 215–43. doi.org/10.1080/10242690210976.

Sambanis, Nicholas, Stergios Skaperdas, and William Wohlforth. 2020. "External Intervention, Identity, and Civil War." *Comparative Political Studies* 53 (14): 2155–82. doi.org/10.1177/0010414020912279.

Sarkees, Meredith Reid. 2010. "The COW Typology of War: Defining and Categorizing Wars (Version 4 of the Data)." The Correlates of War Project. 2010. bit.ly/3GaINxi.

Sarkees, Meredith Reid, and Frank Wayman. 2010. *Resort to War: 1816 - 2007*. Washington DC: CQ Press.

Saveliev, Andrii. 2019a. *Voina v 16. Iz kadetov v «diversanty»*. Moscow: Knizhnyy Mir.

— — —. 2019b. "Prezentatsiia Knigi 'Voina v 16' v Gorode-Geroe Sevastopole." YouTube. March 20, 2019. youtube.com/watch?v=reaWN0L3qMk.

— — —. 2019c. "Prezentatsiia Knigi 'Voina v 16' v Moskve." YouTube. April 18, 2019. youtube.com/watch?v=BvtRYsL8XR4.

— — —. 2019d. "Kak Pogib «Romashka»." Russkaya Vesna. May 2, 2019. bit.ly/3jm9dST, also archived at archive.vn/I2Puo.

SBU. 2014a. "Audiozapys Koordynatora Separatystskykh Aktsii." Security Service of Ukraine on YouTube. April 7, 2014. youtube.com/watch?v=VtWA2Wg59N4.

———. 2014b. "SBU Zatrymala Hromadianyna RF - Koordynatora Separatystskykh Aktsii Na Luhanshchyni." Security Service of Ukraine. April 7, 2014. bit.ly/3jrPDEO, also archived at archive.vn/k6Hzz.

———. 2014c. "GRU Slaviansk 14 04 14." Security Service of Ukraine on YouTube. April 14, 2014. youtube.com/watch?v=xVDx-TqeWj4.

———. 2014d. "Shchodo Zbytoho Litaka (Onovleno)." Security Service of Ukraine on YouTube. July 17, 2014. youtube.com/watch?v=V5E8kDo2n6g.

———. 2014e. "SSU, 'Boeing-777' Plane Crash, 'Buk-M1', 17.07.2014." Security Service of Ukraine. July 18, 2014. youtube.com/watch?v=MVAOTWPmMM4.

———. 2017. "Ispol'zovanie Rossiei Chastnoi Voennoi Kompanii Vagnera." Security Service of Ukraine. October 9, 2017. bit.ly/3E4QRgX.

Schelling, Thomas C. 1966. *Arms and Influence*. New Haven: Yale University Press.

Schneckener, Ulrich. 2021. "Hybrid War in Times of Geopolitics? On the Interpretation and Characterization of the Donbas Conflict." In *Civil War? Interstate War? Hybrid War? Dimensions and Interpretations of the Donbas Conflict in 2014-2020*, edited by Jakob Hauter, 23–59. Stuttgart: ibidem-Verlag.

Schram, Peter. 2021. "Hassling: How States Prevent a Preventive War." *American Journal of Political Science* 65 (2): 294–308. doi.org/10.1111/ajps.12538.

Seawright, Jason. 2016. *Multi-Method Social Science: Combining Qualitative and Quantitative Tools*. Strategies for Social Inquiry. Cambridge: Cambridge University Press. doi.org/10.1017/CBO9781316160831.

Segodnya. 2014a. "Kak Segodnia Mitingovali v Donetske." February 23, 2014. bit.ly/2Wnd85Q, also archived at archive.vn/TbCDU.

———. 2014b. "Poslednie sobytiia Donetska: formiruiut otriady samooborony i okhraniaiut Lenina." February 24, 2014. bit.ly/3vBZrRe, also archived at archive.vn/pQAvS.

———. 2014c. "Donetskii aeroport zachishchaiut pri pomoshchi shturmovoi aviatsii." May 26, 2014. bit.ly/3nkVsnk, also archived at archive.vn/7sLxQ.

———. 2014d. "V Slaviansk i Kramatorsk v''ekhali tanki." June 6, 2014. bit.ly/3nuwwKc, also archived at archive.vn/UKljS.

———. 2014e. "Strel'ba v Dobropol'e: boeviki s ustanovkami 'Grad' i razrukha." June 13, 2014. bit.ly/2Wi4zt6, also archived at archive.vn/YiIqn.

— — —. 2014f. "Pogranichnikov v Donbasse obstrelivaiut minami s territorii RF." July 17, 2014. bit.ly/3GfhO3I, also archived at archive.vn/cbkM8.

— — —. 2014g. "Samye Rezonansnye Sobytiia Dnia v Donbasse: 1 Sentiabria." September 1, 2014. bit.ly/3puiZVh, also archived at archive.vn/EIH78.

Semenchenko, Semen. 2014. "V Boiu Vozle Karlovki Ubito 11 Boitsov Batal'ona Vostok – Semenchenko." Korrespondent. May 26, 2014. bit.ly/3nlSJLy, also archived at archive.ph/qtFJr.

Semenov, Aleksey. 2014. "Voina Spishet Vse." Pskovskaya Guberniya. August 25, 2014. bit.ly/3GdNpT6, also archived at archive.vn/rP63t.

Senekal, Burgert, and Eduan Kotzé. 2019. "Open Source Intelligence (OSINT) for Conflict Monitoring in Contemporary South Africa: Challenges and Opportunities in a Big Data Context." *African Security Review* 28 (1): 19–37. doi.org/10.1080/10246029.2019.1644357.

serg_slavorum. 2015. "Kratkaia Ekskursiia Po Bezlerovskim Mestam Kosmodroma Plesetsk i Goroda Mirnyi." LiveJournal. March 10, 2015. bit.ly/3jnr0ZF, also archived at archive.vn/ugRHn.

Serhatskova, Kateryna. 2014. "V Lagere Batal'ona "Vostok"." Ukrainska Pravda. June 2, 2014. bit.ly/3CaXspG, also archived at archive.vn/aKcYV.

— — —. 2015. "Zanesennyi Vetrom. Kak Elektromekhanik Zakharchenko Vozglavil DNR." Novoye Vremya. March 4, 2015. bit.ly/3AZvf3K, also archived at archive.vn/5tNW3.

Shandra, Alya, and Robert Seely. 2019. "The Surkov Leaks. The Inner Workings of Russia's Hybrid War in Ukraine." London: Royal United Services Institute. bit.ly/3C7Txd8.

Shaposhnikov, Rostyslav. 2014. "Predatel'stvo Generala Khomchaka i Kombata Berezy." YouTube. October 24, 2014. youtube.com/watch?v=WPC0RId3wPQ.

Shapovalov, Aleksandr. 2014. "Desiat' Donskikh Kazakov Pogibli Pod Luganskom." Nezavisimaya Gazeta. May 26, 2014. bit.ly/3vH3FHp, also archived at archive.vn/CDoV3.

Sharii, Anatolii. 2020a. "Boing. «Ptichka Priletela"." YouTube. August 10, 2020. youtube.com/watch?v=3kDfmlkUDcY.

— — —. 2020b. "Untitled Twitter Post." October 17, 2020. archive.vn/7opIa.

Shcherbyna, Serhii. 2014a. "Separatiysty 'Simi.'" Insider. May 15, 2014. bit.ly/3E9XGy0, also archived at archive.vn/16zn5.

— — —. 2014b. "Sviazi DNR: Ten' 'Khoziaev Donbassa.'" Insider. September 12, 2014. bit.ly/3Ed50sL, also archived at archive.vn/OcU9h.

— — —. 2014c. "Sviazi DNR: Firma 'Liuks' i 'Sem'ia' Yanukovicha." Insider. September 27, 2014. bit.ly/3b3BQ2B, also archived at archive.vn/JLR3A.

Shekhovtsov, Anton. 2016. "How Alexander Dugin's Neo-Eurasianists Geared up for the Russian-Ukrainian War in 2005-2013." Anton Shekhovtsov's Blog. January 25, 2016. bit.ly/3E3n740, also archived at archive.vn/6frXL.

Shishkin, Philip. 2014. "Pro-Russian Separatist Takeover Changes Lives in Small Ukraine City." Wall Street Journal. April 23, 2014. on.wsj.com/3nly0Yl, archived at archive.vn/EZLR6.

Shlosberg, Lev. 2014. "Mertvye i Zhivye." Pskovskaya Guberniya. August 25, 2014. bit.ly/3m6VDEJ, also archived at archive.vn/gfL3s.

Sibirtsev, Oleksandr. 2014. "Territorii Dikikh Strelkov." Vesti Reporter. May 2014. bit.ly/3E5osrh, also archived at archive.vn/CR0yT.

Siddi, Marco. 2019. "Italy's 'Middle Power' Approach to Russia." *The International Spectator* 54 (2): 123–38. doi.org/10.1080/03932729.2018.1519765.

Sienkiewicz, Matt. 2015. "Open BUK: Digital Labor, Media Investigation and the Downing of MH17." *Critical Studies in Media Communication* 32 (3): 208–23. doi.org/10.1080/15295036.2015.1050427.

Skripnik, Yevgeniy. n.d. "Odnoklassniki social media page." Accessed September 30, 2020. bit.ly/3nipGtE, also archived at archive.vn/EfMLb.

Slavyansk Delovoy. 2014. "Slavyansk Prostilsya s Shestyu Pogibshimi Zemlyakami v Khode Provedeniya ATO 5 Maya." May 7, 2014. bit.ly/3EeNvIB, also archived at archive.vn/XiHJv.

Smale, Alison. 2014. "Merkel Issues Rebuke to Russia, Setting Caution Aside." The New York Times. November 17, 2014. bit.ly/3JH5du7.

Smith, Dan. 2004. "Trends and Causes of Armed Conflict." In *Transforming Ethnopolitical Conflict*, edited by Alex Austin, Martina Fischer, and Norbert Ropers, 111–27. Wiesbaden: VS Verlag für Sozialwissenschaften. doi.org/10.1007/978-3-663-05642-3_6.

Smith, M.L.R. 2012. "Escalation in Irregular War: Using Strategic Theory to Examine from First Principles." *Journal of Strategic Studies* 35 (5): 613–37. doi.org/10.1080/01402390.2012.706967.

Smoke, Richard. 1977. *War: Controlling Escalation*. Cambridge, MA and London: Harvard University Press.

Smyrnova, Olena. 2014. "Ya Ne Pozvoliu, Chtoby Mne Ukazyvali, Na Kakom Yazyke Mne Razgovarivat'." Fakty. February 24, 2014. bit.ly/3CahQHB, also archived at archive.vn/3ZSFE.

Sokolova, Olena. 2014a. "V Mariupole Mnogotysiachnyi Miting Zaiavil o Provedenii Referenduma." 0629.com.ua. March 8, 2014. bit.ly/3E7X7Vh, also archived at archive.vn/CIxQO.

———. 2014b. "V Mariupole mitinguiushchie razbili stekla i vybili dveri v zdanii prokuratury i gorsoveta." 0629.com.ua. April 5, 2014. bit.ly/3jwOPOO, also archived at archive.vn/7HE7g.

———. 2014c. "V Mariupole DNR Veshchaet o Fashizme Na Tsentral'nom Prospekte." 0629.com.ua. April 26, 2014. bit.ly/30TxnxI, also archived at archive.vn/cfSjZ.

———. 2014d. "V Mariupole na uchastkakh dezhuriat liudi v oranzhevykh zhiletakh (Fotofakt)." 0629.com.ua. May 25, 2014. bit.ly/2XCTebk, also archived at archive.vn/bW37T.

Solntsev, Mykola, and Eduard Okopov. 2014. "«Vostochnyi Front» v Donetske: Separatizm Ne Privedet k Blagopoluchiiu." Novosti Donbassa. March 8, 2014. bit.ly/3nfgRQ4, also archived at archive.vn/n5pt5.

Soshin, Yuriy. 2017. "Ataman Nikolai Kozitsin i «Kazach'ia Natsional'naia Gvardiia»." APN.ru. February 22, 2017. bit.ly/3prjb9r, also archived at archive.vn/8i0v3.

Sotiriou, Stylianos A. 2016. "The Irreversibility of History: The Case of the Ukrainian Crisis (2013–2015)." *Southeast European and Black Sea Studies* 16 (1): 51–70. doi.org/10.1080/14683857.2016.1150700.

Stakhiv, Yevhen. 1995. *Kriz Tiurmy, Pidpillia i Kordony. Povist Moho Zhyttia*. Kyiv: Rada.

State Duma. n.d. "Borodai Aleksandr Yur'evich." Accessed October 26, 2021. bit.ly/3qHgq4e.

Stek, Levko. 2020. "Rossiiskie Boeviki Sbezhali s Donbassa v Krym. Delo MN17." Radio Free Europe/Radio Liberty on YouTube. March 9, 2020. youtube.com/watch?v=Qr4N2I_RlbM.

Still, Keith. 2013. "Static Crowd Density Visuals (100 Square Metres)." Crowd Safety and Risk Analysis. 2013. bit.ly/3bi5emS, also archived at archive.vn/jjjiB.

Stopfake.org. 2014. "Analiz Sobytii v Luganske." June 3, 2014. bit.ly/2ZkkgFa, also archived at archive.vn/wip/4Avmv.

Strubchevskyi, Pavlo, and Sergey Kotkalo. 2015. "V Godovshchinu Nachala Voiny Na Donbasse. Pavel Strubchevskii. 'Kak Eto Bylo.'" Anna News on YouTube. April 5, 2015. youtube.com/watch?v=HoWbK5ySgJM.

Studenna-Skrukwa, Marta. 2014. *Ukraiński Donbas. Oblicza Tożsamości Regionalnej*. Poznań: Nauka i Innowacje.

Suganami, Hidemi. 1996. *On the Causes of War*. Oxford: Clarendon.

Sukhankin, Sergey. 2019. "Unleashing the PMCs and Irregulars in Ukraine: Crimea and Donbas." The Jamestown Foundation. September 3, 2019. bit.ly/3GhRwNW.

— — —. 2020a. "Russian Mercenaries Pour Into Africa and Suffer More Losses (Part One)." The Jamestown Foundation. January 21, 2020. bit.ly/3Gh9q3q.

— — —. 2020b. "Russian Mercenaries Pour Into Africa and Suffer More Losses (Part Two)." The Jamestown Foundation. June 26, 2020. bit.ly/3G8RBU1.

Sundberg, Ralph, Kristine Eck, and Joakim Kreutz. 2012. "Introducing the UCDP Non-State Conflict Dataset." *Journal of Peace Research* 49 (2): 351–62. doi.org/10.1177/0022343311431598.

Surkov, Vladislav, and Aleksandr Boroday. 2021. "ChVK Pegov Surkov i Borodai o Budushchem LDNR, Ukraine, Boinge, Baidene i Chinovnikakh." YouTube. June 12, 2021. youtube.com/watch?v=gYuqBK83l3o.

Sutyagin, Igor. 2015. "Briefing Paper: Russian Forces in Ukraine." Royal United Services Institute. March 2015. bit.ly/3pvCPRq.

Svetikov, Oleksii. 2017. "Osvobozhdenie Lisichanska: Vspomnit' Vsekh Poimenno." Segodnya v Severodonetske. July 23, 2017. bit.ly/3B8V1mn, also archived at archive.vn/mMGE1.

Sviashchenko, Yuliia. 2014a. "V Tsentre Mariupolia Izbili Mitinguiushchikh Za Yedinuiu Ukrainu." 0629.com.ua. April 11, 2014. bit.ly/3cnmCWU, also archived at archive.vn/tN9pw.

— — —. 2014b. "Predstaviteli DNR Zashli v Mariupol'skii Gorsovet i Otravilis' Gazom." 0629.com.ua. May 7, 2014. bit.ly/3wTfP0o, also archived at archive.vn/XcCi8.

— — —. 2014c. "Spisok Pogibshikh v Mariupole 9 Maia Rastet." 0629.com.ua. May 15, 2014. bit.ly/3wV32us, also archived at archive.vn/qPPwG.

Syrian Archive. n.d. "The Syrian Archive Project." Accessed December 11, 2022. syrianarchive.org/.

Taruta, Serhii, and Viktor Shlinchak. 2014. "Sergei Taruta: «Na Donbasse Mnogie Prodolzhaiut Dumat' Tak - Da, Byl «bat'ka», Da, «bat'ka» Grabil, No On Byl Svoi»." Glavkom. April 18, 2014. bit.ly/3DtQUDb, also archived at archive.vn/jAgTR.

TASS. 2014a. "Mer Donetska Podtverdil Gibel' 40 Chelovek v Rezul'tate Spetsoperatsii Kieva." May 27, 2014. bit.ly/3qRxrcl, also archived at archive.vn/ASmYt.

— — —. 2014b. "Pogransluzhba Ukrainy Zaiavila o Shturme Opolchentsami Upravleniia Luganskogo Pogranotriada." June 2, 2014. bit.ly/3DCRuOU, also archived at archive.vn/X7Eh5.

— — —. 2014c. "V DNR Podverdili Fakt Zaderzhaniya Marodnogo Mera Slavyanska." June 10, 2014. bit.ly/3x99vCp, also archived at archive.vn/ob7OC.

Telekanal Donbass. 2014. "V Perestrelke Vozle Voinskoi Chasti v Mariupole Pogiblo Troe." YouTube. April 17, 2014. youtube.com/watch?v=qWMIdh8WvFM.

Teslenko, Lina, and Yaroslav Tynchenko. 2019. "Skilki Voiniv Zahynuly v Ilovaiskomu Otochenni: Vidome Tochne Chyslo i Imena." Novynarnia. August 28, 2019. bit.ly/3oBwkKP, also archived at archive.vn/leQsG.

The Ukrainian Week. 2014. "In the Army Now: Answering Many Why's." July 8, 2014. archive.vn/1v9Xw.

Toler, Aric. 2020a. "How to Verify and Authenticate User-Generated Content." In *Digital Witness: Using Open Source Information for Human Rights Investigation, Documentation, and Accountability*, edited by Sam Dubberley, Alexa Koenig, and Daragh Murray, 185–227. Oxford: Oxford University Press. ebookcentral.proquest.com/lib/ucl/detail.action?docID=6181446.

— — —. 2020b. "Untitled Twitter Post." July 30, 2020. bit.ly/3wTuYyS, also archived at archive.vn/8aXoY.

Trifon, and Danil Bezsonov. 2020a. "Zakhvat Aerodroma." Analiticheskaya Sluzhba Donbassa. February 24, 2020. bit.ly/30DRekG, also archived at archive.vn/SrkG4.

— — —. 2020b. "Krymskaia Vesna." Analiticheskaya Sluzhba Donbassa. February 24, 2020. bit.ly/3Drx7V0, also archived at archive.vn/g1Z5J.

— — —. 2020c. "Russkaia Vesna: Ekskliuzivnoe Interv'iu «Trifona»." Analiticheskaya Sluzhba Donbassa. February 26, 2020. bit.ly/3oBBXZE, also archived at archive.vn/uVveq.

TRK Sigma. 2014. "Mariupol'. Posle Shturma V/Ch No.3057 17.04.14." YouTube. April 17, 2014. youtube.com/watch?v=pQzcuHUTdE8.

Tsarov, Oleh. 2014a. "Oleg Tsarev v Donetske: 'Oni Boiatsia Vas!'" YouTube. April 12, 2014. youtube.com/watch?v=16kDcNCFrGw.

— — —. 2014b. "Oleg Tsarev v Donetske: 'Ya Nikuda Ne Uedu!'" YouTube. April 12, 2014. youtube.com/watch?v=Rk8tuwC6ePI.

— — —. 2014c. "Oleg Tsarev v Luganske: 'My Dolzhny Byt' Kak Kulak!'" YouTube. April 12, 2014. youtube.com/watch?v=I9iDfo4V0Cw.

———. 2014d. "Oleg Tsarev v Luganske: 'Ya Schitaiu Etu Vlast' Nezakonnoi.'" YouTube. April 12, 2014. youtube.com/watch?v=jiFOg7IlNa0.

TSN. 2014a. "V Mariupole Separatisty Ob''iavili 'Narodnym Merom' Reketira Pod Sledstviem." March 28, 2014. bit.ly/3CqT4SH, also archived at archive.vn/bq6h3.

———. 2014b. "Liashko Zapostil Foto 'Ministra Oborony Separatistov' v Trusakh." May 7, 2014. bit.ly/3qNlYuk, also archived at archive.vn/qEwI4.

———. 2014c. "Ukrainskie Desantniki Ubili Odnogo i Ranili 14 Terroristov v Luganske." June 10, 2014. bit.ly/3wZBsfB, also archived at archive.vn/dSd2d.

———. 2019a. "5 Rokiv Viiny Za 2 Khvylyny." YouTube. April 14, 2019. youtube.com/watch?v=ciJJhpQVhp0.

———. 2019b. "Ataman 'Terets': Kontrrazvedka Razoblachila Rossiianina, Kotoryi Byl 'Komendantom' Okkupirovannogo Kramatorska i Zakhvatyval Ukrainskie Tserkvi v Krymu." October 18, 2019. bit.ly/3hnSKNN, also archived at archive.vn/Tzm3m.

Tsukur, Mykola, and Natalia Dvali. 2015. "Byvshii Separatist, a Seichas Boets ATO: V Fevrale 2014-go Yefremov Pri Mne Govoril, Chto Privez 70 Tysiach Pasportov RF Dlia Zhitelei Luganska." Gordon. May 11, 2015. bit.ly/30zxZsc, also archived at archive.vn/p5q6b.

Tsygankov, Andrei. 2015. "Vladimir Putin's Last Stand: The Sources of Russia's Ukraine Policy." *Post-Soviet Affairs* 31 (4): 279–303. doi.org/10.1080/1060586X.2015.1005903.

Tumanov, Grigoriy. 2016. "Tenevoi Blok." Kommersant Vlast. February 29, 2016. bit.ly/3cnK86c, also archived at archive.vn/cTOfP.

Turchynov, Oleksandr. 2014a. "Turchinov Grozit Donbassu 'Antiterroristicheskimi Merami.'" YouTube. April 7, 2014. youtube.com/watch?v=DhXsPxLWr7k.

———. 2014b. "O. Turchynov: My ne damo Rosii povtoryty krymskyi stsenarii u skhidnomu rehioni Ukrainy." YouTube. April 13, 2014. youtube.com/watch?v=qrV0JmNLf-c.

UCDP. n.d.a. "Ukraine: Donetsk." Accessed October 26, 2021. Uppsala Conflict Data Program (UCDP). bit.ly/3GqKE0P, archived at archive.vn/8lrMI.

———. n.d.b. "Ukraine: Lugansk." Accessed October 26, 2021. Uppsala Conflict Data Program (UCDP). bit.ly/3nuBbwT, archived at archive.vn/oh51t.

———. n.d.c. "Ukraine: Novorossiya." Accessed October 26, 2021. Uppsala Conflict Data Program (UCDP). bit.ly/3pEl6Y4, archived at archive.vn/qnp2R.

UINP. 2022. "Informatsiino-Metodychni Materialy Do Dnia Heroiv Nebesnoi Sotni, Rozrobleni Natsionalnym Muzeiem Revoliutsii Hidnosti." Ukrainian Institute of National Memory. February 18, 2022. bit.ly/3YwhjLF, also archived at archive.vn/5CHjL.

UK Government. 2019. "Intelligence Collection, Analysis and Dissemination Policy Framework." Ministry of Justice, HM Prison & Probation Service. bit.ly/3w40lFu.

Ukraine@war. 2015. "Google Earth Shows Russians Crossed Border to Attack Ukrainian Camp at Zelenopole." Blogspot. January 29, 2015. bit.ly/3nFWkpr, also archived at archive.vn/8paSw.

Ukrainian Foreign Ministry. 2014. "Geneva Statement on Ukraine." Mission of Ukraine to the North Atlantic Treaty Organization. April 17, 2014. bit.ly/3oH0WLe, archived at archive.vn/vcq7M.

Ukrainska Pravda. 2014a. "Luganskuiu OGA shutrmovali, yest' postradavshie." February 22, 2014. bit.ly/3nA93db, also archived at archive.vn/zOgiI.

— — —. 2014b. "V sotssetiakh verbuiut rossiian dlia aktsii na Donbasse i Odesse." March 3, 2014. bit.ly/3CwHN3u, also archived at archive.vn/pgBxJ.

— — —. 2014c. "V Luganske prorossiiskie aktivisty izbili Yevromaidan i zakhvatili OGA." March 9, 2014. bit.ly/32c0lcF, also archived at archive.vn/R428b.

— — —. 2014d. "V Bakhchisarae Pokhishchennyi Komandir Sdal Voennuiu Chast' Zakhvatchikam." March 10, 2014. bit.ly/3FvTitU, also archived at archive.vn/BPFO4.

— — —. 2014e. "Yarema i Timoshenko srochno letiat v Donetsk, glava SBU - v Lugansk." April 7, 2014. bit.ly/2Z2AbrC, also archived at archive.vn/zrCJk.

— — —. 2014f. "Donetskie Separatisty Poobeshchali Osvobodit' Zdanie SBU i Slozhit' Oruzhie - Yarema." April 8, 2014. bit.ly/3DADup8, also archived at archive.vn/NiWWH.

— — —. 2014g. "Zakhvativshie zdanie SBU v Luganske otpravili svoikh na peregovory s vlast'iu." April 8, 2014. bit.ly/3kPcxqs, also archived at archive.vn/sSVAO.

— — —. 2014h. "Separatisty Pokinuli Zdanie SBU v Donetske, Ischezlo Oruzhie - Istochnik." April 8, 2014. bit.ly/3FuKGnd, also archived at archive.vn/jcfqd.

— — —. 2014i. "Yarema nadeetsia, chto k 11 utra v Donetskoi OGA separatistov uzhe ne budet." April 9, 2014. bit.ly/3cthNeu, also archived at archive.vn/y8TEY.

―――. 2014j. "Akhmetov Predlozhil Separatistam Byt' Posrednikom." April 10, 2014. bit.ly/3CDmGMF, also archived at archive.vn/fLxjM.

―――. 2014k. "Luganskie separatisty uzhe khotiat amnistiiu dlia 'Berkuta.'" April 11, 2014. bit.ly/3oE5NN4, also archived at archive.vn/UiQXc.

―――. 2014l. "SBU Razyskivaet Rossiiskogo Podpolkovnika, Kotoryi Zakhvatyval Militsiiu v Gorlovke." April 18, 2014. bit.ly/3nyOnCd, also archived at archive.vn/lCQxt.

―――. 2014m. "1 voennyi pogib i 3 raneny v boiu mezhdu Rubezhnym i Druzheliubovkoi." May 23, 2014. bit.ly/3oJXxuX, also archived at archive.vn/uYjm0.

―――. 2014n. "Ot Terroristov Osvobodili Yeshche 2 Goroda - Artemovsk i Druzhkovku." July 6, 2014. bit.ly/3oML3Td, also archived at archive.vn/NKHd0.

―――. 2014o. "Voennykh vozle Zelenopol'ia obstreliali so storony granitsy s RF." July 11, 2014. bit.ly/3HBMxsi, also archived at archive.vn/1rZBQ.

United Nations. 2020. "Berkeley Protocol on Digital Open Source Investigations." UC Berkeley School of Law Human Rights Center and OHCHR. bit.ly/3zSzD7H.

Utov, Mikhail. 2019. "Donbasskii Gruz-200 ChVK «Vagnera». Chast' 1." May 7, 2019. bit.ly/3HFGzGI, archived at archive.vn/XJoKh.

Vasquez, John A. 1993. *The War Puzzle*. Cambridge: Cambridge University Press.

Veselova, Viktoria. 2017. "Krymskiy 'Gruz 200:' Krymchane, Pogibshiye v Boyakh Za 'DNR' i 'LNR.'" Radio Free Europe/Radio Liberty. May 17, 2017. bit.ly/30ONzAk, also archived at archive.vn/besao.

Vesti. 2014a. "Luganskii oblsovet priznal kievskuiu vlast' nelegitimnoi." March 2, 2014. bit.ly/3kZqzFN, also archived at archive.vn/eTwSt.

―――. 2014b. "V Donetskuiu OGA Zavezli Avtomaty Kalashnikova. Protestuiushchie Govoriat, Chto 'Otstupat' Teper' Nekuda.'" April 7, 2014. bit.ly/3nBhxRc, also archived at archive.vn/caeoL.

―――. 2014c. "Avakov rasskazal o rezul'tatakh nochnoi spetsoperatsii v Mariupole." April 17, 2014. bit.ly/3cChY7w, also archived at archive.vn/LKVRy.

―――. 2014d. "V Mariupole Podschityvaiut Pogibshikh i Zhdut Zachistki Goroda." May 7, 2014. bit.ly/3l0CX8u, also archived at archive.vn/6jqsG.

―――. 2014e. "Avakov Rasskazal o Gibeli 21 Cheloveka s Oboikh Storon v Perestrelke v Mariupole." May 9, 2014. bit.ly/3xcdON3, also archived at archive.vn/OEwSs.

— — —. 2014f. "V Mariupole 9 maia pogibli sem' chelovek i 39 postradali." May 9, 2014. bit.ly/3CzpLNW, also archived at archive.vn/kdygt.

— — —. 2014g. "V Slavianske iz artillerii obstreliali detskuiu bol'nitsu." May 30, 2014. bit.ly/3nFELFP, also archived at archive.vn/256Lf.

Vesti.ru. 2014. "Donetskim Opolchentsam Ne Udalos' Zakhvatit' Tankovuiu Bazu v Artemovske." June 20, 2014. bit.ly/30S2REw, also archived at archive.vn/XYIio.

VICE News. 2014. "The New Rebel Offensive: Russian Roulette (Dispatch 72)." YouTube. September 2, 2014. youtube.com/watch?v=hgrSb8G57cI.

VK. 2014. "Evgen Zloy Profile Page Snapshot." April 24, 2014. archive.vn/r1YNQ.

Votinova, Anna. 2014. "Voronezhtsy Na Mitinge: Derzhis', Lugansk! Voronezh s Toboi!" Bloknot Voronezh. March 29, 2014. bit.ly/3nBoy4u, also archived at archive.vn/2hxul.

Voyskovye Chasti Rossii. n.d. "Voiskovaia Chast' 27777 (18-ia OMSBr)." Accessed September 1, 2020. bit.ly/30JTZk4, also archived at archive.vn/9xV7l.

Wheatley, Ben. 2018. "British Open Source Intelligence (OSINT) and the Holocaust in the Soviet Union: Persecution, Extermination and Partisan Warfare." *Intelligence and National Security* 33 (3): 422–38. doi.org/10.1080/02684527.2017.1410516.

Wikimapia. n.d. "Turbaza 'Yaseny.'" Accessed August 4, 2021. bit.ly/3oPS8CD, archived at archive.vn/j0MF8.

Wilson, Andrew. 2014. *Ukraine Crisis. What It Means for the West*. New Haven and London: Yale University Press.

— — —. 2016. "The Donbas in 2014: Explaining Civil Conflict Perhaps, but Not Civil War." *Europe-Asia Studies* 68 (4): 631–52. doi.org/10.1080/09668136.2016.1176994.

yadocent. 2014. "Pavshie v Luganske." LiveJournal. June 4, 2014. bit.ly/3DG3ajX, also archived at archive.vn/zSG0F.

Yefremov, Oleksandr. 2014a. "Yefremov Na Mitinge v Luganske 2.03.2014." YouTube. March 2, 2014. youtube.com/watch?v=OgHNzOGC2UA.

— — —. 2014b. "Lider parlamentskoi fraktsii Partii regionov schitaet, chto vooruzhennyi zakhvat SBU v Luganske – eto mnenie mnogikh liudei." Ostrov. April 7, 2014. bit.ly/32dVg3y, also archived at archive.vn/xznO9.

— — —. 2014c. "Vystuplenie Aleksandra Yefremova v Verkhovnoi Rade Ukrainy, 12.05.2014." YouTube. May 12, 2014. youtube.com/watch?v=c0DI9UmwDJw.

YouTube. 2012. "Rossiia, A280 - Ukraina, M14. [Taganrog - Mariupol']." December 6, 2012. youtube.com/watch?v=zheX2iflqUg.

———. 2014a. "'Aktsiya 'Antimaydanovtsev' + Tsirk Ot Shtepy, v Den Traura, 23.02.2014, g.Slavyansk (Donetskaya Obl.)." February 23, 2014. youtube.com/watch?v=qxLpBLH-ohM.

———. 2014b. "Miting v Donetske 23 Fevralia 2014. Chto Na Samom Dele Dumaiut Zhiteli Donetska." February 23, 2014. youtube.com/watch?v=2aklurujd9A.

———. 2014c. "MVI 0094." March 1, 2014. youtube.com/watch?v=laUFb_7ZgBs.

———. 2014d. "Miting V Luganske. 1 Marta 2014." March 1, 2014. youtube.com/watch?v=ckVkZDf_34g.

———. 2014e. "Miting Na Ploshchadi Lenina v Donetske 1 Marta 2014 Goda." March 1, 2014. youtube.com/watch?v=rOTNZyCvOEs.

———. 2014f. "Russkaia Vesna - Lugansk 1 Marta 2014." March 1, 2014. youtube.com/watch?v=I6pNxaRlaUg.

———. 2014g. "Shestvie / Mirnyi Miting v Donetske 1 Marta 2014 Goda." March 1, 2014. youtube.com/watch?v=3GFrijU8NvE.

———. 2014h. "Dveri." March 2, 2014. youtube.com/watch?v=EN6mZfuSfI8.

———. 2014i. "Mitingi v Donetske Prodolzhaiutsia. 3 Marta 2014." March 3, 2014. youtube.com/watch?v=KadxzCjEXSg.

———. 2014j. "Shturm DonODA." March 3, 2014. youtube.com/watch?v=AMDYy2bTGMg.

———. 2014k. "Antifashistskii Miting v Mariupole 08.03.2014." March 8, 2014. youtube.com/watch?v=yXpTwi56Z6I.

———. 2014l. "Obrashchenie Yugo-Vostoka." March 16, 2014. youtube.com/watch?v=6E_Tx1ZtxnQ.

———. 2014m. "Gorsovet Mariupol'. 18.03.14. Viacheslav Kuklin." March 18, 2014. youtube.com/watch?v=eN-Md2OjFQw.

———. 2014n. "Vnimanie! Mobilizatsiia Yugo-Vostoka Ukrainy!" April 1, 2014. youtube.com/watch?v=M8s1IetITWs.

———. 2014o. "6 Aprelia 2014 Sobytiia v Donetske. Polnoe Video." April 6, 2014. youtube.com/watch?v=RsFeWotGFxM.

———. 2014p. "06 Aprelia 2014 Shturm - Zakhvat SBU Luganskoi Oblasti." April 6, 2014. youtube.com/watch?v=_NuCnoXJ5Vo.

———. 2014q. "V Donetske 6 Aprelia 2014 Zakhvat Gorodskoi Administratsii." April 6, 2014. youtube.com/watch?v=fFeA1t6oQQk.

———. 2014r. "Donetsk 6 Aprelia 2014 Chast' 5 Narod Shturmuet OblGosAdministratsiiu Donetska." April 6, 2014. youtube.com/watch?v=8p3G2dUDs4c.

———. 2014s. "Donetsk 6 Aprelia 2014 Chast' 12 Obsuzhdenie Plana Deistvii s Militsiei." April 6, 2014. youtube.com/watch?v=W_5zuSwAlI8.

———. 2014t. "Donetsk 6 Aprelia 2014 Chast' 14 Obrashchenie Glav Soprotivleniia Donbasa!!!" April 6, 2014. youtube.com/watch?v=LWJLnCov3gA.

———. 2014u. "Donetsk 7 Aprelia 2014 Noch' Oblastnaia Administratsiia Donetskoi." April 6, 2014. youtube.com/watch?v=wH4jI6p4_R4.

———. 2014v. "Lugansk, 06.04.2014. Zakhvat Zdaniia SBU." April 6, 2014. youtube.com/watch?v=yJQO3GOZPTg.

———. 2014w. "Shturm Obladministratsii v Donetske. 06.04.2014 / Storming of the Regional Administration in Donetsk." April 6, 2014. youtube.com/watch?v=XgzV8XIycqU.

———. 2014x. "Provozglashenie Donetskoi Narodnoi Respubliki 07.04.2014." April 7, 2014. youtube.com/watch?v=SRJ1YqjMu3s.

———. 2014y. "V Donetske Vybrali Chlenov Vremennogo Pravitel'stva." April 8, 2014. youtube.com/watch?v=5C6YafI992w.

———. 2014z. "Donetsk 8 Aprelia 2014." April 8, 2014. youtube.com/watch?v=DzSIYR9zojQ.

———. 2014aa. "Zakhvat SBU Donetsk 07.04.2014." April 8, 2014. youtube.com/watch?v=Ir_u2B-VUwc.

———. 2014ab. "Rinat Akhmetov i Nikolai Levchenko Vozle Donetskoi OGA. 8.04.2014." April 8, 2014. youtube.com/watch?v=01eWab_Wvvc.

———. 2014ac. "Zdanie SBU g. Luganska 09.04.2014g., 18:30." April 9, 2014. youtube.com/watch?v=57ukdTFwXgU.

———. 2014ad. "Press-Konferentsiia Yugo-Vostochnoi Armii 09.04.14." April 9, 2014. youtube.com/watch?v=Pp3AKWSKVQ4.

———. 2014ae. "Press Konferentsiia Vremennogo Pravitel'stva DNR." April 10, 2014. youtube.com/watch?v=lT4MhwcBwrI.

———. 2014af. "Press-Konferentsiia Pravitel'stva Donetskoi Narodnoi Respubliki. 10.04.2014." April 10, 2014. youtube.com/watch?v=VKxEYpoAB_Q.

———. 2014ag. "Zakhvat UVD g.Slaviansk." April 12, 2014. youtube.com/watch?v=F_1Aji1GFXM.

———. 2014ah. "Slaviansk Shturm Gorotdela 12 04 2014." April 12, 2014. youtube.com/watch?v=QDXqnVqGlGI.

———. 2014ai. "Kramatorsk, Zakhvat Otdela MVD." April 13, 2014. youtube.com/watch?v=VGLr8-6Dpxs.

———. 2014aj. "Bezler I.N. (BYeS) v Gorlovke. (Zakhvat Raiotdela) 14 04 2014." April 14, 2014. youtube.com/watch?v=ElFPsRUqE8Y.

———. 2014ak. "Kramatorsk i Slaviansk,16 04 2014 Samooborona Poluchila BMD." April 16, 2014. youtube.com/watch?v=BDqm7UWumz8.

———. 2014al. "Shou Na BMD v Slavianske 16.04.2014." April 16, 2014. youtube.com/watch?v=96knzHmsIO0.

———. 2014am. "Fragmenty Poezdki Rebiat Shkoly Biznesa LIDYeR k Nikolaiu Tarasenko." April 25, 2014. youtube.com/watch?v=HVEVY7hqjrU.

———. 2014an. "Antratsit 05.05.2014 Pribytie Vezhlivykh Kazakov." May 5, 2014. youtube.com/watch?v=A2Ux-I_EDlw.

———. 2014ao. "Lugansk Antratsit v Gorod Priekhali Russkie Kazaki." May 6, 2014. youtube.com/watch?v=dEhNvhXrUO4.

———. 2014ap. "Vstrecha s Predstaviteliami DNR v Mariupole 18.05.2014." May 18, 2014. youtube.com/watch?v=6YQaOQZTVIQ.

———. 2014aq. "Rasstrel Ukrainskimi Vertoletami Svoikh Ukrainskikh Chastei v Volnovakha (Blagodatnoe) 22 Maia 2014." May 22, 2014. youtube.com/watch?v=psCnGMEL4d0.

———. 2014ar. "Pokhorony Geroev Stakhanova." May 24, 2014. youtube.com/watch?v=Z5_X-IcdepQ.

———. 2014as. "Obrashchenie Komendanta DNR k Meru Mariupolia i Gorozhanam. 28.05.2014." May 28, 2014. youtube.com/watch?v=hj5w7-zs-cE.

———. 2014at. "2 06 14 Lugansk Shturm Pogranchasti Boitsami Armii Luganskoi Narodnoi Respubliki." June 2, 2014. youtube.com/watch?v=z0498KjrFBY.

———. 2014au. "Geroi Novorossii - Edvard «Piterskii»." June 5, 2014. youtube.com/watch?v=r0BItX3Z_zw.

———. 2014av. "Kolonna Boevikov v Luganske 11 Iiunia." June 11, 2014. youtube.com/watch?v=hIiQ7Yh719w.

———. 2014aw. "Makeevka. Kolonna Tankov. 12.06.14." June 12, 2014. youtube.com/watch?v=q977zU2J1ww.

———. 2014ax. "Torez Tanki k Opolcheniiu Pribylo Podkreplenie 12.06.2014." June 12, 2014. youtube.com/watch?v=v73d1bq837I.

———. 2014ay. "Dobropol'e, Sozhzhennaia Ustanovka GRAD." June 13, 2014. youtube.com/watch?v=4y1Vr-beV6c.

———. 2014az. "Dobropol'e Obstrel Gradom." June 14, 2014. youtube.com/watch?v=m2Ul_mpEfkU.

―――. 2014ba. "Yak Ponomarov Pochynav Svoiu Kareru." June 16, 2014. youtube.com/watch?v=EzctVapvW-Q.

―――. 2014bb. "Kolona 1." June 20, 2014. youtube.com/watch?v=PSs7Rs_VJqM.

―――. 2014bc. "Tanki i BTR v Gorlovke 20.06.2014." June 20, 2014. youtube.com/watch?v=Z_Jp8nF6L1w.

―――. 2014bd. "Torez. Motoryzovana Kolona Boiovykiv Rukhaietsia Cherez Misto." June 21, 2014. youtube.com/watch?v=89IVKu1aH94.

―――. 2014be. "Donetsk V Raione Krasnodona Stoiat Rossiiskie Tanki 4 Iiulia 2014." July 4, 2014. youtube.com/watch?v=Wp4a0K4QYeI.

―――. 2014bf. "Tanki Pod Flagom Kryma V"ekhali v Krasnodon." July 4, 2014. youtube.com/watch?v=bRkCZ4rzhSQ.

―――. 2014bg. "Krasnodon Rossiiskie Tanki Voshli v Gorod 04 07 2014 (Nesusvetnaia Radost' Zhitelei)." July 9, 2014. youtube.com/watch?v=JbZSAKY9UpI.

―――. 2014bh. "Kurginian - Donetsk 7 Iiulia 2014, Polnaia Versiia Press-Konferentsii, Sliv Strelkova I.I., DNR i NOD." July 9, 2014. youtube.com/watch?v=WD00ClwCqWw.

―――. 2014bi. "Aleksandr Borodai, Igor' Strelkov. Donetsk, Press-Konferentsiia 10 Iiulia 2014." July 10, 2014. youtube.com/watch?v=1-Z_dJRHfB8.

―――. 2014bj. "TV 'Sut' Vremeni - DNR'. Vypusk 10: Osetinskaia 'Sut' Vremeni' - v Batal'one 'Vostok.'" July 10, 2014. youtube.com/watch?v=gYzMBoVC63g.

―――. 2014bk. "Po Trasse Tanki Grokhotali." July 11, 2014. youtube.com/watch?v=oDcVn37Xv0g.

―――. 2014bl. "13.07.14. Kolonna Bronetekhniki LNR Na Ulitsakh Luganska." July 12, 2014. youtube.com/watch?v=h0TAhMAsknM.

―――. 2014bm. "Ukraina.Russkie Tanki,SAU 2S1 'Gvozdika' v Yenakievo 15.07. Donetsk. Putin Ustroil Skidki v Voentorge." July 15, 2014. youtube.com/watch?v=J93t4oIIeAw.

―――. 2014bn. "DNR, Donetsk. U Batal'ona 'Vostok' Poiavilas' Trofeinaia Bronetekhnika. 16.07.2014." July 16, 2014. youtube.com/watch?v=wGAhIs2x2Bg.

―――. 2014bo. "Donetsk, Kuibyshevskii Raion Posle Obstrela 19 07 2014." July 19, 2014. youtube.com/watch?v=yRIgwjBgxpE.

―――. 2014bp. "Lugansk. Krasnodon - Molodogvardeisk. Bol'shaia Kolona Rossiiskoi Voennoi Tekhniki 02.09.2014." September 3, 2014. youtube.com/watch?v=A_JiDaoMC0I.

―――. 2014bq. "Kolonna Rossiiskikh Voisk Vozle Luganska (03.09.14)." September 7, 2014. youtube.com/watch?v=ewliSdAKO30.

———. 2014br. "Krasnoiarsk Pogruzka Tanka v Samolet An 124 100 Otpravka v Taganrog 31 05 2014g." October 16, 2014. youtube.com/watch?v=jcd68FktZUU.

———. 2014bs. "Kramatorsk. Zakhvat Kolonny Ukrainskoi Bronetekhniki 16.04.2014 g." October 19, 2014. youtube.com/watch?v=M1bvYNjihDs.

———. 2014bt. "Opolchenets Novorossii 'Prapor' v Studii ARI TV Ch.1." November 9, 2014. youtube.com/watch?v=9RVq3bAQE0I.

———. 2015a. "[1146] Torez Kolonna BTR i Tankov 21 Iiunia DNR." February 11, 2015. youtube.com/watch?v=R4xYaYgOUGM.

———. 2015b. "Donetsk Live No.196: Igor' Khakimzianov." September 17, 2015. youtube.com/watch?v=3pPFE5OQLbQ.

———. 2016a. "Donetsk.7 Aprelia,2014.Vziatie SBU,Arkhiv 2." March 26, 2016. youtube.com/watch?v=z-43BuMUiCM.

———. 2016b. "T-90A u Sela Lysoe Ukraina." November 21, 2016. youtube.com/watch?v=RbZQ71614lY.

———. 2017a. "Interv'iu s Pervym Ministrom Oborony DNR | Igor' Khakimzianov." June 24, 2017. youtube.com/watch?v=T4D51UWXBnE.

———. 2017b. "Slaviansk, 16.04.2014." July 6, 2017. youtube.com/watch?v=h_Gx3S38dQE.

———. 2019a. "Volnovakha 21 Maia 2014 Goda." May 1, 2019. youtube.com/watch?v=sgclTfjJhmA.

———. 2019b. "Volnovakha 22 Maia 2014 Goda - Rezul'tat." May 1, 2019. youtube.com/watch?v=o65wNQIESGI.

———. 2020a. "RSOTM, Vladlen i Tikhii | Gruppa Strelkova: Operatsiia Slaviansk." April 5, 2020. youtube.com/watch?v=_VORIU9Tpu8.

———. 2020b. "RSOTM, Vladlen i Igor' Strelkov | Operatsiia Slaviansk." April 13, 2020. youtube.com/watch?v=Gkfl47Xh1O4.

Yurchenko, Yuliya. 2018. *Ukraine and the Empire of Capital: From Marketisation to Armed Conflict*. London: Pluto Press.

Zaks, Sherry. 2021. "Updating Bayesian(s): A Critical Evaluation of Bayesian Process Tracing." *Political Analysis* 29 (1): 58–74. doi.org/10.1017/pan.2020.10.

Zdryliuk, Bronislava, and Valentina Murakhovska. 2014. "Rodychi Abvera umovliaiut yoho zdatisia." Gazeta.ua. May 8, 2014. bit.ly/2mlWEwu, also archived at archive.vn/YZjbx.

Zhegulev, Ilya. 2013. "Rassledovanie: Kak Lichnyi Kulinar Putina Nakormit Armiiu Za 92 Mlrd Rublei." Forbes Russia. March 18, 2013. bit.ly/3H8KKwP, also archived at archive.ph/ddEKv.

Zhezhera, Liudmyla. 2014. "Mariupol'tsev «uslyshali» v Krymu. Aksenov Napisal Obrashchenie k Zhiteliam Goroda." 0629.com.ua. March 4, 2014. bit.ly/3oPCHdH, also archived at archive.vn/Nih2t.

Zhuchkovskiy, Aleksandr. 2018. *85 Dney Slavyanska*. Nizhniy Novgorod: Chornaya Sotnya.

Zhychko, Vera. 2014. "Osada Voinskoi Chasti v Mariupole: «My Budem Otstrelivat'sia Do Poslednego Patrona. No Nam Nuzhna Pomoshch'!»." Fakty. April 18, 2014. bit.ly/3czua8T, also archived at archive.vn/mFp3x.

Zhyrokhov, Mykhailo. 2016a. "Piat' Shturmov Artemovskoi Bazy: Istoriia Pervykh Pobed VSU." Liga.Net. 2016. bit.ly/3CFg4NS, also archived at archive.vn/bIMAf.

— — —. 2016b. "Tochka ukrainskogo nevozvrata: krovavyi chetverg 22 maia 2014." Fraza. May 22, 2016. bit.ly/32pdoaU; archived at archive.vn/imAyv.

— — —. 2016c. "Istoriia pervykh pobed: shturm Luganskogo pogranotriada." Fraza. September 16, 2016. bit.ly/2Z4F9nV, archived at archive.vn/CBXOz.

— — —. 2017. "Zabytye Srazheniia Leta 2014 Goda: Boi v Prigranich'e." Fraza. May 5, 2017. bit.ly/30Vixa6, also archived at archive.vn/Q7itn.

— — —. 2020. "'Russkaia Vesna' v Mariupole: Kak Boeviki Atakovali Gorod." Apostrof. May 9, 2020. bit.ly/3qXQwcI, also archived at archive.vn/WoL8V.

Zhyvotov, Oleh. 2018. "Stenogramma Doprosa Svidetelia Po Delu Yefremova." Strana.ua. October 25, 2018. bit.ly/30K7oJt, also archived at archive.vn/RO9Uj.

Zhyvotov, Oleh, and Bohdan Butkevych. 2016. "Polkovnyk Oleh Zhyvotov: «My ne zdavaly luhanske SBU»." Tyzhden.ua. March 25, 2016. bit.ly/3DG4Dqx, also archived at archive.vn/Ja8Kp.

SOVIET AND POST-SOVIET POLITICS AND SOCIETY
Edited by Dr. Andreas Umland | ISSN 1614-3515

1 Андреас Умланд (ред.) | Воплощение Европейской конвенции по правам человека в России. Философские, юридические и эмпирические исследования | ISBN 3-89821-387-0

2 Christian Wipperfürth | Russland – ein vertrauenswürdiger Partner? Grundlagen, Hintergründe und Praxis gegenwärtiger russischer Außenpolitik | Mit einem Vorwort von Heinz Timmermann | ISBN 3-89821-401-X

3 Manja Hussner | Die Übernahme internationalen Rechts in die russische und deutsche Rechtsordnung. Eine vergleichende Analyse zur Völkerrechtsfreundlichkeit der Verfassungen der Russländischen Föderation und der Bundesrepublik Deutschland | Mit einem Vorwort von Rainer Arnold | ISBN 3-89821-438-9

4 Matthew Tejada | Bulgaria's Democratic Consolidation and the Kozloduy Nuclear Power Plant (KNPP). The Unattainability of Closure | With a foreword by Richard J. Crampton | ISBN 3-89821-439-7

5 Марк Григорьевич Меерович | Квадратные метры, определяющие сознание. Государственная жилищная политика в СССР. 1921 – 1941 гг | ISBN 3-89821-474-5

6 Andrei P. Tsygankov, Pavel A.Tsygankov (Eds.) | New Directions in Russian International Studies | ISBN 3-89821-422-2

7 Марк Григорьевич Меерович | Как власть народ к труду приучала. Жилище в СССР – средство управления людьми. 1917 – 1941 гг. | С предисловием Елены Осокиной | ISBN 3-89821-495-8

8 David J. Galbreath | Nation-Building and Minority Politics in Post-Socialist States. Interests, Influence and Identities in Estonia and Latvia | With a foreword by David J. Smith | ISBN 3-89821-467-2

9 Алексей Юрьевич Безугольный | Народы Кавказа в Вооруженных силах СССР в годы Великой Отечественной войны 1941-1945 гг. | С предисловием Николая Бугая | ISBN 3-89821-475-3

10 Вячеслав Лихачев и Владимир Прибыловский (ред.) | Русское Национальное Единство, 1990-2000. В 2-х томах | ISBN 3-89821-523-7

11 Николай Бугай (ред.) | Народы стран Балтии в условиях сталинизма (1940-е – 1950-е годы). Документированная история | ISBN 3-89821-525-3

12 Ingmar Bredies (Hrsg.) | Zur Anatomie der Orange Revolution in der Ukraine. Wechsel des Elitenregimes oder Triumph des Parlamentarismus? | ISBN 3-89821-524-5

13 Anastasia V. Mitrofanova | The Politicization of Russian Orthodoxy. Actors and Ideas | With a foreword by William C. Gay | ISBN 3-89821-481-8

14 Nathan D. Larson | Alexander Solzhenitsyn and the Russo-Jewish Question | ISBN 3-89821-483-4

15 Guido Houben | Kulturpolitik und Ethnizität. Staatliche Kunstförderung im Russland der neunziger Jahre | Mit einem Vorwort von Gert Weisskirchen | ISBN 3-89821-542-3

16 Leonid Luks | Der russische „Sonderweg"? Aufsätze zur neuesten Geschichte Russlands im europäischen Kontext | ISBN 3-89821-496-6

17 Евгений Мороз | История «Мёртвой воды» – от страшной сказки к большой политике. Политическое неоязычество в постсоветской России | ISBN 3-89821-551-2

18 Александр Верховский и Галина Кожевникова (ред.) | Этническая и религиозная интолерантность в российских СМИ. Результаты мониторинга 2001-2004 гг. | ISBN 3-89821-569-5

19 Christian Ganzer | Sowjetisches Erbe und ukrainische Nation. Das Museum der Geschichte des Zaporoger Kosakentums auf der Insel Chortycja | Mit einem Vorwort von Frank Golczewski | ISBN 3-89821-504-0

20 Эльза-Баир Гучинова | Помнить нельзя забыть. Антропология депортационной травмы калмыков | С предисловием Кэролайн Хамфри | ISBN 3-89821-506-7

21 Юлия Лидерман | Мотивы «проверки» и «испытания» в постсоветской культуре. Советское прошлое в российском кинематографе 1990-х годов | С предисловием Евгения Марголита | ISBN 3-89821-511-3

22 Tanya Lokshina, Ray Thomas, Mary Mayer (Eds.) | The Imposition of a Fake Political Settlement in the Northern Caucasus. The 2003 Chechen Presidential Election | ISBN 3-89821-436-2

23 Timothy McCajor Hall, Rosie Read (Eds.) | Changes in the Heart of Europe. Recent Ethnographies of Czechs, Slovaks, Roma, and Sorbs | With an afterword by Zdeněk Salzmann | ISBN 3-89821-606-5

24   Christian Autengruber | Die politischen Parteien in Bulgarien und Rumänien. Eine vergleichende Analyse seit Beginn der 90er Jahre | Mit einem Vorwort von Dorothée de Nève | ISBN 3-89821-476-1

25   Annette Freyberg-Inan with Radu Cristescu | The Ghosts in Our Classrooms, or: John Dewey Meets Ceauşescu. The Promise and the Failures of Civic Education in Romania | ISBN 3-89821-416-8

26   John B. Dunlop | The 2002 Dubrovka and 2004 Beslan Hostage Crises. A Critique of Russian Counter-Terrorism | With a foreword by Donald N. Jensen | ISBN 3-89821-608-X

27   Peter Koller | Das touristische Potenzial von Kam"janec'–Podil's'kyj. Eine fremdenverkehrsgeographische Untersuchung der Zukunftsperspektiven und Maßnahmenplanung zur Destinationsentwicklung des „ukrainischen Rothenburg" | Mit einem Vorwort von Kristiane Klemm | ISBN 3-89821-640-3

28   Françoise Daucé, Elisabeth Sieca-Kozlowski (Eds.) | Dedovshchina in the Post-Soviet Military. Hazing of Russian Army Conscripts in a Comparative Perspective | With a foreword by Dale Herspring | ISBN 3-89821-616-0

29   Florian Strasser | Zivilgesellschaftliche Einflüsse auf die Orange Revolution. Die gewaltlose Massenbewegung und die ukrainische Wahlkrise 2004 | Mit einem Vorwort von Egbert Jahn | ISBN 3-89821-648-9

30   Rebecca S. Katz | The Georgian Regime Crisis of 2003-2004. A Case Study in Post-Soviet Media Representation of Politics, Crime and Corruption | ISBN 3-89821-413-3

31   Vladimir Kantor | Willkür oder Freiheit. Beiträge zur russischen Geschichtsphilosophie | Ediert von Dagmar Herrmann sowie mit einem Vorwort versehen von Leonid Luks | ISBN 3-89821-589-X

32   Laura A. Victoir | The Russian Land Estate Today. A Case Study of Cultural Politics in Post-Soviet Russia | With a foreword by Priscilla Roosevelt | ISBN 3-89821-426-5

33   Ivan Katchanovski | Cleft Countries. Regional Political Divisions and Cultures in Post-Soviet Ukraine and Moldova | With a foreword by Francis Fukuyama | ISBN 3-89821-558-X

34   Florian Mühlfried | Postsowjetische Feiern. Das Georgische Bankett im Wandel | Mit einem Vorwort von Kevin Tuite | ISBN 3-89821-601-2

35   Roger Griffin, Werner Loh, Andreas Umland (Eds.) | Fascism Past and Present, West and East. An International Debate on Concepts and Cases in the Comparative Study of the Extreme Right | With an afterword by Walter Laqueur | ISBN 3-89821-674-8

36   Sebastian Schlegel | Der „Weiße Archipel". Sowjetische Atomstädte 1945-1991 | Mit einem Geleitwort von Thomas Bohn | ISBN 3-89821-679-9

37   Vyacheslav Likhachev | Political Anti-Semitism in Post-Soviet Russia. Actors and Ideas in 1991-2003 | Edited and translated from Russian by Eugene Veklerov | ISBN 3-89821-529-6

38   Josette Baer (Ed.) | Preparing Liberty in Central Europe. Political Texts from the Spring of Nations 1848 to the Spring of Prague 1968 | With a foreword by Zdeněk V. David | ISBN 3-89821-546-6

39   Михаил Лукьянов | Российский консерватизм и реформа, 1907-1914 | С предисловием Марка Д. Стейнберга | ISBN 3-89821-503-2

40   Nicola Melloni | Market Without Economy. The 1998 Russian Financial Crisis | With a foreword by Eiji Furukawa | ISBN 3-89821-407-9

41   Dmitrij Chmelnizki | Die Architektur Stalins | Bd. 1: Studien zu Ideologie und Stil | Bd. 2: Bilddokumentation | Mit einem Vorwort von Bruno Flierl | ISBN 3-89821-515-6

42   Katja Yafimava | Post-Soviet Russian-Belarussian Relationships. The Role of Gas Transit Pipelines | With a foreword by Jonathan P. Stern | ISBN 3-89821-655-1

43   Boris Chavkin | Verflechtungen der deutschen und russischen Zeitgeschichte. Aufsätze und Archivfunde zu den Beziehungen Deutschlands und der Sowjetunion von 1917 bis 1991 | Ediert von Markus Edlinger sowie mit einem Vorwort versehen von Leonid Luks | ISBN 3-89821-756-6

44   Anastasija Grynenko in Zusammenarbeit mit Claudia Dathe | Die Terminologie des Gerichtswesens der Ukraine und Deutschlands im Vergleich. Eine übersetzungswissenschaftliche Analyse juristischer Fachbegriffe im Deutschen, Ukrainischen und Russischen | Mit einem Vorwort von Ulrich Hartmann | ISBN 3-89821-691-8

45   Anton Burkov | The Impact of the European Convention on Human Rights on Russian Law. Legislation and Application in 1996-2006 | With a foreword by Françoise Hampson | ISBN 978-3-89821-639-5

46   Stina Torjesen, Indra Overland (Eds.) | International Election Observers in Post-Soviet Azerbaijan. Geopolitical Pawns or Agents of Change? | ISBN 978-3-89821-743-9

47   Taras Kuzio | Ukraine – Crimea – Russia. Triangle of Conflict | ISBN 978-3-89821-761-3

48   Claudia Šabić | „Ich erinnere mich nicht, aber L'viv!" Zur Funktion kultureller Faktoren für die Institutionalisierung und Entwicklung einer ukrainischen Region | Mit einem Vorwort von Melanie Tatur | ISBN 978-3-89821-752-1

49 *Marlies Bilz* | Tatarstan in der Transformation. Nationaler Diskurs und Politische Praxis 1988-1994 | Mit einem Vorwort von Frank Golczewski | ISBN 978-3-89821-722-4

50 *Марлен Ларюэль (ред.)* | Современные интерпретации русского национализма | ISBN 978-3-89821-795-8

51 *Sonja Schüler* | Die ethnische Dimension der Armut. Roma im postsozialistischen Rumänien | Mit einem Vorwort von Anton Sterbling | ISBN 978-3-89821-776-7

52 *Галина Кожевникова* | Радикальный национализм в России и противодействие ему. Сборник докладов Центра «Сова» за 2004-2007 гг. | С предисловием Александра Верховского | ISBN 978-3-89821-721-7

53 *Галина Кожевникова и Владимир Прибыловский* | Российская власть в биографиях I. Высшие должностные лица РФ в 2004 г. | ISBN 978-3-89821-796-5

54 *Галина Кожевникова и Владимир Прибыловский* | Российская власть в биографиях II. Члены Правительства РФ в 2004 г. | ISBN 978-3-89821-797-2

55 *Галина Кожевникова и Владимир Прибыловский* | Российская власть в биографиях III. Руководители федеральных служб и агентств РФ в 2004 г.| ISBN 978-3-89821-798-9

56 *Ileana Petroniu* | Privatisierung in Transformationsökonomien. Determinanten der Restrukturierungs-Bereitschaft am Beispiel Polens, Rumäniens und der Ukraine | Mit einem Vorwort von Rainer W. Schäfer | ISBN 978-3-89821-790-3

57 *Christian Wipperfürth* | Russland und seine GUS-Nachbarn. Hintergründe, aktuelle Entwicklungen und Konflikte in einer ressourcenreichen Region| ISBN 978-3-89821-801-6

58 *Togzhan Kassenova* | From Antagonism to Partnership. The Uneasy Path of the U.S.-Russian Cooperative Threat Reduction | With a foreword by Christoph Bluth | ISBN 978-3-89821-707-1

59 *Alexander Höllwerth* | Das sakrale eurasische Imperium des Aleksandr Dugin. Eine Diskursanalyse zum postsowjetischen russischen Rechtsextremismus | Mit einem Vorwort von Dirk Uffelmann | ISBN 978-3-89821-813-9

60 *Олег Рябов* | «Россия-Матушка». Национализм, гендер и война в России XX века | С предисловием Елены Гощило | ISBN 978-3-89821-487-2

61 *Ivan Maistrenko* | Borot'bism. A Chapter in the History of the Ukrainian Revolution | With a new Introduction by Chris Ford | Translated by George S. N. Luckyj with the assistance of Ivan L. Rudnytsky | Second, Revised and Expanded Edition ISBN 978-3-8382-1107-7

62 *Maryna Romanets* | Anamorphosic Texts and Reconfigured Visions. Improvised Traditions in Contemporary Ukrainian and Irish Literature | ISBN 978-3-89821-576-3

63 *Paul D'Anieri and Taras Kuzio (Eds.)* | Aspects of the Orange Revolution I. Democratization and Elections in Post-Communist Ukraine | ISBN 978-3-89821-698-2

64 *Bohdan Harasymiw in collaboration with Oleh S. Ilnytzkyj (Eds.)* | Aspects of the Orange Revolution II. Information and Manipulation Strategies in the 2004 Ukrainian Presidential Elections | ISBN 978-3-89821-699-9

65 *Ingmar Bredies, Andreas Umland and Valentin Yakushik (Eds.)* | Aspects of the Orange Revolution III. The Context and Dynamics of the 2004 Ukrainian Presidential Elections | ISBN 978-3-89821-803-0

66 *Ingmar Bredies, Andreas Umland and Valentin Yakushik (Eds.)* | Aspects of the Orange Revolution IV. Foreign Assistance and Civic Action in the 2004 Ukrainian Presidential Elections | ISBN 978-3-89821-808-5

67 *Ingmar Bredies, Andreas Umland and Valentin Yakushik (Eds.)* | Aspects of the Orange Revolution V. Institutional Observation Reports on the 2004 Ukrainian Presidential Elections | ISBN 978-3-89821-809-2

68 *Taras Kuzio (Ed.)* | Aspects of the Orange Revolution VI. Post-Communist Democratic Revolutions in Comparative Perspective | ISBN 978-3-89821-820-7

69 *Tim Bohse* | Autoritarismus statt Selbstverwaltung. Die Transformation der kommunalen Politik in der Stadt Kaliningrad 1990-2005 | Mit einem Geleitwort von Stefan Troebst | ISBN 978-3-89821-782-8

70 *David Rupp* | Die Rußländische Föderation und die russischsprachige Minderheit in Lettland. Eine Fallstudie zur Anwaltspolitik Moskaus gegenüber den russophonen Minderheiten im „Nahen Ausland" von 1991 bis 2002 | Mit einem Vorwort von Helmut Wagner | ISBN 978-3-89821-778-1

71 *Taras Kuzio* | Theoretical and Comparative Perspectives on Nationalism. New Directions in Cross-Cultural and Post-Communist Studies | With a foreword by Paul Robert Magocsi | ISBN 978-3-89821-815-3

72 *Christine Teichmann* | Die Hochschultransformation im heutigen Osteuropa. Kontinuität und Wandel bei der Entwicklung des postkommunistischen Universitätswesens | Mit einem Vorwort von Oskar Anweiler | ISBN 978-3-89821-842-9

73 Julia Kusznir | Der politische Einfluss von Wirtschaftseliten in russischen Regionen. Eine Analyse am Beispiel der Erdöl- und Erdgasindustrie, 1992-2005 | Mit einem Vorwort von Wolfgang Eichwede | ISBN 978-3-89821-821-4

74 Alena Vysotskaya | Russland, Belarus und die EU-Osterweiterung. Zur Minderheitenfrage und zum Problem der Freizügigkeit des Personenverkehrs | Mit einem Vorwort von Katlijn Malfliet | ISBN 978-3-89821-822-1

75 Heiko Pleines (Hrsg.) | Corporate Governance in post-sozialistischen Volkswirtschaften | ISBN 978-3-89821-766-8

76 Stefan Ihrig | Wer sind die Moldawier? Rumänismus versus Moldowanismus in Historiographie und Schulbüchern der Republik Moldova, 1991-2006 | Mit einem Vorwort von Holm Sundhaussen | ISBN 978-3-89821-466-7

77 Galina Kozhevnikova in collaboration with Alexander Verkhovsky and Eugene Veklerov | Ultra-Nationalism and Hate Crimes in Contemporary Russia. The 2004-2006 Annual Reports of Moscow's SOVA Center | With a foreword by Stephen D. Shenfield | ISBN 978-3-89821-868-9

78 Florian Küchler | The Role of the European Union in Moldova's Transnistria Conflict | With a foreword by Christopher Hill | ISBN 978-3-89821-850-4

79 Bernd Rechel | The Long Way Back to Europe. Minority Protection in Bulgaria | With a foreword by Richard Crampton | ISBN 978-3-89821-863-4

80 Peter W. Rodgers | Nation, Region and History in Post-Communist Transitions. Identity Politics in Ukraine, 1991-2006 | With a foreword by Vera Tolz | ISBN 978-3-89821-903-7

81 Stephanie Solywoda | The Life and Work of Semen L. Frank. A Study of Russian Religious Philosophy | With a foreword by Philip Walters | ISBN 978-3-89821-457-5

82 Vera Sokolova | Cultural Politics of Ethnicity. Discourses on Roma in Communist Czechoslovakia | ISBN 978-3-89821-864-1

83 Natalya Shevchik Ketenci | Kazakhstani Enterprises in Transition. The Role of Historical Regional Development in Kazakhstan's Post-Soviet Economic Transformation | ISBN 978-3-89821-831-3

84 Martin Malek, Anna Schor-Tschudnowskaja (Hgg.) | Europa im Tschetschenienkrieg. Zwischen politischer Ohnmacht und Gleichgültigkeit | Mit einem Vorwort von Lipchan Basajewa | ISBN 978-3-89821-676-0

85 Stefan Meister | Das postsowjetische Universitätswesen zwischen nationalem und internationalem Wandel. Die Entwicklung der regionalen Hochschule in Russland als Gradmesser der Systemtransformation | Mit einem Vorwort von Joan DeBardeleben | ISBN 978-3-89821-891-7

86 Konstantin Sheiko in collaboration with Stephen Brown | Nationalist Imaginings of the Russian Past. Anatolii Fomenko and the Rise of Alternative History in Post-Communist Russia | With a foreword by Donald Ostrowski | ISBN 978-3-89821-915-0

87 Sabine Jenni | Wie stark ist das „Einige Russland"? Zur Parteibindung der Eliten und zum Wahlerfolg der Machtpartei im Dezember 2007 | Mit einem Vorwort von Klaus Armingeon | ISBN 978-3-89821-961-7

88 Thomas Borén | Meeting-Places of Transformation. Urban Identity, Spatial Representations and Local Politics in Post-Soviet St Petersburg | ISBN 978-3-89821-739-2

89 Aygul Ashirova | Stalinismus und Stalin-Kult in Zentralasien. Turkmenistan 1924-1953 | Mit einem Vorwort von Leonid Luks | ISBN 978-3-89821-987-7

90 Leonid Luks | Freiheit oder imperiale Größe? Essays zu einem russischen Dilemma | ISBN 978-3-8382-0011-8

91 Christopher Gilley | The 'Change of Signposts' in the Ukrainian Emigration. A Contribution to the History of Sovietophilism in the 1920s | With a foreword by Frank Golczewski | ISBN 978-3-89821-965-5

92 Philipp Casula, Jeronim Perovic (Eds.) | Identities and Politics During the Putin Presidency. The Discursive Foundations of Russia's Stability | With a foreword by Heiko Haumann | ISBN 978-3-8382-0015-6

93 Marcel Viëtor | Europa und die Frage nach seinen Grenzen im Osten. Zur Konstruktion ‚europäischer Identität' in Geschichte und Gegenwart | Mit einem Vorwort von Albrecht Lehmann | ISBN 978-3-8382-0045-3

94 Ben Hellman, Andrei Rogachevskii | Filming the Unfilmable. Casper Wrede's 'One Day in the Life of Ivan Denisovich' | Second, Revised and Expanded Edition | ISBN 978-3-8382-0044-6

95 Eva Fuchslocher | Vaterland, Sprache, Glaube. Orthodoxie und Nationenbildung am Beispiel Georgiens | Mit einem Vorwort von Christina von Braun | ISBN 978-3-89821-884-9

96 Vladimir Kantor | Das Westlertum und der Weg Russlands. Zur Entwicklung der russischen Literatur und Philosophie | Ediert von Dagmar Herrmann | Mit einem Beitrag von Nikolaus Lobkowicz | ISBN 978-3-8382-0102-3

97 Kamran Musayev | Die postsowjetische Transformation im Baltikum und Südkaukasus. Eine vergleichende Untersuchung der politischen Entwicklung Lettlands und Aserbaidschans 1985-2009 | Mit einem Vorwort von Leonid Luks | Ediert von Sandro Henschel | ISBN 978-3-8382-0103-0

98 *Tatiana Zhurzhenko* | Borderlands into Bordered Lands. Geopolitics of Identity in Post-Soviet Ukraine | With a foreword by Dieter Segert | ISBN 978-3-8382-0042-2

99 *Кирилл Галушко, Лидия Смола (ред.)* | Пределы падения – варианты украинского будущего. Аналитико-прогностические исследования | ISBN 978-3-8382-0148-1

100 *Michael Minkenberg (Ed.)* | Historical Legacies and the Radical Right in Post-Cold War Central and Eastern Europe | With an afterword by Sabrina P. Ramet | ISBN 978-3-8382-0124-5

101 *David-Emil Wickström* | Rocking St. Petersburg. Transcultural Flows and Identity Politics in the St. Petersburg Popular Music Scene | With a foreword by Yngvar B. Steinholt | Second, Revised and Expanded Edition | ISBN 978-3-8382-0100-9

102 *Eva Zabka* | Eine neue „Zeit der Wirren"? Der spät- und postsowjetische Systemwandel 1985-2000 im Spiegel russischer gesellschaftspolitischer Diskurse | Mit einem Vorwort von Margareta Mommsen | ISBN 978-3-8382-0161-0

103 *Ulrike Ziemer* | Ethnic Belonging, Gender and Cultural Practices. Youth Identitites in Contemporary Russia | With a foreword by Anoop Nayak | ISBN 978-3-8382-0152-8

104 *Ksenia Chepikova* | ‚Einiges Russland' - eine zweite KPdSU? Aspekte der Identitätskonstruktion einer postsowjetischen „Partei der Macht" | Mit einem Vorwort von Torsten Oppelland | ISBN 978-3-8382-0311-9

105 *Леонид Люкс* | Западничество или евразийство? Демократия или идеократия? Сборник статей об исторических дилеммах России | С предисловием Владимира Кантора | ISBN 978-3-8382-0211-2

106 *Anna Dost* | Das russische Verfassungsrecht auf dem Weg zum Föderalismus und zurück. Zum Konflikt von Rechtsnormen und -wirklichkeit in der Russländischen Föderation von 1991 bis 2009 | Mit einem Vorwort von Alexander Blankenagel | ISBN 978-3-8382-0292-1

107 *Philipp Herzog* | Sozialistische Völkerfreundschaft, nationaler Widerstand oder harmloser Zeitvertreib? Zur politischen Funktion der Volkskunst im sowjetischen Estland | Mit einem Vorwort von Andreas Kappeler | ISBN 978-3-8382-0216-7

108 *Marlène Laruelle (Ed.)* | Russian Nationalism, Foreign Policy, and Identity Debates in Putin's Russia. New Ideological Patterns after the Orange Revolution | ISBN 978-3-8382-0325-6

109 *Michail Logvinov* | Russlands Kampf gegen den internationalen Terrorismus. Eine kritische Bestandsaufnahme des Bekämpfungsansatzes | Mit einem Geleitwort von Hans-Henning Schröder und einem Vorwort von Eckhard Jesse | ISBN 978-3-8382-0329-4

110 *John B. Dunlop* | The Moscow Bombings of September 1999. Examinations of Russian Terrorist Attacks at the Onset of Vladimir Putin's Rule | Second, Revised and Expanded Edition | ISBN 978-3-8382-0388-1

111 *Андрей А. Ковалёв* | Свидетельство из-за кулис российской политики I. Можно ли делать добро из зла? (Воспоминания и размышления о последних советских и первых послесоветских годах) | With a foreword by Peter Reddaway | ISBN 978-3-8382-0302-7

112 *Андрей А. Ковалёв* | Свидетельство из-за кулис российской политики II. Угроза для себя и окружающих (Наблюдения и предостережения относительно происходящего после 2000 г.) | ISBN 978-3-8382-0303-4

113 *Bernd Kappenberg* | Zeichen setzen für Europa. Der Gebrauch europäischer lateinischer Sonderzeichen in der deutschen Öffentlichkeit | Mit einem Vorwort von Peter Schlobinski | ISBN 978-3-89821-749-1

114 *Ivo Mijnssen* | The Quest for an Ideal Youth in Putin's Russia I. Back to Our Future! History, Modernity, and Patriotism according to Nashi, 2005-2013 | With a foreword by Jeronim Perović | Second, Revised and Expanded Edition | ISBN 978-3-8382-0368-3

115 *Jussi Lassila* | The Quest for an Ideal Youth in Putin's Russia II. The Search for Distinctive Conformism in the Political Communication of Nashi, 2005-2009 | With a foreword by Kirill Postoutenko | Second, Revised and Expanded Edition | ISBN 978-3-8382-0415-4

116 *Valerio Trabandt* | Neue Nachbarn, gute Nachbarschaft? Die EU als internationaler Akteur am Beispiel ihrer Demokratieförderung in Belarus und der Ukraine 2004-2009 | Mit einem Vorwort von Jutta Joachim | ISBN 978-3-8382-0437-6

117 *Fabian Pfeiffer* | Estlands Außen- und Sicherheitspolitik I. Der estnische Atlantizismus nach der wiedererlangten Unabhängigkeit 1991-2004 | Mit einem Vorwort von Helmut Hubel | ISBN 978-3-8382-0127-6

118 *Jana Podßuweit* | Estlands Außen- und Sicherheitspolitik II. Handlungsoptionen eines Kleinstaates im Rahmen seiner EU-Mitgliedschaft (2004-2008) | Mit einem Vorwort von Helmut Hubel | ISBN 978-3-8382-0440-6

119 *Karin Pointner* | Estlands Außen- und Sicherheitspolitik III. Eine gedächtnispolitische Analyse estnischer Entwicklungskooperation 2006-2010 | Mit einem Vorwort von Karin Liebhart | ISBN 978-3-8382-0435-2

120 *Ruslana Vovk* | Die Offenheit der ukrainischen Verfassung für das Völkerrecht und die europäische Integration | Mit einem Vorwort von Alexander Blankenagel | ISBN 978-3-8382-0481-9

121 *Mykhaylo Banakh* | Die Relevanz der Zivilgesellschaft bei den postkommunistischen Transformationsprozessen in mittel- und osteuropäischen Ländern. Das Beispiel der spät- und postsowjetischen Ukraine 1986-2009 | Mit einem Vorwort von Gerhard Simon | ISBN 978-3-8382-0499-4

122 *Michael Moser* | Language Policy and the Discourse on Languages in Ukraine under President Viktor Yanukovych (25 February 2010–28 October 2012) | ISBN 978-3-8382-0497-0 (Paperback edition) | ISBN 978-3-8382-0507-6 (Hardcover edition)

123 *Nicole Krome* | Russischer Netzwerkkapitalismus Restrukturierungsprozesse in der Russischen Föderation am Beispiel des Luftfahrtunternehmens „Aviastar" | Mit einem Vorwort von Petra Stykow | ISBN 978-3-8382-0534-2

124 *David R. Marples* | 'Our Glorious Past'. Lukashenka's Belarus and the Great Patriotic War | ISBN 978-3-8382-0574-8 (Paperback edition) | ISBN 978-3-8382-0675-2 (Hardcover edition)

125 *Ulf Walther* | Russlands „neuer Adel". Die Macht des Geheimdienstes von Gorbatschow bis Putin | Mit einem Vorwort von Hans-Georg Wieck | ISBN 978-3-8382-0584-7

126 *Simon Geissbühler (Hrsg.)* | Kiew – Revolution 3.0. Der Euromaidan 2013/14 und die Zukunftsperspektiven der Ukraine | ISBN 978-3-8382-0581-6 (Paperback edition) | ISBN 978-3-8382-0681-3 (Hardcover edition)

127 *Andrey Makarychev* | Russia and the EU in a Multipolar World. Discourses, Identities, Norms | With a foreword by Klaus Segbers | ISBN 978-3-8382-0629-5

128 *Roland Scharff* | Kasachstan als postsowjetischer Wohlfahrtsstaat. Die Transformation des sozialen Schutzsystems | Mit einem Vorwort von Joachim Ahrens | ISBN 978-3-8382-0622-6

129 *Katja Grupp* | Bild Lücke Deutschland. Kaliningrader Studierende sprechen über Deutschland | Mit einem Vorwort von Martin Schulz | ISBN 978-3-8382-0552-6

130 *Konstantin Sheiko, Stephen Brown* | History as Therapy. Alternative History and Nationalist Imaginings in Russia, 1991-2014 | ISBN 978-3-8382-0665-3

131 *Elisa Kriza* | Alexander Solzhenitsyn: Cold War Icon, Gulag Author, Russian Nationalist? A Study of the Western Reception of his Literary Writings, Historical Interpretations, and Political Ideas | With a foreword by Andrei Rogatchevski | ISBN 978-3-8382-0589-2 (Paperback edition) | ISBN 978-3-8382-0690-5 (Hardcover edition)

132 *Serghei Golunov* | The Elephant in the Room. Corruption and Cheating in Russian Universities | ISBN 978-3-8382-0570-0

133 *Manja Hussner, Rainer Arnold (Hgg.)* | Verfassungsgerichtsbarkeit in Zentralasien I. Sammlung von Verfassungstexten | ISBN 978-3-8382-0595-3

134 *Nikolay Mitrokhin* | Die „Russische Partei". Die Bewegung der russischen Nationalisten in der UdSSR 1953-1985 | Aus dem Russischen übertragen von einem Übersetzerteam unter der Leitung von Larisa Schippel | ISBN 978-3-8382-0024-8

135 *Manja Hussner, Rainer Arnold (Hgg.)* | Verfassungsgerichtsbarkeit in Zentralasien II. Sammlung von Verfassungstexten | ISBN 978-3-8382-0597-7

136 *Manfred Zeller* | Das sowjetische Fieber. Fußballfans im poststalinistischen Vielvölkerreich | Mit einem Vorwort von Nikolaus Katzer | ISBN 978-3-8382-0757-5

137 *Kristin Schreiter* | Stellung und Entwicklungspotential zivilgesellschaftlicher Gruppen in Russland. Menschenrechtsorganisationen im Vergleich | ISBN 978-3-8382-0673-8

138 *David R. Marples, Frederick V. Mills (Eds.)* | Ukraine's Euromaidan. Analyses of a Civil Revolution | ISBN 978-3-8382-0660-8

139 *Bernd Kappenberg* | Setting Signs for Europe. Why Diacritics Matter for European Integration | With a foreword by Peter Schlobinski | ISBN 978-3-8382-0663-9

140 *René Lenz* | Internationalisierung, Kooperation und Transfer. Externe bildungspolitische Akteure in der Russischen Föderation | Mit einem Vorwort von Frank Ettrich | ISBN 978-3-8382-0751-3

141 *Juri Plusnin, Yana Zausaeva, Natalia Zhidkevich, Artemy Pozanenko* | Wandering Workers. Mores, Behavior, Way of Life, and Political Status of Domestic Russian Labor Migrants | Translated by Julia Kazantseva | ISBN 978-3-8382-0653-0

142 *David J. Smith (Eds.)* | Latvia – A Work in Progress? 100 Years of State- and Nation-Building | ISBN 978-3-8382-0648-6

143 *Инна Чувычкина (ред.)* | Экспортные нефте- и газопроводы на постсоветском пространстве. Анализ трубопроводной политики в свете теории международных отношений | ISBN 978-3-8382-0822-0

144 *Johann Zajaczkowski* | Russland – eine pragmatische Großmacht? Eine rollentheoretische Untersuchung russischer Außenpolitik am Beispiel der Zusammenarbeit mit den USA nach 9/11 und des Georgienkrieges von 2008 | Mit einem Vorwort von Siegfried Schieder | ISBN 978-3-8382-0837-4

145 *Boris Popivanov* | Changing Images of the Left in Bulgaria. The Challenge of Post-Communism in the Early 21st Century | ISBN 978-3-8382-0667-7

146 *Lenka Krátká* | A History of the Czechoslovak Ocean Shipping Company 1948-1989. How a Small, Landlocked Country Ran Maritime Business During the Cold War | ISBN 978-3-8382-0666-0

147 *Alexander Sergunin* | Explaining Russian Foreign Policy Behavior. Theory and Practice | ISBN 978-3-8382-0752-0

148 *Darya Malyutina* | Migrant Friendships in a Super-Diverse City. Russian-Speakers and their Social Relationships in London in the 21st Century | With a foreword by Claire Dwyer | ISBN 978-3-8382-0652-3

149 *Alexander Sergunin, Valery Konyshev* | Russia in the Arctic. Hard or Soft Power? | ISBN 978-3-8382-0753-7

150 *John J. Maresca* | Helsinki Revisited. A Key U.S. Negotiator's Memoirs on the Development of the CSCE into the OSCE | With a foreword by Hafiz Pashayev | ISBN 978-3-8382-0852-7

151 *Jardar Østbø* | The New Third Rome. Readings of a Russian Nationalist Myth | With a foreword by Pål Kolstø | ISBN 978-3-8382-0870-1

152 *Simon Kordonsky* | Socio-Economic Foundations of the Russian Post-Soviet Regime. The Resource-Based Economy and Estate-Based Social Structure of Contemporary Russia | With a foreword by Svetlana Barsukova | ISBN 978-3-8382-0775-9

153 *Duncan Leitch* | Assisting Reform in Post-Communist Ukraine 2000–2012. The Illusions of Donors and the Disillusion of Beneficiaries | With a foreword by Kataryna Wolczuk | ISBN 978-3-8382-0844-2

154 *Abel Polese* | Limits of a Post-Soviet State. How Informality Replaces, Renegotiates, and Reshapes Governance in Contemporary Ukraine | With a foreword by Colin Williams | ISBN 978-3-8382-0845-9

155 *Mikhail Suslov (Ed.)* | Digital Orthodoxy in the Post-Soviet World. The Russian Orthodox Church and Web 2.0 | With a foreword by Father Cyril Hovorun | ISBN 978-3-8382-0871-8

156 *Leonid Luks* | Zwei „Sonderwege"? Russisch-deutsche Parallelen und Kontraste (1917-2014). Vergleichende Essays | ISBN 978-3-8382-0823-7

157 *Vladimir V. Karacharovskiy, Ovsey I. Shkaratan, Gordey A. Yastrebov* | Towards a New Russian Work Culture. Can Western Companies and Expatriates Change Russian Society? | With a foreword by Elena N. Danilova | Translated by Julia Kazantseva | ISBN 978-3-8382-0902-9

158 *Edmund Griffiths* | Aleksandr Prokhanov and Post-Soviet Esotericism | ISBN 978-3-8382-0963-0

159 *Timm Beichelt, Susann Worschech (Eds.)* | Transnational Ukraine? Networks and Ties that Influence(d) Contemporary Ukraine | ISBN 978-3-8382-0944-9

160 *Mieste Hotopp-Riecke* | Die Tataren der Krim zwischen Assimilation und Selbstbehauptung. Der Aufbau des krimtatarischen Bildungswesens nach Deportation und Heimkehr (1990-2005) | Mit einem Vorwort von Swetlana Czerwonnaja | ISBN 978-3-89821-940-2

161 *Olga Bertelsen (Ed.)* | Revolution and War in Contemporary Ukraine. The Challenge of Change | ISBN 978-3-8382-1016-2

162 *Natalya Ryabinska* | Ukraine's Post-Communist Mass Media. Between Capture and Commercialization | With a foreword by Marta Dyczok | ISBN 978-3-8382-1011-7

163 *Alexandra Cotofana, James M. Nyce (Eds.)* | Religion and Magic in Socialist and Post-Socialist Contexts. Historic and Ethnographic Case Studies of Orthodoxy, Heterodoxy, and Alternative Spirituality | With a foreword by Patrick L. Michelson | ISBN 978-3-8382-0989-0

164 *Nozima Akhrarkhodjaeva* | The Instrumentalisation of Mass Media in Electoral Authoritarian Regimes. Evidence from Russia's Presidential Election Campaigns of 2000 and 2008 | ISBN 978-3-8382-1013-1

165 *Yulia Krasheninnikova* | Informal Healthcare in Contemporary Russia. Sociographic Essays on the Post-Soviet Infrastructure for Alternative Healing Practices | ISBN 978-3-8382-0970-8

166 *Peter Kaiser* | Das Schachbrett der Macht. Die Handlungsspielräume eines sowjetischen Funktionärs unter Stalin am Beispiel des Generalsekretärs des Komsomol Aleksandr Kosarev (1929-1938) | Mit einem Vorwort von Dietmar Neutatz | ISBN 978-3-8382-1052-0

167 *Oksana Kim* | The Effects and Implications of Kazakhstan's Adoption of International Financial Reporting Standards. A Resource Dependence Perspective | With a foreword by Svetlana Vlady | ISBN 978-3-8382-0987-6

168 *Anna Sanina* | Patriotic Education in Contemporary Russia. Sociological Studies in the Making of the Post-Soviet Citizen | With a foreword by Anna Oldfield | ISBN 978-3-8382-0993-7

169 *Rudolf Wolters* | Spezialist in Sibirien Faksimile der 1933 erschienenen ersten Ausgabe | Mit einem Vorwort von Dmitrij Chmelnizki | ISBN 978-3-8382-0515-1

170 *Michal Vít, Magdalena M. Baran (Eds.)* | Transregional versus National Perspectives on Contemporary Central European History. Studies on the Building of Nation-States and Their Cooperation in the 20th and 21st Century | With a foreword by Petr Vágner | ISBN 978-3-8382-1015-5

171 *Philip Gamaghelyan* | Conflict Resolution Beyond the International Relations Paradigm. Evolving Designs as a Transformative Practice in Nagorno-Karabakh and Syria | With a foreword by Susan Allen | ISBN 978-3-8382-1057-5

172 *Maria Shagina* | Joining a Prestigious Club. Cooperation with Europarties and Its Impact on Party Development in Georgia, Moldova, and Ukraine 2004–2015 | With a foreword by Kataryna Wolczuk | ISBN 978-3-8382-1084-1

173 *Alexandra Cotofana, James M. Nyce (Eds.)* | Religion and Magic in Socialist and Post-Socialist Contexts II. Baltic, Eastern European, and Post-USSR Case Studies | With a foreword by Anita Stasulane | ISBN 978-3-8382-0990-6

174 *Barbara Kunz* | Kind Words, Cruise Missiles, and Everything in Between. The Use of Power Resources in U.S. Policies towards Poland, Ukraine, and Belarus 1989–2008 | With a foreword by William Hill | ISBN 978-3-8382-1065-0

175 *Eduard Klein* | Bildungskorruption in Russland und der Ukraine. Eine komparative Analyse der Performanz staatlicher Antikorruptionsmaßnahmen im Hochschulsektor am Beispiel universitärer Aufnahmeprüfungen | Mit einem Vorwort von Heiko Pleines | ISBN 978-3-8382-0995-1

176 *Markus Soldner* | Politischer Kapitalismus im postsowjetischen Russland. Die politische, wirtschaftliche und mediale Transformation in den 1990er Jahren | Mit einem Vorwort von Wolfgang Ismayr | ISBN 978-3-8382-1222-7

177 *Anton Oleinik* | Building Ukraine from Within. A Sociological, Institutional, and Economic Analysis of a Nation-State in the Making | ISBN 978-3-8382-1150-3

178 *Peter Rollberg, Marlene Laruelle (Eds.)* | Mass Media in the Post-Soviet World. Market Forces, State Actors, and Political Manipulation in the Informational Environment after Communism | ISBN 978-3-8382-1116-9

179 *Mikhail Minakov* | Development and Dystopia. Studies in Post-Soviet Ukraine and Eastern Europe | With a foreword by Alexander Etkind | ISBN 978-3-8382-1112-1

180 *Aijan Sharshenova* | The European Union's Democracy Promotion in Central Asia. A Study of Political Interests, Influence, and Development in Kazakhstan and Kyrgyzstan in 2007–2013 | With a foreword by Gordon Crawford | ISBN 978-3-8382-1151-0

181 *Andrey Makarychev, Alexandra Yatsyk (Eds.)* | Boris Nemtsov and Russian Politics. Power and Resistance | With a foreword by Zhanna Nemtsova | ISBN 978-3-8382-1122-0

182 *Sophie Falsini* | The Euromaidan's Effect on Civil Society. Why and How Ukrainian Social Capital Increased after the Revolution of Dignity | With a foreword by Susann Worschech | ISBN 978-3-8382-1131-2

183 *Valentyna Romanova, Andreas Umland (Eds.)* | Ukraine's Decentralization. Challenges and Implications of the Local Governance Reform after the Euromaidan Revolution | ISBN 978-3-8382-1162-6

184 *Leonid Luks* | A Fateful Triangle. Essays on Contemporary Russian, German and Polish History | ISBN 978-3-8382-1143-5

185 *John B. Dunlop* | The February 2015 Assassination of Boris Nemtsov and the Flawed Trial of his Alleged Killers. An Exploration of Russia's "Crime of the 21st Century" | ISBN 978-3-8382-1188-6

186 *Vasile Rotaru* | Russia, the EU, and the Eastern Partnership. Building Bridges or Digging Trenches? | ISBN 978-3-8382-1134-3

187 *Marina Lebedeva* | Russian Studies of International Relations. From the Soviet Past to the Post-Cold-War Present | With a foreword by Andrei P. Tsygankov | ISBN 978-3-8382-0851-0

188 *Tomasz Stępniewski, George Soroka (Eds.)* | Ukraine after Maidan. Revisiting Domestic and Regional Security | ISBN 978-3-8382-1075-9

189 *Petar Cholakov* | Ethnic Entrepreneurs Unmasked. Political Institutions and Ethnic Conflicts in Contemporary Bulgaria | ISBN 978-3-8382-1189-3

190 *A. Salem, G. Hazeldine, D. Morgan (Eds.)* | Higher Education in Post-Communist States. Comparative and Sociological Perspectives | ISBN 978-3-8382-1183-1

191 *Igor Torbakov* | After Empire. Nationalist Imagination and Symbolic Politics in Russia and Eurasia in the Twentieth and Twenty-First Century | With a foreword by Serhii Plokhy | ISBN 978-3-8382-1217-3

192 *Aleksandr Burakovskiy* | Jewish-Ukrainian Relations in Late and Post-Soviet Ukraine. Articles, Lectures and Essays from 1986 to 2016 | ISBN 978-3-8382-1210-4

193 *Natalia Shapovalova, Olga Burlyuk (Eds.)* | Civil Society in Post-Euromaidan Ukraine. From Revolution to Consolidation | With a foreword by Richard Youngs | ISBN 978-3-8382-1216-6

194 *Franz Preissler* | Positionsverteidigung, Imperialismus oder Irredentismus? Russland und die „Russischsprachigen", 1991–2015 | ISBN 978-3-8382-1262-3

195 *Marian Madeła* | Der Reformprozess in der Ukraine 2014-2017. Eine Fallstudie zur Reform der öffentlichen Verwaltung | Mit einem Vorwort von Martin Malek | ISBN 978-3-8382-1266-1

196 *Anke Giesen* | „Wie kann denn der Sieger ein Verbrecher sein?" Eine diskursanalytische Untersuchung der russlandweiten Debatte über Konzept und Verstaatlichungsprozess der Lagergedenkstätte „Perm'-36" im Ural | ISBN 978-3-8382-1284-5

197 *Victoria Leukavets* | The Integration Policies of Belarus and Ukraine vis-à-vis the EU and Russia. A Comparative Analysis Through the Prism of a Two-Level Game Approach | ISBN 978-3-8382-1247-0

198 *Oksana Kim* | The Development and Challenges of Russian Corporate Governance I. The Roles and Functions of Boards of Directors | With a foreword by Sheila M. Puffer | ISBN 978-3-8382-1287-6

199 *Thomas D. Grant* | International Law and the Post-Soviet Space I. Essays on Chechnya and the Baltic States | With a foreword by Stephen M. Schwebel | ISBN 978-3-8382-1279-1

200 *Thomas D. Grant* | International Law and the Post-Soviet Space II. Essays on Ukraine, Intervention, and Non-Proliferation | ISBN 978-3-8382-1280-7

201 *Slavomír Michálek, Michal Štefansky* | The Age of Fear. The Cold War and Its Influence on Czechoslovakia 1945–1968 | ISBN 978-3-8382-1285-2

202 *Iulia-Sabina Joja* | Romania's Strategic Culture 1990–2014. Continuity and Change in a Post-Communist Country's Evolution of National Interests and Security Policies | With a foreword by Heiko Biehl | ISBN 978-3-8382-1286-9

203 *Andrei Rogatchevski, Yngvar B. Steinholt, Arve Hansen, David-Emil Wickström* | War of Songs. Popular Music and Recent Russia-Ukraine Relations | With a foreword by Artemy Troitsky | ISBN 978-3-8382-1173-2

204 *Maria Lipman (Ed.)* | Russian Voices on Post-Crimea Russia. An Almanac of Counterpoint Essays from 2015–2018 | ISBN 978-3-8382-1251-7

205 *Ksenia Maksimovtsova* | Language Conflicts in Contemporary Estonia, Latvia, and Ukraine. A Comparative Exploration of Discourses in Post-Soviet Russian-Language Digital Media | With a foreword by Ammon Cheskin | ISBN 978-3-8382-1282-1

206 *Michal Vít* | The EU's Impact on Identity Formation in East-Central Europe between 2004 and 2013. Perceptions of the Nation and Europe in Political Parties of the Czech Republic, Poland, and Slovakia | With a foreword by Andrea Pető | ISBN 978-3-8382-1275-3

207 *Per A. Rudling* | Tarnished Heroes. The Organization of Ukrainian Nationalists in the Memory Politics of Post-Soviet Ukraine | ISBN 978-3-8382-0999-9

208 *Kaja Gadowska, Peter Solomon (Eds.)* | Legal Change in Post-Communist States. Progress, Reversions, Explanations | ISBN 978-3-8382-1312-5

209 *Paweł Kowal, Georges Mink, Iwona Reichardt (Eds.)* | Three Revolutions: Mobilization and Change in Contemporary Ukraine I. Theoretical Aspects and Analyses on Religion, Memory, and Identity | ISBN 978-3-8382-1321-7

210 *Paweł Kowal, Georges Mink, Adam Reichardt, Iwona Reichardt (Eds.)* | Three Revolutions: Mobilization and Change in Contemporary Ukraine II. An Oral History of the Revolution on Granite, Orange Revolution, and Revolution of Dignity | ISBN 978-3-8382-1323-1

211 *Li Bennich-Björkman, Sergiy Kurbatov (Eds.)* | When the Future Came. The Collapse of the USSR and the Emergence of National Memory in Post-Soviet History Textbooks | ISBN 978-3-8382-1335-4

212 *Olga R. Gulina* | Migration as a (Geo-)Political Challenge in the Post-Soviet Space. Border Regimes, Policy Choices, Visa Agendas | With a foreword by Nils Muižnieks | ISBN 978-3-8382-1338-5

213 *Sanna Turoma, Kaarina Aitamurto, Slobodanka Vladiv-Glover (Eds.)* | Religion, Expression, and Patriotism in Russia. Essays on Post-Soviet Society and the State. ISBN 978-3-8382-1346-0

214 *Vasif Huseynov* | Geopolitical Rivalries in the "Common Neighborhood". Russia's Conflict with the West, Soft Power, and Neoclassical Realism | With a foreword by Nicholas Ross Smith | ISBN 978-3-8382-1277-7

215 *Mikhail Suslov* | Geopolitical Imagination. Ideology and Utopia in Post-Soviet Russia | With a foreword by Mark Bassin | ISBN 978-3-8382-1361-3

216 *Alexander Etkind, Mikhail Minakov (Eds.)* | Ideology after Union. Political Doctrines, Discourses, and Debates in Post-Soviet Societies | ISBN 978-3-8382-1388-0

217 *Jakob Mischke, Oleksandr Zabirko (Hgg.)* | Protestbewegungen im langen Schatten des Kreml. Aufbruch und Resignation in Russland und der Ukraine | ISBN 978-3-8382-0926-5

218 *Oksana Huss* | How Corruption and Anti-Corruption Policies Sustain Hybrid Regimes. Strategies of Political Domination under Ukraine's Presidents in 1994-2014 | With a foreword by Tobias Debiel and Andrea Gawrich | ISBN 978-3-8382-1430-6

219 *Dmitry Travin, Vladimir Gel'man, Otar Marganiya* | The Russian Path. Ideas, Interests, Institutions, Illusions | With a foreword by Vladimir Ryzhkov | ISBN 978-3-8382-1421-4

220 *Gergana Dimova* | Political Uncertainty. A Comparative Exploration | With a foreword by Todor Yalamov and Rumena Filipova | ISBN 978-3-8382-1385-9

221 *Torben Waschke* | Russland in Transition. Geopolitik zwischen Raum, Identität und Machtinteressen | Mit einem Vorwort von Andreas Dittmann | ISBN 978-3-8382-1480-1

222 *Steven Jobbitt, Zsolt Bottlik, Marton Berki (Eds.)* | Power and Identity in the Post-Soviet Realm. Geographies of Ethnicity and Nationality after 1991 | ISBN 978-3-8382-1399-6

223 *Daria Buteiko* | Erinnerungsort. Ort des Gedenkens, der Erholung oder der Einkehr? Kommunismus-Erinnerung am Beispiel der Gedenkstätte Berliner Mauer sowie des Soloveckij-Klosters und -Museumsparks | ISBN 978-3-8382-1367-5

224 *Olga Bertelsen (Ed.)* | Russian Active Measures. Yesterday, Today, Tomorrow | With a foreword by Jan Goldman | ISBN 978-3-8382-1529-7

225 *David Mandel* | "Optimizing" Higher Education in Russia. University Teachers and their Union "Universitetskaya solidarnost'" | ISBN 978-3-8382-1519-8

226 *Mikhail Minakov, Gwendolyn Sasse, Daria Isachenko (Eds.)* | Post-Soviet Secessionism. Nation-Building and State-Failure after Communism | ISBN 978-3-8382-1538-9

227 *Jakob Hauter (Ed.)* | Civil War? Interstate War? Hybrid War? Dimensions and Interpretations of the Donbas Conflict in 2014–2020 | With a foreword by Andrew Wilson | ISBN 978-3-8382-1383-5

228 *Tima T. Moldogaziev, Gene A. Brewer, J. Edward Kellough (Eds.)* | Public Policy and Politics in Georgia. Lessons from Post-Soviet Transition | With a foreword by Dan Durning | ISBN 978-3-8382-1535-8

229 *Oxana Schmies (Ed.)* | NATO's Enlargement and Russia. A Strategic Challenge in the Past and Future | With a foreword by Vladimir Kara-Murza | ISBN 978-3-8382-1478-8

230 *Christopher Ford* | Ukapisme – Une Gauche perdue. Le marxisme anti-colonial dans la révolution ukrainienne 1917-1925 | Avec une préface de Vincent Présumey | ISBN 978-3-8382-0899-2

231 *Anna Kutkina* | Between Lenin and Bandera. Decommunization and Multivocality in Post-Euromaidan Ukraine | With a foreword by Juri Mykkänen | ISBN 978-3-8382-1506-8

232 *Lincoln E. Flake* | Defending the Faith. The Russian Orthodox Church and the Demise of Religious Pluralism | With a foreword by Peter Martland | ISBN 978-3-8382-1378-1

233 *Nikoloz Samkharadze* | Russia's Recognition of the Independence of Abkhazia and South Ossetia. Analysis of a Deviant Case in Moscow's Foreign Policy | With a foreword by Neil MacFarlane | ISBN 978-3-8382-1414-6

234 *Arve Hansen* | Urban Protest. A Spatial Perspective on Kyiv, Minsk, and Moscow | With a foreword by Julie Wilhelmsen | ISBN 978-3-8382-1495-5

235 *Eleonora Narvselius, Julie Fedor (Eds.)* | Diversity in the East-Central European Borderlands. Memories, Cityscapes, People | ISBN 978-3-8382-1523-5

236 *Regina Elsner* | The Russian Orthodox Church and Modernity. A Historical and Theological Investigation into Eastern Christianity between Unity and Plurality | With a foreword by Mikhail Suslov | ISBN 978-3-8382-1568-6

237 *Bo Petersson* | The Putin Predicament. Problems of Legitimacy and Succession in Russia | With a foreword by J. Paul Goode | ISBN 978-3-8382-1050-6

238 *Jonathan Otto Pohl* | The Years of Great Silence. The Deportation, Special Settlement, and Mobilization into the Labor Army of Ethnic Germans in the USSR, 1941–1955 | ISBN 978-3-8382-1630-0

239 *Mikhail Minakov (Ed.)* | Inventing Majorities. Ideological Creativity in Post-Soviet Societies | ISBN 978-3-8382-1641-6

240 *Robert M. Cutler* | Soviet and Post-Soviet Foreign Policies I. East-South Relations and the Political Economy of the Communist Bloc, 1971–1991 | With a foreword by Roger E. Kanet | ISBN 978-3-8382-1654-6

241 *Izabella Agardi* | On the Verge of History. Life Stories of Rural Women from Serbia, Romania, and Hungary, 1920–2020 | With a foreword by Andrea Pető | ISBN 978-3-8382-1602-7

242 *Sebastian Schäffer (Ed.)* | Ukraine in Central and Eastern Europe. Kyiv's Foreign Affairs and the International Relations of the Post-Communist Region | With a foreword by Pavlo Klimkin and Andreas Umland| ISBN 978-3-8382-1615-7

243 *Volodymyr Dubrovskyi, Kalman Mizsei, Mychailo Wynnyckyj (Eds.)* | Eight Years after the Revolution of Dignity. What Has Changed in Ukraine during 2013–2021? | With a foreword by Yaroslav Hrytsak | ISBN 978-3-8382-1560-0

244 *Rumena Filipova* | Constructing the Limits of Europe Identity and Foreign Policy in Poland, Bulgaria, and Russia since 1989 | With forewords by Harald Wydra and Gergana Yankova-Dimova | ISBN 978-3-8382-1649-2

245 *Oleksandra Keudel* | How Patronal Networks Shape Opportunities for Local Citizen Participation in a Hybrid Regime A Comparative Analysis of Five Cities in Ukraine | With a foreword by Sabine Kropp | ISBN 978-3-8382-1671-3

246 *Jan Claas Behrends, Thomas Lindenberger, Pavel Kolar (Eds.)* | Violence after Stalin Institutions, Practices, and Everyday Life in the Soviet Bloc 1953–1989 | ISBN 978-3-8382-1637-9

247 *Leonid Luks* | Macht und Ohnmacht der Utopien Essays zur Geschichte Russlands im 20. und 21. Jahrhundert | ISBN 978-3-8382-1677-5

248 *Iuliia Barshadska* | Brüssel zwischen Kyjiw und Moskau Das auswärtige Handeln der Europäischen Union im ukrainisch-russischen Konflikt 2014-2019 | Mit einem Vorwort von Olaf Leiße | ISBN 978-3-8382-1667-6

249 *Valentyna Romanova* | Decentralisation and Multilevel Elections in Ukraine Reform Dynamics and Party Politics in 2010–2021 | With a foreword by Kimitaka Matsuzato | ISBN 978-3-8382-1700-0

250 *Alexander Motyl* | National Questions. Theoretical Reflections on Nations and Nationalism in Eastern Europe | ISBN 978-3-8382-1675-1

251 *Marc Dietrich* | A Cosmopolitan Model for Peacebuilding. The Ukrainian Cases of Crimea and the Donbas | With a foreword by Rémi Baudouï | ISBN 978-3-8382-1687-4

252 *Eduard Baidaus* | An Unsettled Nation. Moldova in the Geopolitics of Russia, Romania, and Ukraine | With forewords by John-Paul Himka and David R. Marples | ISBN 978-3-8382-1582-2

253 *Igor Okunev, Petr Oskolkov (Eds.)* | Transforming the Administrative Matryoshka. The Reform of Autonomous Okrugs in the Russian Federation, 2003–2008 | With a foreword by Vladimir Zorin | ISBN 978-3-8382-1721-5

254 *Winfried Schneider-Deters* | Ukraine's Fateful Years 2013–2019. Vol. I: The Popular Uprising in Winter 2013/2014 | ISBN 978-3-8382-1725-3

255 *Winfried Schneider-Deters* | Ukraine's Fateful Years 2013–2019. Vol. II: The Annexation of Crimea and the War in Donbas | ISBN 978-3-8382-1726-0

256 *Robert M. Cutler* | Soviet and Post-Soviet Russian Foreign Policies II. East-West Relations in Europe and the Political Economy of the Communist Bloc, 1971–1991 | With a foreword by Roger E. Kanet | ISBN 978-3-8382-1727-7

257 *Robert M. Cutler* | Soviet and Post-Soviet Russian Foreign Policies III. East-West Relations in Europe and Eurasia in the Post-Cold War Transition, 1991–2001 | With a foreword by Roger E. Kanet | ISBN 978-3-8382-1728-4

258 *Paweł Kowal, Iwona Reichardt, Kateryna Pryshchepa (Eds.)* | Three Revolutions: Mobilization and Change in Contemporary Ukraine III. Archival Records and Historical Sources on the 1990 Revolution on Granite | ISBN 978-3-8382-1376-7

259 *Mikhail Minakov (Ed.)* | Philosophy Unchained. Developments in Post-Soviet Philosophical Thought. | With a foreword by Christopher Donohue | ISBN 978-3-8382-1768-0

260 *David Dalton* | The Ukrainian Oligarchy After the Euromaidan. How Ukraine's Political Economy Regime Survived the Crisis | With a foreword by Andrew Wilson | ISBN 978-3-8382-1740-6

261 *Andreas Heinemann-Grüder (Ed.)* | Who are the Fighters? Irregular Armed Groups in the Russian-Ukrainian War in 2014–2015 | ISBN 978-3-8382-1777-2

262 *Taras Kuzio (Ed.)* | Russian Disinformation and Western Scholarship. Bias and Prejudice in Journalistic, Expert, and Academic Analyses of East European and Eurasian Affairs | ISBN 978-3-8382-1685-0

263 *Darius Furmonavicius* | LithuaniaTransforms the West. Lithuania's Liberation from Soviet Occupation and the Enlargement of NATO (1988–2022) | With a foreword by Vytautas Landsbergis | ISBN 978-3-8382-1779-6

264 *Dirk Dalberg* | Politisches Denken im tschechoslowakischen Dissens. Egon Bondy, Miroslav Kusý, Milan Šimečka und Petr Uhl (1968-1989) | ISBN 978-3-8382-1318-7

265 *Леонид Люкс* | К столетию «философского парохода». Мыслители «первой» русской эмиграции о русской революции и о тоталитарных соблазнах XX века | ISBN 978-3-8382-1775-8

266 *Daviti Mtchedlishvili* | The EU and the South Caucasus. European Neighborhood Policies between Eclecticism and Pragmatism, 1991-2021 | With a foreword by Nicholas Ross Smith | ISBN 978-3-8382-1735-2

267 *Bohdan Harasymiw* | Post-Euromaidan Ukraine. Domestic Power Struggles and War of National Survival in 2014–2022 | ISBN 978-3-8382-1798-7

268 *Nadiia Koval, Denys Tereshchenko (Eds.)* | Russian Cultural Diplomacy under Putin. Rossotrudnichestvo, the "Russkiy Mir" Foundation, and the Gorchakov Fund in 2007–2022 | ISBN 978-3-8382-1801-4

269 *Izabela Kazejak* | Jews in Post-War Wrocław and L'viv. Official Policies and Local Responses in Comparative Perspective, 1945-1970s | ISBN 978-3-8382-1802-1

270 *Jakob Hauter* | Russia's Overlooked Invasion. The Causes of the 2014 Outbreak of War in Ukraine's Donbas | With a foreword by Hiroaki Kuromiya | ISBN 978-3-8382-1803-8

271 *Anton Shekhovtsov* | Russian Political Warfare. Essays on Kremlin Propaganda in Europe and the Neighbourhood, 2020-2023 | With a foreword by Nathalie Loiseau | ISBN 978-3-8382-1821-2

272 *Андреа Пето* | Насилие и Молчание. Красная армия в Венгрии во Второй Мировой войне | ISBN 978-3-8382-1636-2

***ibidem**.eu*